Say I Love You.

5

by
Kanae Hazuki

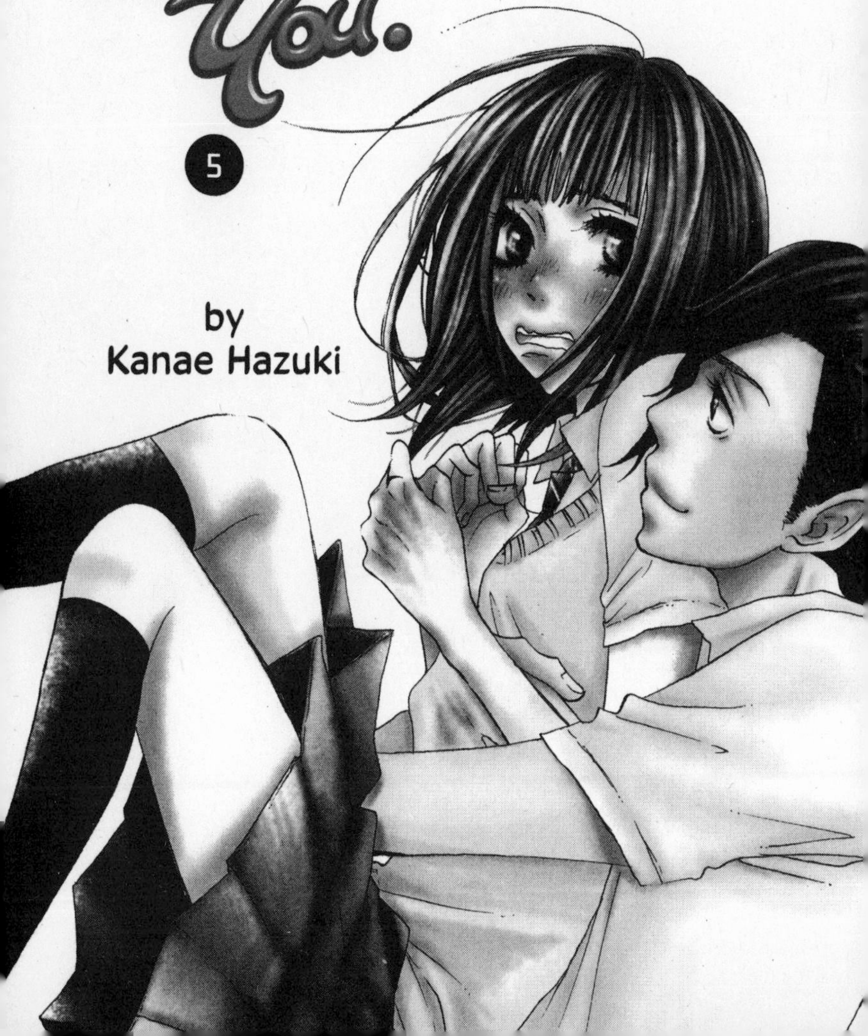

Kanae Hazuki
presents

Chapter 17

4

Chapter 18

45

Chapter 19

83

Chapter 20

122

CHARACTERS

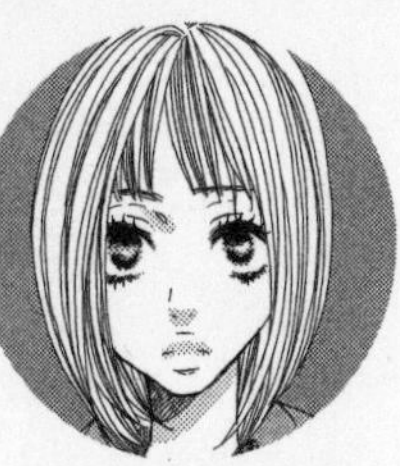

Mei Tachibana

A girl who hasn't had a single friend, let alone a boyfriend, in sixteen years, and has lived her life trusting no one. She finds herself attracted to Yamato, who, for some reason, just won't leave her alone, and they start dating.

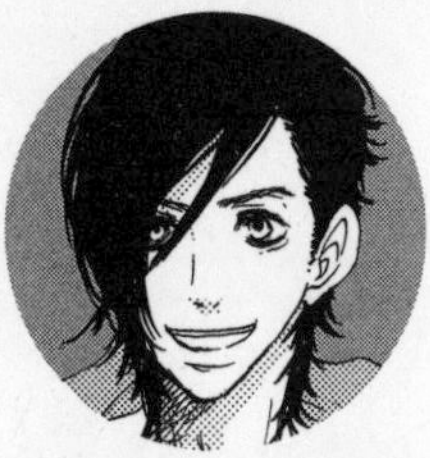

Yamato Kurosawa

The most popular boy at Mei's school. He has the love of many girls, yet for some reason, he is obsessed with Mei, the brooding weirdo girl from another class.

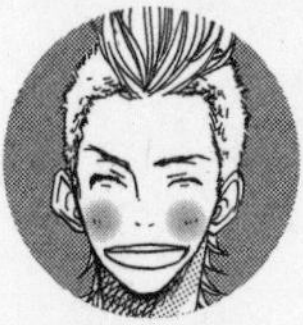

Kai

Yamato's classmate from middle school who had been the victim of bullying. For his own reasons, he started high school a year late. He is a regular customer at Mei's work, and he loves the Land amusement park.

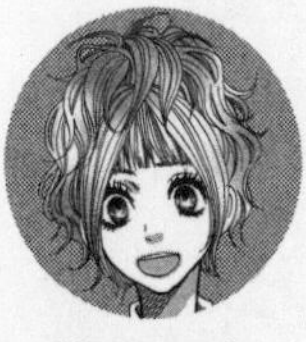

Megumi

An amateur model who has her sights set on Yamato. She transferred to his school, got him a modeling job, and the two gradually got closer. Has she not given up on Yamato yet?

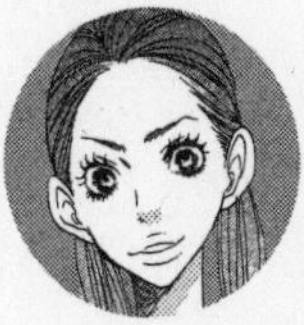

Aiko

She likes Yamato and was jealous of Mei, but now that she has seen Mei trying so hard to confront her own insecurities, she has decided to cheer her on. They were put in the same class in their second year of high school.

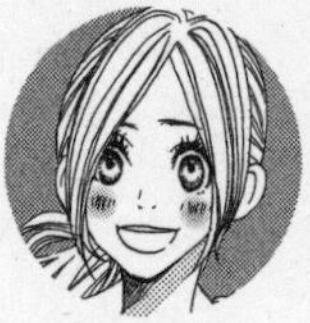

Asami

A girl who treats Mei as a real friend. She had a thing for Yamato, but now she is dating his friend Nakanishi. She and Mei were put in different classes in their second year of high school.

STORY

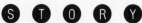

Mei Tachibana spent sixteen years without a single friend or boyfriend. One day she accidentally injured Yamato Kurosawa, the most popular boy in her school. Ironically, that made him like her, and he unilaterally decided that they were friends. He even kissed her like he meant it. Mei had a very difficult time opening her heart, but she was gradually drawn in by Yamato's kindness and sincerity, and they started dating. Mei realized that she was in love, and she began to awaken to her femininity, but then Megumi, an amateur model who had her eyes on Yamato, transferred to their school. For the first time, Mei sensed a rift between herself and Yamato, but managed to overcome that as well. Meanwhile, Yamato's classmate from middle school is one of the new first years at their school?!

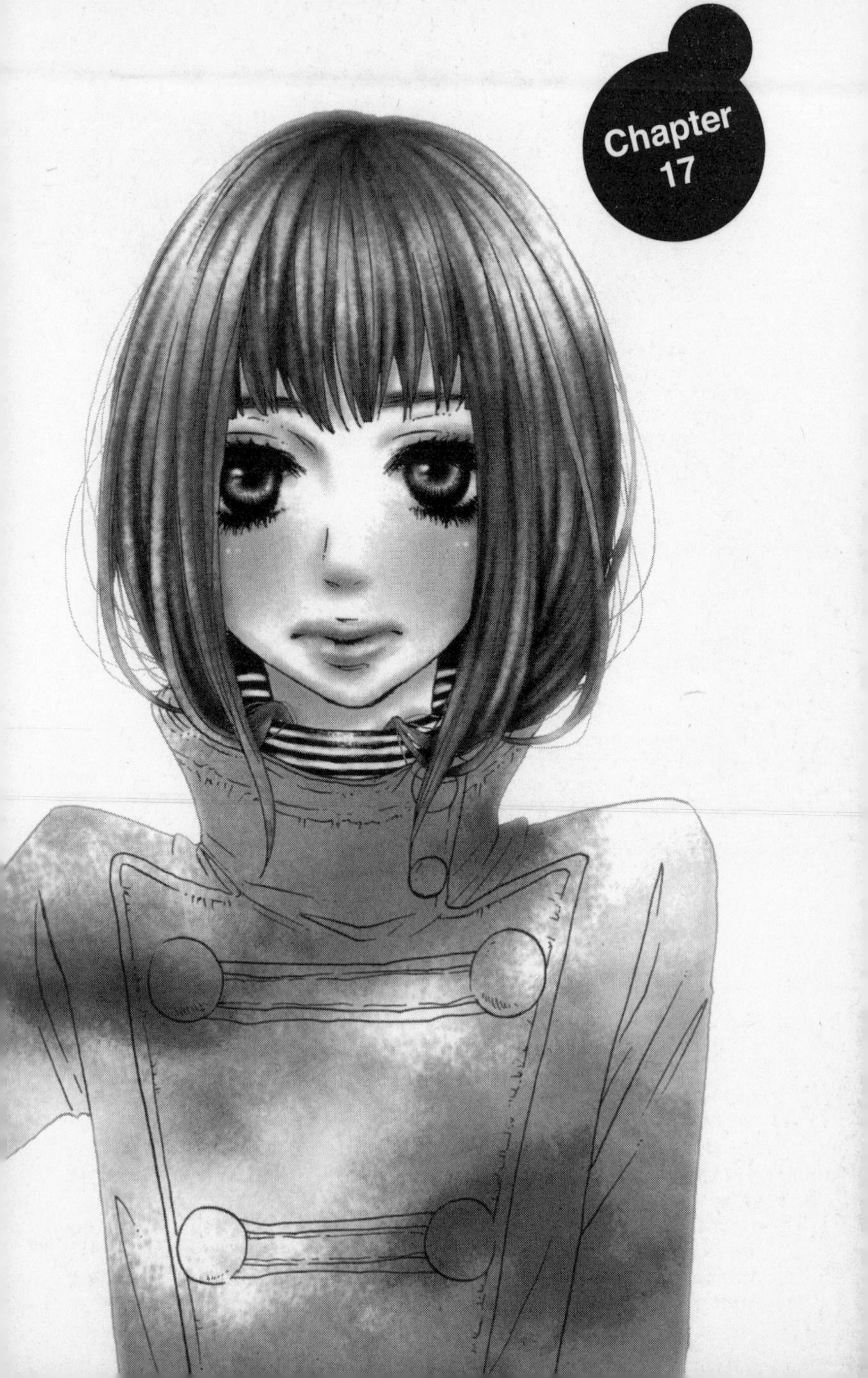
Chapter
17

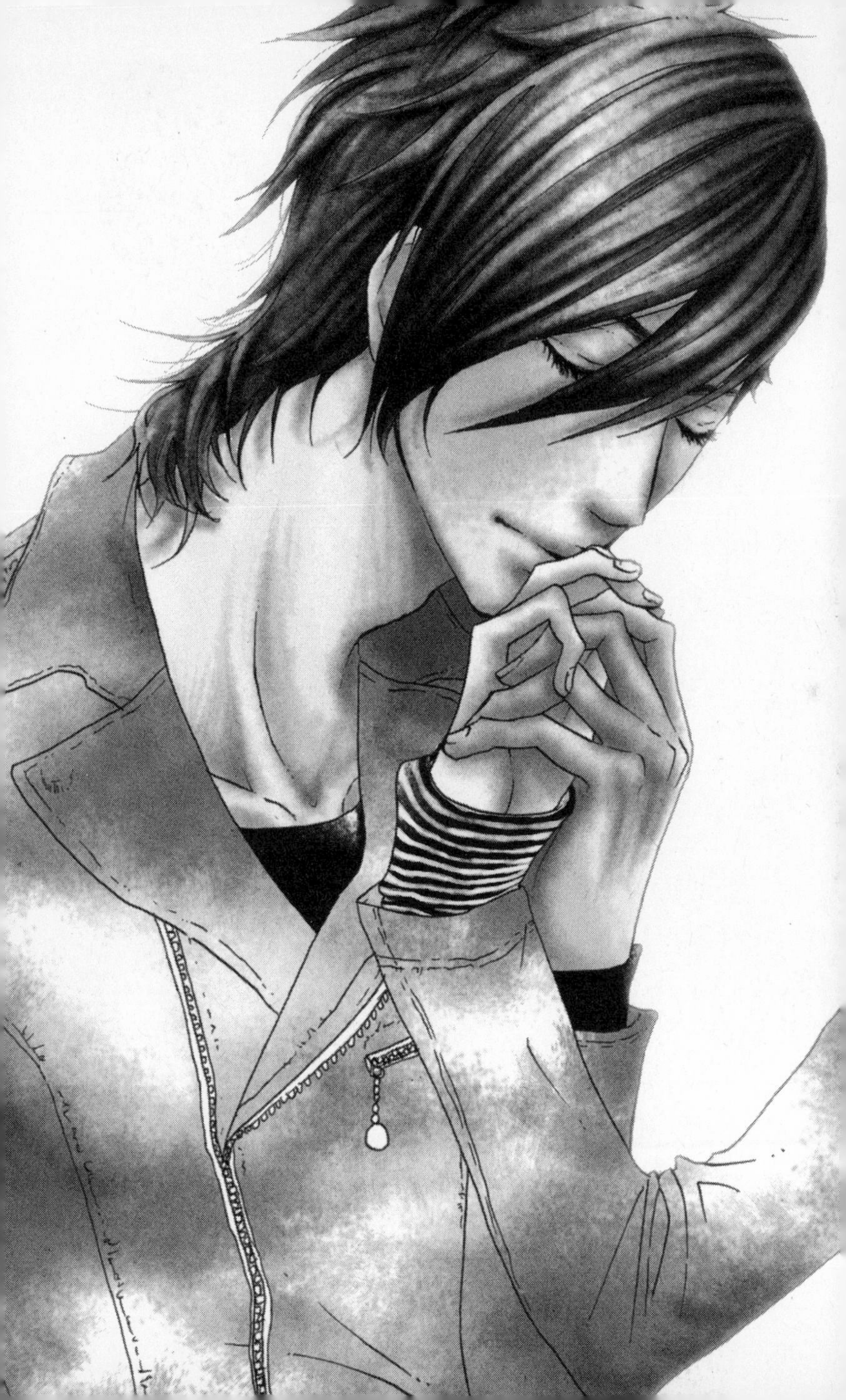

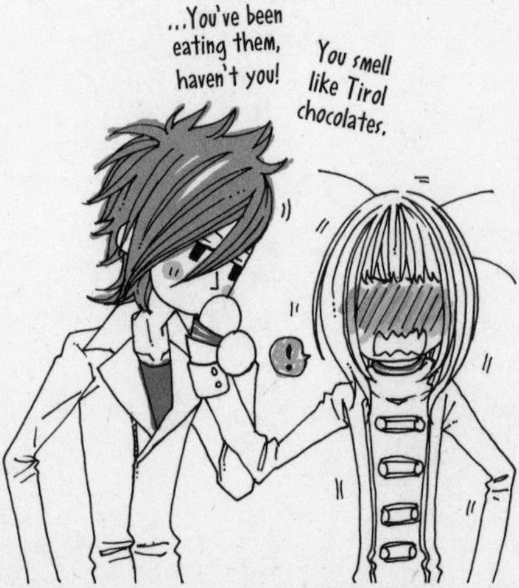
You smell like Tirol chocolates.
...You've been eating them, haven't you!

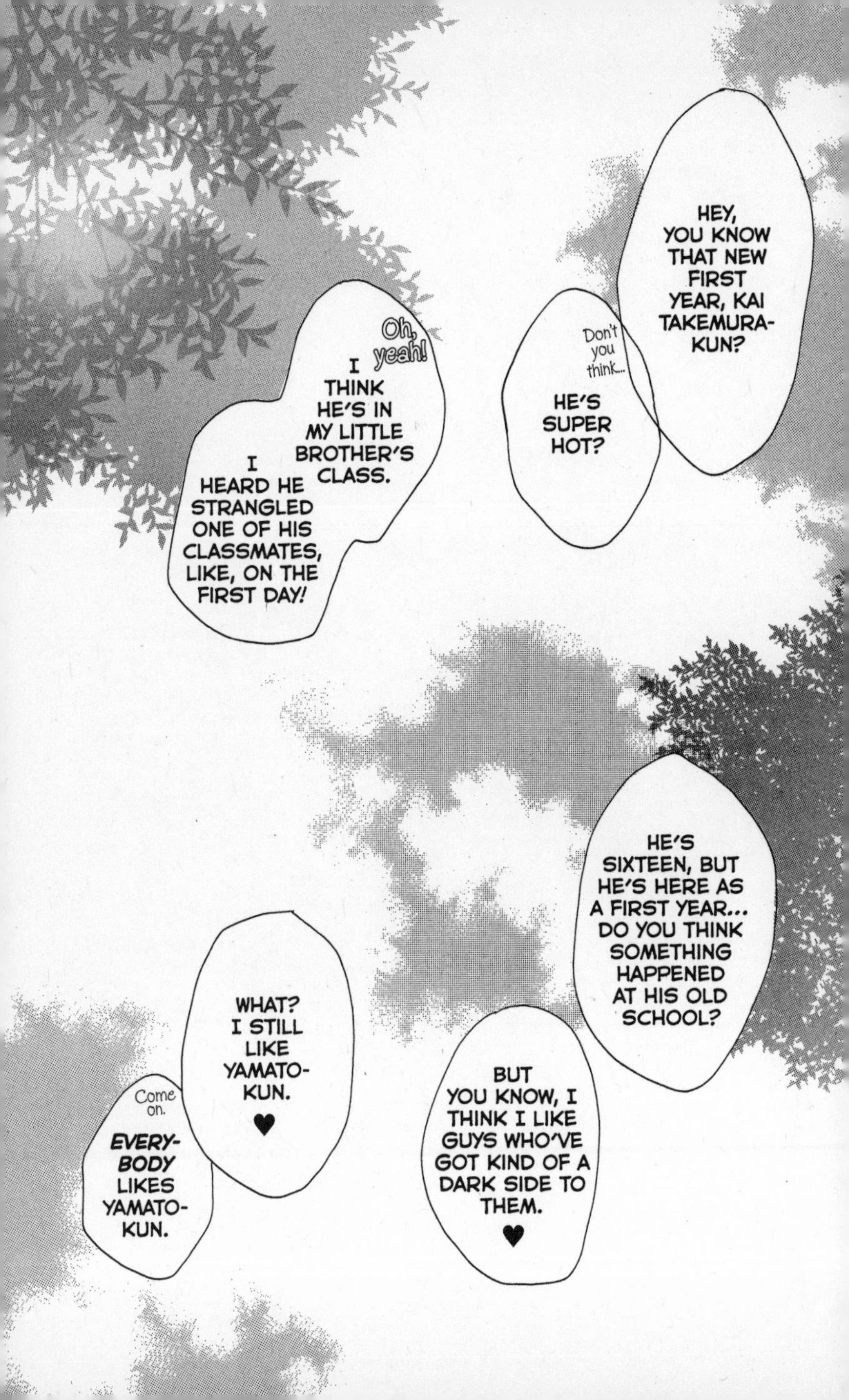
HEY, YOU KNOW THAT NEW FIRST YEAR, KAI TAKEMURA-KUN?
Don't you think...
HE'S SUPER HOT?
Oh, yeah!
I THINK HE'S IN MY LITTLE BROTHER'S CLASS.
I HEARD HE STRANGLED ONE OF HIS CLASSMATES, LIKE, ON THE FIRST DAY!
HE'S SIXTEEN, BUT HE'S HERE AS A FIRST YEAR... DO YOU THINK SOMETHING HAPPENED AT HIS OLD SCHOOL?
BUT YOU KNOW, I THINK I LIKE GUYS WHO'VE GOT KIND OF A DARK SIDE TO THEM. ♥
WHAT? I STILL LIKE YAMATO-KUN. ♥
Come on.
EVERYBODY LIKES YAMATO-KUN.

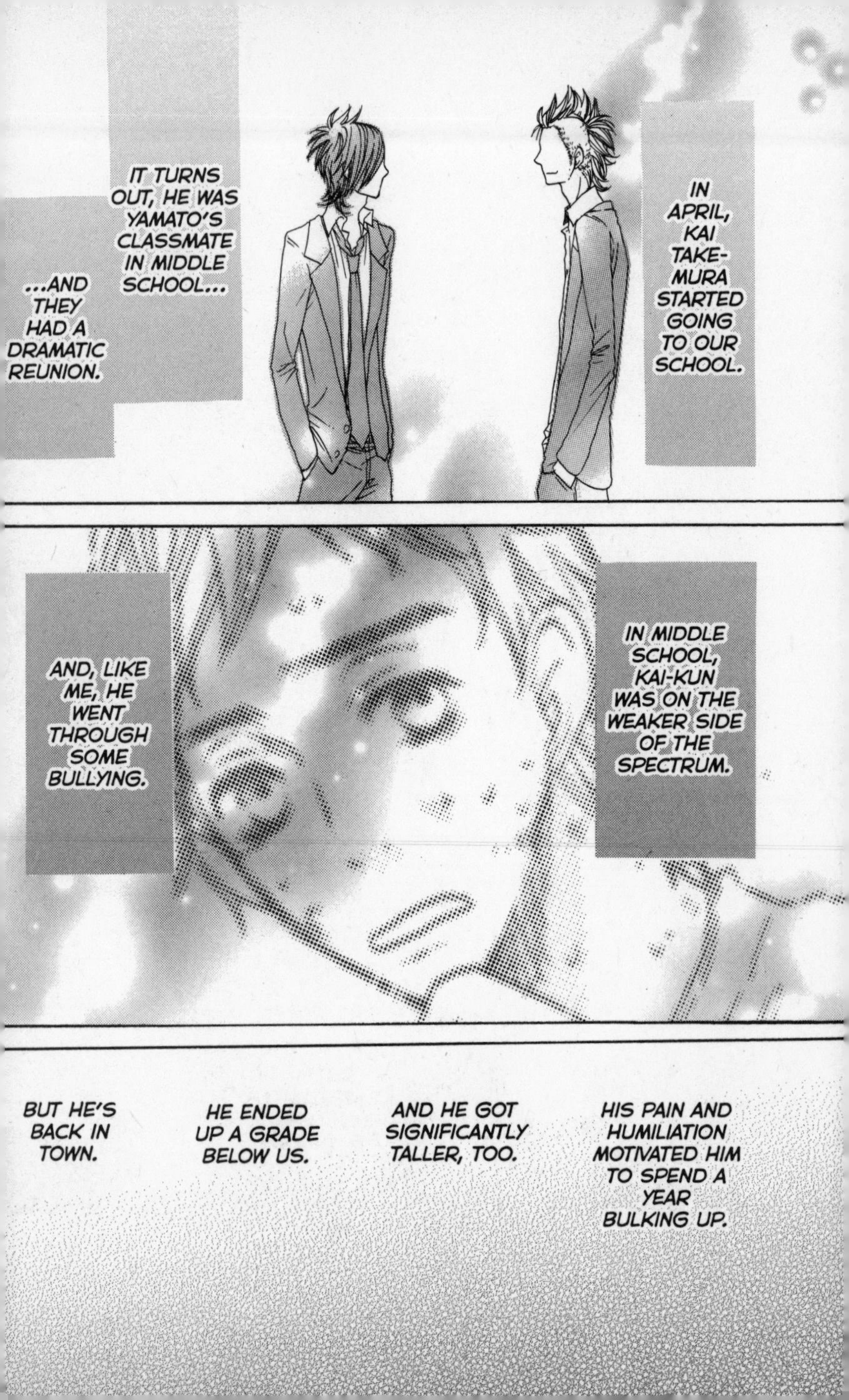
IN APRIL, KAI TAKE-MURA STARTED GOING TO OUR SCHOOL.
IT TURNS OUT, HE WAS YAMATO'S CLASSMATE IN MIDDLE SCHOOL...
...AND THEY HAD A DRAMATIC REUNION.
IN MIDDLE SCHOOL, KAI-KUN WAS ON THE WEAKER SIDE OF THE SPECTRUM.
AND, LIKE ME, HE WENT THROUGH SOME BULLYING.
HIS PAIN AND HUMILIATION MOTIVATED HIM TO SPEND A YEAR BULKING UP.
AND HE GOT SIGNIFICANTLY TALLER, TOO.
HE ENDED UP A GRADE BELOW US.
BUT HE'S BACK IN TOWN.

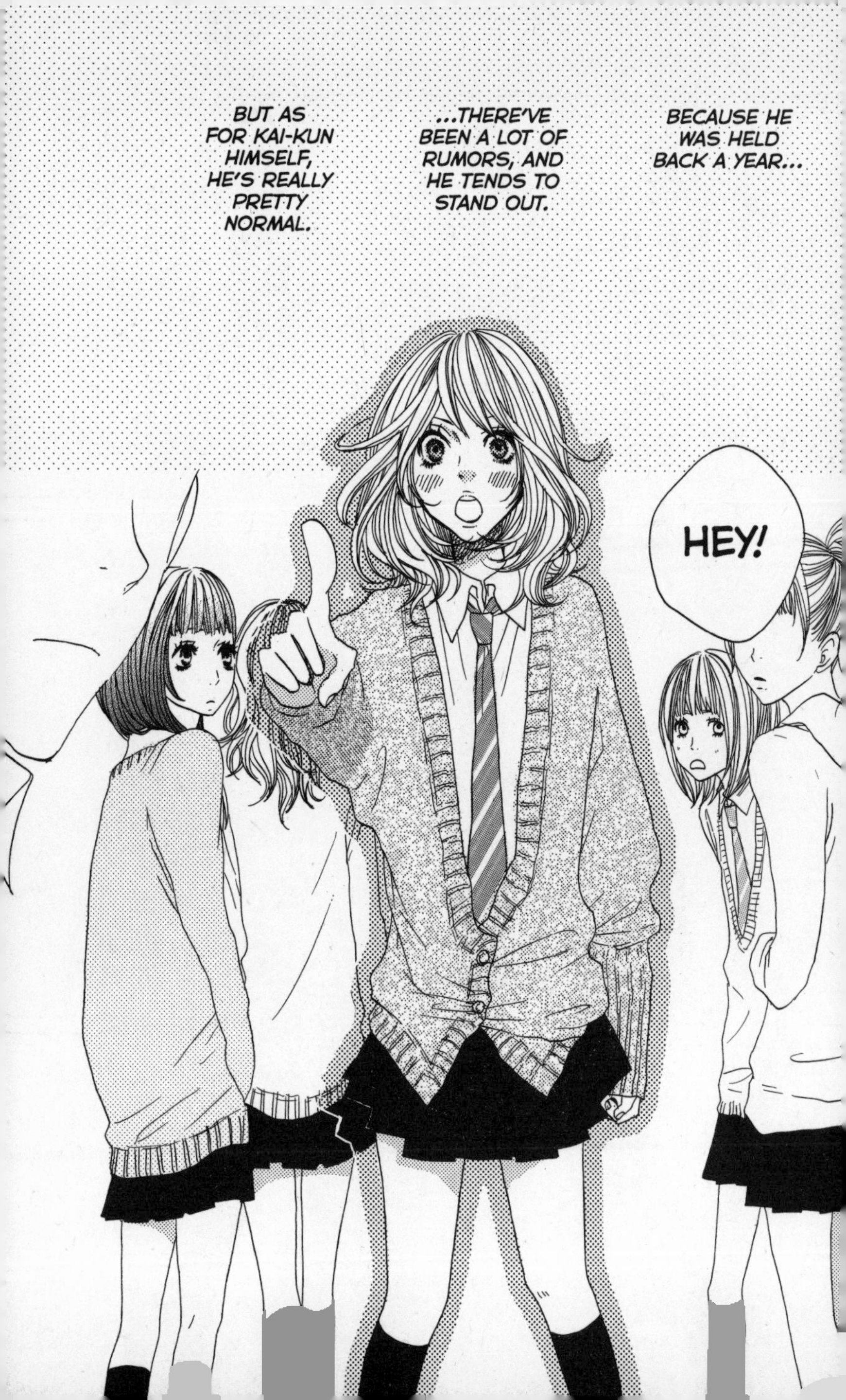
BECAUSE HE WAS HELD BACK A YEAR...
...THERE'VE BEEN A LOT OF RUMORS, AND HE TENDS TO STAND OUT.
BUT AS FOR KAI-KUN HIMSELF, HE'S REALLY PRETTY NORMAL.
HEY!

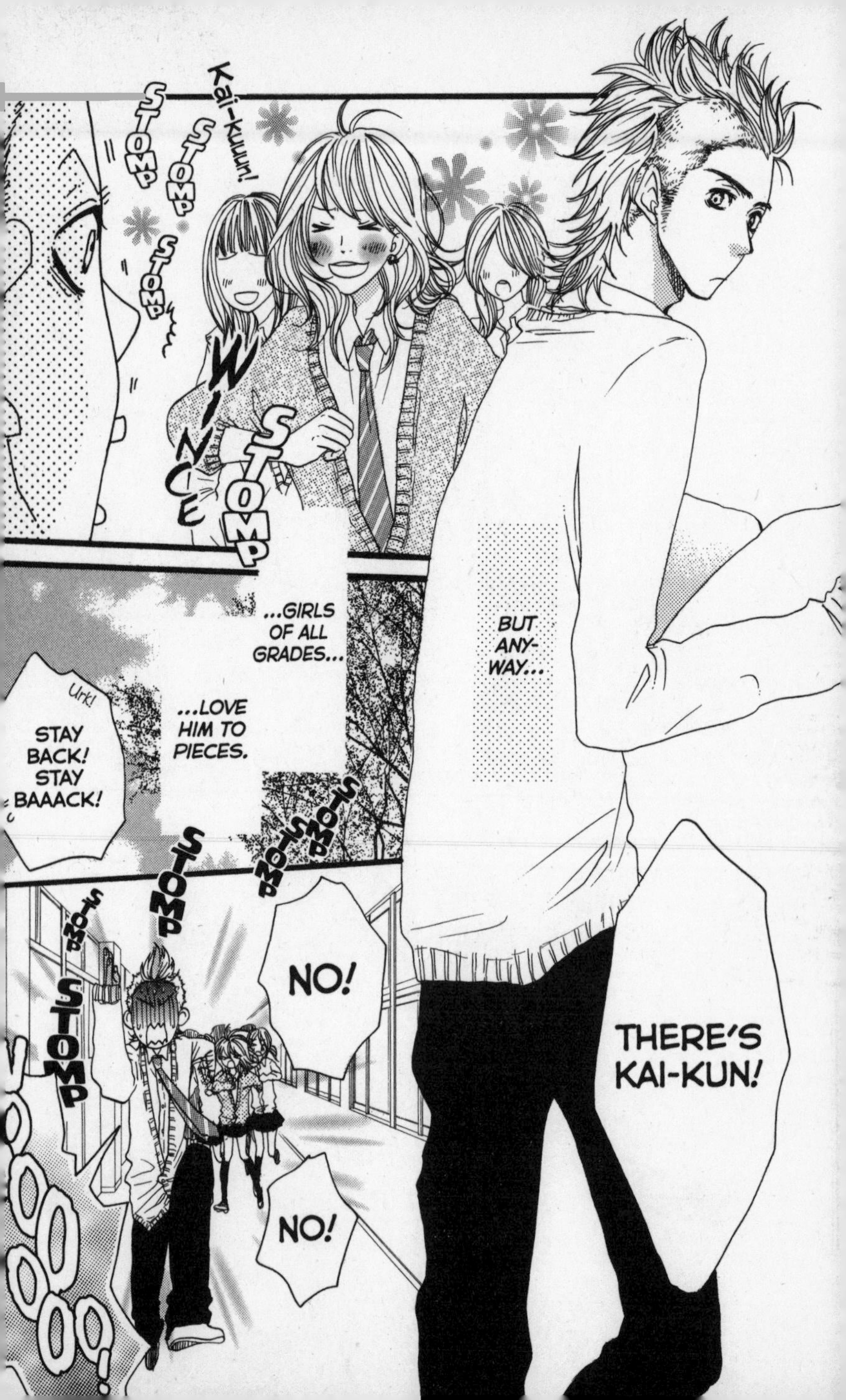
BUT ANYWAY...
THERE'S KAI-KUN!
Kai-kuuun!
STOMP
STOMP
STOMP
WINCE
STOMP
...GIRLS OF ALL GRADES...
...LOVE HIM TO PIECES.
Urk!
STAY BACK! STAY BAAACK!
STOMP
STOMP
STOMP
STOMP
NO!
NO!
STOMP
STOMP

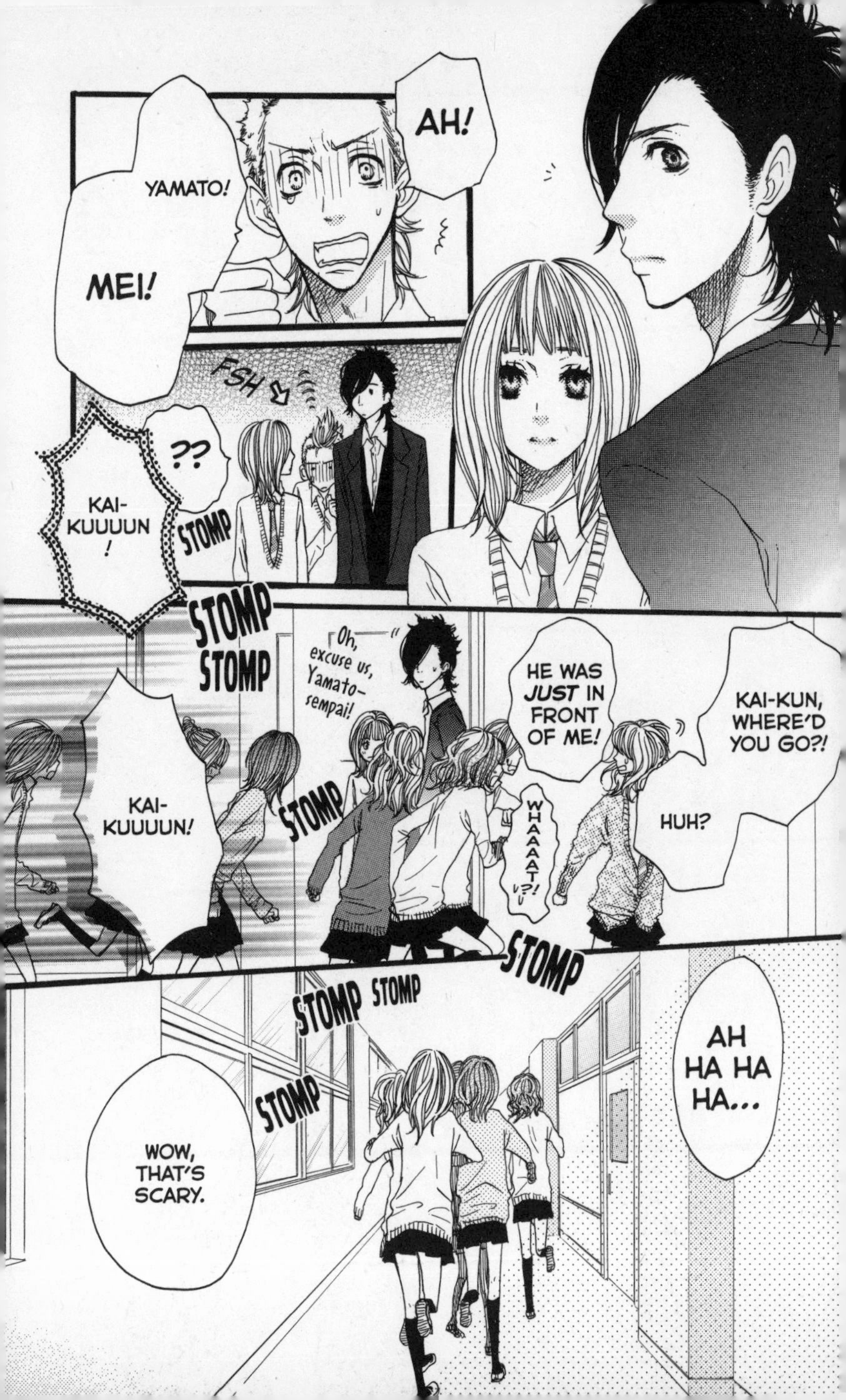
AH!
YAMATO!
MEI!
FSH
??
STOMP
KAI-KUUUUN!
KAI-KUN, WHERE'D YOU GO?!
HUH?
HE WAS JUST IN FRONT OF ME!
WHAAAAAT?!
Oh, excuse us, Yamato-sempai!
STOMP
STOMP
STOMP
KAI-KUUUUN!
STOMP
AH HA HA HA...
STOMP STOMP
STOMP
WOW, THAT'S SCARY.

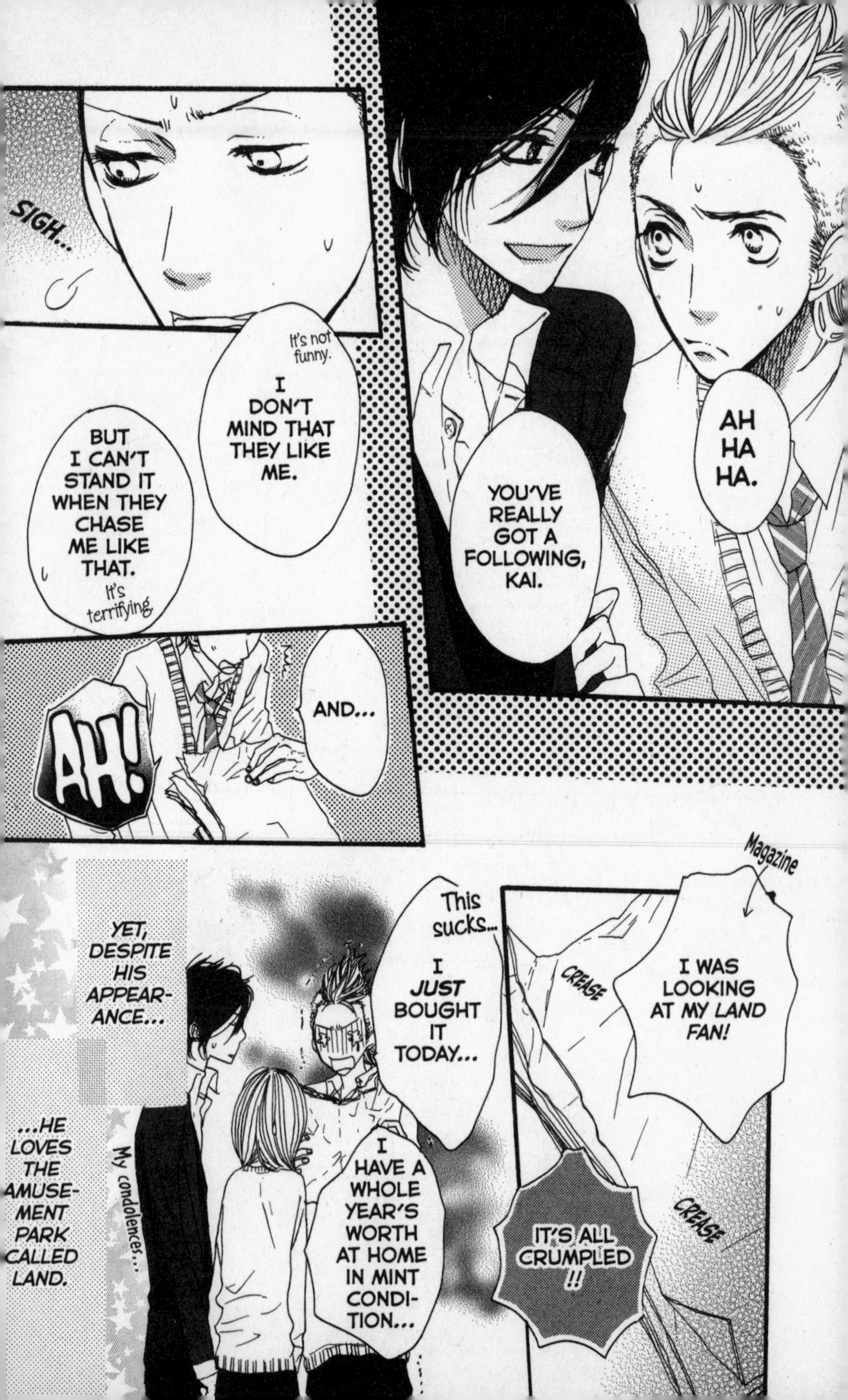
AH HA HA.
YOU'VE REALLY GOT A FOLLOWING, KAI.
SIGH...
It's not funny.
I DON'T MIND THAT THEY LIKE ME.
BUT I CAN'T STAND IT WHEN THEY CHASE ME LIKE THAT.
It's terrifying
AND...
AH!
Magazine
I WAS LOOKING AT MY LAND FAN!
CREASE
CREASE
IT'S ALL CRUMPLED !!
This sucks...
I JUST BOUGHT IT TODAY...
I HAVE A WHOLE YEAR'S WORTH AT HOME IN MINT CONDITION...
My condolences...
YET, DESPITE HIS APPEARANCE...
...HE LOVES THE AMUSEMENT PARK CALLED LAND.

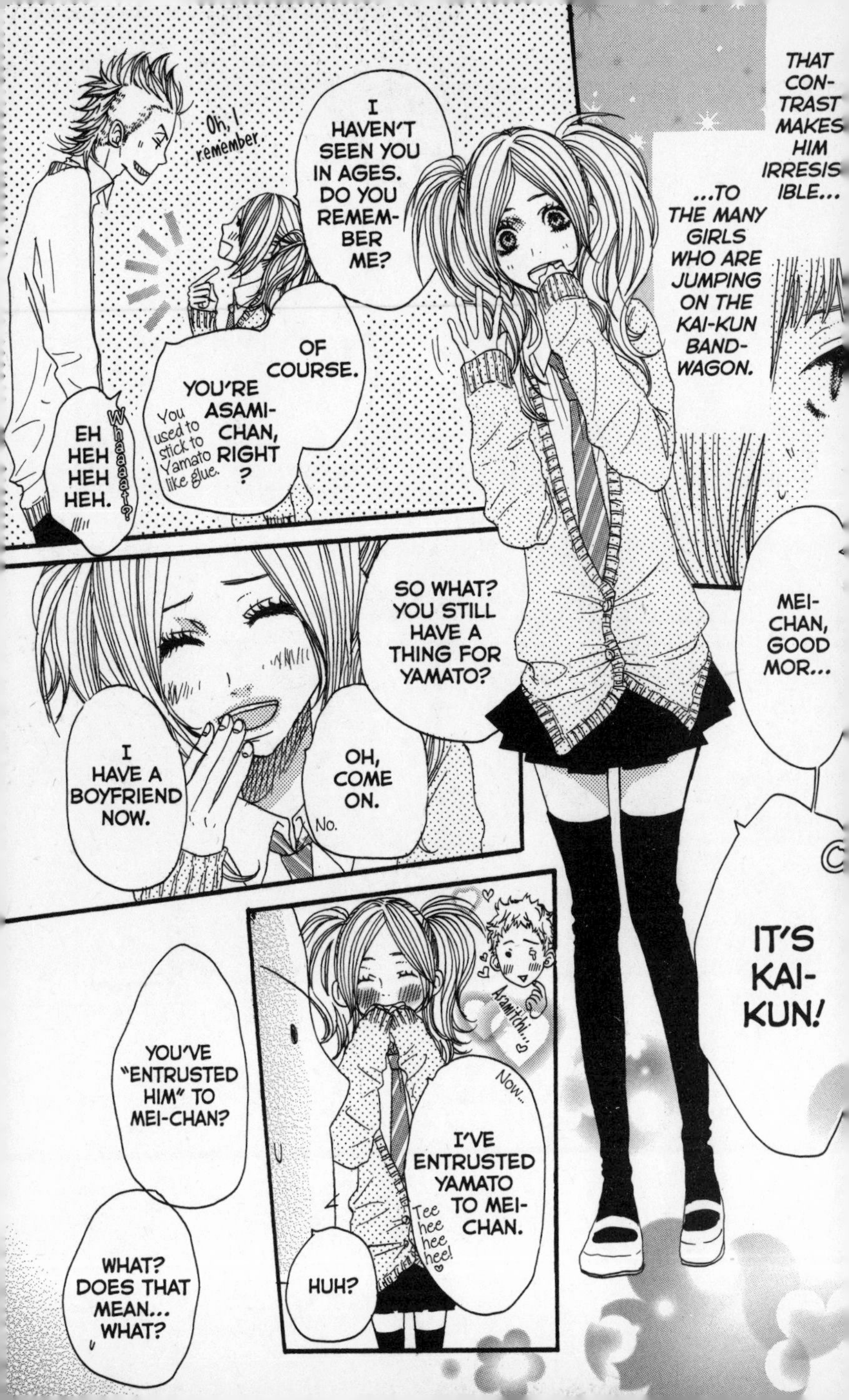
THAT CONTRAST MAKES HIM IRRESISTIBLE...
...TO THE MANY GIRLS WHO ARE JUMPING ON THE KAI-KUN BANDWAGON.
MEI-CHAN, GOOD MOR...
IT'S KAI-KUN!
I HAVEN'T SEEN YOU IN AGES. DO YOU REMEMBER ME?
Oh, I remember.
OF COURSE. YOU'RE ASAMI-CHAN, RIGHT?
You used to stick to Yamato like glue.
EH HEH HEH HEH.
Whaaaaat?
SO WHAT? YOU STILL HAVE A THING FOR YAMATO?
OH, COME ON.
No.
I HAVE A BOYFRIEND NOW.
I'VE ENTRUSTED YAMATO TO MEI-CHAN.
Now...
Tee hee hee hee!
Aramitchi...
HUH?
YOU'VE "ENTRUSTED HIM" TO MEI-CHAN?
WHAT? DOES THAT MEAN... WHAT?

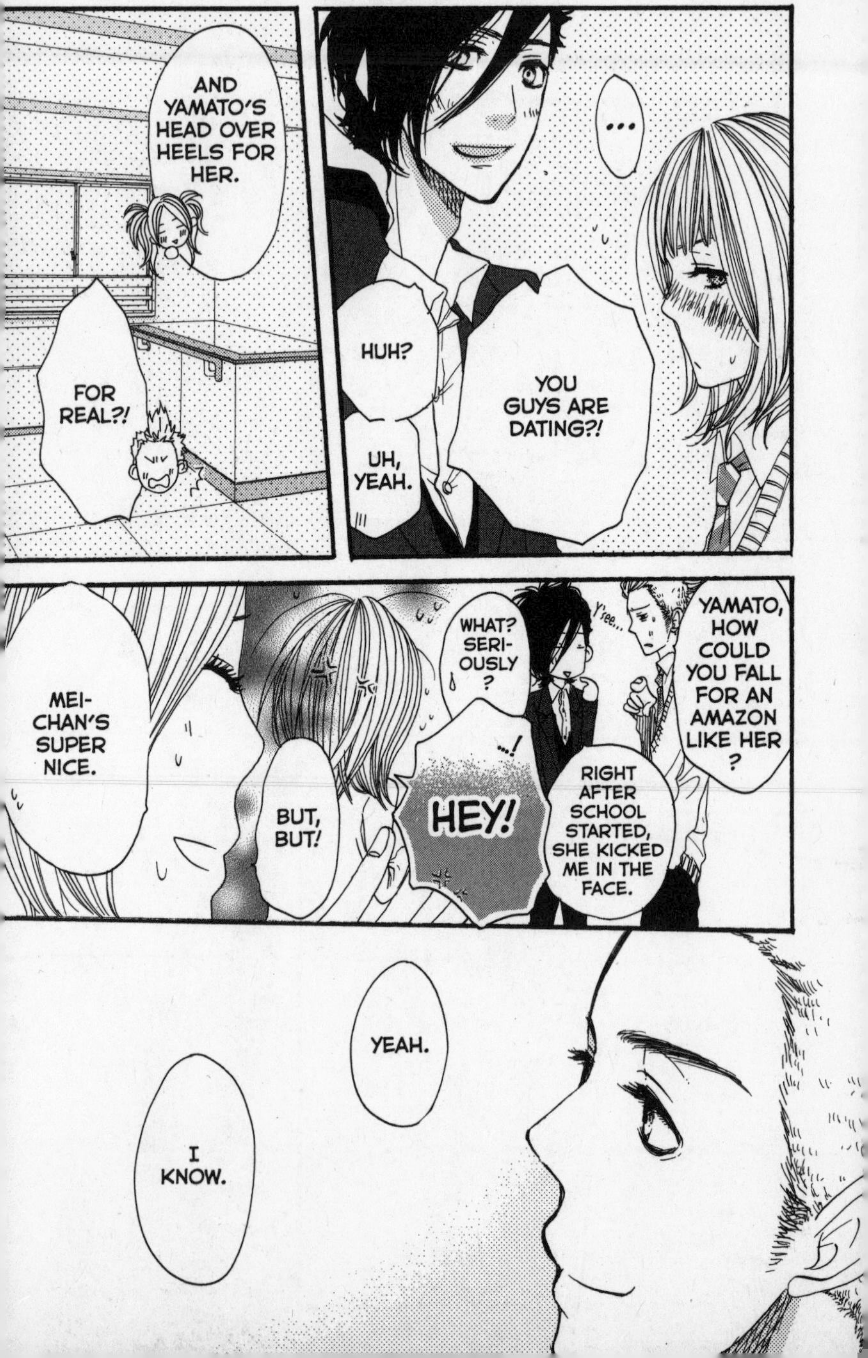
...
YOU GUYS ARE DATING?!
HUH?
UH, YEAH.
AND YAMATO'S HEAD OVER HEELS FOR HER.
FOR REAL?!
YAMATO, HOW COULD YOU FALL FOR AN AMAZON LIKE HER?
Y'see...
WHAT? SERIOUSLY?
RIGHT AFTER SCHOOL STARTED, SHE KICKED ME IN THE FACE.
...!
HEY!
BUT, BUT!
MEI-CHAN'S SUPER NICE.
YEAH.
I KNOW.

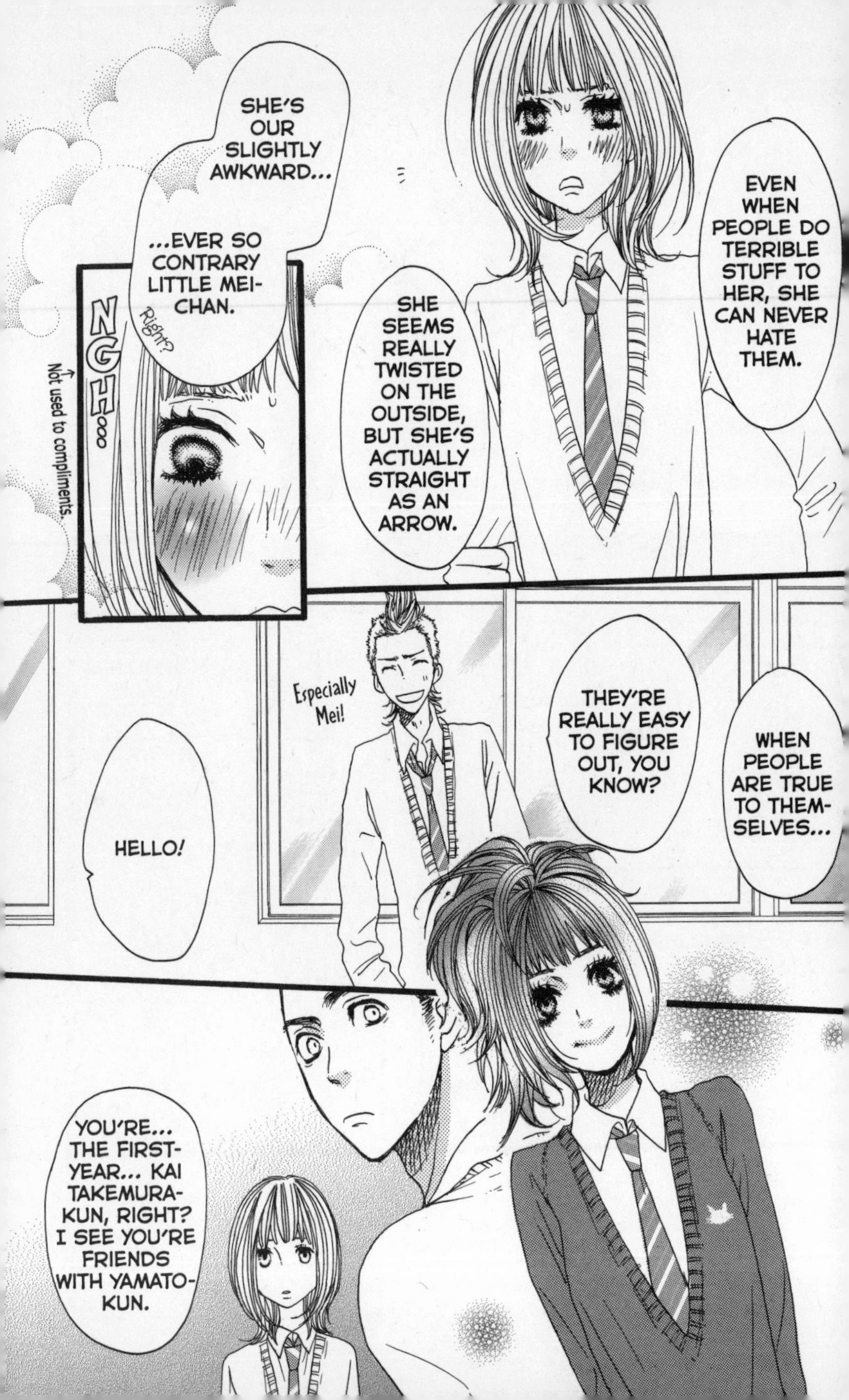
EVEN WHEN PEOPLE DO TERRIBLE STUFF TO HER, SHE CAN NEVER HATE THEM.
SHE SEEMS REALLY TWISTED ON THE OUTSIDE, BUT SHE'S ACTUALLY STRAIGHT AS AN ARROW.
SHE'S OUR SLIGHTLY AWKWARD...
...EVER SO CONTRARY LITTLE MEI-CHAN.
Right?
NGHooo
Not used to compliments.
WHEN PEOPLE ARE TRUE TO THEM-SELVES...
THEY'RE REALLY EASY TO FIGURE OUT, YOU KNOW?
Especially Mei!
HELLO!
YOU'RE... THE FIRST-YEAR... KAI TAKEMURA-KUN, RIGHT? I SEE YOU'RE FRIENDS WITH YAMATO-KUN.

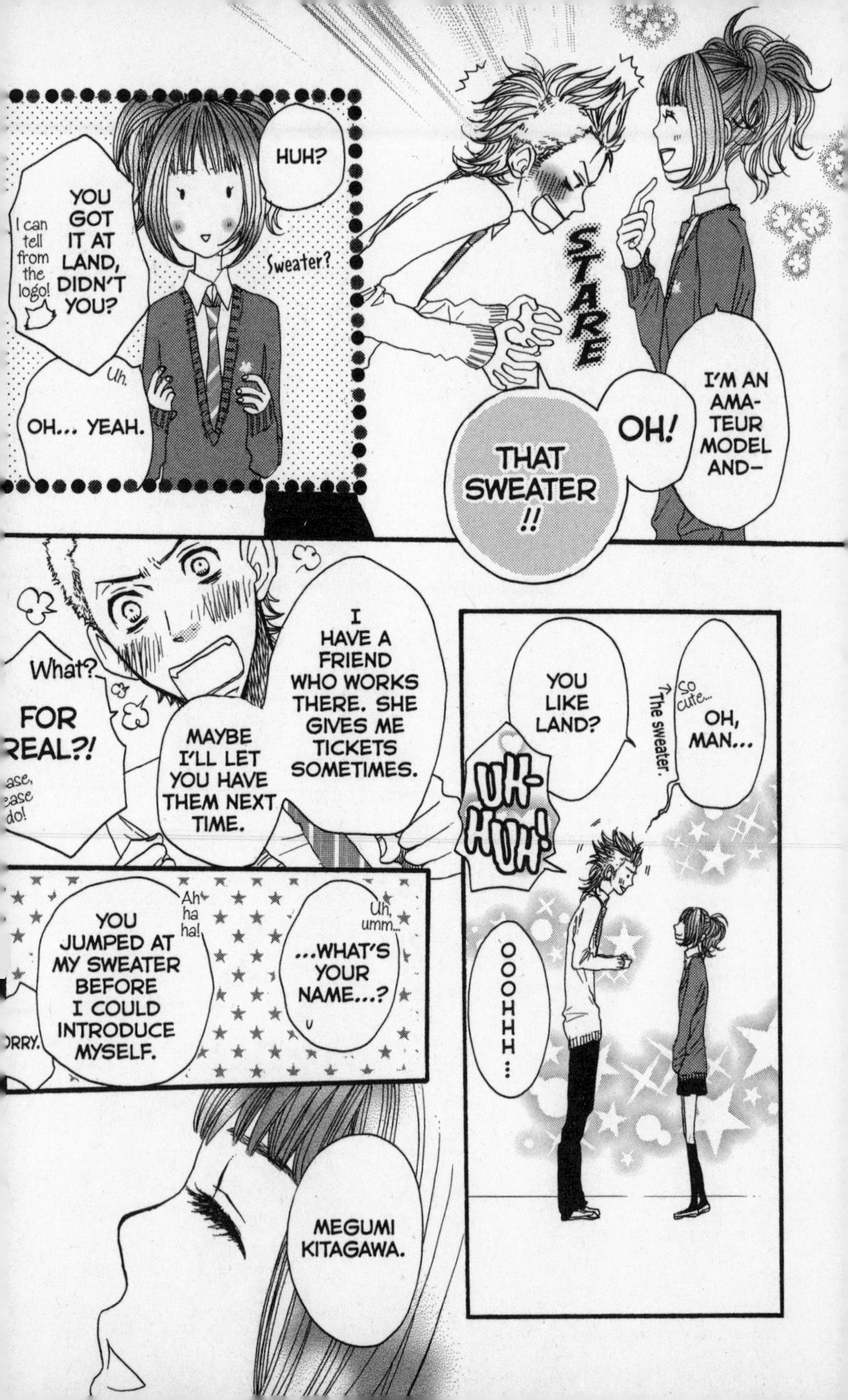
I'M AN AMATEUR MODEL AND—
OH!
THAT SWEATER!!
STARE
HUH?
Sweater?
YOU GOT IT AT LAND, DIDN'T YOU?
I can tell from the logo!
Uh.
OH... YEAH.
OH, MAN...
So cute...
The sweater.
YOU LIKE LAND?
UH-HUH!
OOOHHH...
I HAVE A FRIEND WHO WORKS THERE. SHE GIVES ME TICKETS SOMETIMES.
MAYBE I'LL LET YOU HAVE THEM NEXT TIME.
What?
FOR REAL?!
Uh, umm...
...WHAT'S YOUR NAME...?
Ah ha ha!
YOU JUMPED AT MY SWEATER BEFORE I COULD INTRODUCE MYSELF.
MEGUMI KITAGAWA.

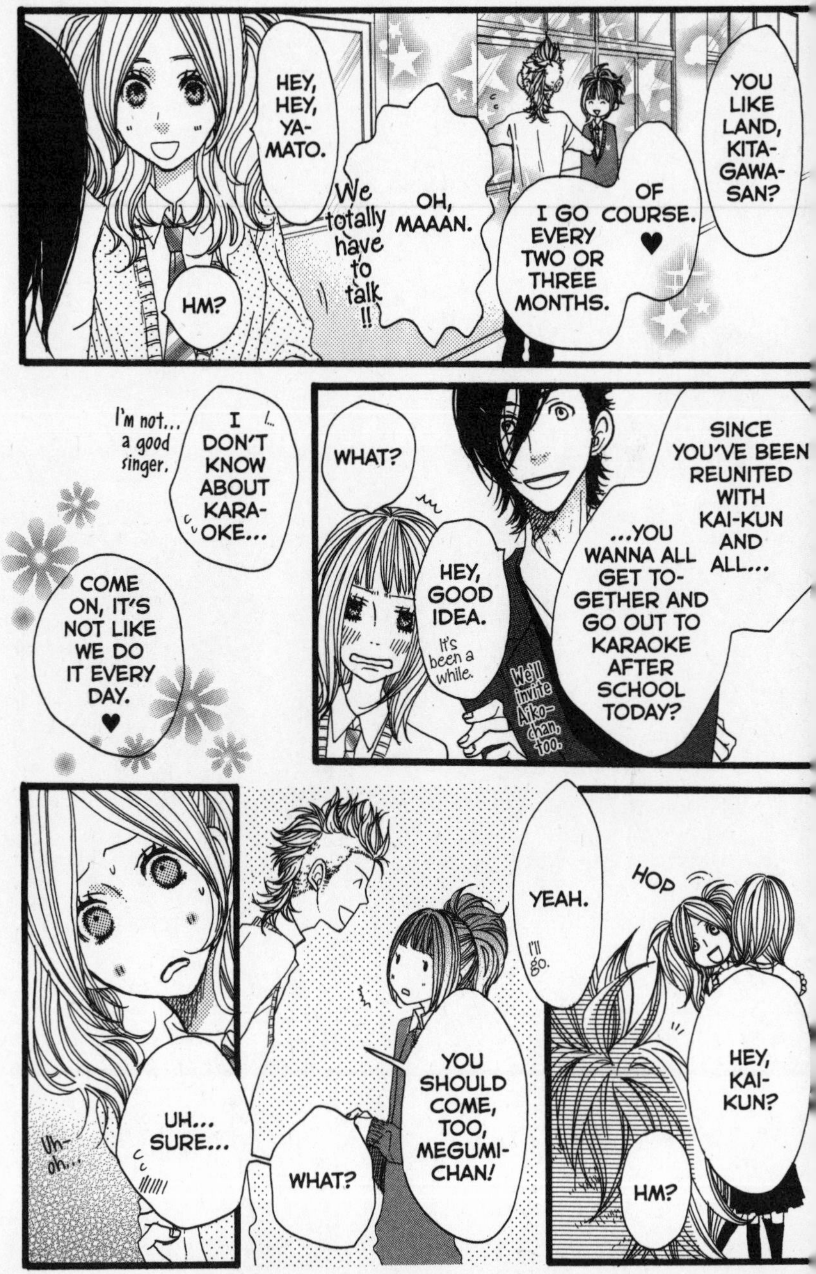

YOU LIKE LAND, KITAGAWA-SAN?
OF COURSE. I GO EVERY TWO OR THREE MONTHS. ♥
OH, MAAAN.
We totally have to talk!!
HEY, HEY, YAMATO.
HM?
SINCE YOU'VE BEEN REUNITED WITH KAI-KUN AND ALL...
...YOU WANNA ALL GET TOGETHER AND GO OUT TO KARAOKE AFTER SCHOOL TODAY?
We'll invite Aiko-chan, too.
WHAT?
HEY, GOOD IDEA.
It's been a while.
I...
I DON'T KNOW ABOUT KARAOKE...
I'm not... a good singer.
COME ON, IT'S NOT LIKE WE DO IT EVERY DAY. ♥
YEAH.
I'll go.
HOP
HEY, KAI-KUN?
HM?
YOU SHOULD COME, TOO, MEGUMI-CHAN!
WHAT?
UH... SURE...
Uh-oh...

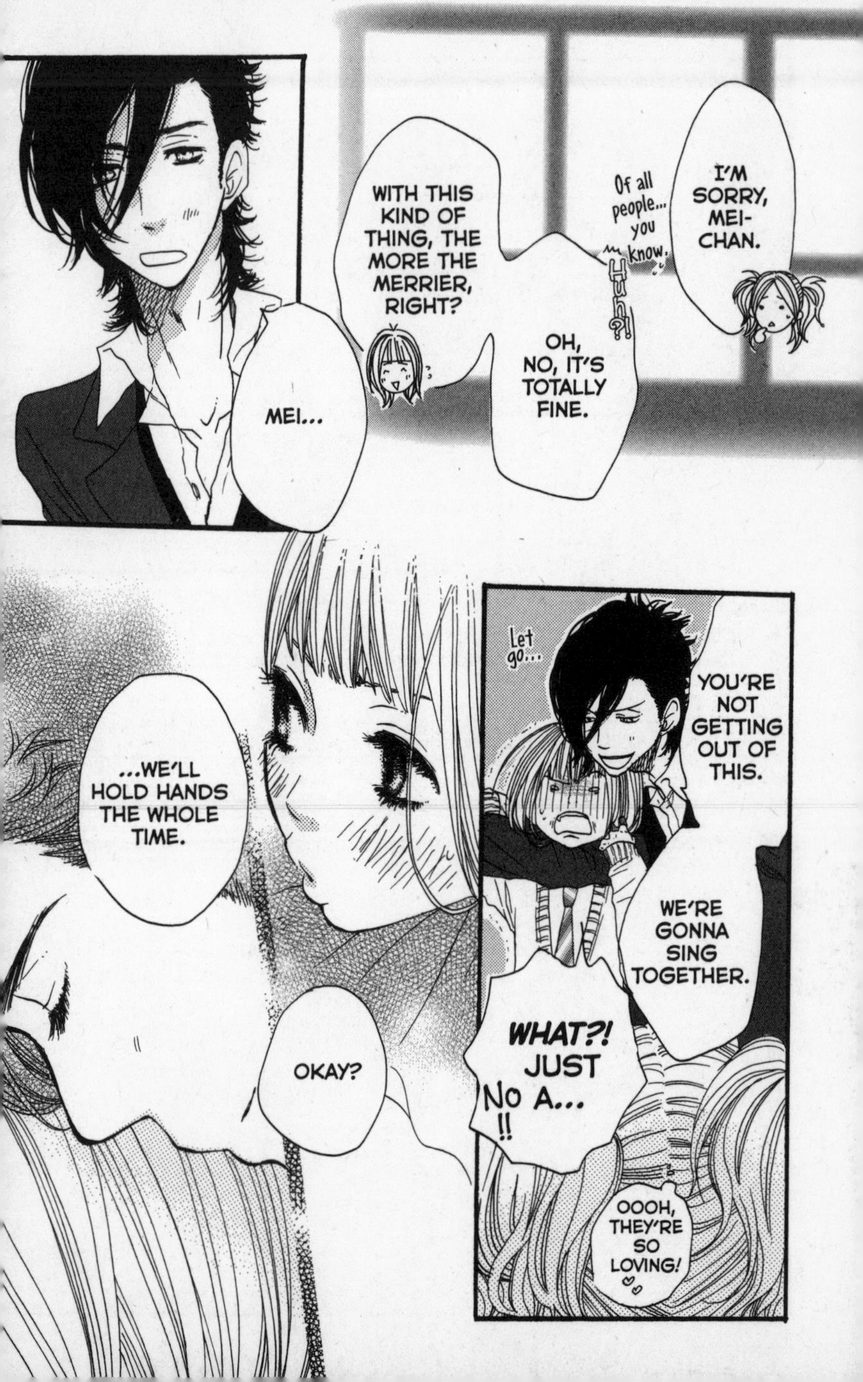
I'M SORRY, MEI-CHAN.
Of all people... you know.
Huh?!
OH, NO, IT'S TOTALLY FINE.
WITH THIS KIND OF THING, THE MORE THE MERRIER, RIGHT?
MEI...
Let go...
YOU'RE NOT GETTING OUT OF THIS.
WE'RE GONNA SING TOGETHER.
WHAT?! JUST A...
No !!
OOOH, THEY'RE SO LOVING!
...WE'LL HOLD HANDS THE WHOLE TIME.
OKAY?

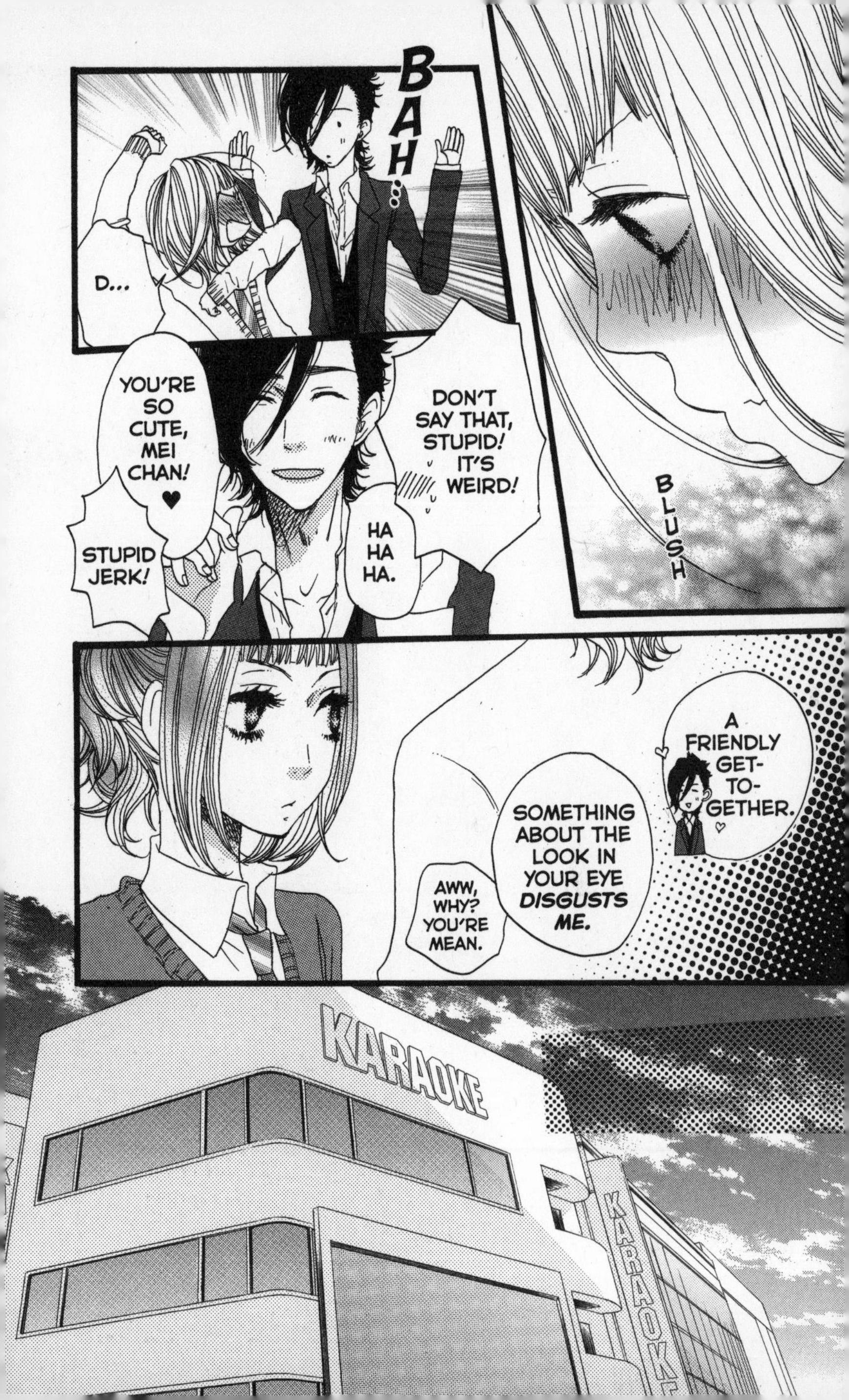
BLUSH
BAH...
D...
DON'T SAY THAT, STUPID! IT'S WEIRD!
YOU'RE SO CUTE, MEI CHAN! ♥
HA HA HA.
STUPID JERK!
A FRIENDLY GET-TOGETHER.
SOMETHING ABOUT THE LOOK IN YOUR EYE *DISGUSTS ME.*
AWW, WHY? YOU'RE MEAN.
KARAOKE
KARAOKE

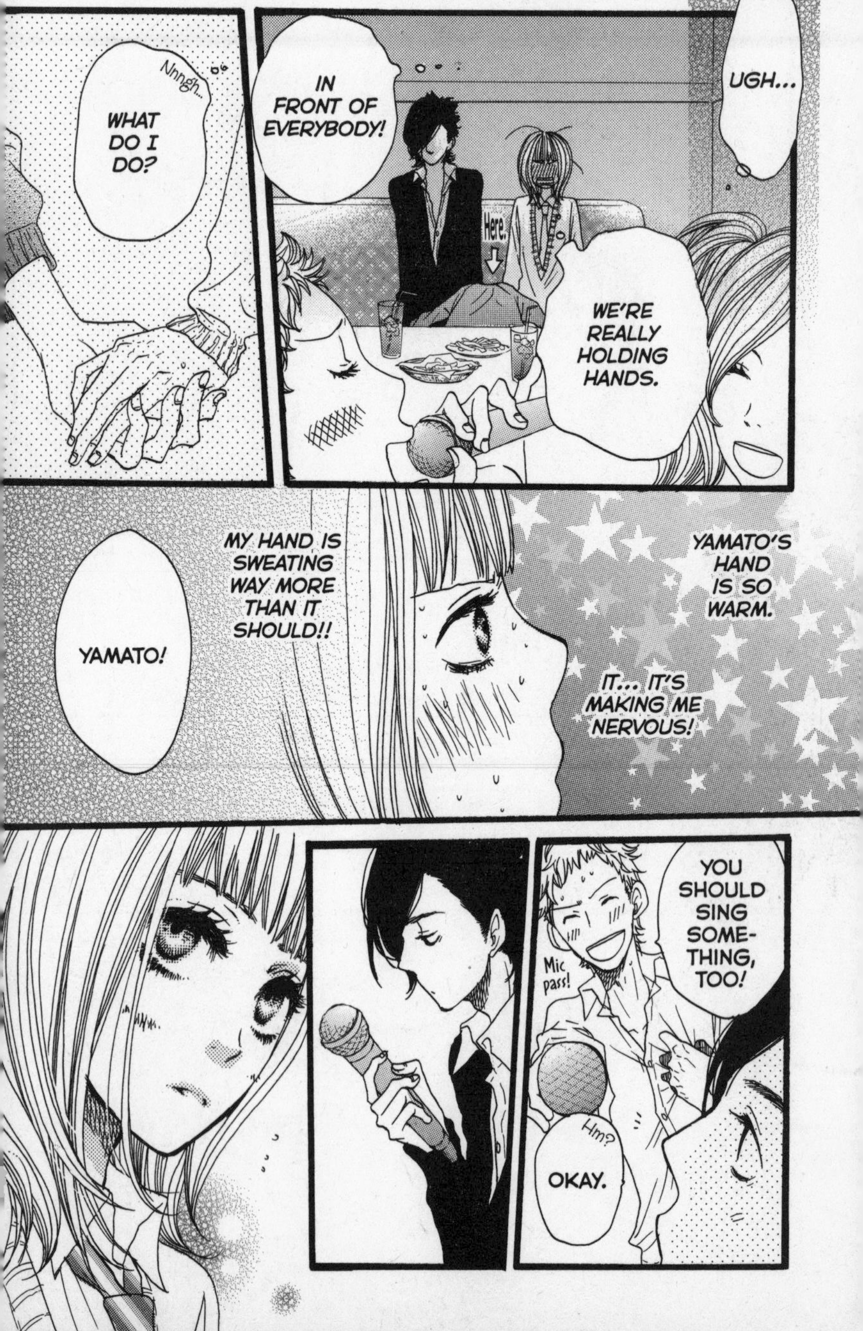
UGH...
IN FRONT OF EVERYBODY!
WE'RE REALLY HOLDING HANDS.
Here.
Nnngh..
WHAT DO I DO?
YAMATO'S HAND IS SO WARM.
IT... IT'S MAKING ME NERVOUS!
MY HAND IS SWEATING WAY MORE THAN IT SHOULD!!
YAMATO!
YOU SHOULD SING SOMETHING, TOO!
Mic pass!
Hm?
OKAY.

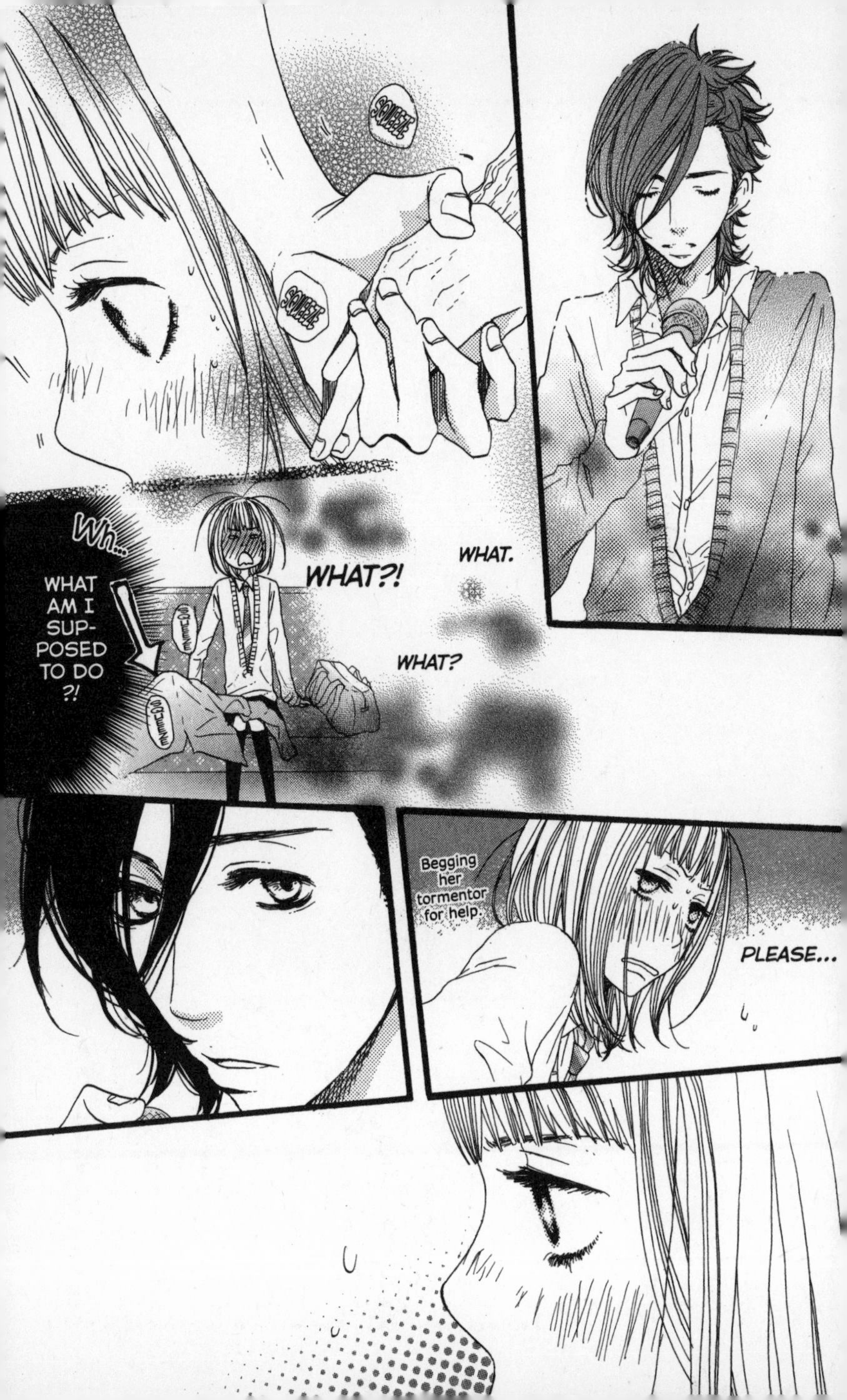
SQUEEZE
SQUEEZE
WHAT.
WHAT?!
WHAT?
Wh...
WHAT AM I SUP-POSED TO DO?!
SQUEEZE
SQUEEZE
PLEASE...
Begging her tormentor for help.

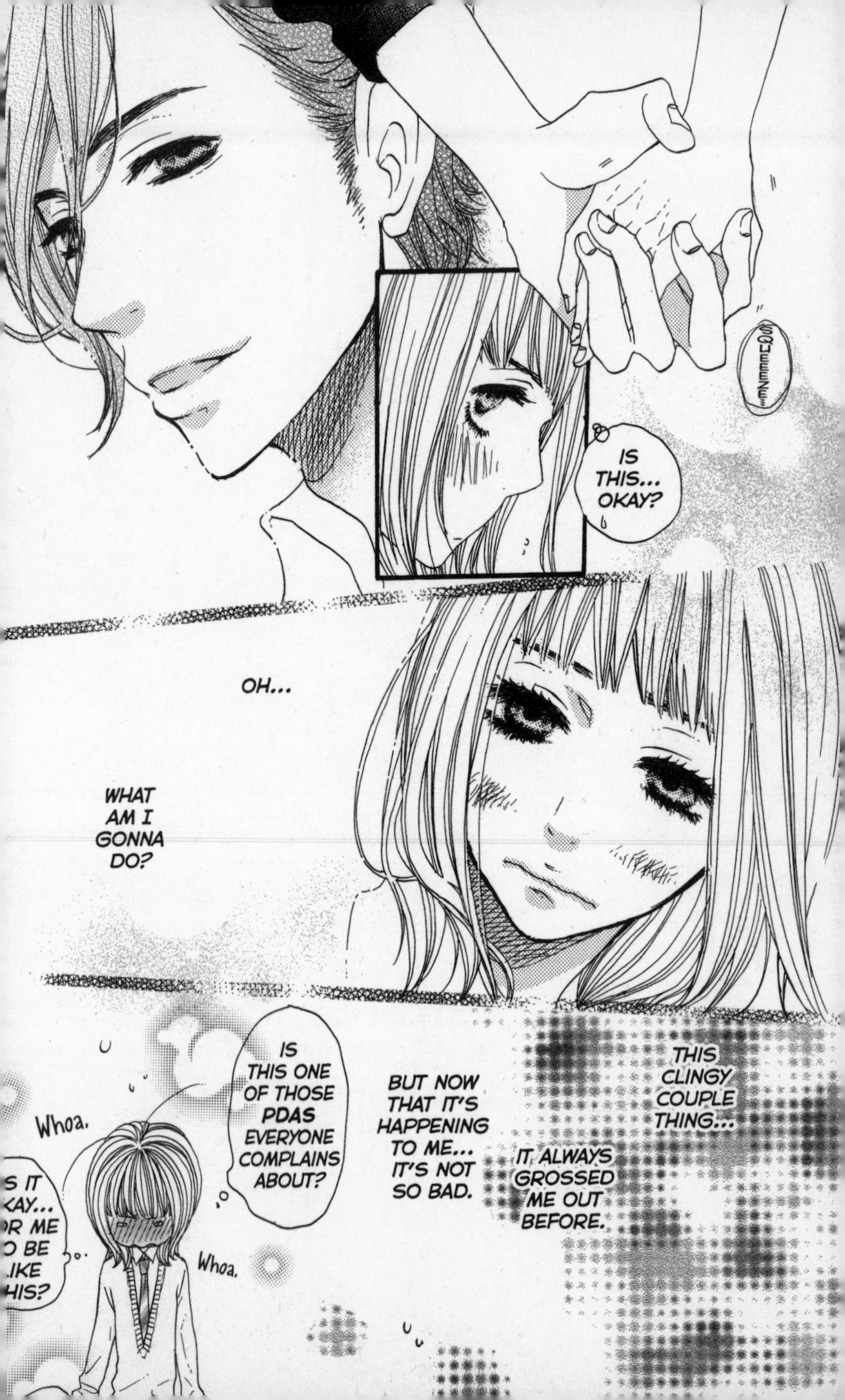
SQUEEZE...
IS THIS... OKAY?
OH...
WHAT AM I GONNA DO?
THIS CLINGY COUPLE THING...
IT ALWAYS GROSSED ME OUT BEFORE.
BUT NOW THAT IT'S HAPPENING TO ME... IT'S NOT SO BAD.
IS THIS ONE OF THOSE PDAS EVERYONE COMPLAINS ABOUT?
Whoa.
Whoa.
S IT KAY... OR ME O BE IKE HIS?

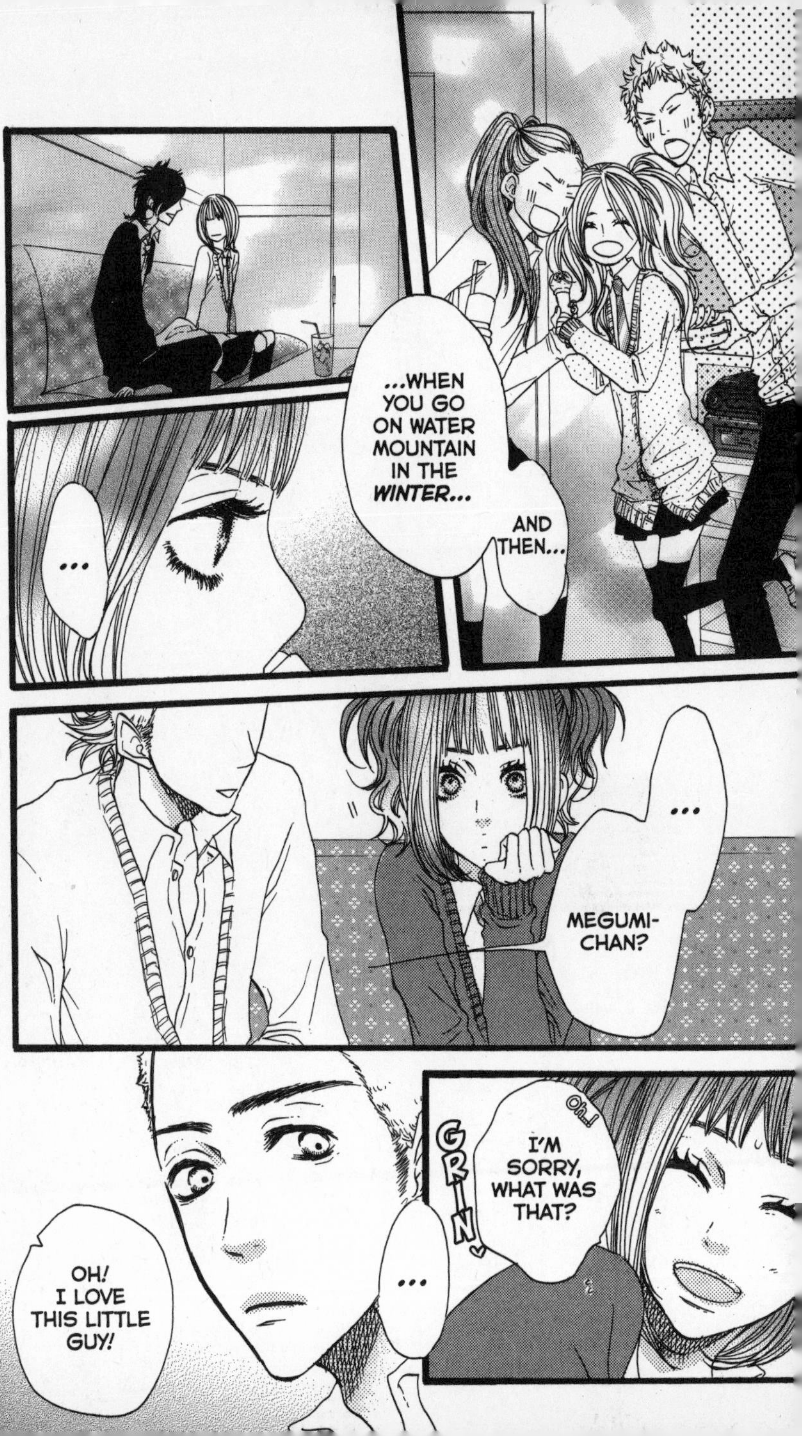
...WHEN YOU GO ON WATER MOUNTAIN IN THE *WINTER*...
AND THEN...
...
...
MEGUMI-CHAN?
Oh!
GRIN
I'M SORRY, WHAT WAS THAT?
...
OH! I LOVE THIS LITTLE GUY!

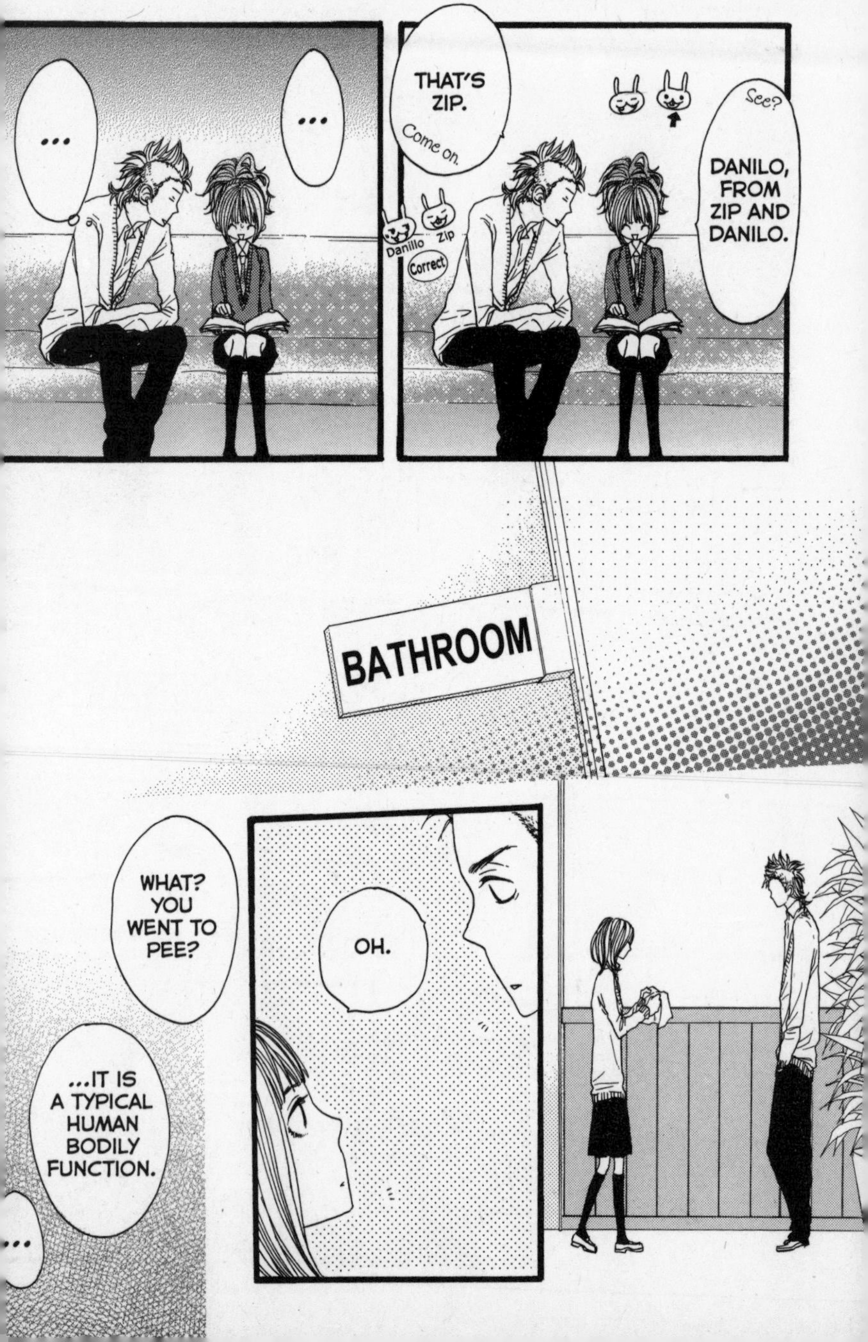
See?
DANILO, FROM ZIP AND DANILO.
THAT'S ZIP.
Come on.
Danillo
Zip
Correct
...
...
BATHROOM
OH.
WHAT? YOU WENT TO PEE?
...IT IS A TYPICAL HUMAN BODILY FUNCTION.
...

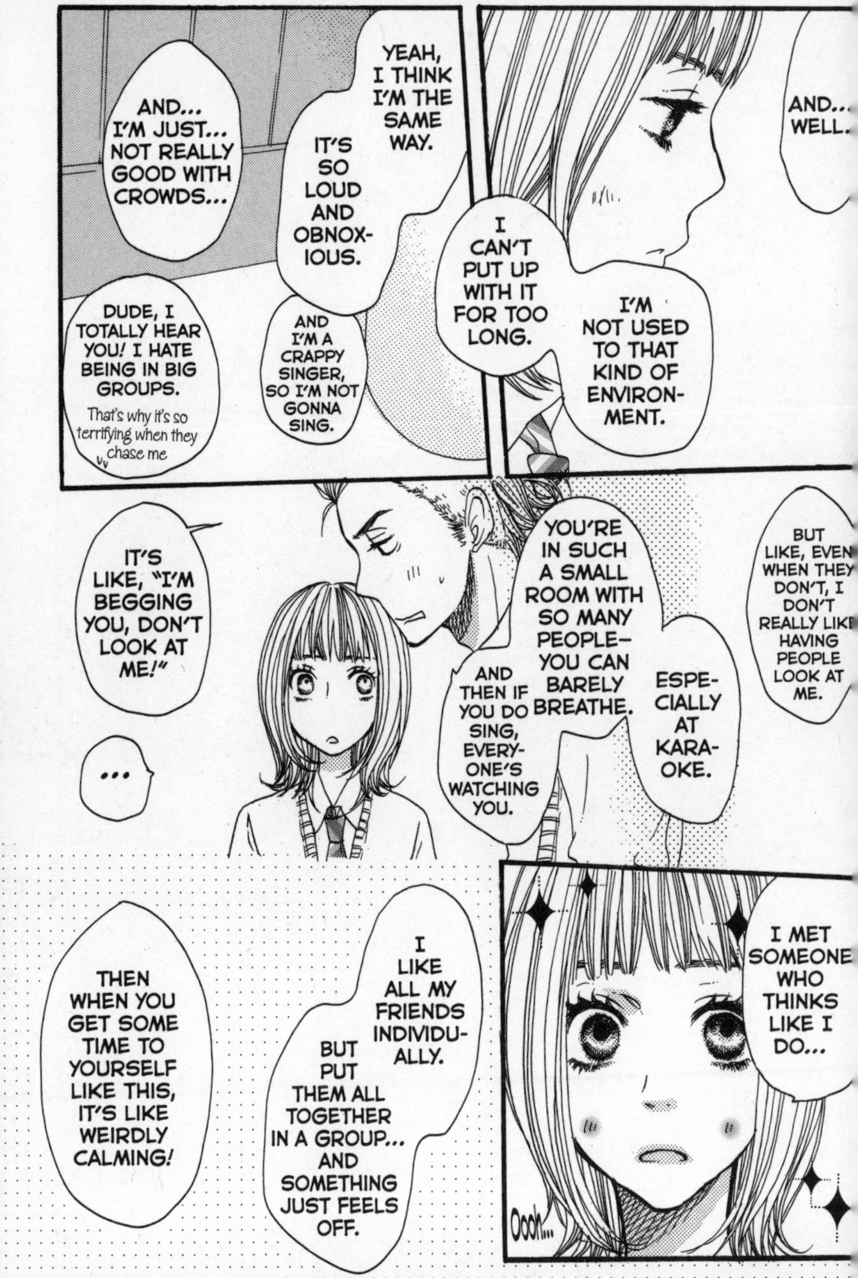
AND... WELL.
I'M NOT USED TO THAT KIND OF ENVIRONMENT.
I CAN'T PUT UP WITH IT FOR TOO LONG.
YEAH, I THINK I'M THE SAME WAY.
IT'S SO LOUD AND OBNOXIOUS.
AND... I'M JUST... NOT REALLY GOOD WITH CROWDS...
AND I'M A CRAPPY SINGER, SO I'M NOT GONNA SING.
DUDE, I TOTALLY HEAR YOU! I HATE BEING IN BIG GROUPS.
That's why it's so terrifying when they chase me
BUT LIKE, EVEN WHEN THEY DON'T, I DON'T REALLY LIKE HAVING PEOPLE LOOK AT ME.
ESPECIALLY AT KARAOKE.
YOU'RE IN SUCH A SMALL ROOM WITH SO MANY PEOPLE—YOU CAN BARELY BREATHE.
AND THEN IF YOU DO SING, EVERYONE'S WATCHING YOU.
IT'S LIKE, "I'M BEGGING YOU, DON'T LOOK AT ME!"
...
I MET SOMEONE WHO THINKS LIKE I DO...
Oooh...
I LIKE ALL MY FRIENDS INDIVIDUALLY.
BUT PUT THEM ALL TOGETHER IN A GROUP... AND SOMETHING JUST FEELS OFF.
THEN WHEN YOU GET SOME TIME TO YOURSELF LIKE THIS, IT'S LIKE WEIRDLY CALMING!

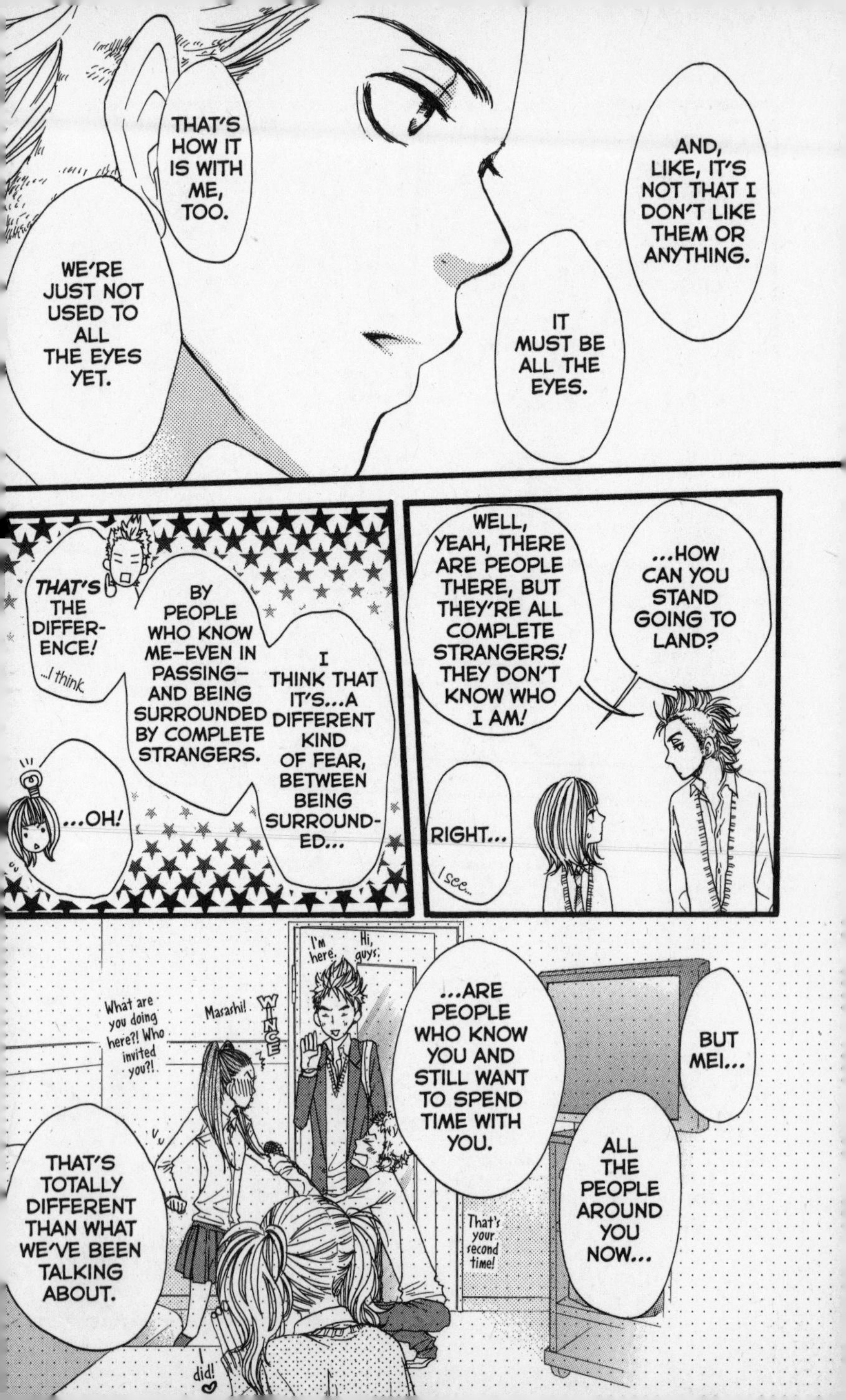
AND, LIKE, IT'S NOT THAT I DON'T LIKE THEM OR ANYTHING.
IT MUST BE ALL THE EYES.
THAT'S HOW IT IS WITH ME, TOO.
WE'RE JUST NOT USED TO ALL THE EYES YET.
...HOW CAN YOU STAND GOING TO LAND?
WELL, YEAH, THERE ARE PEOPLE THERE, BUT THEY'RE ALL COMPLETE STRANGERS! THEY DON'T KNOW WHO I AM!
RIGHT...
I see...
I THINK THAT IT'S...A DIFFERENT KIND OF FEAR, BETWEEN BEING SURROUNDED...
BY PEOPLE WHO KNOW ME—EVEN IN PASSING—AND BEING SURROUNDED BY COMPLETE STRANGERS.
THAT'S THE DIFFERENCE!
...I think
...OH!
BUT MEI...
ALL THE PEOPLE AROUND YOU NOW...
...ARE PEOPLE WHO KNOW YOU AND STILL WANT TO SPEND TIME WITH YOU.
Hi, guys.
I'm here.
WINCE
Marashi!
What are you doing here?! Who invited you?!
That's your second time!
I did!
THAT'S TOTALLY DIFFERENT THAN WHAT WE'VE BEEN TALKING ABOUT.

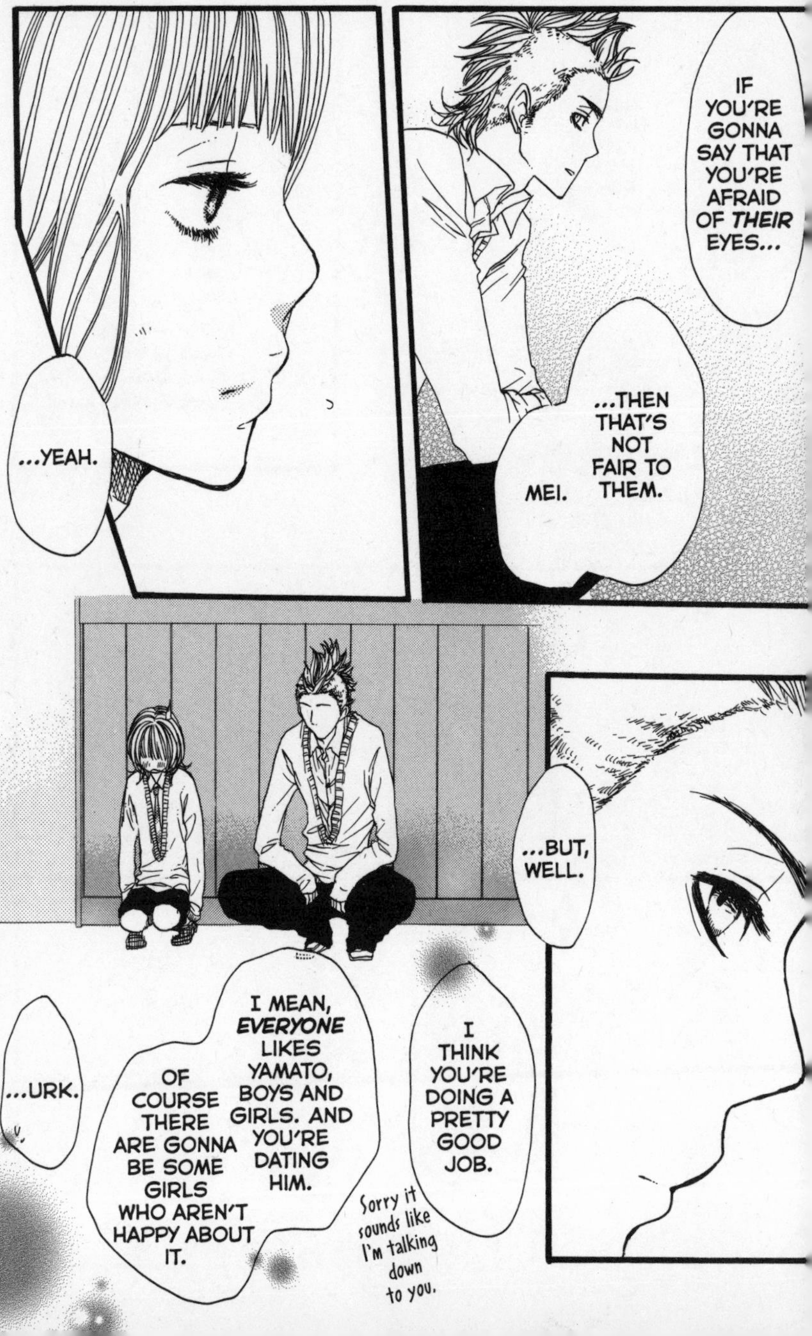
IF YOU'RE GONNA SAY THAT YOU'RE AFRAID OF *THEIR* EYES...
...THEN THAT'S NOT FAIR TO THEM.
MEI.
...YEAH.
...BUT, WELL.
I THINK YOU'RE DOING A PRETTY GOOD JOB.
I MEAN, *EVERYONE* LIKES YAMATO, BOYS AND GIRLS. AND YOU'RE DATING HIM.
OF COURSE THERE ARE GONNA BE SOME GIRLS WHO AREN'T HAPPY ABOUT IT.
Sorry it sounds like I'm talking down to you.
...URK.

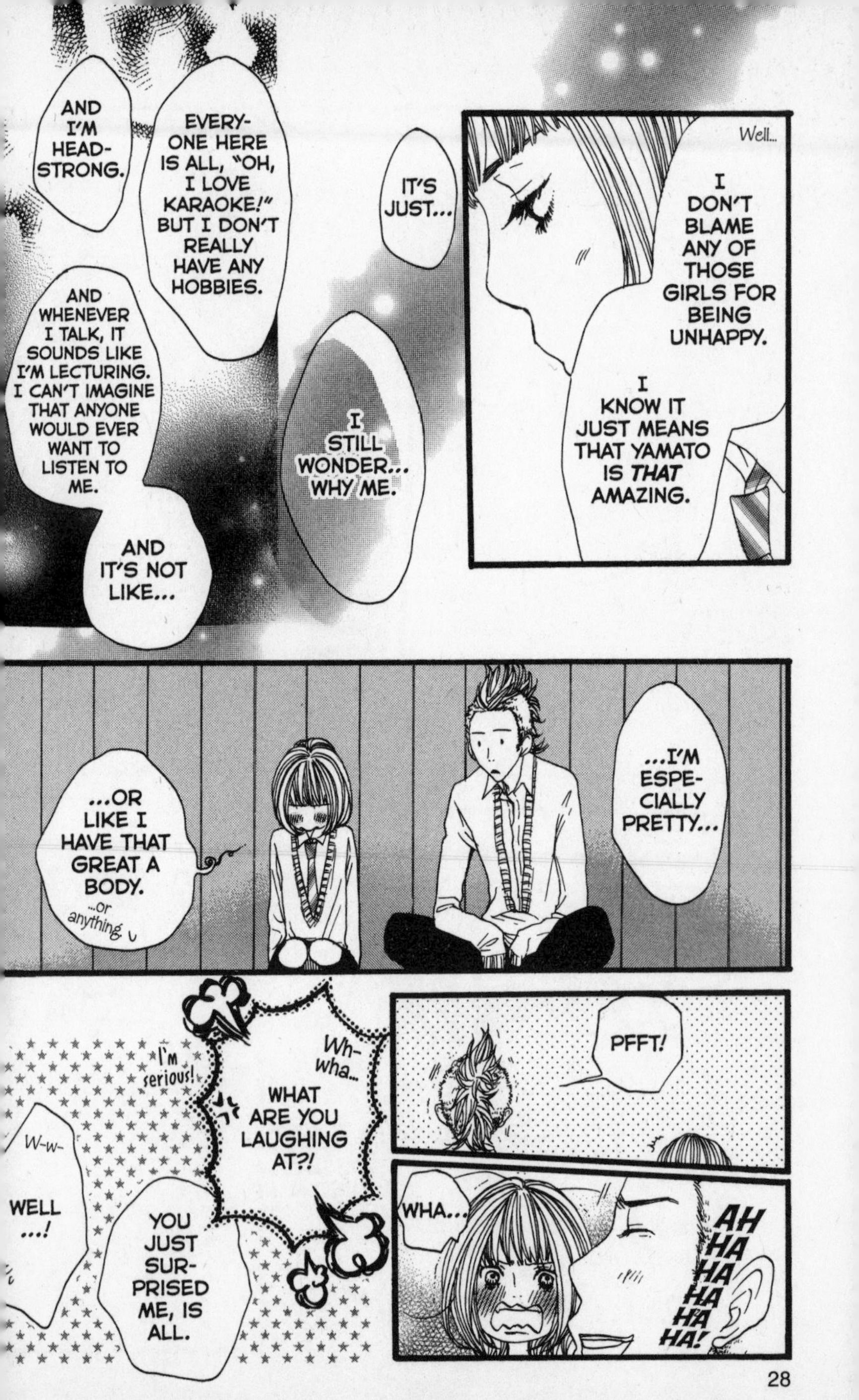
Well...
I DON'T BLAME ANY OF THOSE GIRLS FOR BEING UNHAPPY.
I KNOW IT JUST MEANS THAT YAMATO IS *THAT* AMAZING.
IT'S JUST...
I STILL WONDER... WHY ME.
EVERY-ONE HERE IS ALL, "OH, I LOVE KARAOKE!" BUT I DON'T REALLY HAVE ANY HOBBIES.
AND I'M HEAD-STRONG.
AND WHENEVER I TALK, IT SOUNDS LIKE I'M LECTURING. I CAN'T IMAGINE THAT ANYONE WOULD EVER WANT TO LISTEN TO ME.
AND IT'S NOT LIKE...
...I'M ESPE-CIALLY PRETTY...
...OR LIKE I HAVE THAT GREAT A BODY.
...or anything.
PFFT!
WHA...
AH HA HA HA HA HA!
Wh-wha...
WHAT ARE YOU LAUGHING AT?!
I'm serious!
W-w-
WELL ...!
YOU JUST SUR-PRISED ME, IS ALL.

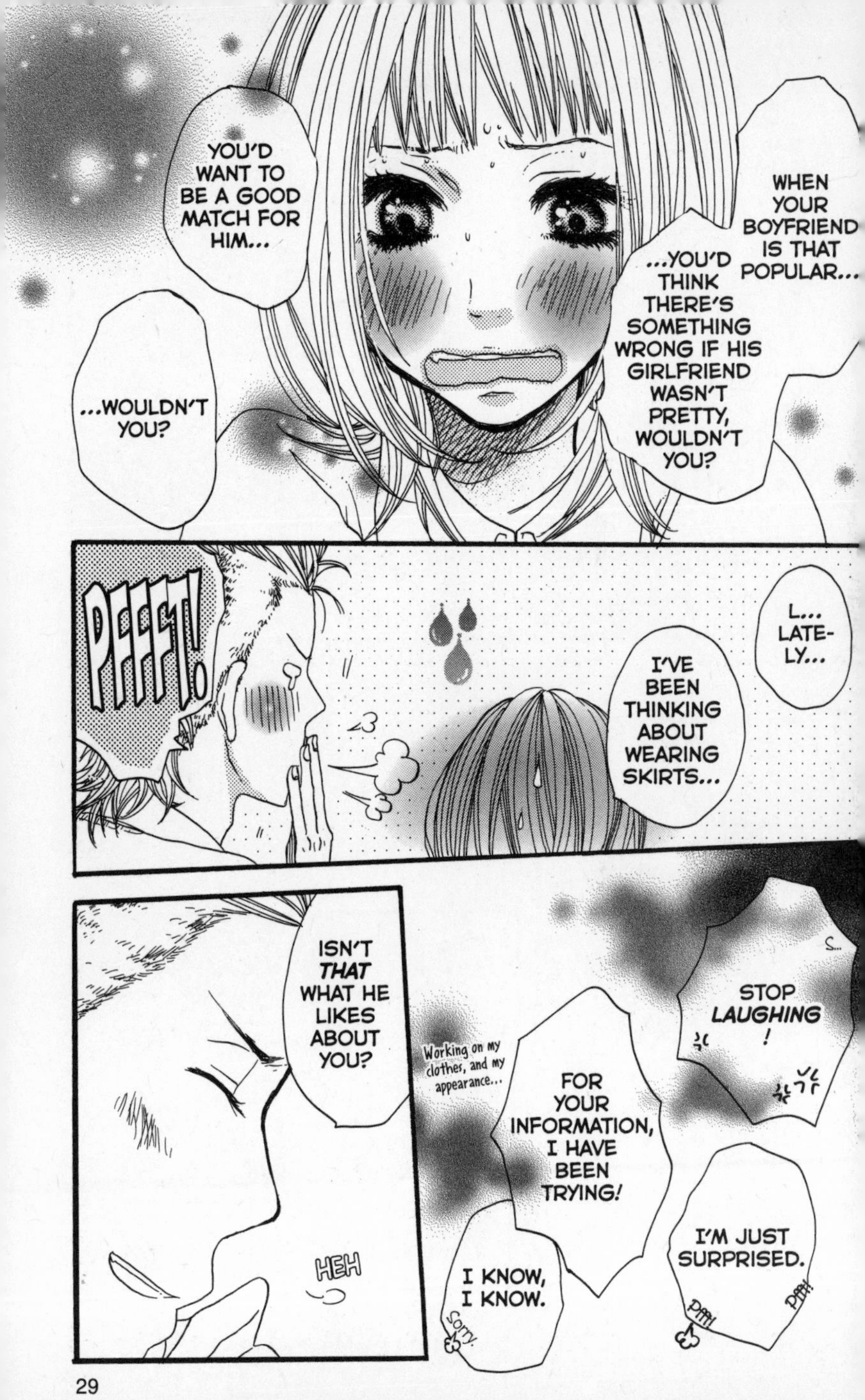
WHEN YOUR BOYFRIEND IS THAT POPULAR...
...YOU'D THINK THERE'S SOMETHING WRONG IF HIS GIRLFRIEND WASN'T PRETTY, WOULDN'T YOU?
YOU'D WANT TO BE A GOOD MATCH FOR HIM...
...WOULDN'T YOU?
L... LATE-LY...
I'VE BEEN THINKING ABOUT WEARING SKIRTS...
PFFFT!
S...
STOP *LAUGHING*!
FOR YOUR INFORMATION, I HAVE BEEN TRYING!
Working on my clothes, and my appearance...
I'M JUST SURPRISED.
Pfft!
Pfft!
I KNOW, I KNOW.
Sorry.
ISN'T *THAT* WHAT HE LIKES ABOUT YOU?
HEH

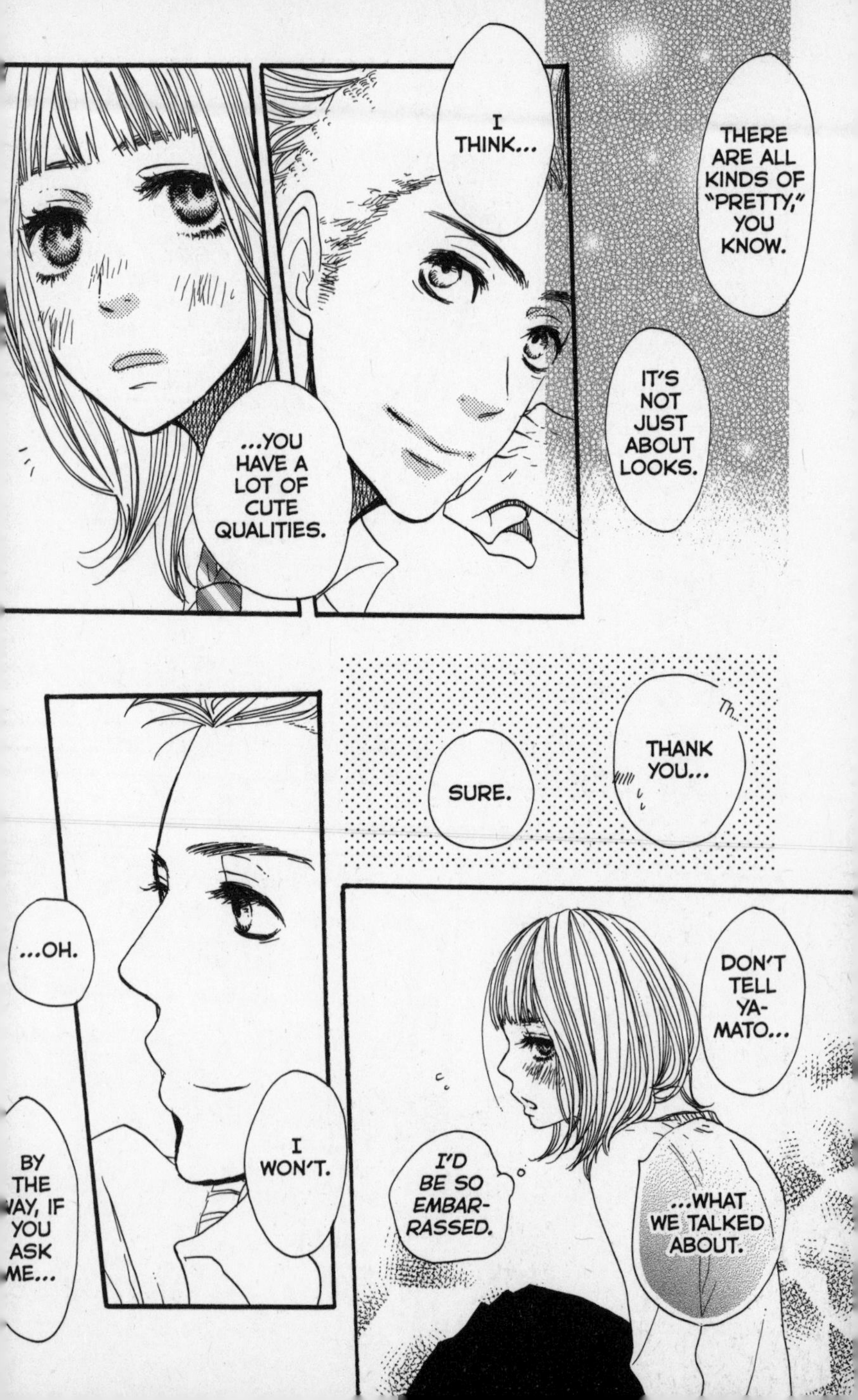
THERE ARE ALL KINDS OF "PRETTY," YOU KNOW.
IT'S NOT JUST ABOUT LOOKS.
I THINK...
...YOU HAVE A LOT OF CUTE QUALITIES.
Th..
THANK YOU...
SURE.
DON'T TELL YA-MATO...
...WHAT WE TALKED ABOUT.
I'D BE SO EMBAR-RASSED.
I WON'T.
...OH.
BY THE WAY, IF YOU ASK ME...

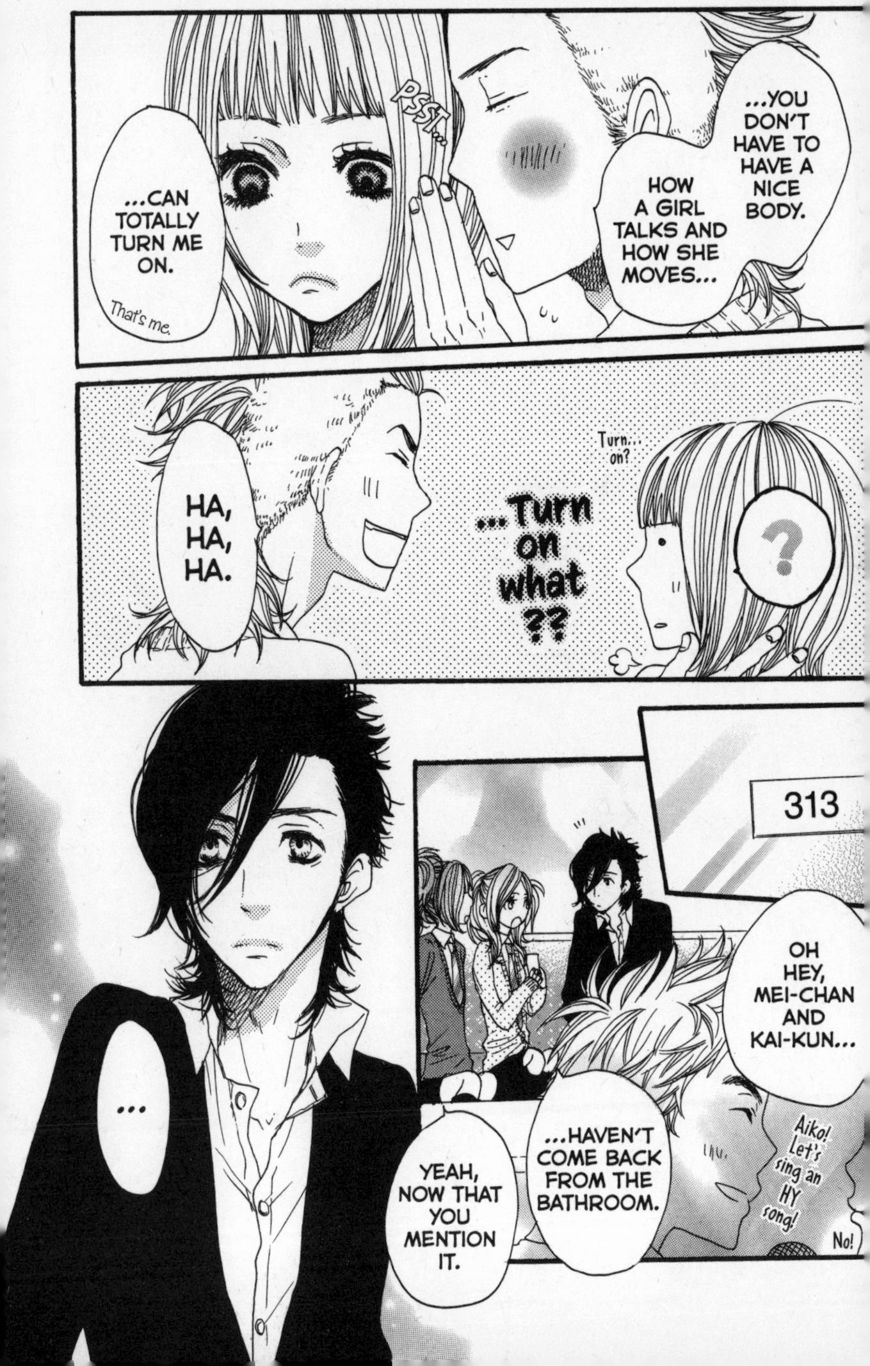
...YOU DON'T HAVE TO HAVE A NICE BODY.
HOW A GIRL TALKS AND HOW SHE MOVES...
PSST...
...CAN TOTALLY TURN ME ON.
That's me.
Turn... on?
...Turn on what ??
HA, HA, HA.
313
OH HEY, MEI-CHAN AND KAI-KUN...
Aiko! Let's sing an HY song!
No!
...HAVEN'T COME BACK FROM THE BATHROOM.
YEAH, NOW THAT YOU MENTION IT.
...

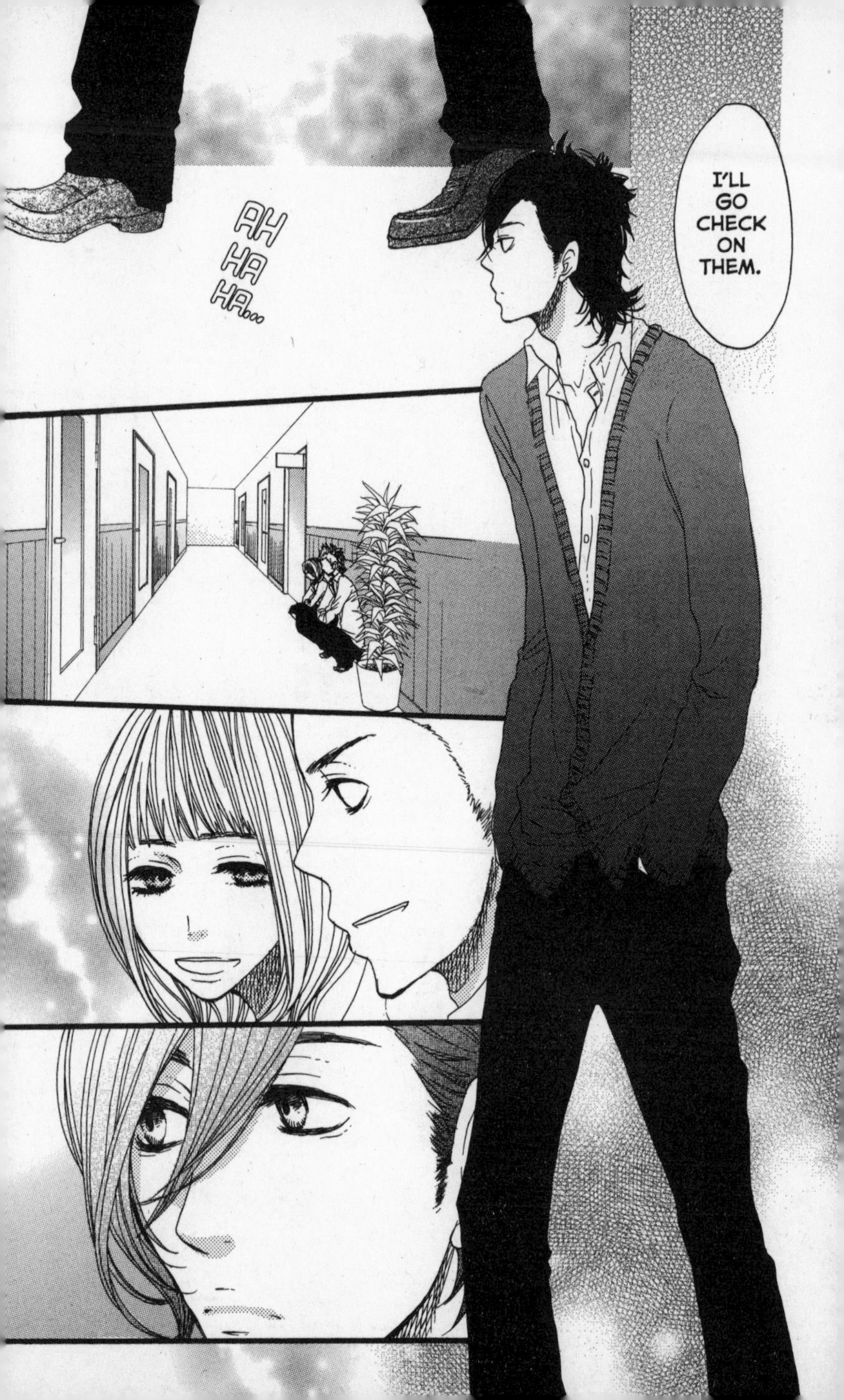
I'LL GO CHECK ON THEM.
AH HA HA...

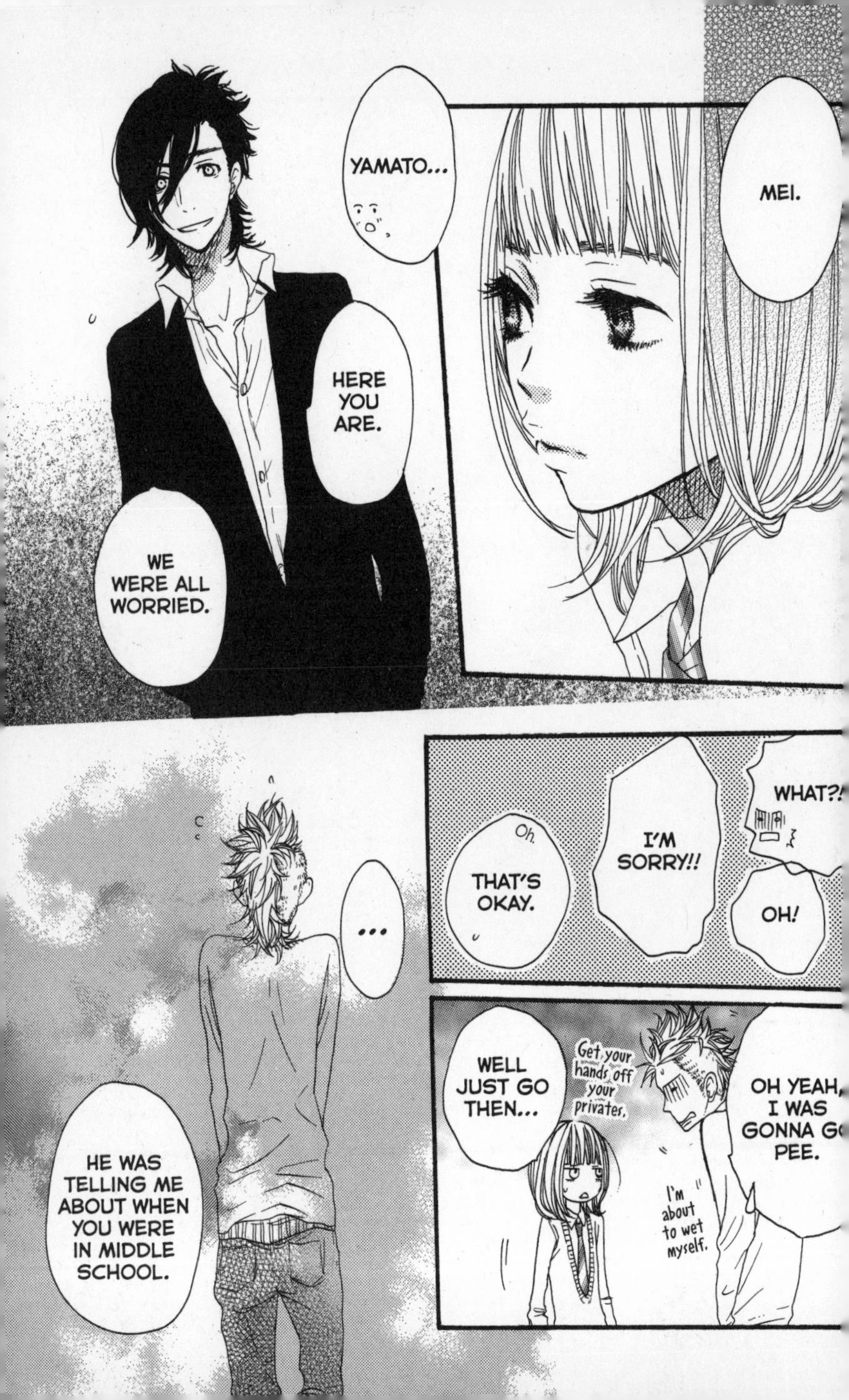
MEI.
YAMATO...
HERE YOU ARE.
WE WERE ALL WORRIED.
WHAT?!
OH!
I'M SORRY!!
Oh.
THAT'S OKAY.
OH YEAH, I WAS GONNA GO PEE.
I'm about to wet myself.
Get your hands off your privates.
WELL JUST GO THEN...
...
HE WAS TELLING ME ABOUT WHEN YOU WERE IN MIDDLE SCHOOL.

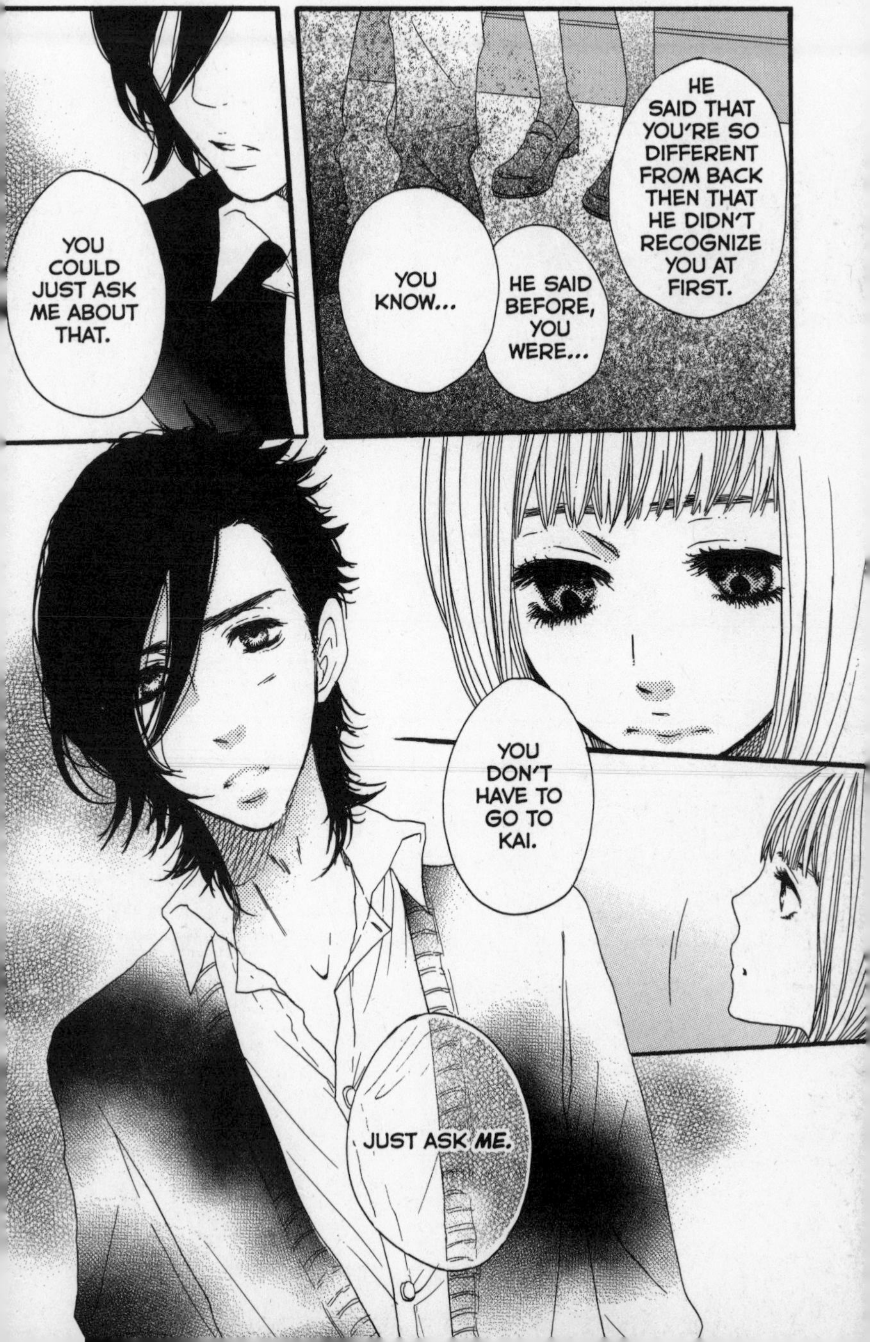
HE SAID THAT YOU'RE SO DIFFERENT FROM BACK THEN THAT HE DIDN'T RECOGNIZE YOU AT FIRST.
HE SAID BEFORE, YOU WERE...
YOU KNOW...
YOU COULD JUST ASK ME ABOUT THAT.
YOU DON'T HAVE TO GO TO KAI.
JUST ASK *ME.*

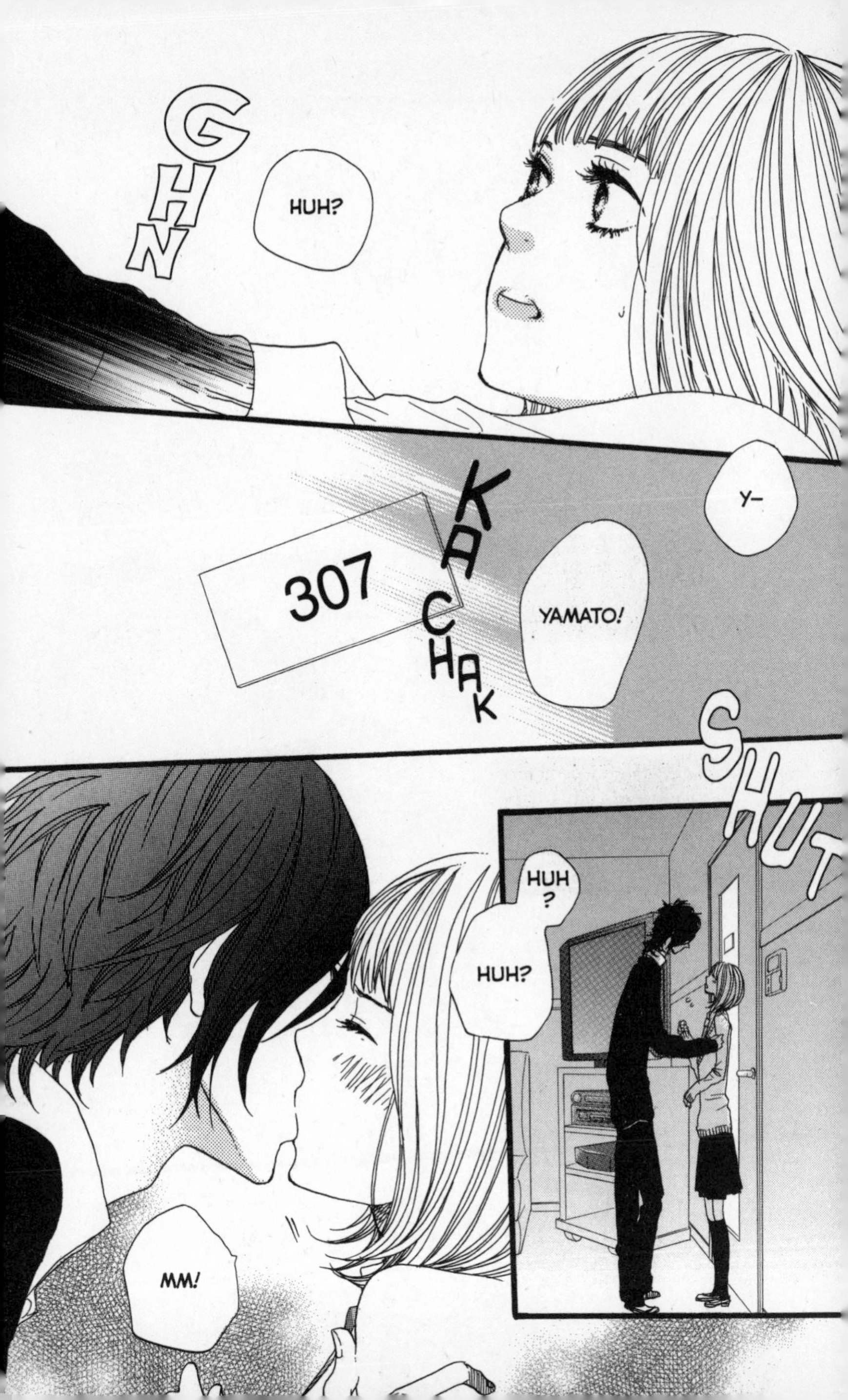
HUH?
GHN
Y–
YAMATO!
KACHAK
307
SHUT
HUH ?
HUH?
MM!

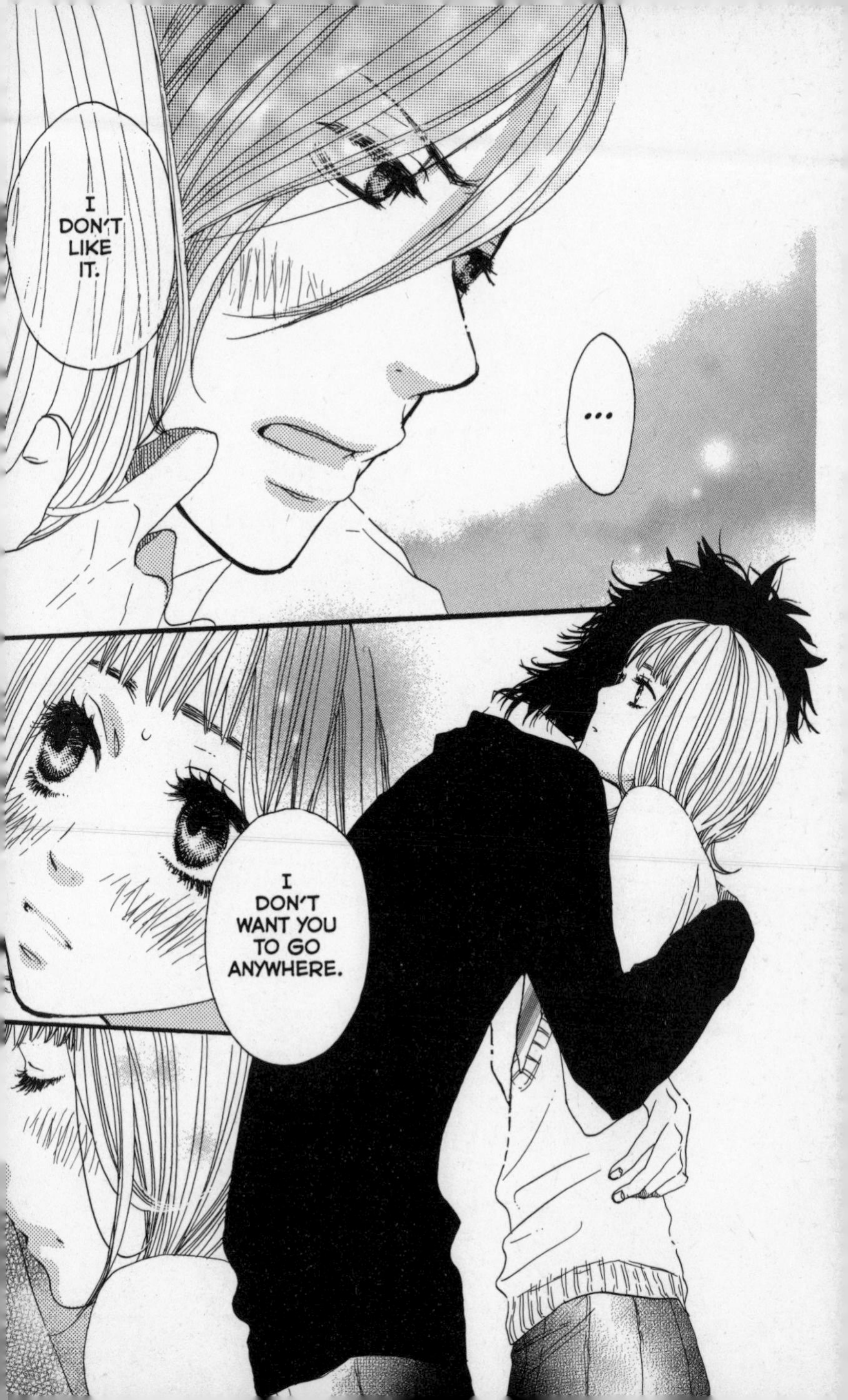
...
I DON'T LIKE IT.
I DON'T WANT YOU TO GO ANYWHERE.

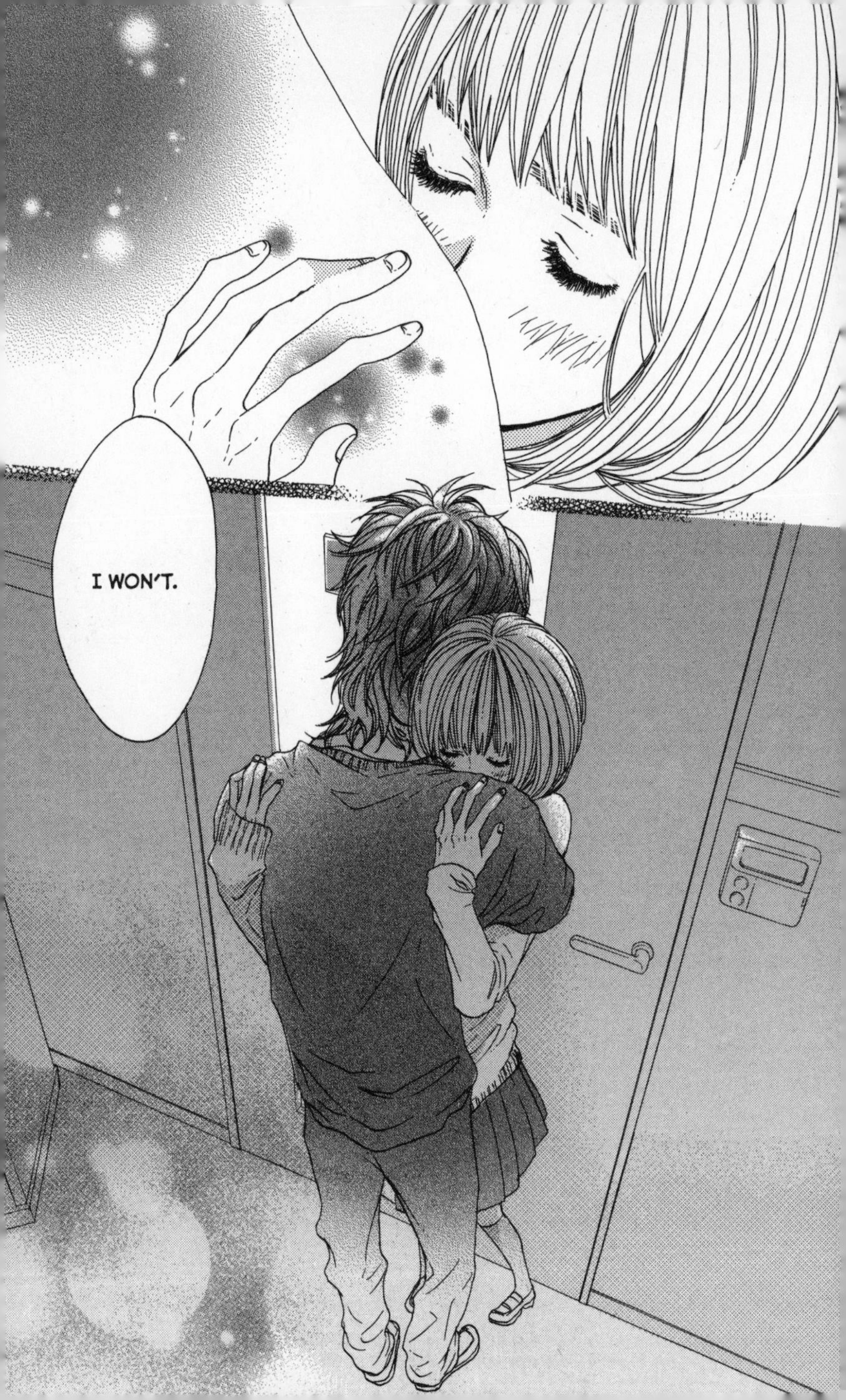
I WON'T.

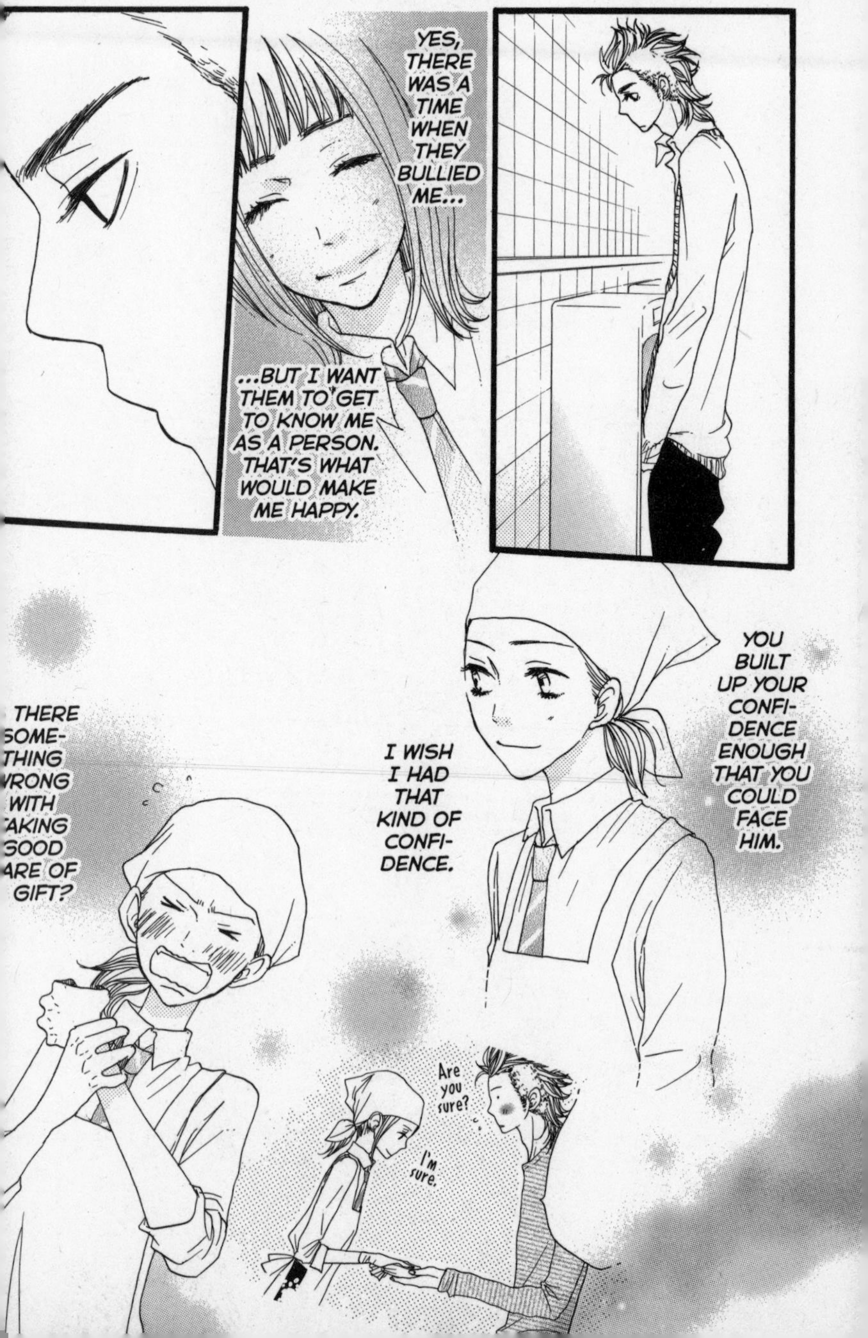
YES, THERE WAS A TIME WHEN THEY BULLIED ME...
...BUT I WANT THEM TO GET TO KNOW ME AS A PERSON. THAT'S WHAT WOULD MAKE ME HAPPY.
YOU BUILT UP YOUR CONFI-DENCE ENOUGH THAT YOU COULD FACE HIM.
I WISH I HAD THAT KIND OF CONFI-DENCE.
Are you sure?
I'm sure.
THERE SOME-THING VRONG WITH AKING GOOD ARE OF GIFT?

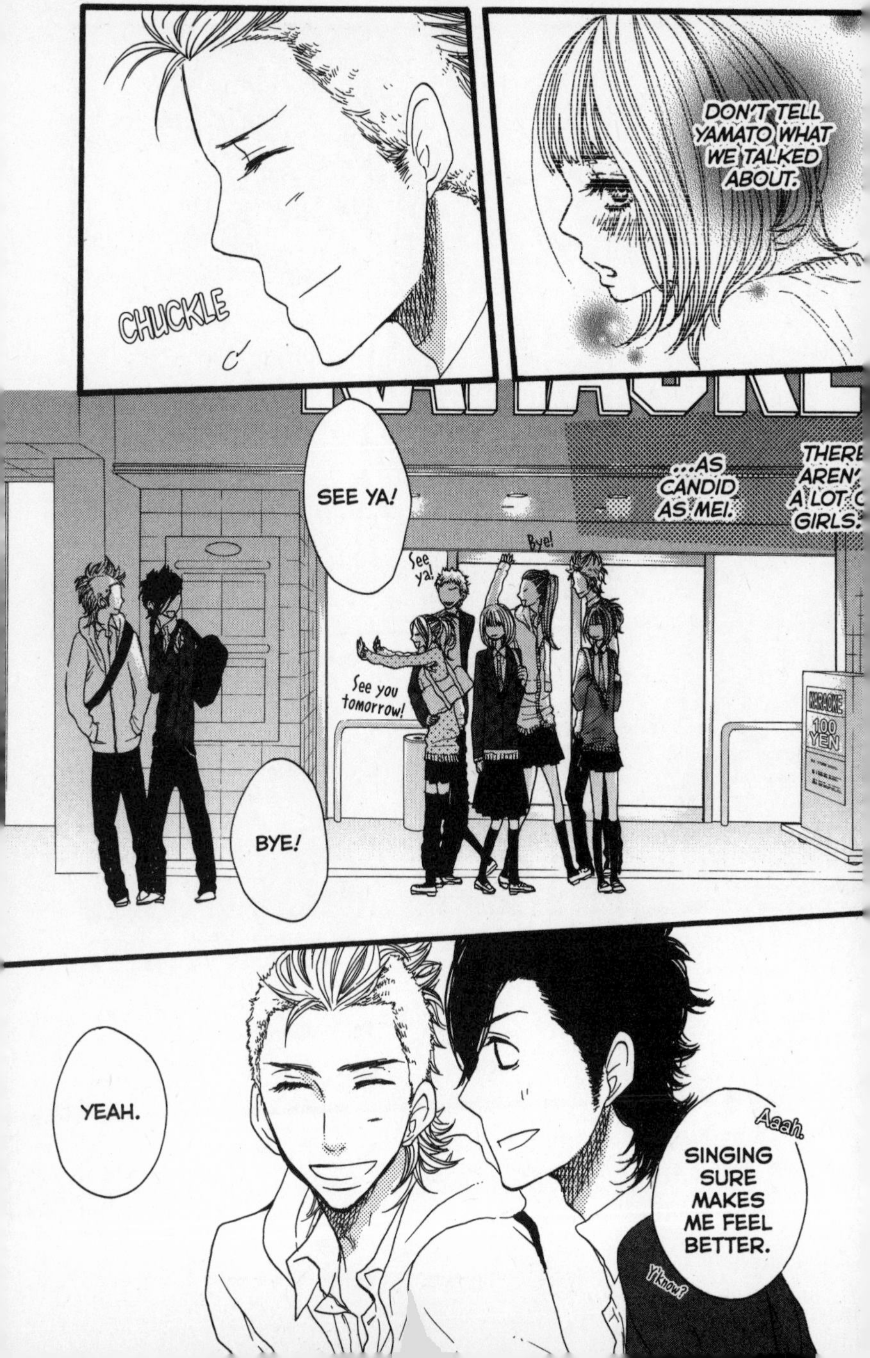
DON'T TELL YAMATO WHAT WE TALKED ABOUT.
CHUCKLE
THERE AREN' A LOT GIRLS.
...AS CANDID AS MEI.
Bye!
See ya!
SEE YA!
See you tomorrow!
KARAOKE 100 YEN
BYE!
Aaah.
SINGING SURE MAKES ME FEEL BETTER.
Y'know?
YEAH.

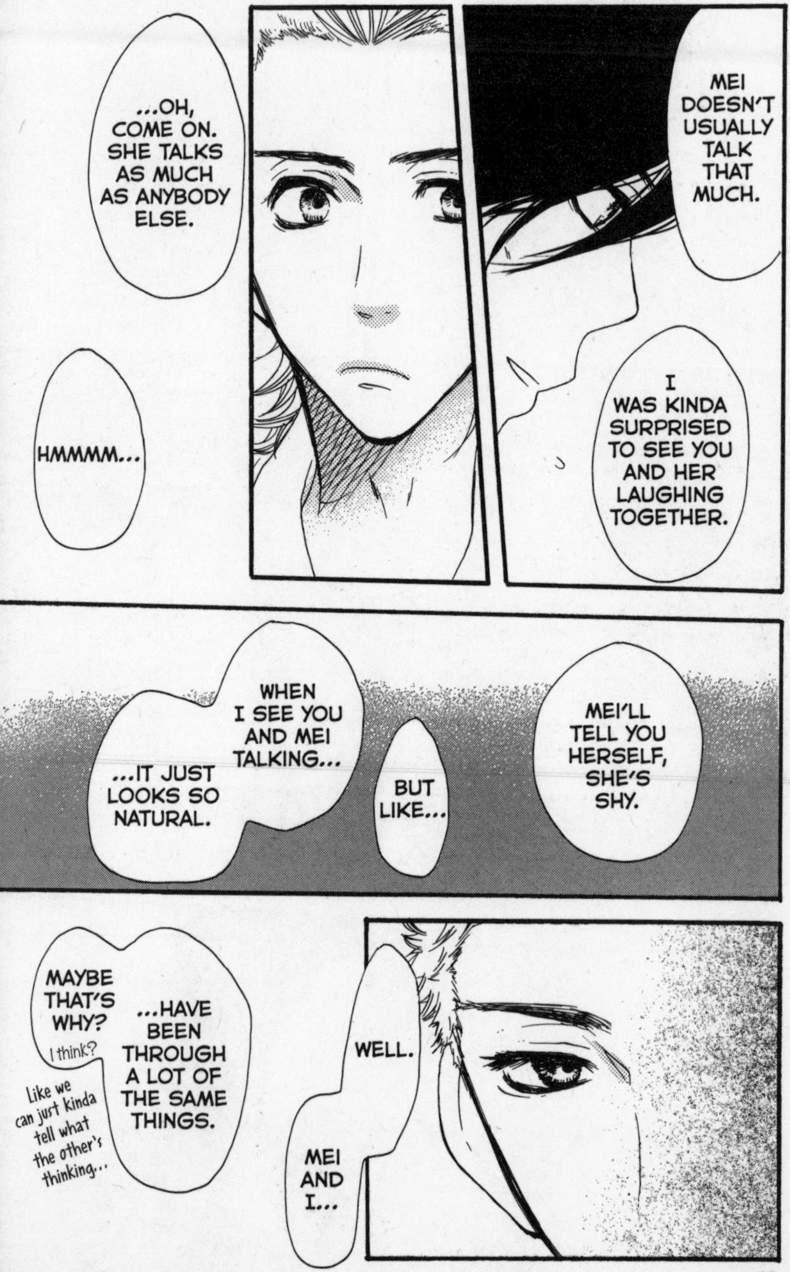
MEI DOESN'T USUALLY TALK THAT MUCH.
I WAS KINDA SURPRISED TO SEE YOU AND HER LAUGHING TOGETHER.
...OH, COME ON. SHE TALKS AS MUCH AS ANYBODY ELSE.
HMMMM...
MEI'LL TELL YOU HERSELF, SHE'S SHY.
BUT LIKE...
WHEN I SEE YOU AND MEI TALKING...
...IT JUST LOOKS SO NATURAL.
WELL.
MEI AND I...
...HAVE BEEN THROUGH A LOT OF THE SAME THINGS.
MAYBE THAT'S WHY?
I think?
Like we can just kinda tell what the other's thinking...

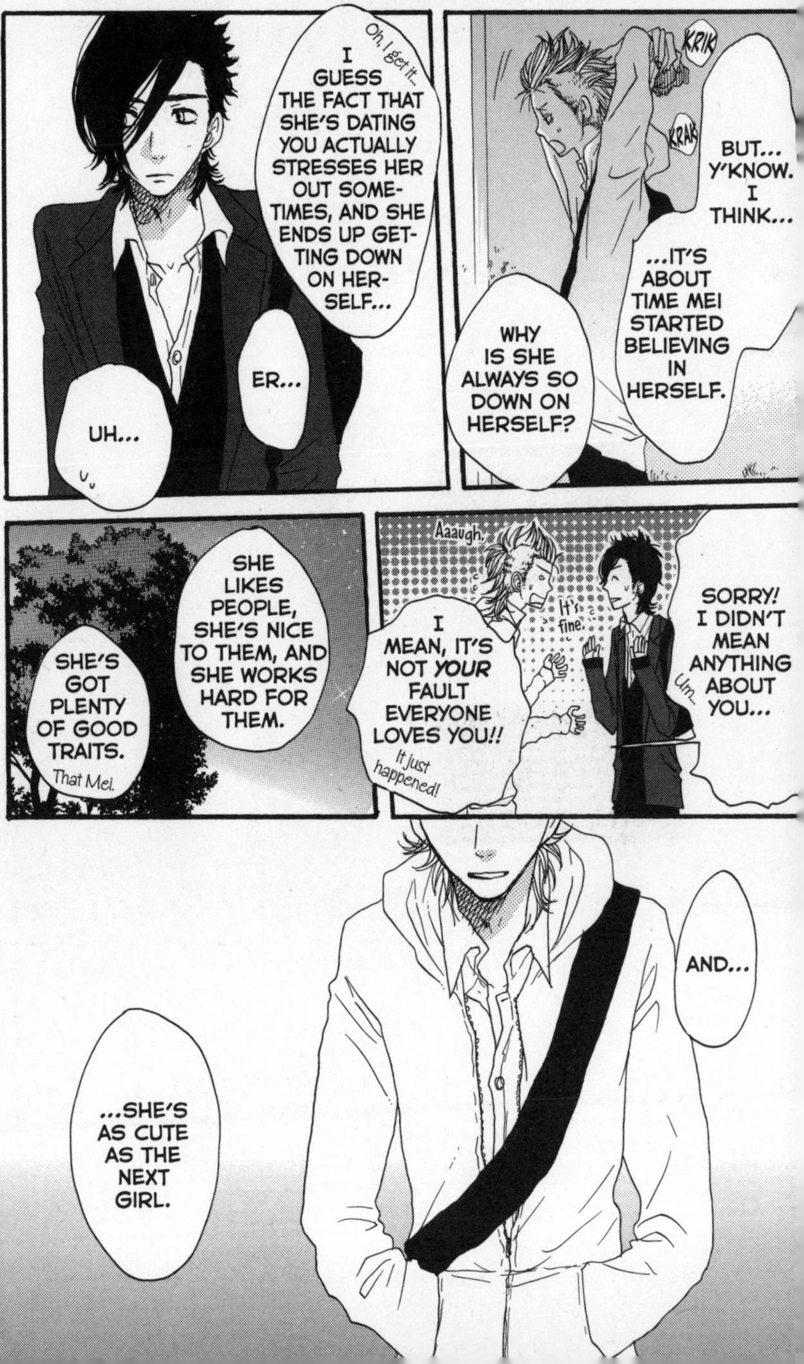
KRIK
KRAK
BUT... Y'KNOW. I THINK...
...IT'S ABOUT TIME MEI STARTED BELIEVING IN HERSELF.
WHY IS SHE ALWAYS SO DOWN ON HERSELF?
Oh, I get it...
I GUESS THE FACT THAT SHE'S DATING YOU ACTUALLY STRESSES HER OUT SOME-TIMES, AND SHE ENDS UP GET-TING DOWN ON HER-SELF...
ER...
UH...
SORRY! I DIDN'T MEAN ANYTHING ABOUT YOU...
Um...
It's fine.
Aaaugh.
I MEAN, IT'S NOT *YOUR* FAULT EVERYONE LOVES YOU!!
It just happened!
SHE LIKES PEOPLE, SHE'S NICE TO THEM, AND SHE WORKS HARD FOR THEM.
SHE'S GOT PLENTY OF GOOD TRAITS.
That Mei.
AND...
...SHE'S AS CUTE AS THE NEXT GIRL.

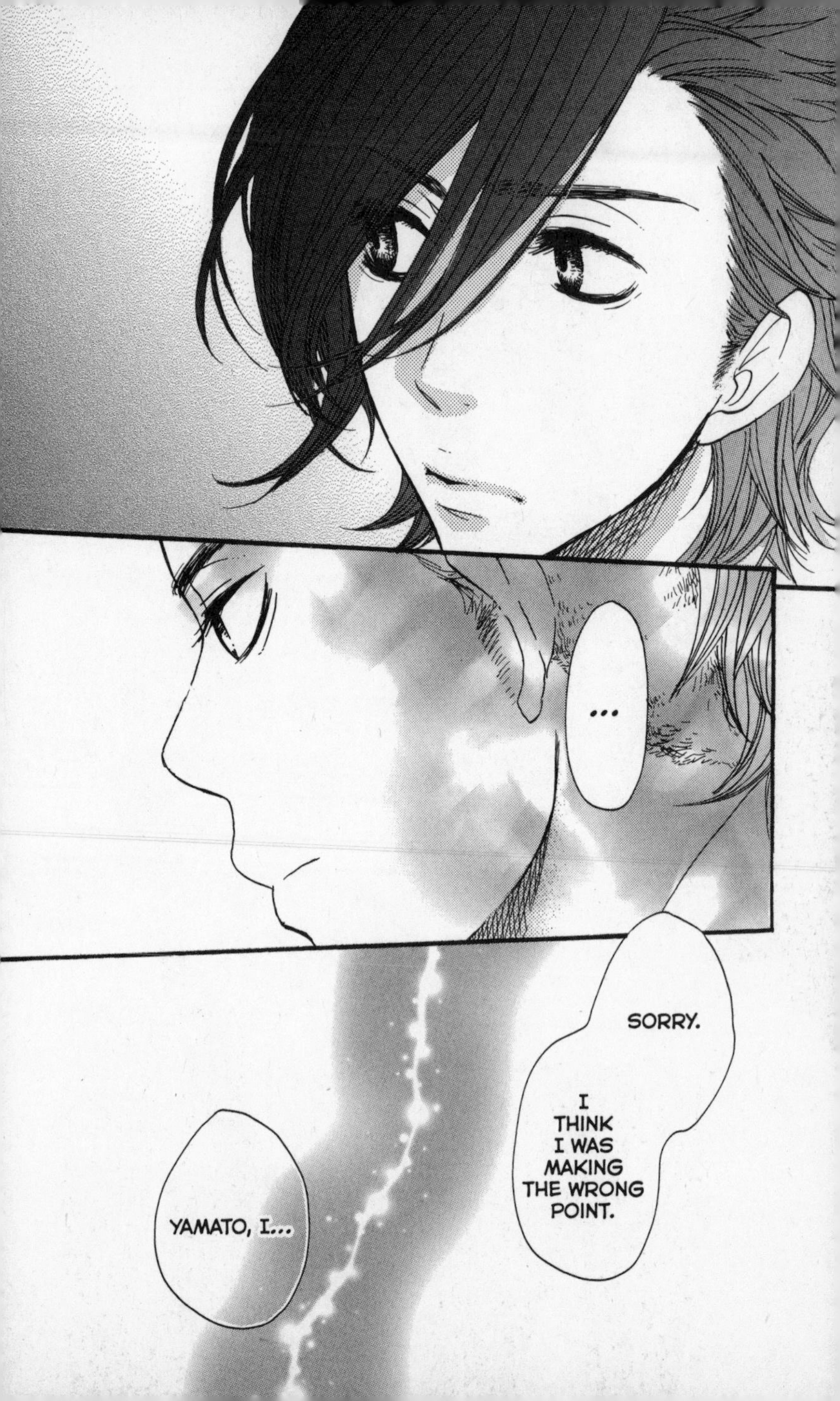
...
SORRY.
I THINK I WAS MAKING THE WRONG POINT.
YAMATO, I...

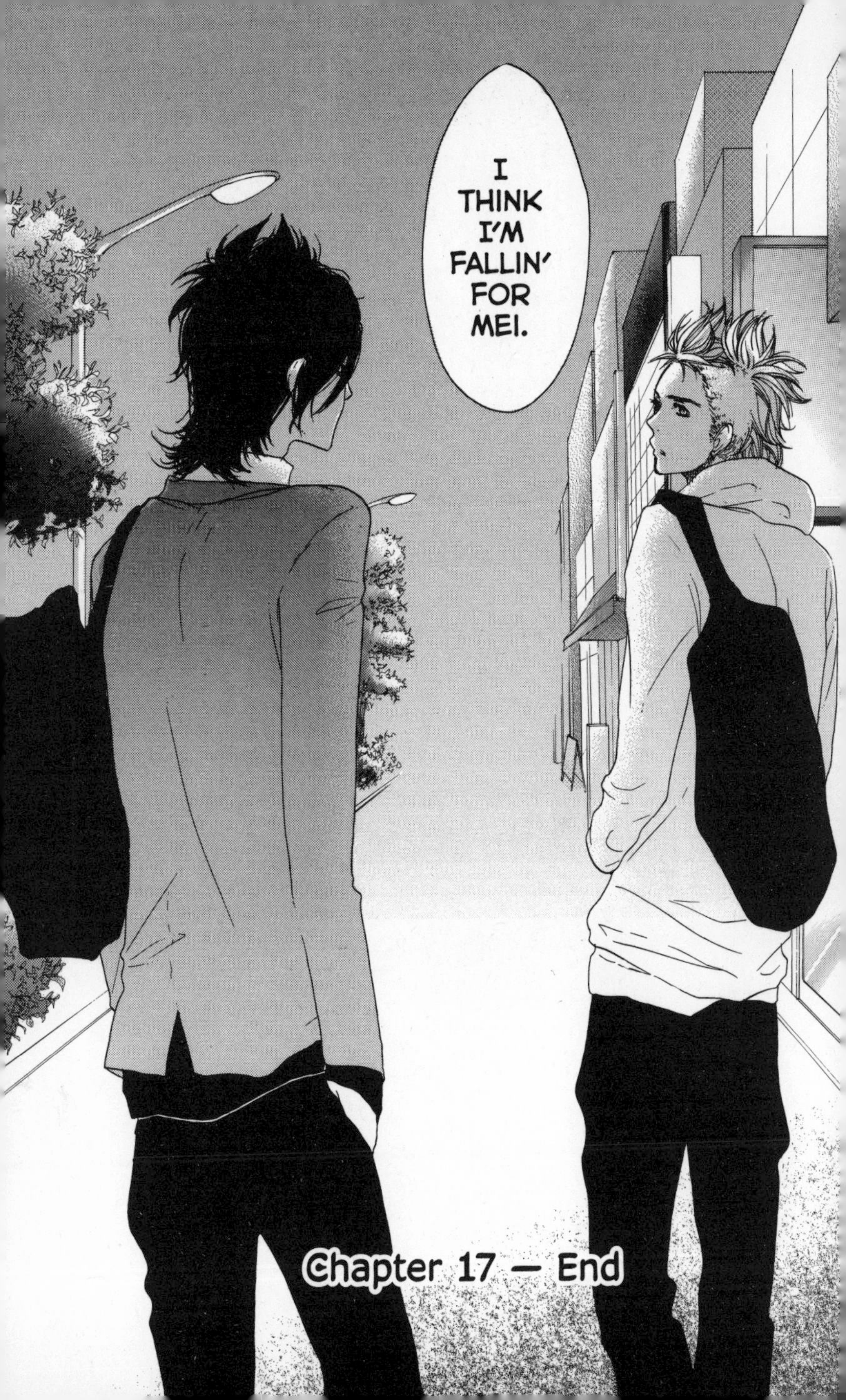
I THINK I'M FALLIN' FOR MEI.
Chapter 17 — End

Love a
duck.

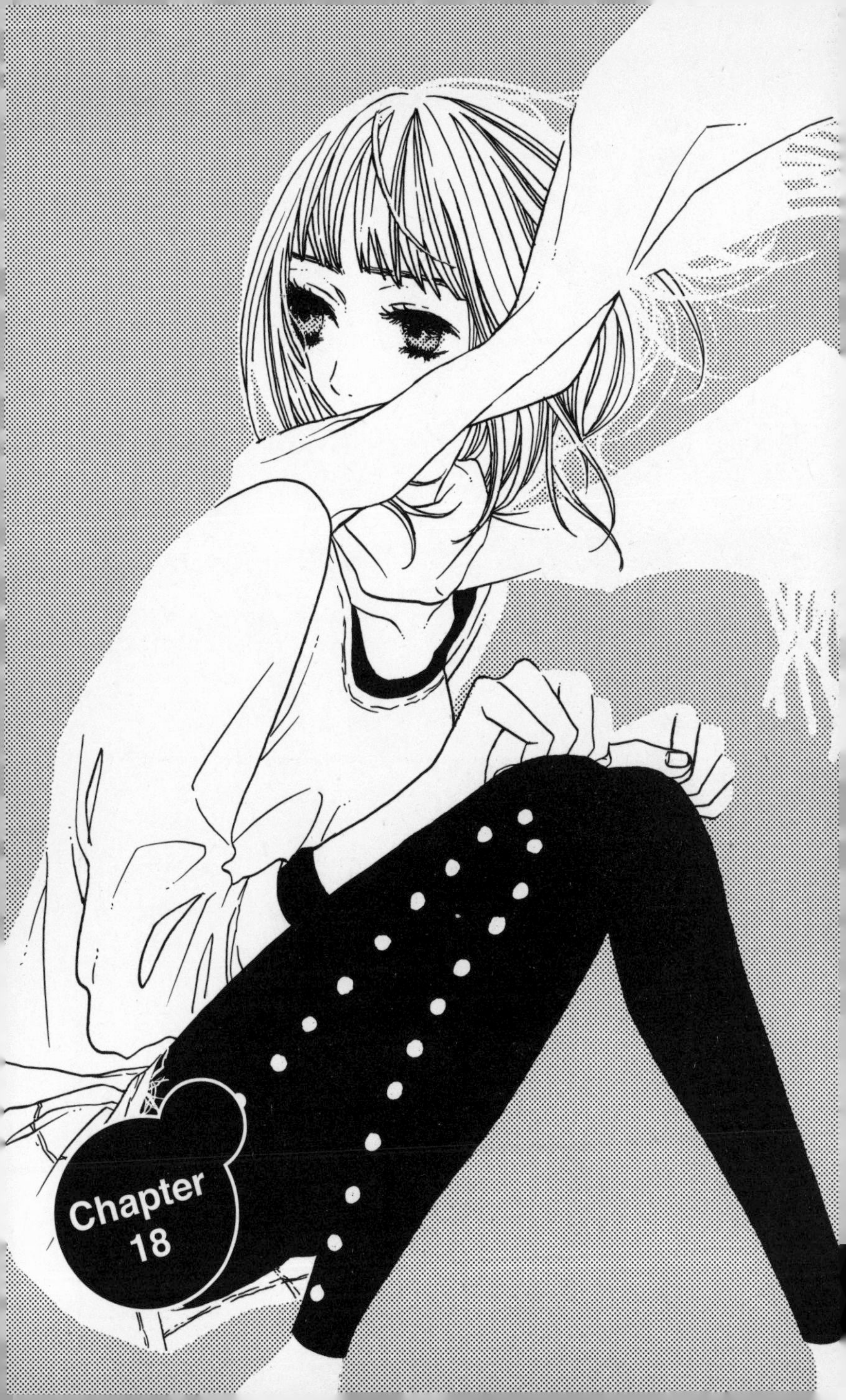
Chapter
18

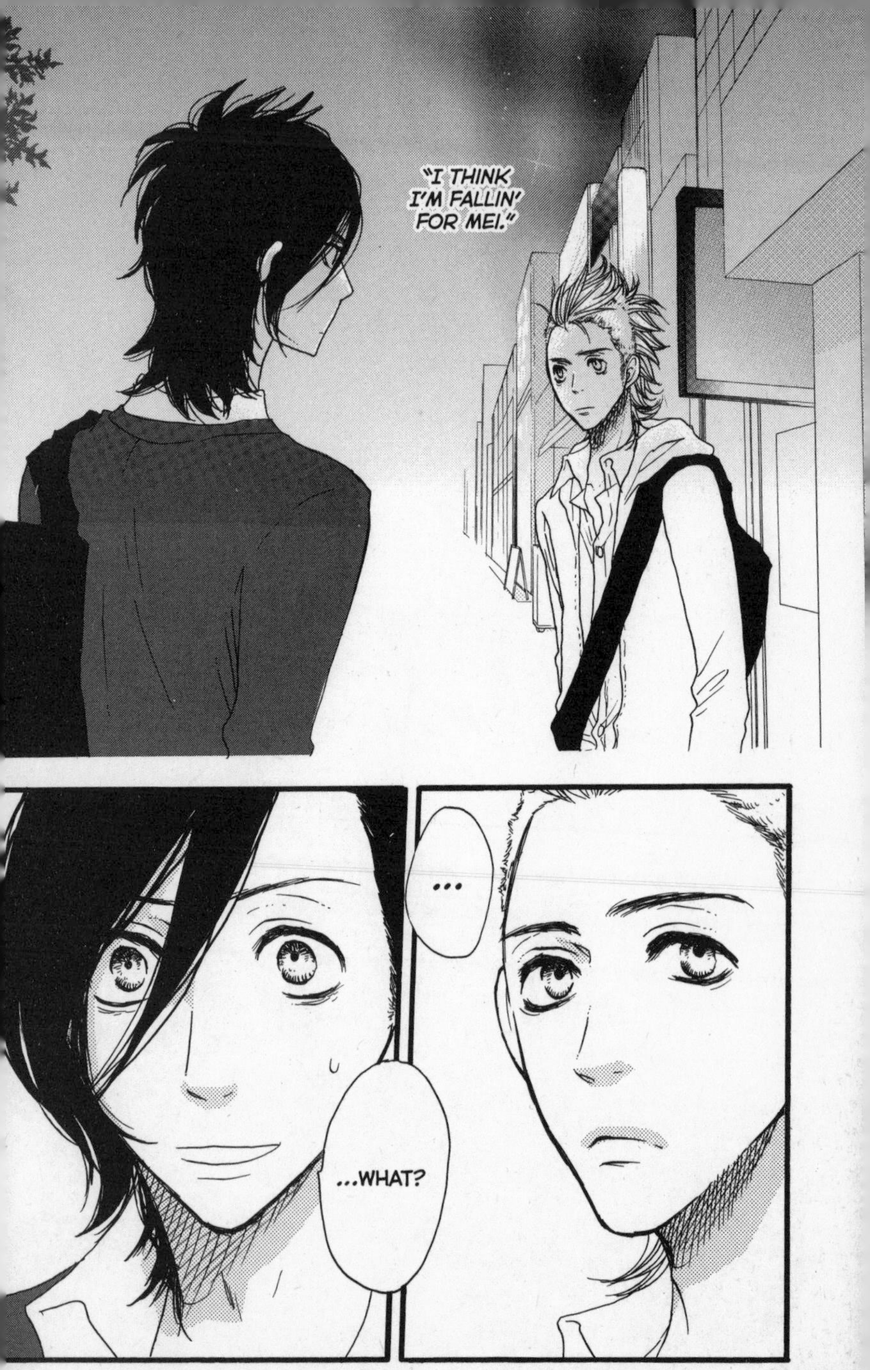
"I THINK I'M FALLIN' FOR MEI."
...
...WHAT?

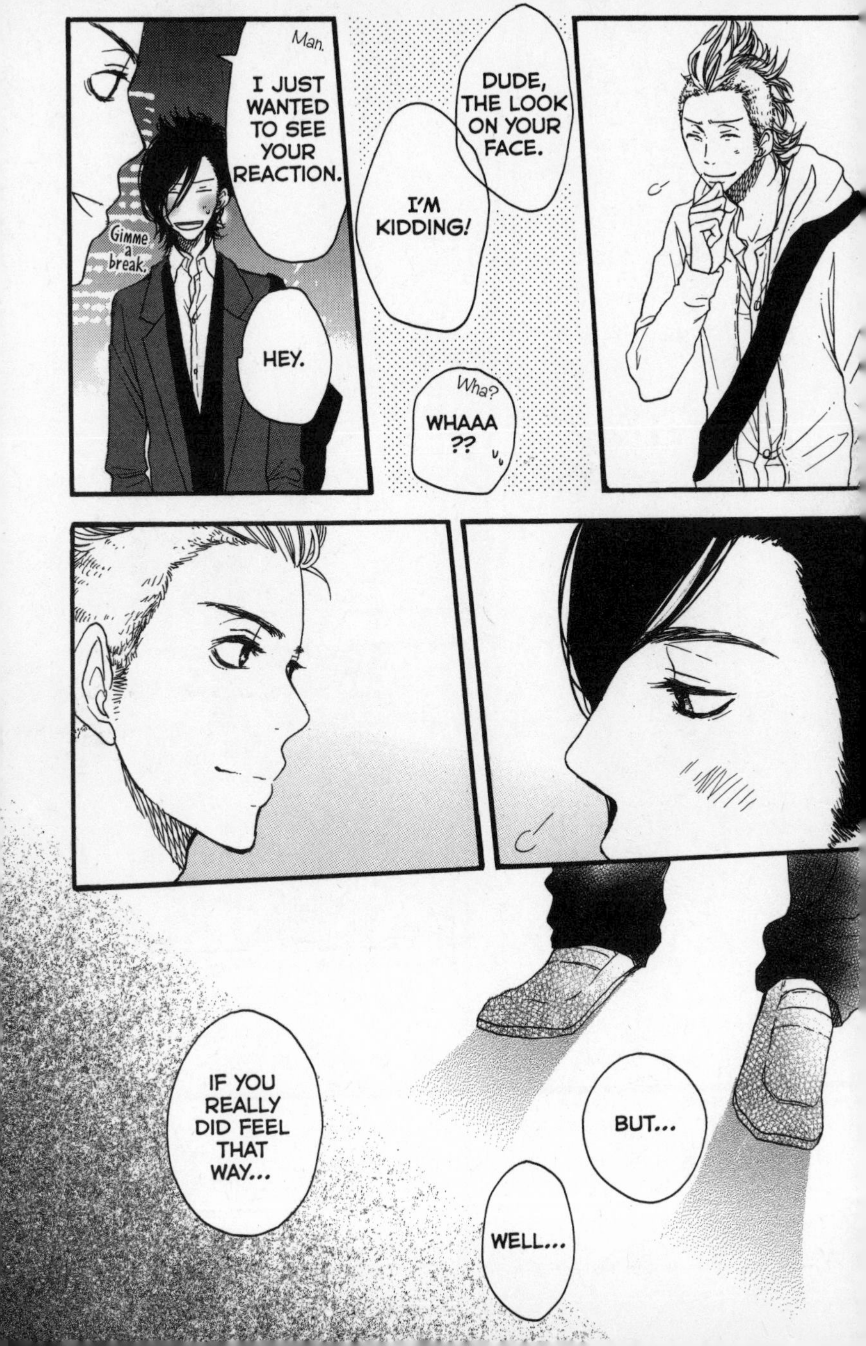
DUDE, THE LOOK ON YOUR FACE.
I'M KIDDING!
Wha? WHAAA ??
Man.
I JUST WANTED TO SEE YOUR REACTION.
Gimme a break.
HEY.
BUT...
WELL...
IF YOU REALLY DID FEEL THAT WAY...

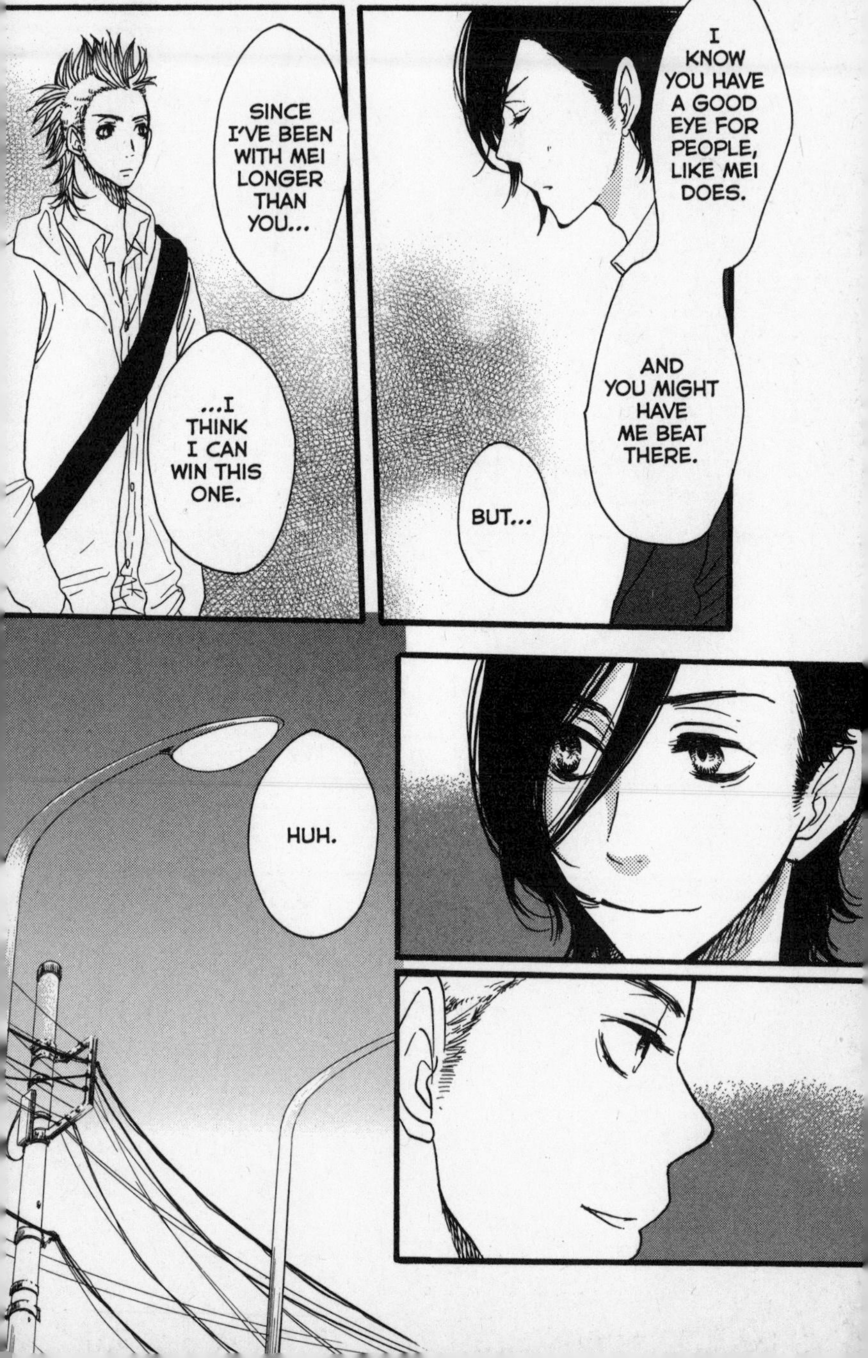
I KNOW YOU HAVE A GOOD EYE FOR PEOPLE, LIKE MEI DOES.
AND YOU MIGHT HAVE ME BEAT THERE.
BUT...
SINCE I'VE BEEN WITH MEI LONGER THAN YOU...
...I THINK I CAN WIN THIS ONE.
HUH.

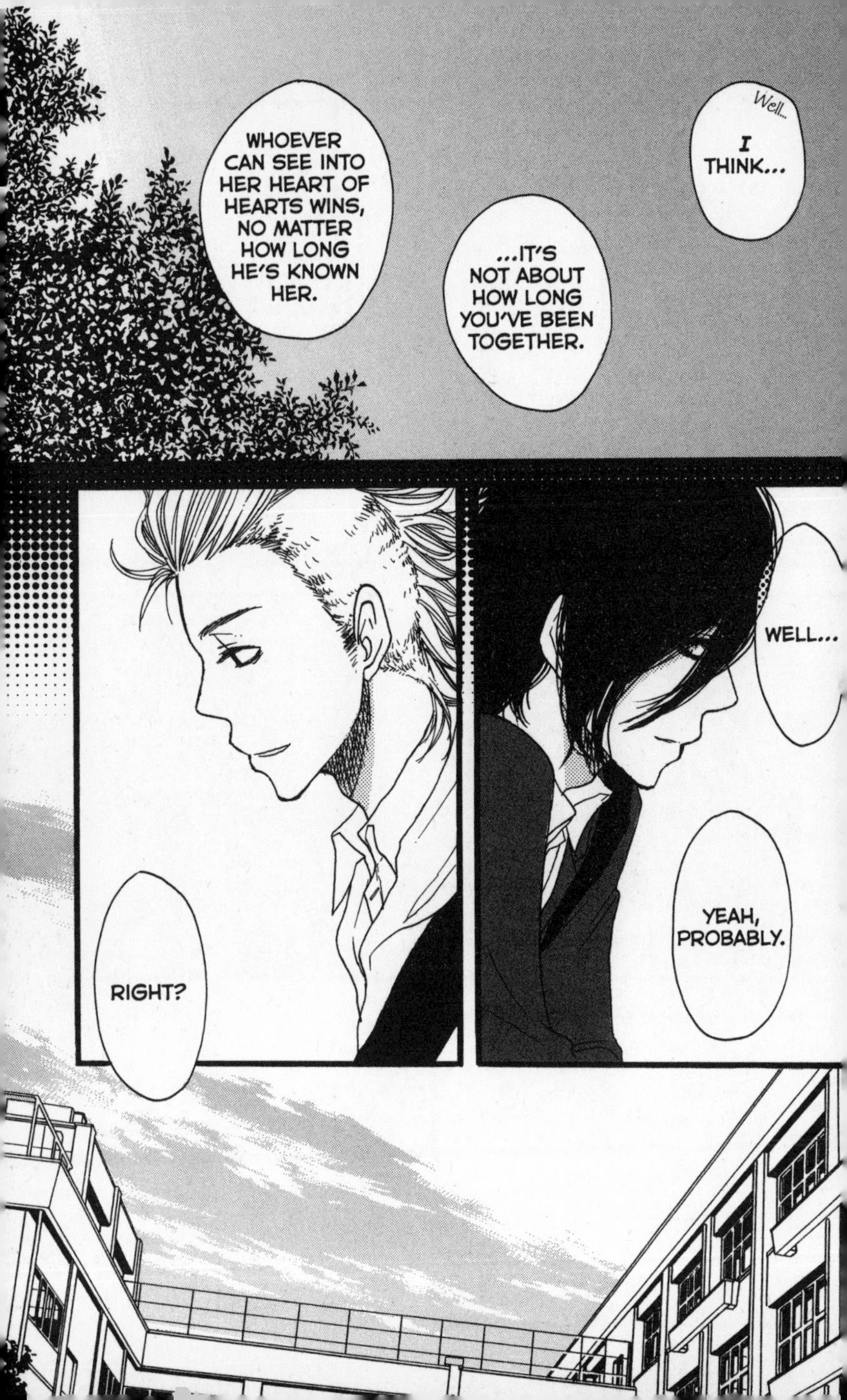
Well...
I THINK...
...IT'S NOT ABOUT HOW LONG YOU'VE BEEN TOGETHER.
WHOEVER CAN SEE INTO HER HEART OF HEARTS WINS, NO MATTER HOW LONG HE'S KNOWN HER.
WELL...
YEAH, PROBABLY.
RIGHT?

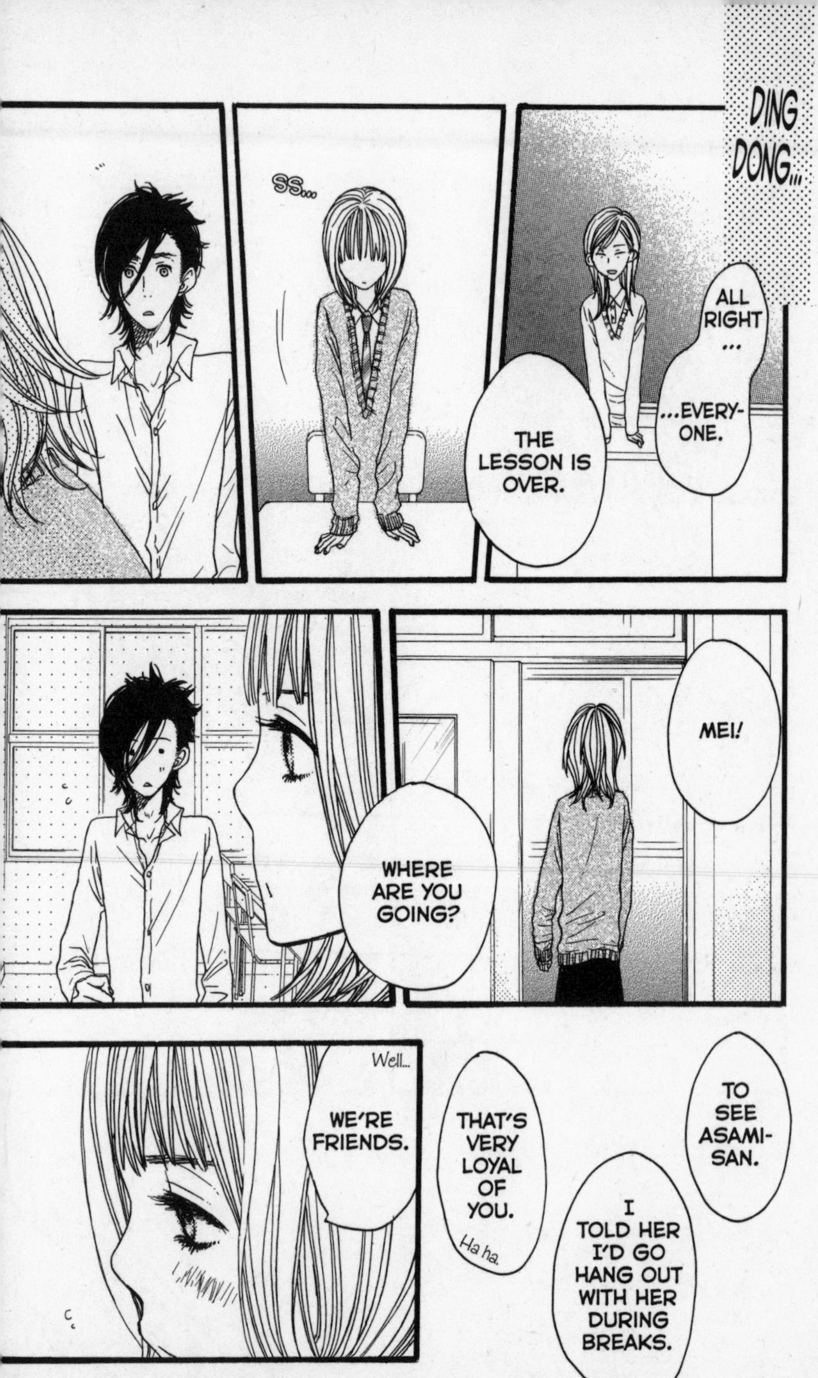
DING DONG...
ALL RIGHT...
...EVERYONE.
THE LESSON IS OVER.
SS...
MEI!
WHERE ARE YOU GOING?
TO SEE ASAMI-SAN.
I TOLD HER I'D GO HANG OUT WITH HER DURING BREAKS.
THAT'S VERY LOYAL OF YOU.
Ha ha.
Well...
WE'RE FRIENDS.

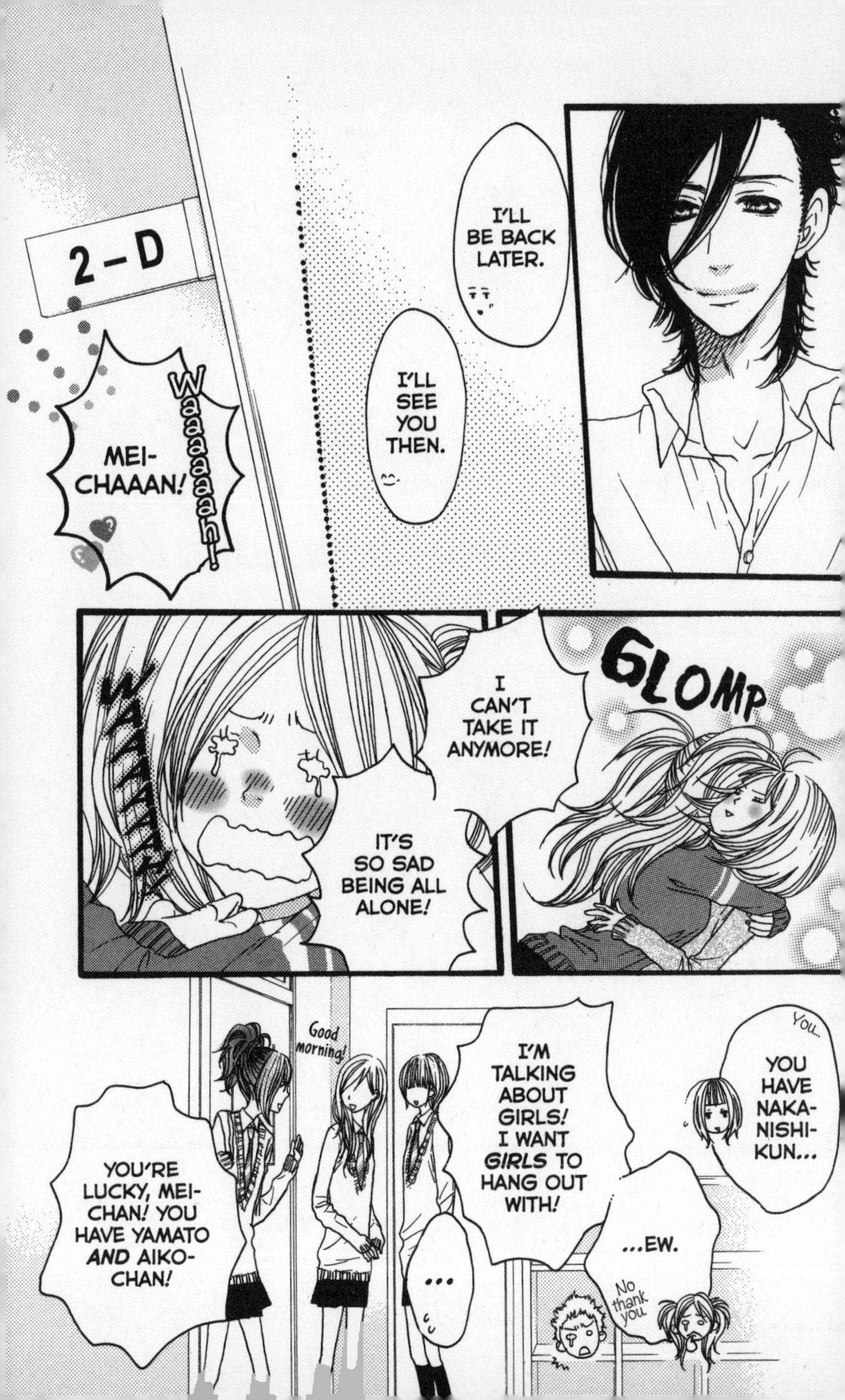
I'LL BE BACK LATER.
I'LL SEE YOU THEN.
2-D
MEI-CHAAAN!
Waaaaaaah!
GLOMP
I CAN'T TAKE IT ANYMORE!
IT'S SO SAD BEING ALL ALONE!
You...
YOU HAVE NAKA-NISHI-KUN...
...EW.
No thank you.
I'M TALKING ABOUT GIRLS! I WANT *GIRLS* TO HANG OUT WITH!
...
Good morning!
YOU'RE LUCKY, MEI-CHAN! YOU HAVE YAMATO *AND* AIKO-CHAN!

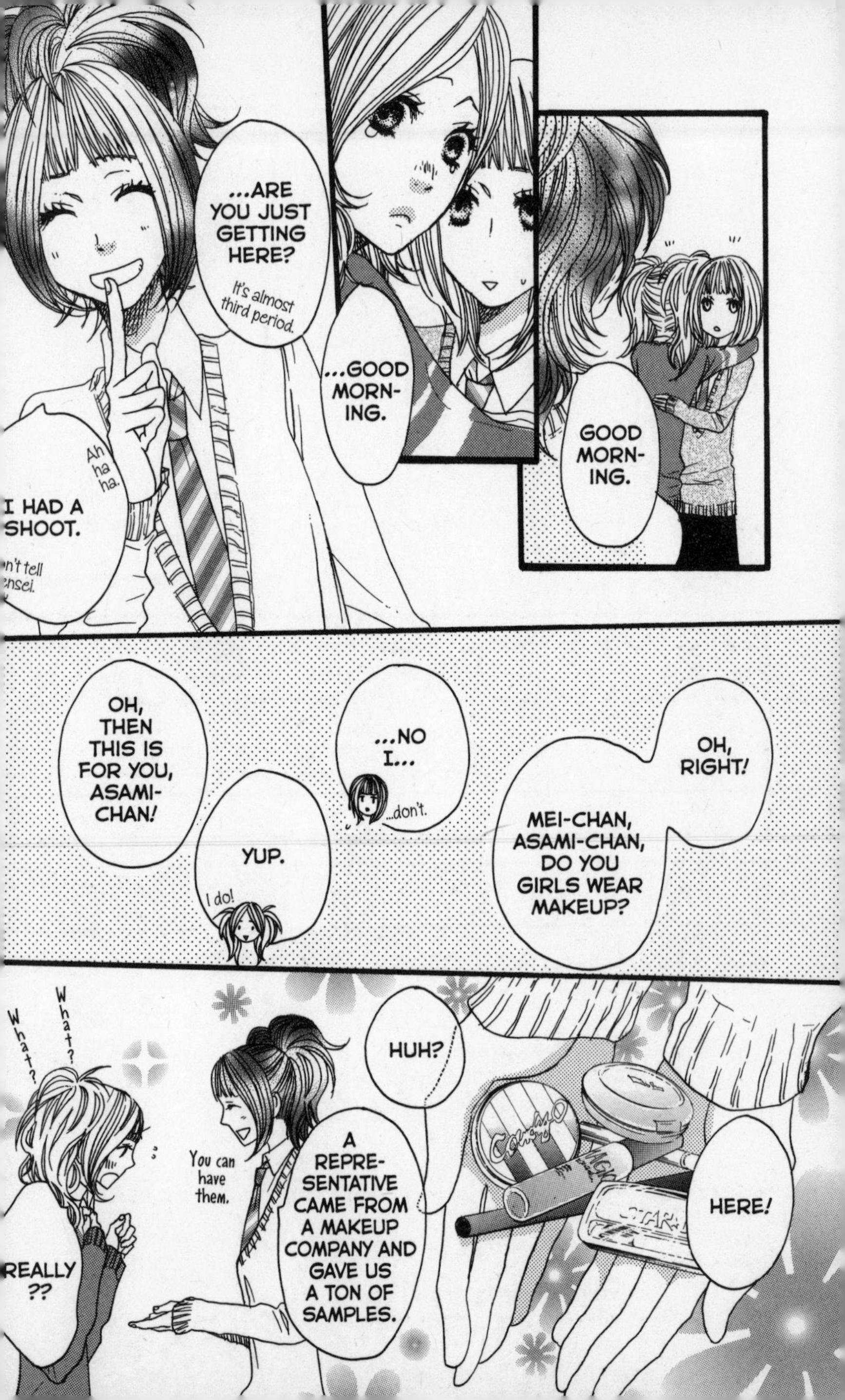
GOOD MORNING.
...GOOD MORNING.
...ARE YOU JUST GETTING HERE?
It's almost third period.
Ah ha ha.
I HAD A SHOOT.
n't tell nsei.
OH, RIGHT!
MEI-CHAN, ASAMI-CHAN, DO YOU GIRLS WEAR MAKEUP?
...NO I...
...don't.
YUP.
I do!
OH, THEN THIS IS FOR YOU, ASAMI-CHAN!
HERE!
HUH?
A REPRESENTATIVE CAME FROM A MAKEUP COMPANY AND GAVE US A TON OF SAMPLES.
You can have them.
REALLY??
What?
What?

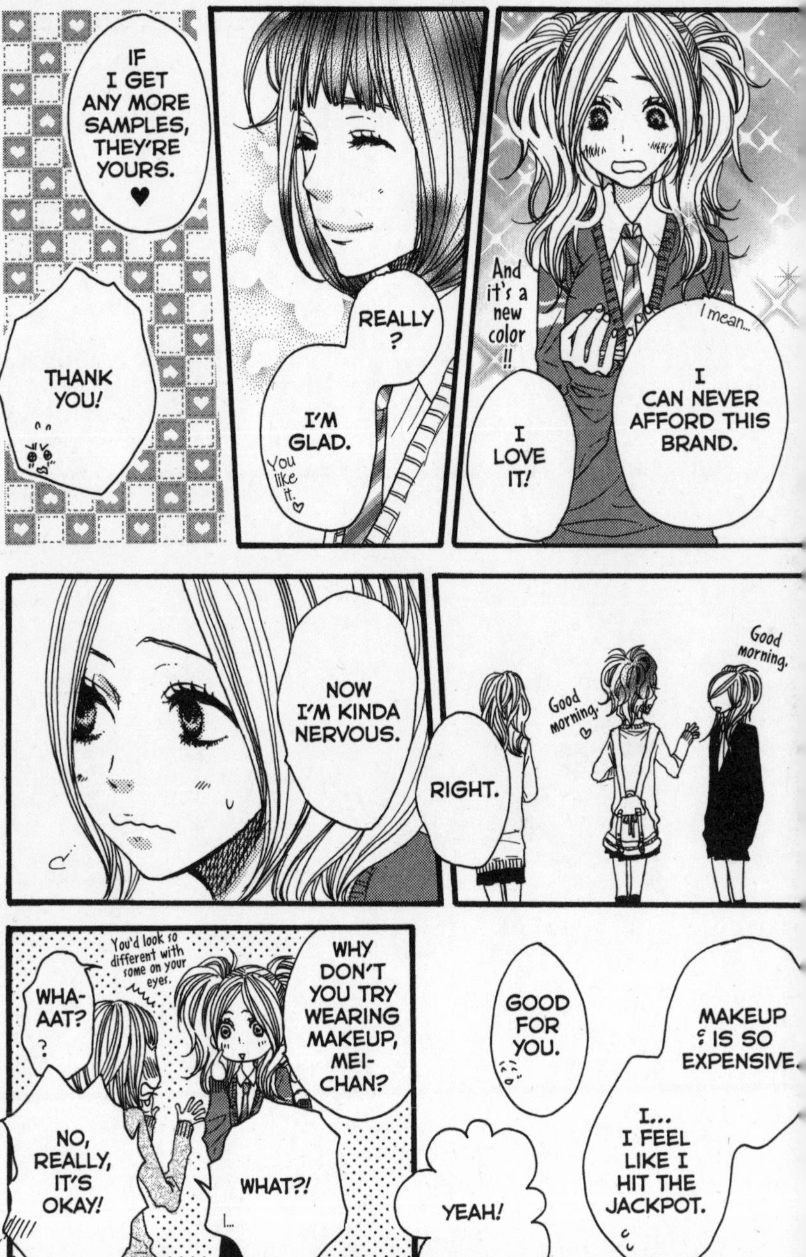
I mean...
I CAN NEVER AFFORD THIS BRAND.
And it's a new color!!
I LOVE IT!
REALLY?
I'M GLAD.
You like it. ♥
IF I GET ANY MORE SAMPLES, THEY'RE YOURS. ♥
THANK YOU!
Good morning.
Good morning. ♥
RIGHT.
NOW I'M KINDA NERVOUS.
MAKEUP IS SO EXPENSIVE.
I... I FEEL LIKE I HIT THE JACKPOT.
GOOD FOR YOU.
YEAH! ♥
WHY DON'T YOU TRY WEARING MAKEUP, MEI-CHAN?
You'd look so different with some on your eyes.
WHA-AAT?
WHAT?!
I...
NO, REALLY, IT'S OKAY!

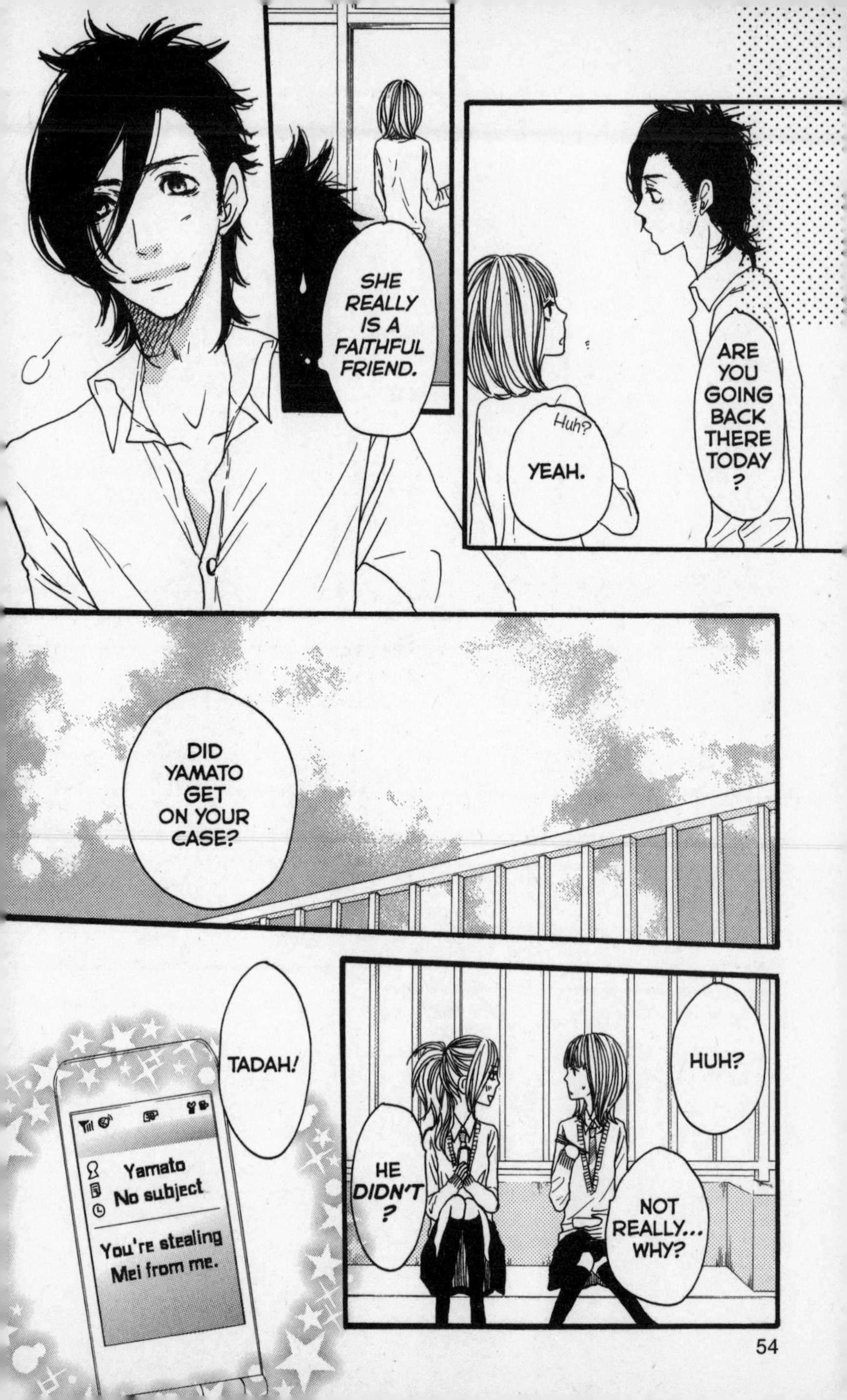
ARE YOU GOING BACK THERE TODAY?
Huh?
YEAH.
SHE REALLY IS A FAITHFUL FRIEND.
DID YAMATO GET ON YOUR CASE?
HUH?
NOT REALLY... WHY?
HE DIDN'T?
TADAH!
Yamato
No subject
You're stealing Mei from me.

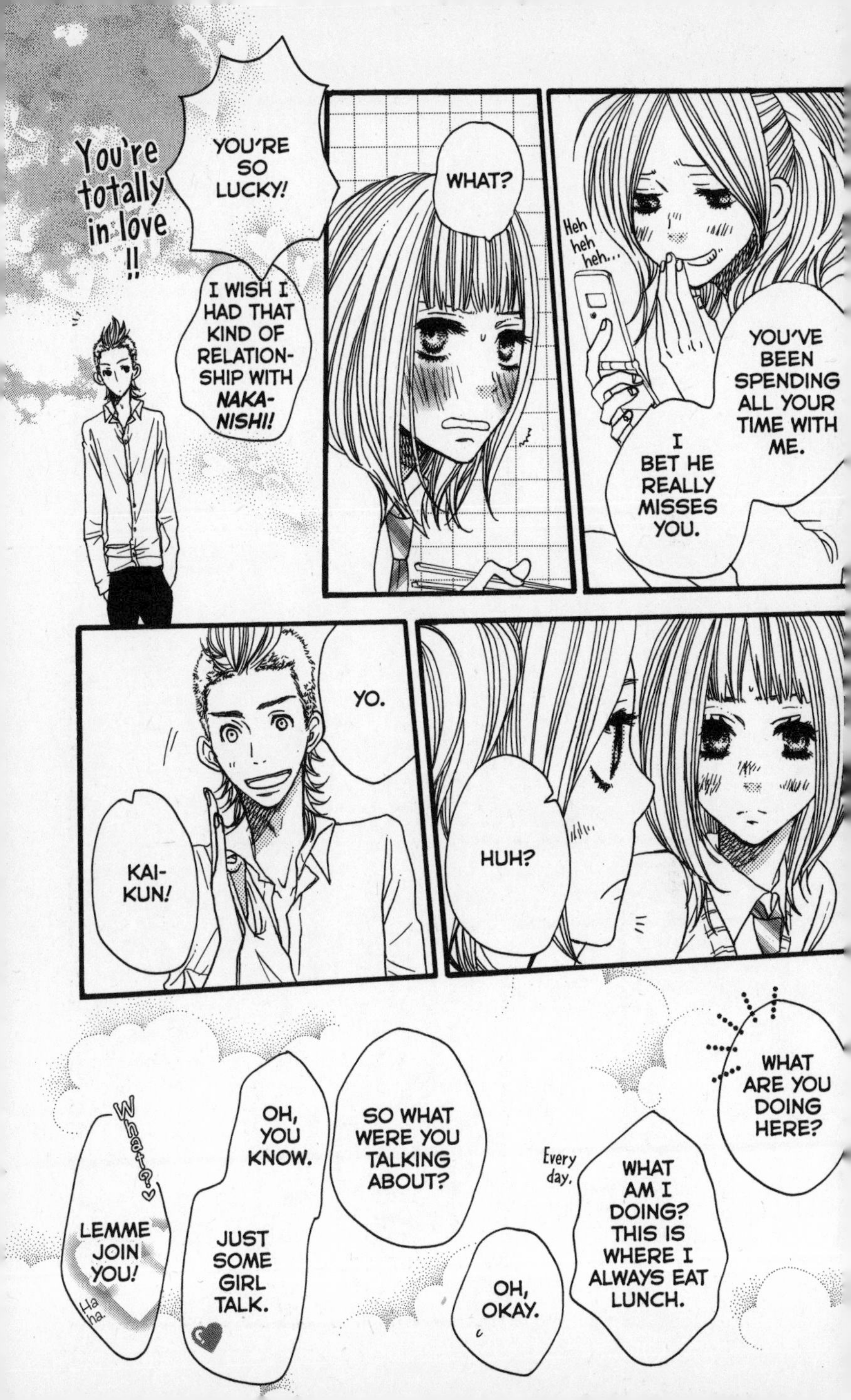
Heh heh heh...
YOU'VE BEEN SPENDING ALL YOUR TIME WITH ME.
I BET HE REALLY MISSES YOU.
WHAT?
YOU'RE SO LUCKY!
You're totally in love !!
I WISH I HAD THAT KIND OF RELATIONSHIP WITH NAKA-NISHI!
HUH?
YO.
KAI-KUN!
WHAT ARE YOU DOING HERE?
WHAT AM I DOING? THIS IS WHERE I ALWAYS EAT LUNCH.
Every day.
OH, OKAY.
SO WHAT WERE YOU TALKING ABOUT?
OH, YOU KNOW.
JUST SOME GIRL TALK.
What?♡
LEMME JOIN YOU!
Ha ha.

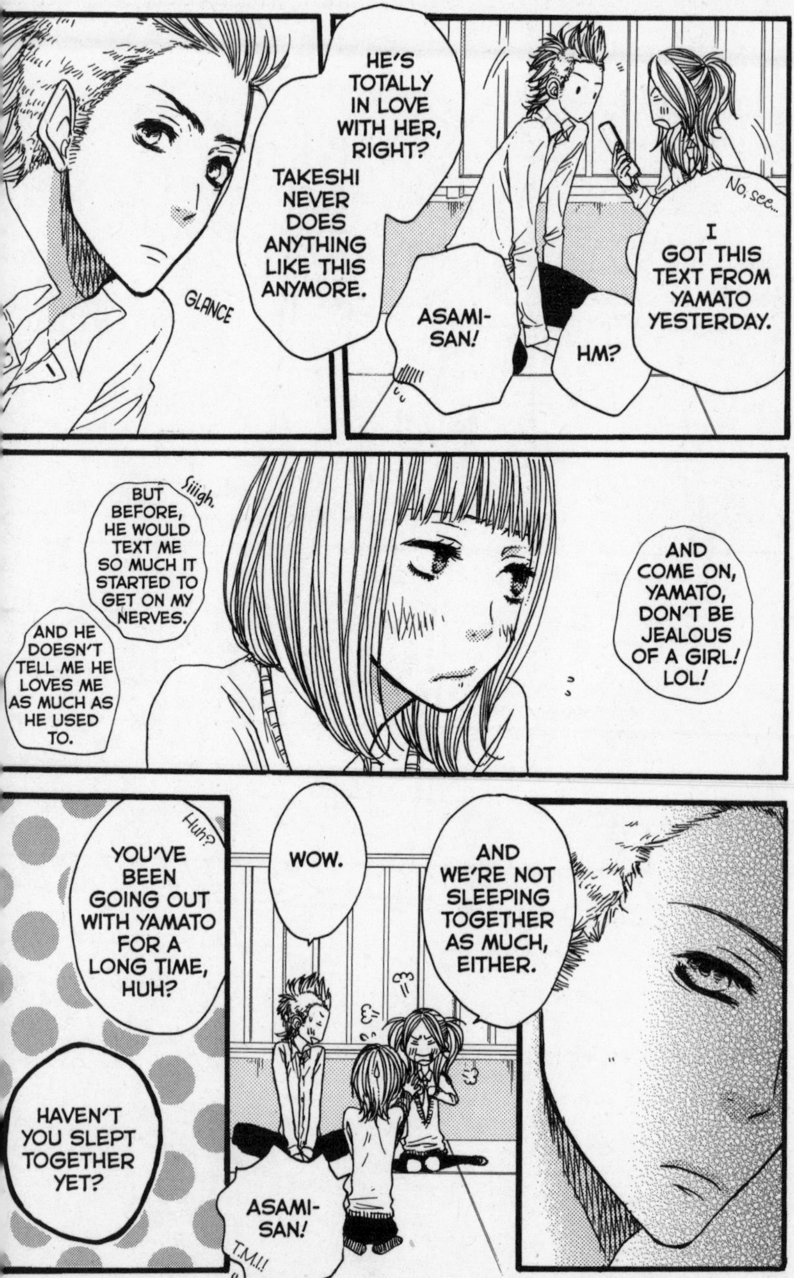

No, see...
I GOT THIS TEXT FROM YAMATO YESTERDAY.
HM?
ASAMI-SAN!
HE'S TOTALLY IN LOVE WITH HER, RIGHT?
TAKESHI NEVER DOES ANYTHING LIKE THIS ANYMORE.
GLANCE
AND COME ON, YAMATO, DON'T BE JEALOUS OF A GIRL! LOL!
Siiigh.
BUT BEFORE, HE WOULD TEXT ME SO MUCH IT STARTED TO GET ON MY NERVES.
AND HE DOESN'T TELL ME HE LOVES ME AS MUCH AS HE USED TO.
AND WE'RE NOT SLEEPING TOGETHER AS MUCH, EITHER.
WOW.
ASAMI-SAN!
T.M.I.!
Huh?
YOU'VE BEEN GOING OUT WITH YAMATO FOR A LONG TIME, HUH?
HAVEN'T YOU SLEPT TOGETHER YET?

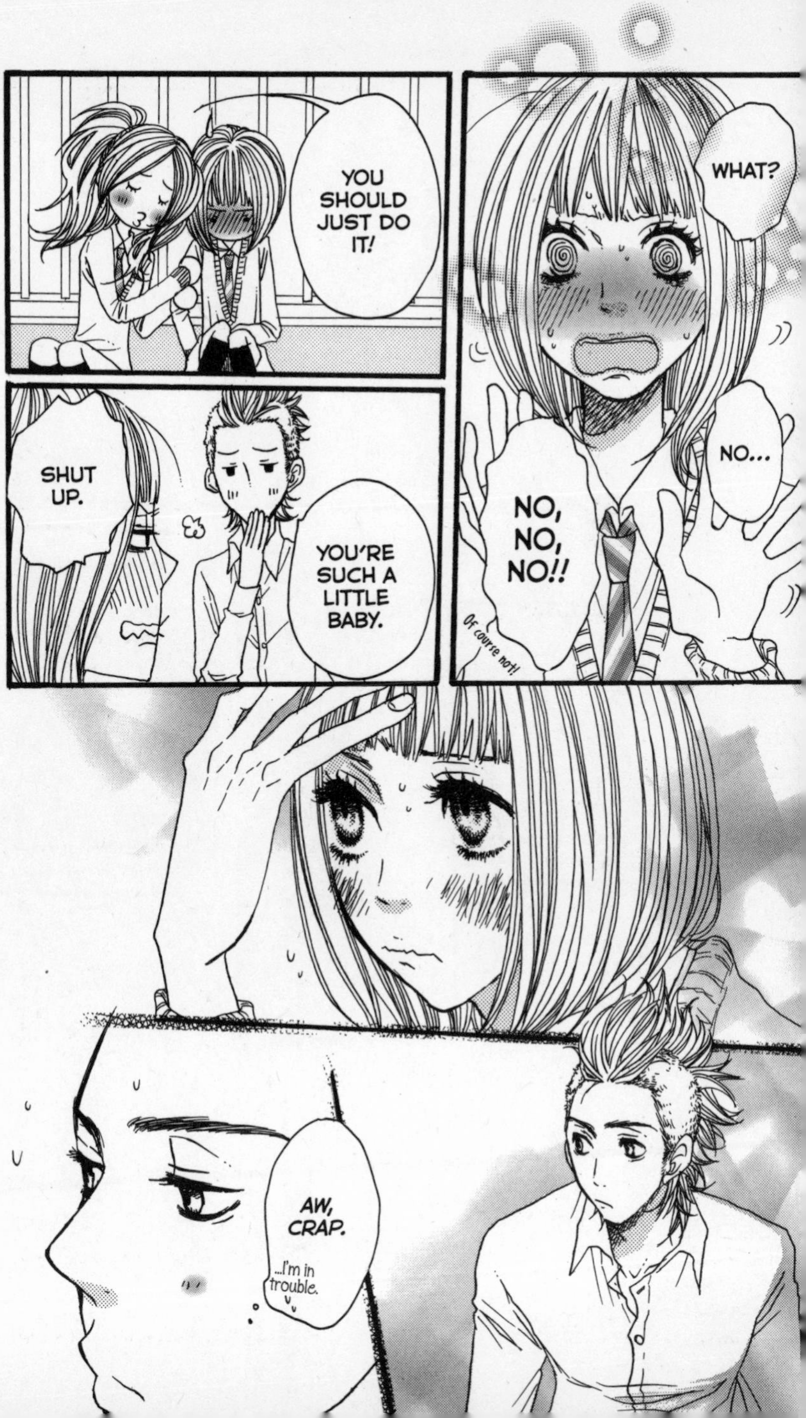
WHAT?
NO...
NO, NO, NO!!
Of course not!
YOU SHOULD JUST DO IT!
YOU'RE SUCH A LITTLE BABY.
SHUT UP.
AW, CRAP.
...I'm in trouble.

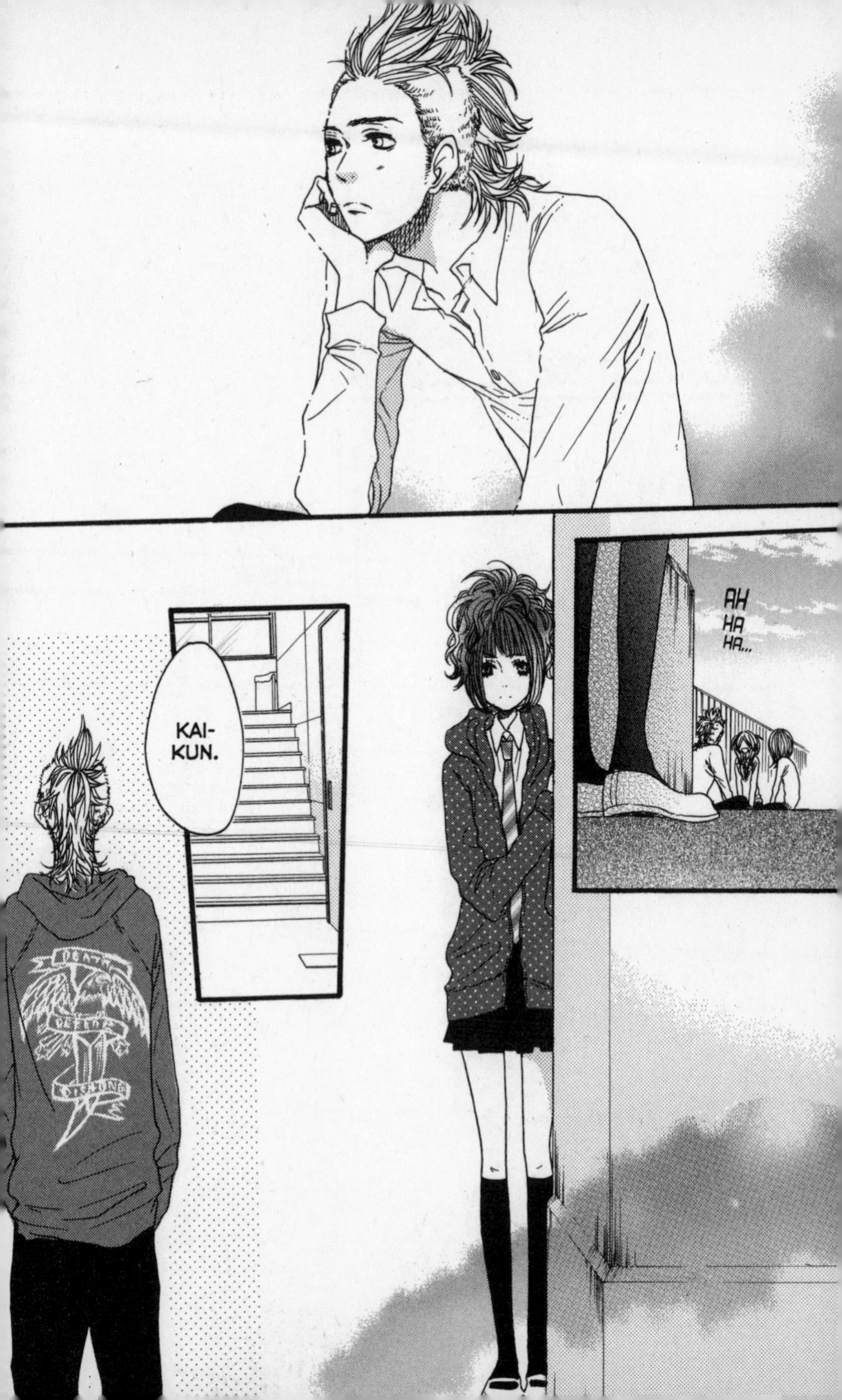
AH HA HA...
KAI-KUN.

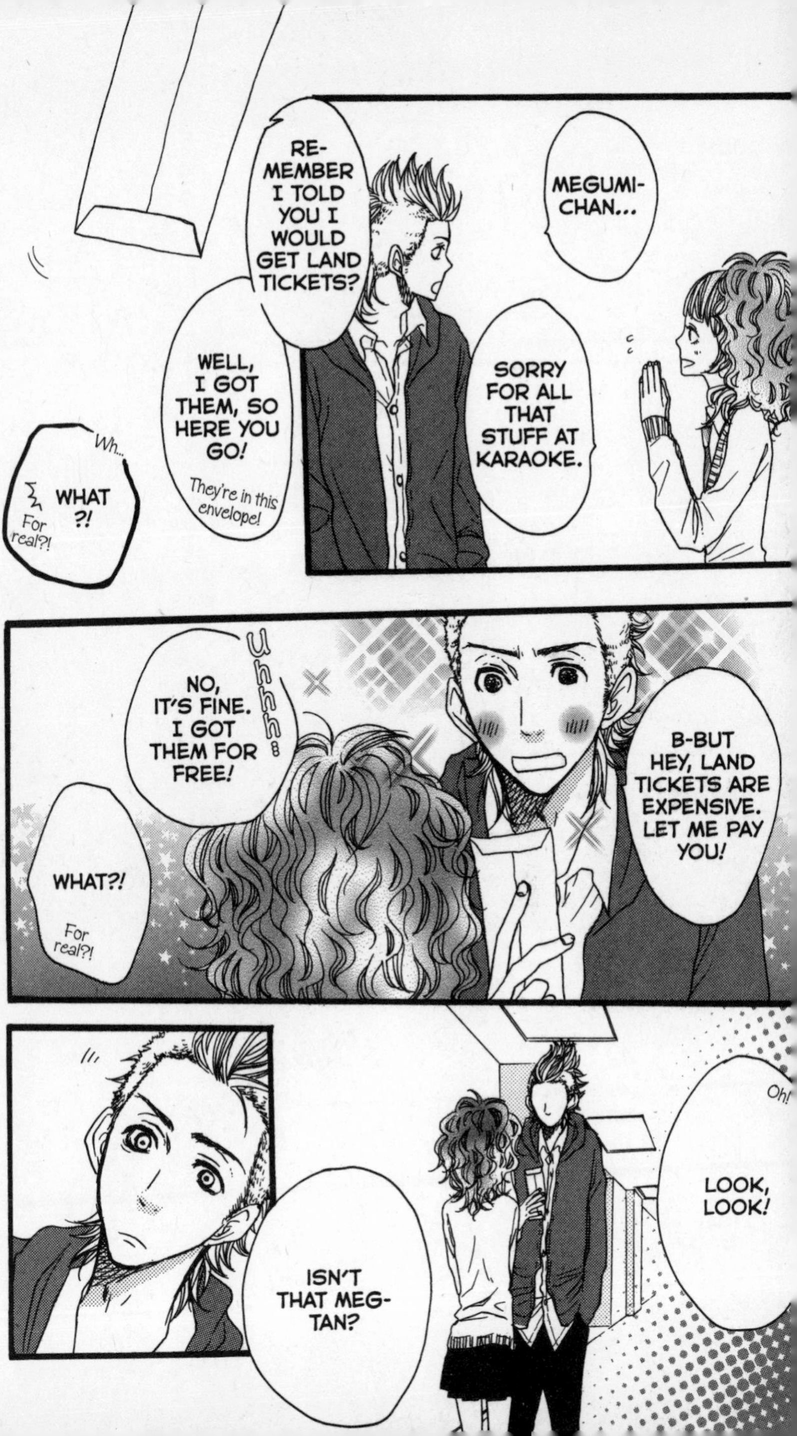
MEGUMI-CHAN...
SORRY FOR ALL THAT STUFF AT KARAOKE.
RE-MEMBER I TOLD YOU I WOULD GET LAND TICKETS?
WELL, I GOT THEM, SO HERE YOU GO!
They're in this envelope!
Wh...
WHAT?!
For real?!
B-BUT HEY, LAND TICKETS ARE EXPENSIVE. LET ME PAY YOU!
Uhhh...
NO, IT'S FINE. I GOT THEM FOR FREE!
WHAT?!
For real?!
Oh!
LOOK, LOOK!
ISN'T THAT MEG-TAN?

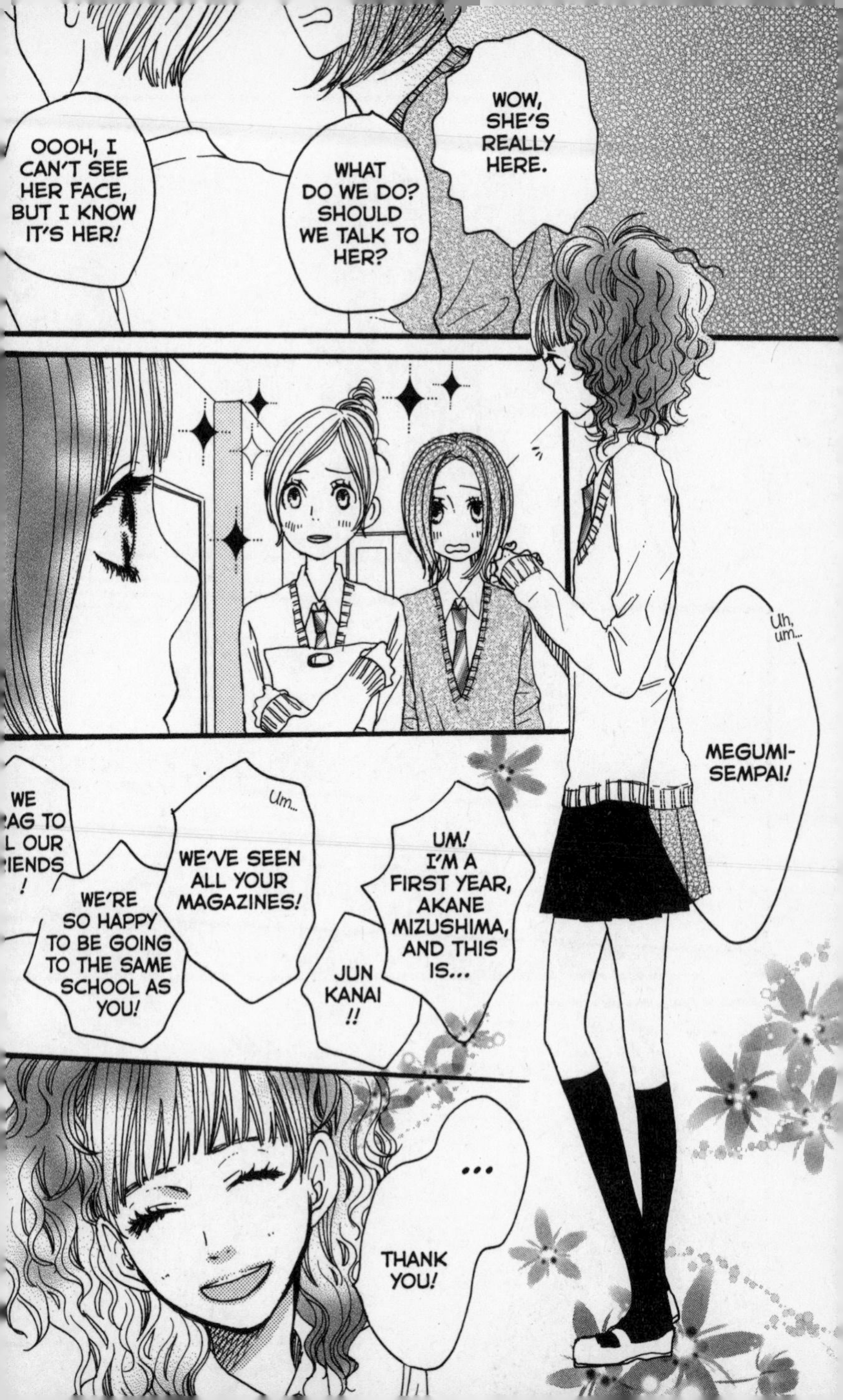

WOW, SHE'S REALLY HERE.
WHAT DO WE DO? SHOULD WE TALK TO HER?
OOOH, I CAN'T SEE HER FACE, BUT I KNOW IT'S HER!
Uh, um...
MEGUMI-SEMPAI!
UM! I'M A FIRST YEAR, AKANE MIZUSHIMA, AND THIS IS...
JUN KANAI!!
Um...
WE'VE SEEN ALL YOUR MAGAZINES!
WE'RE SO HAPPY TO BE GOING TO THE SAME SCHOOL AS YOU!
WE AG TO L OUR IENDS!
...
THANK YOU!

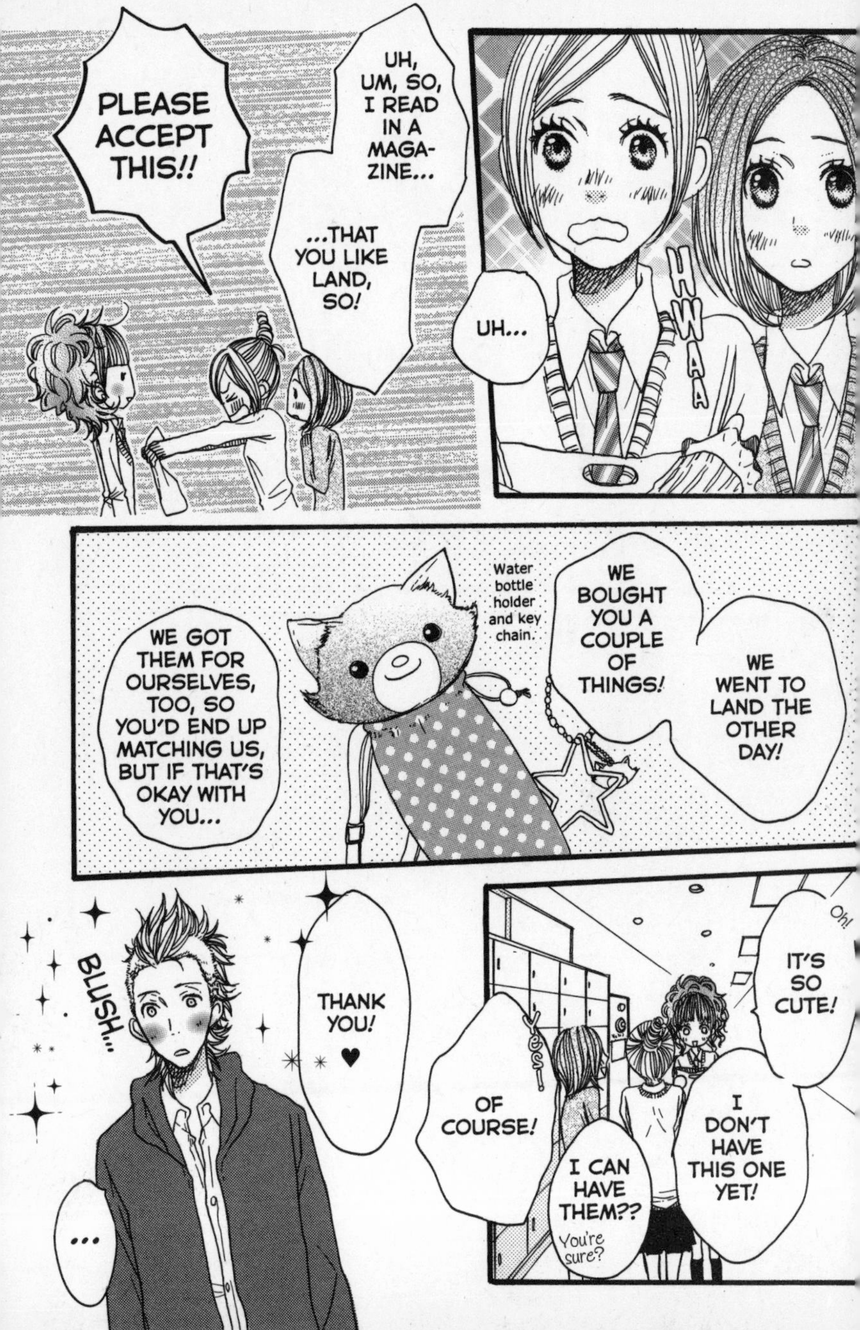
UH...
HWAA
UH, UM, SO, I READ IN A MAGAZINE...
...THAT YOU LIKE LAND, SO!
PLEASE ACCEPT THIS!!
WE WENT TO LAND THE OTHER DAY!
WE BOUGHT YOU A COUPLE OF THINGS!
Water bottle holder and key chain.
WE GOT THEM FOR OURSELVES, TOO, SO YOU'D END UP MATCHING US, BUT IF THAT'S OKAY WITH YOU...
Oh!
IT'S SO CUTE!
I DON'T HAVE THIS ONE YET!
I CAN HAVE THEM??
You're sure?
YES!
OF COURSE!
THANK YOU! ♥
BLUSH...
...

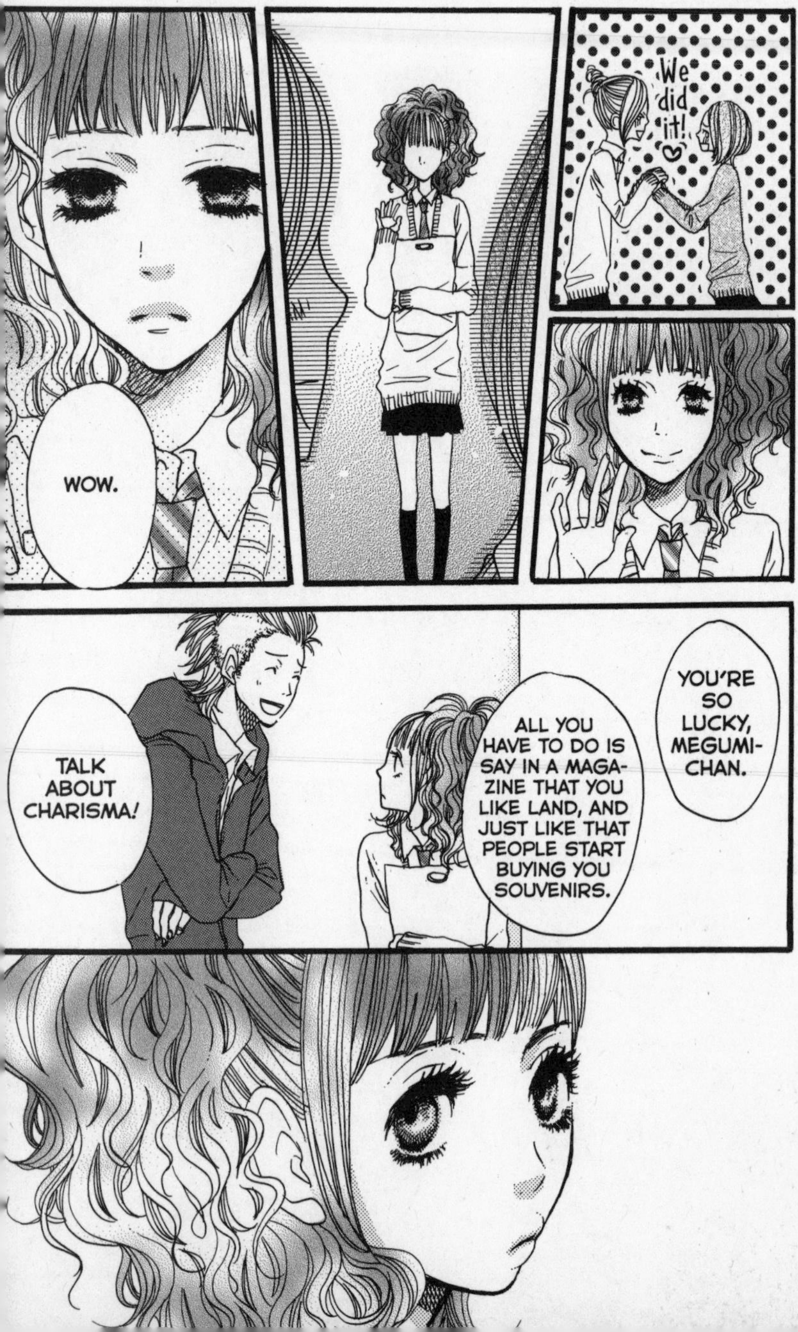
We did it!
WOW.
YOU'RE SO LUCKY, MEGUMI-CHAN.
ALL YOU HAVE TO DO IS SAY IN A MAGAZINE THAT YOU LIKE LAND, AND JUST LIKE THAT PEOPLE START BUYING YOU SOUVENIRS.
TALK ABOUT CHARISMA!

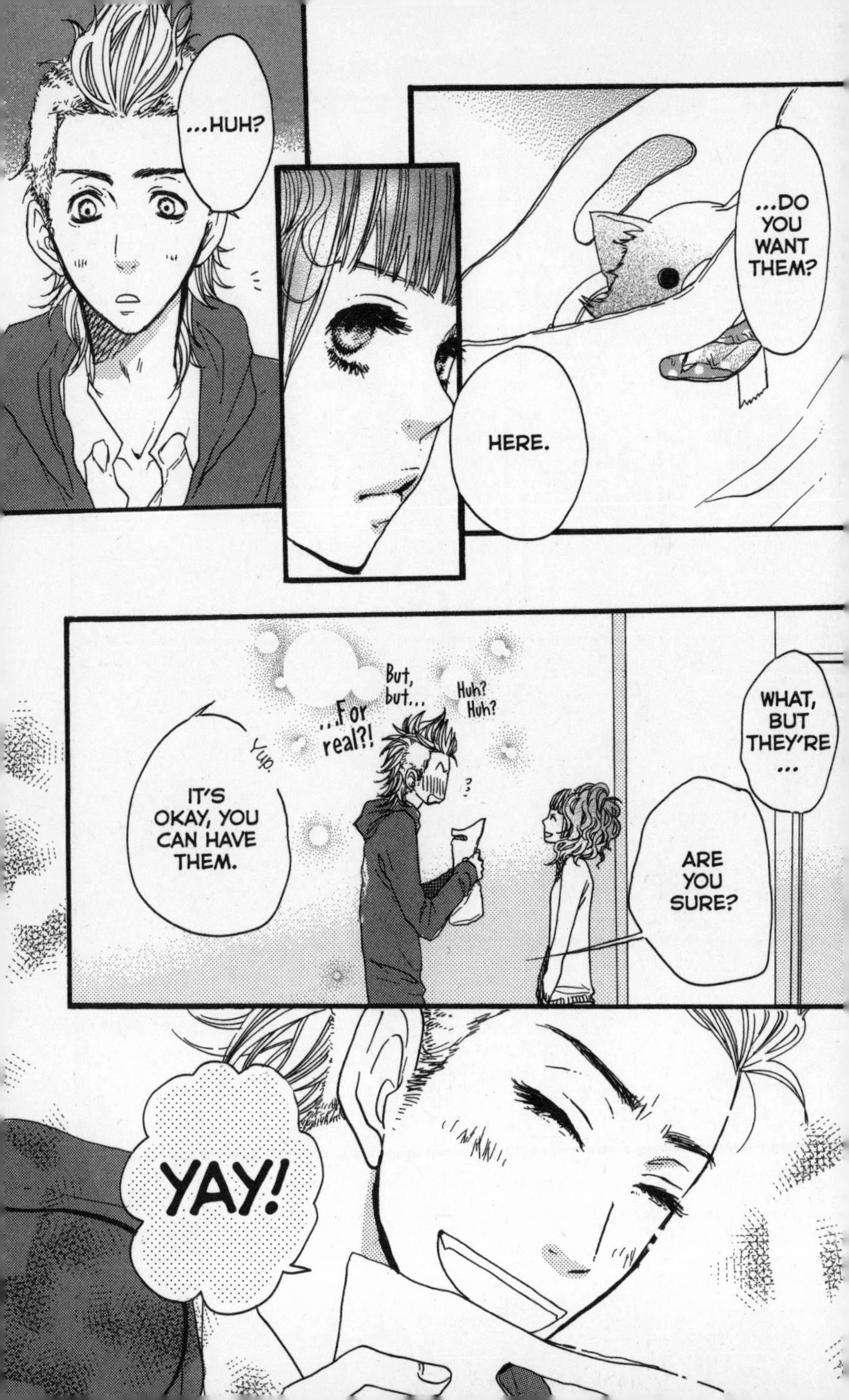
...DO YOU WANT THEM?
HERE.
...HUH?
WHAT, BUT THEY'RE ...
ARE YOU SURE?
Huh? Huh?
But, but...
...For real?!
Yup.
IT'S OKAY, YOU CAN HAVE THEM.
YAY!

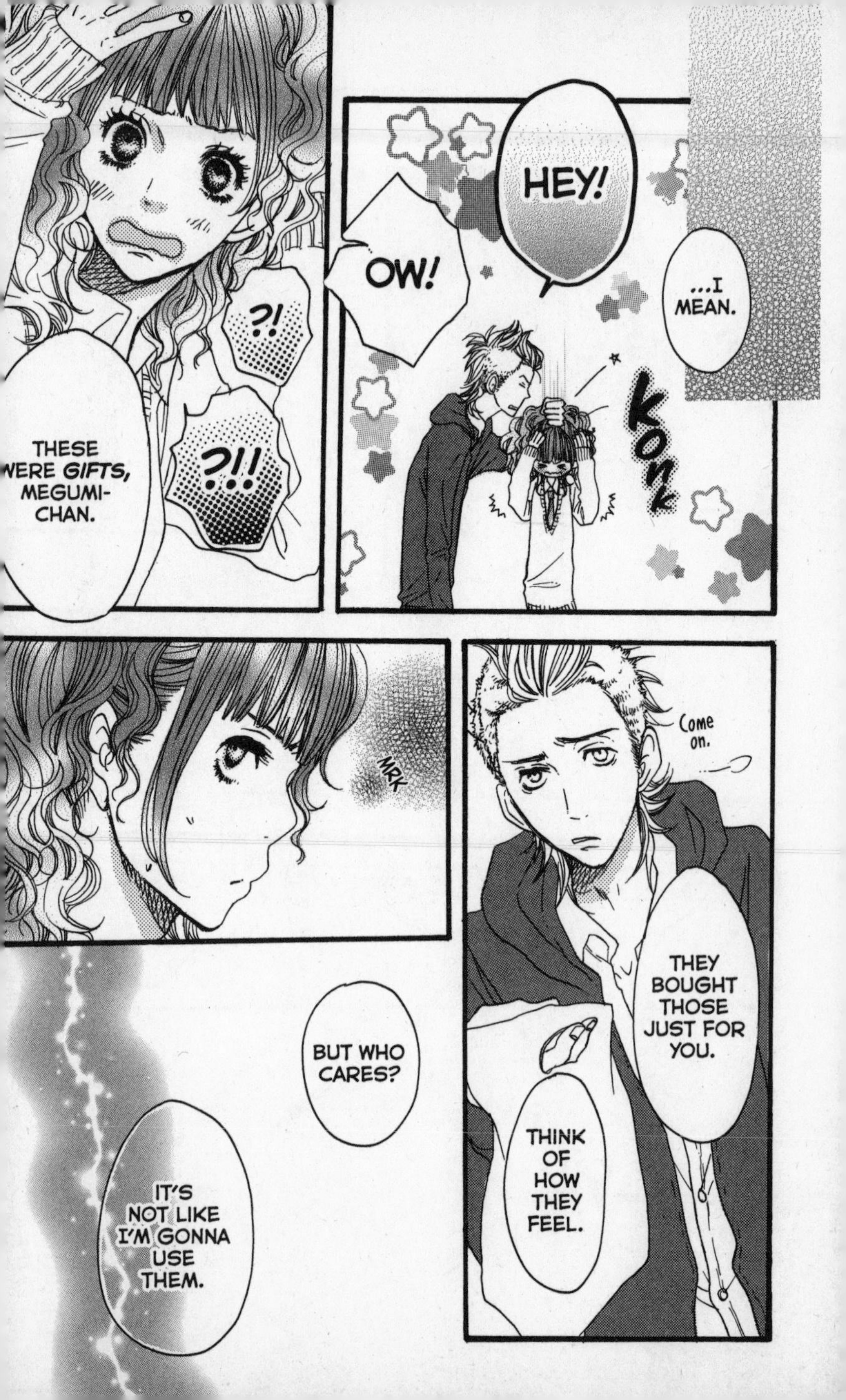
...I MEAN.
HEY!
OW!
KONK
?!
?!!
THESE WERE GIFTS, MEGUMI-CHAN.
Come on.
THEY BOUGHT THOSE JUST FOR YOU.
THINK OF HOW THEY FEEL.
MRK
BUT WHO CARES?
IT'S NOT LIKE I'M GONNA USE THEM.

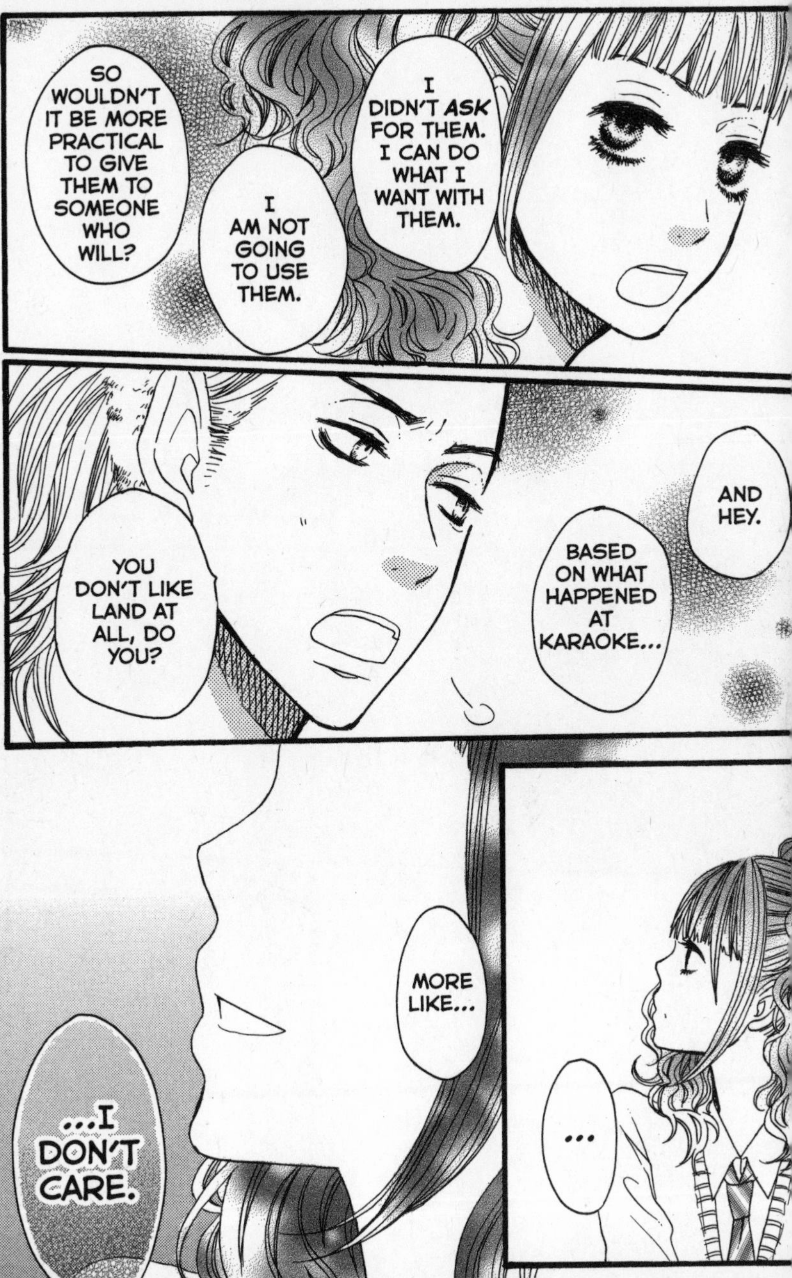
I DIDN'T ASK FOR THEM. I CAN DO WHAT I WANT WITH THEM.
I AM NOT GOING TO USE THEM.
SO WOULDN'T IT BE MORE PRACTICAL TO GIVE THEM TO SOMEONE WHO WILL?
AND HEY.
BASED ON WHAT HAPPENED AT KARAOKE...
YOU DON'T LIKE LAND AT ALL, DO YOU?
...
MORE LIKE...
...I DON'T CARE.

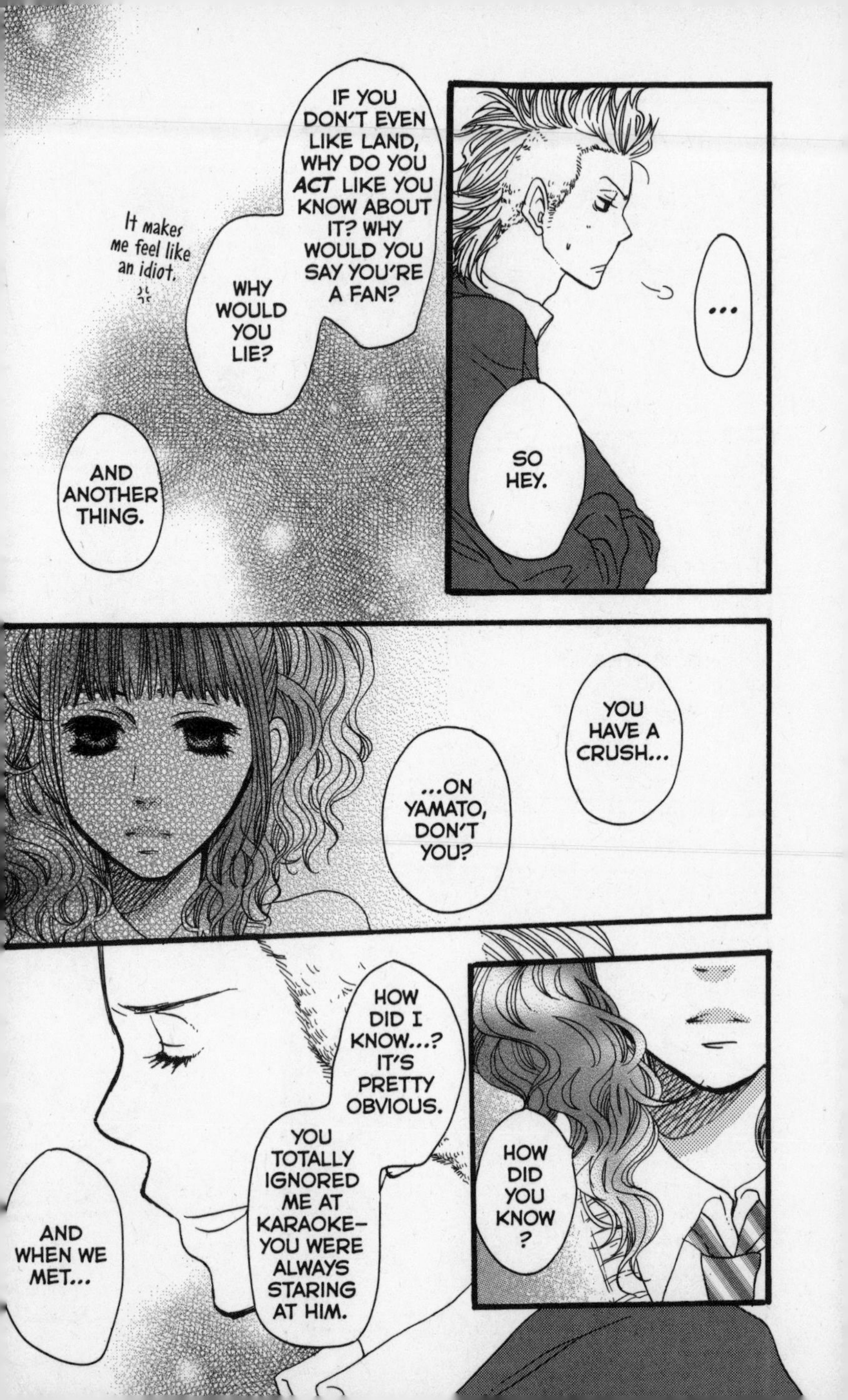
...
SO HEY.
IF YOU DON'T EVEN LIKE LAND, WHY DO YOU ACT LIKE YOU KNOW ABOUT IT? WHY WOULD YOU SAY YOU'RE A FAN?
WHY WOULD YOU LIE?
It makes me feel like an idiot.
AND ANOTHER THING.
YOU HAVE A CRUSH...
...ON YAMATO, DON'T YOU?
HOW DID YOU KNOW?
HOW DID I KNOW...? IT'S PRETTY OBVIOUS.
YOU TOTALLY IGNORED ME AT KARAOKE-YOU WERE ALWAYS STARING AT HIM.
AND WHEN WE MET...

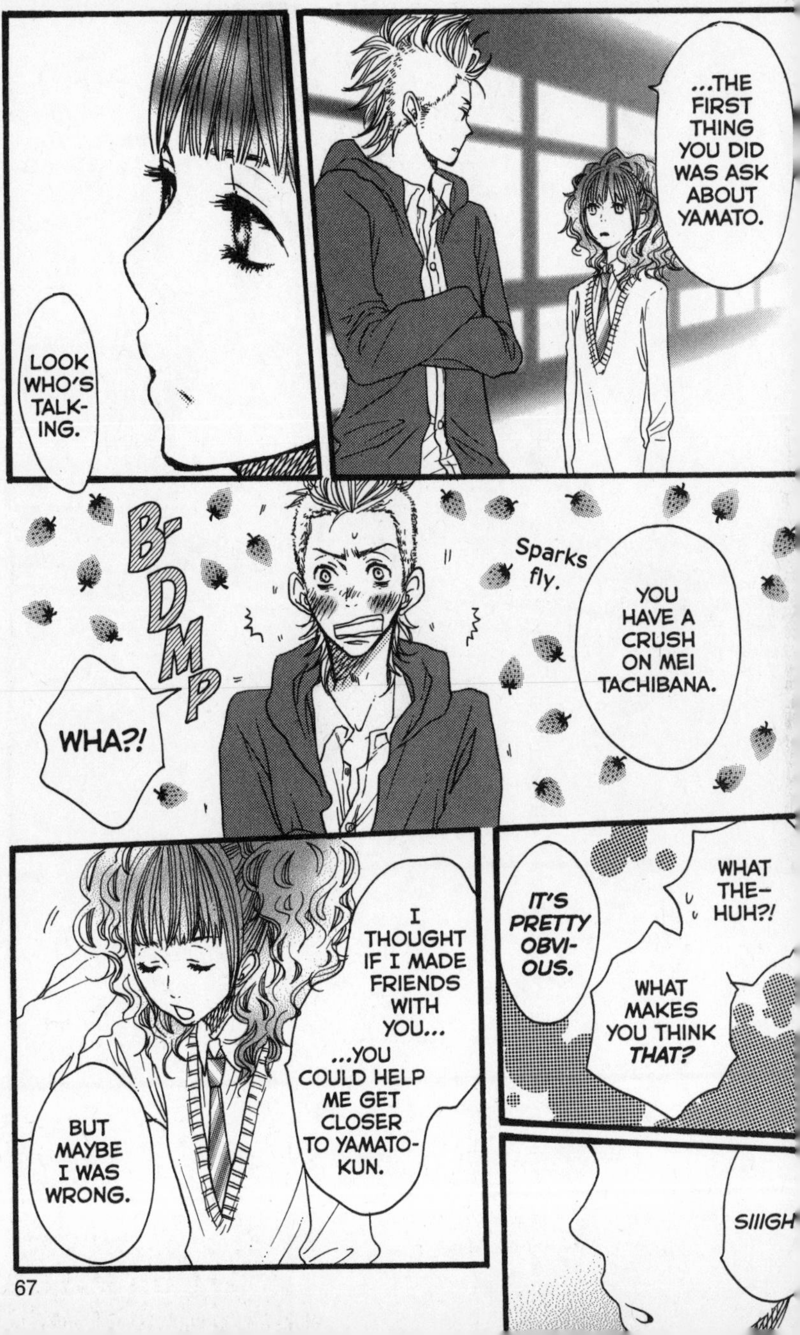
...THE FIRST THING YOU DID WAS ASK ABOUT YAMATO.
LOOK WHO'S TALK-ING.
YOU HAVE A CRUSH ON MEI TACHIBANA.
Sparks fly.
B-DMP
WHA?!
WHAT THE— HUH?!
WHAT MAKES YOU THINK *THAT?*
IT'S PRETTY OBVI-OUS.
SIIIGH
I THOUGHT IF I MADE FRIENDS WITH YOU...
...YOU COULD HELP ME GET CLOSER TO YAMATO-KUN.
BUT MAYBE I WAS WRONG.

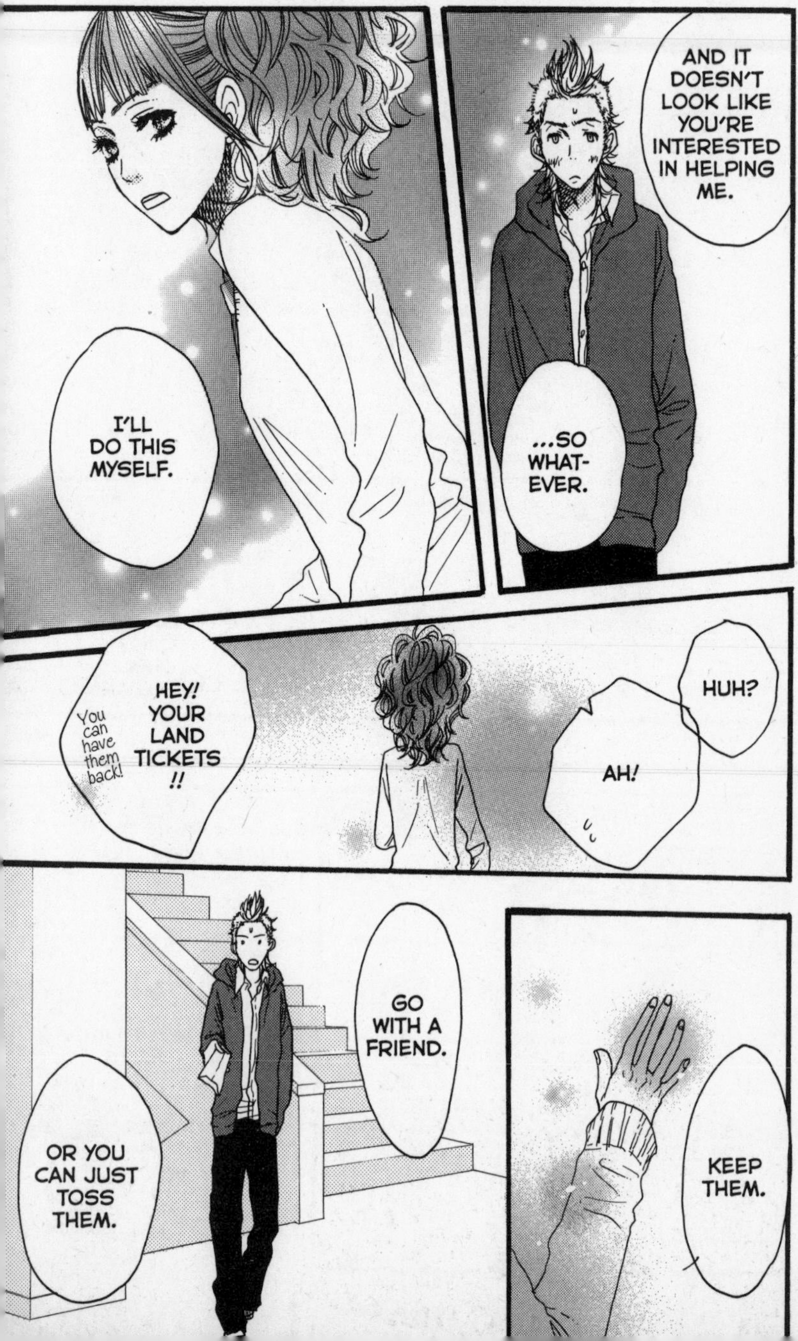
AND IT DOESN'T LOOK LIKE YOU'RE INTERESTED IN HELPING ME.
...SO WHAT-EVER.
I'LL DO THIS MYSELF.
HUH?
AH!
HEY! YOUR LAND TICKETS !!
You can have them back!
KEEP THEM.
GO WITH A FRIEND.
OR YOU CAN JUST TOSS THEM.

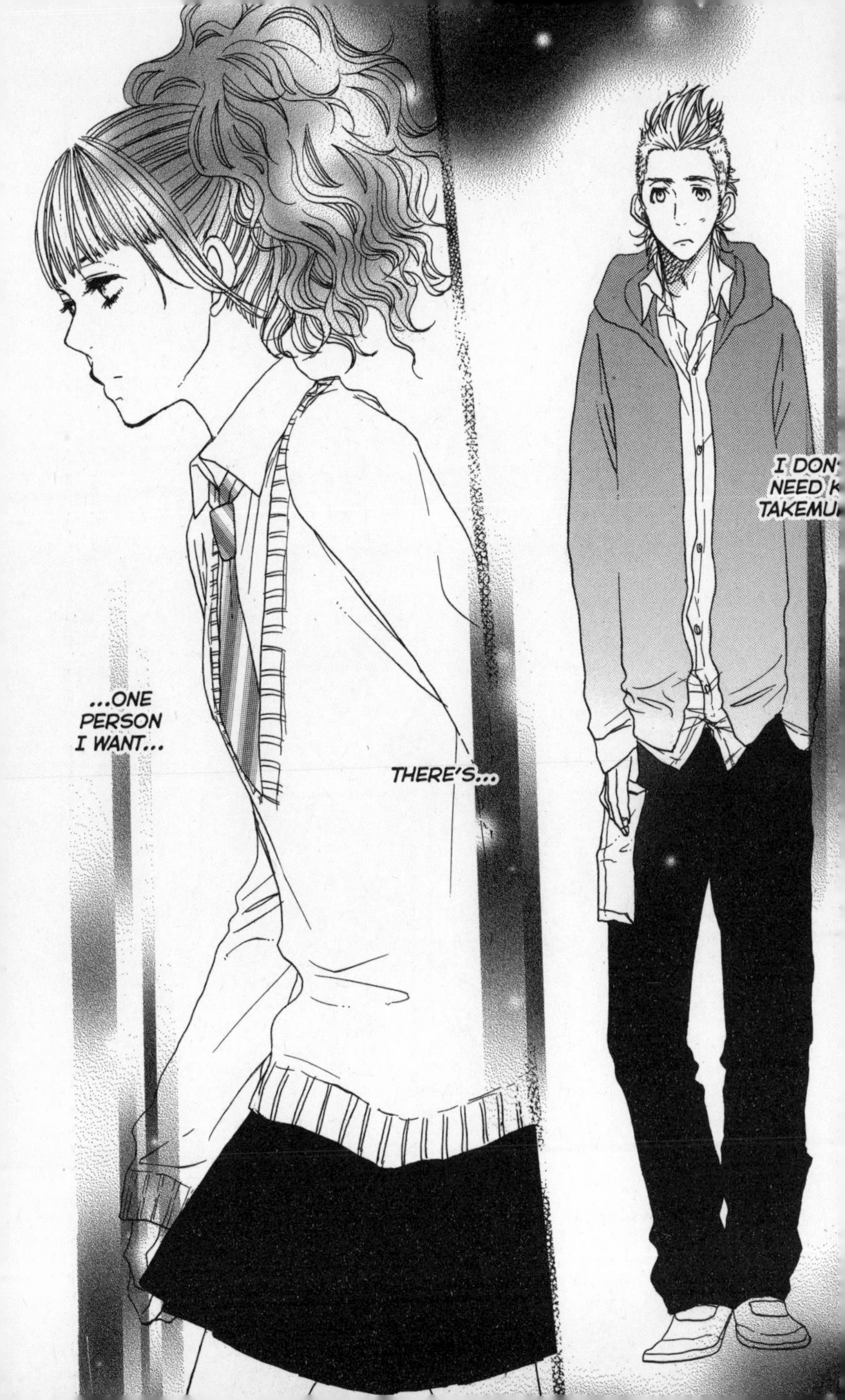
I DON
NEED K
TAKEMU
THERE'S...
...ONE PERSON I WANT...

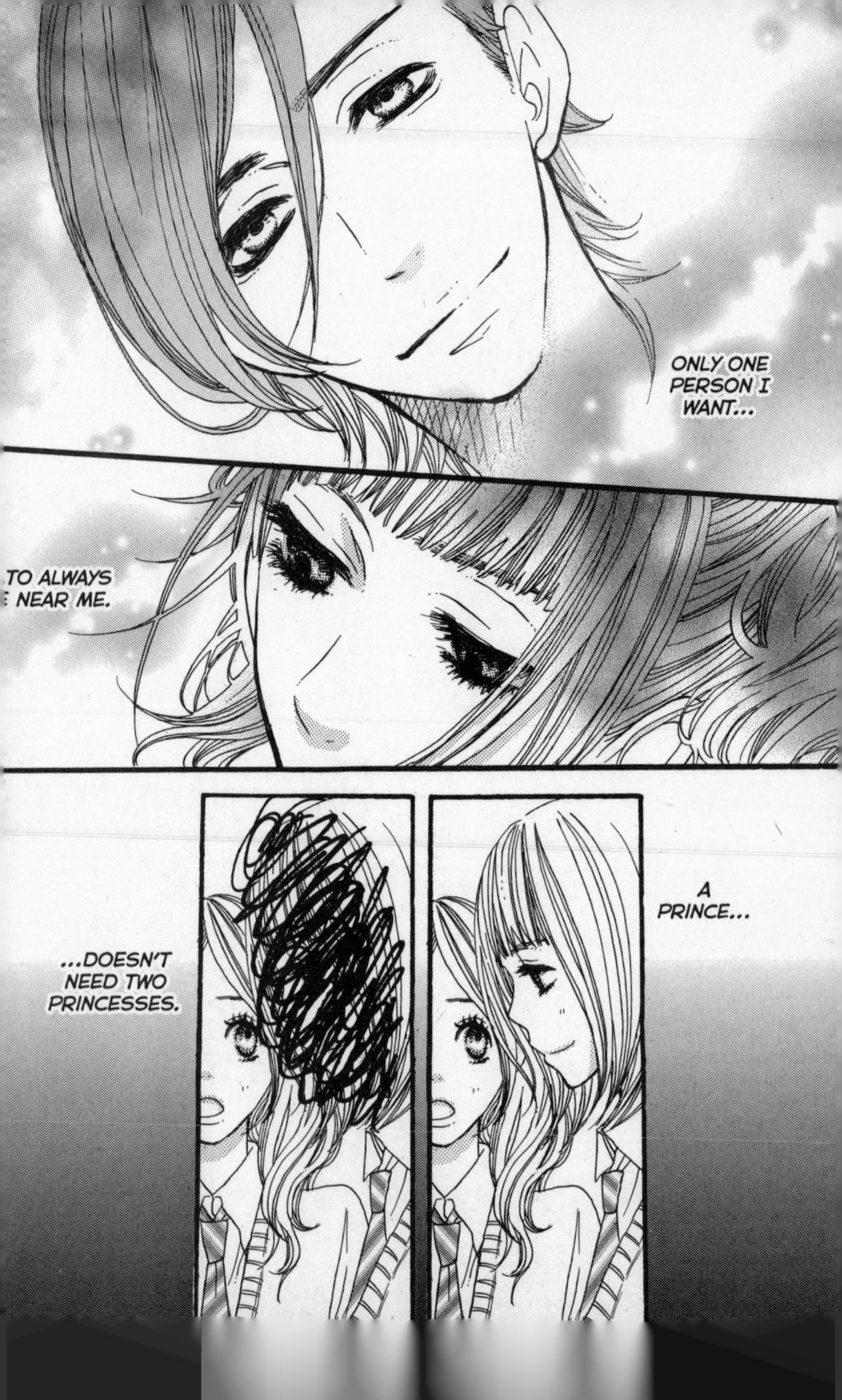
ONLY ONE PERSON I WANT...
TO ALWAYS
NEAR ME.
A PRINCE...
...DOESN'T NEED TWO PRINCESSES.

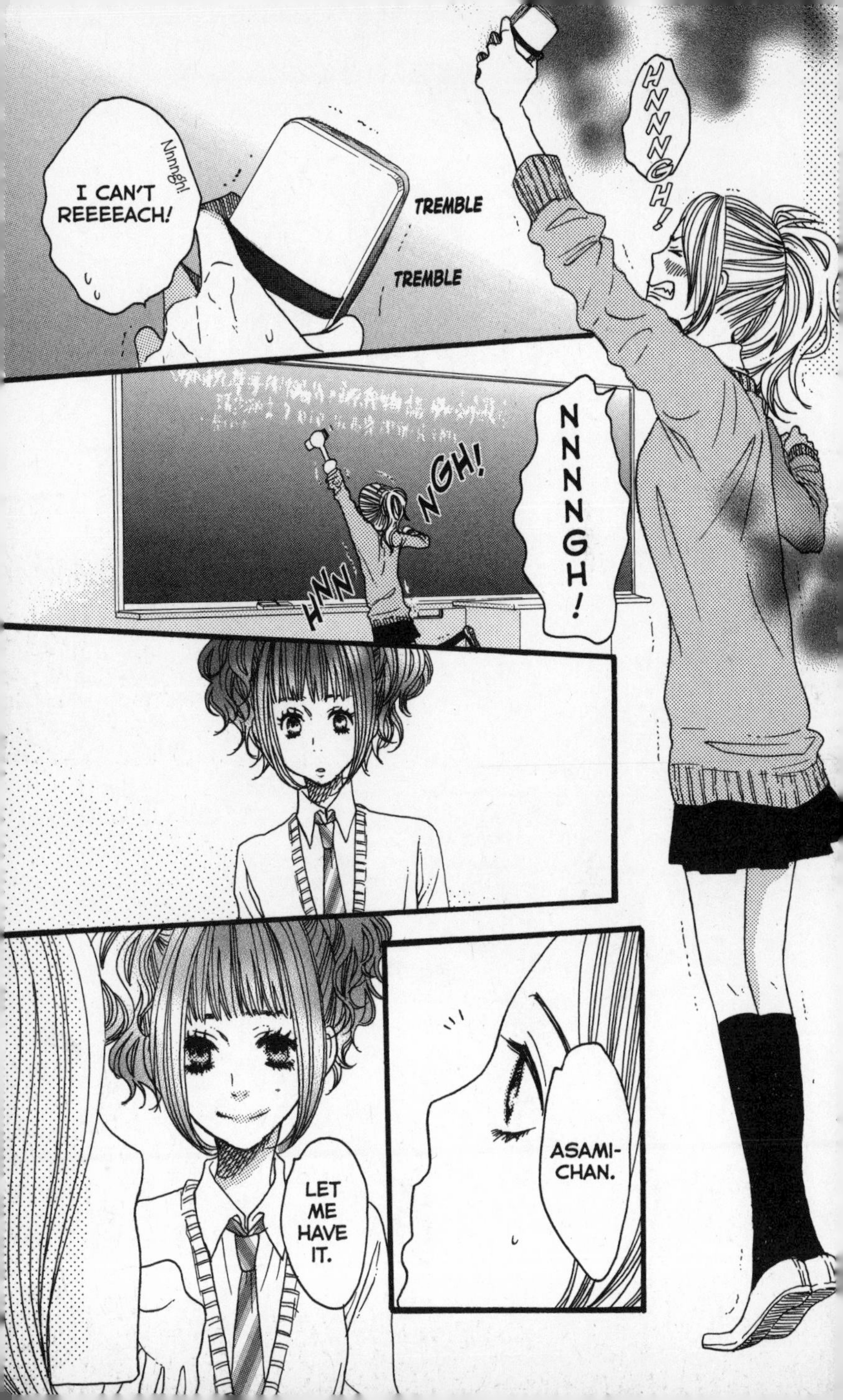
HNNNGH!
NNNNGH!
Nnnngh!
I CAN'T REEEEACH!
TREMBLE
TREMBLE
HNN NGH!
ASAMI-CHAN.
LET ME HAVE IT.

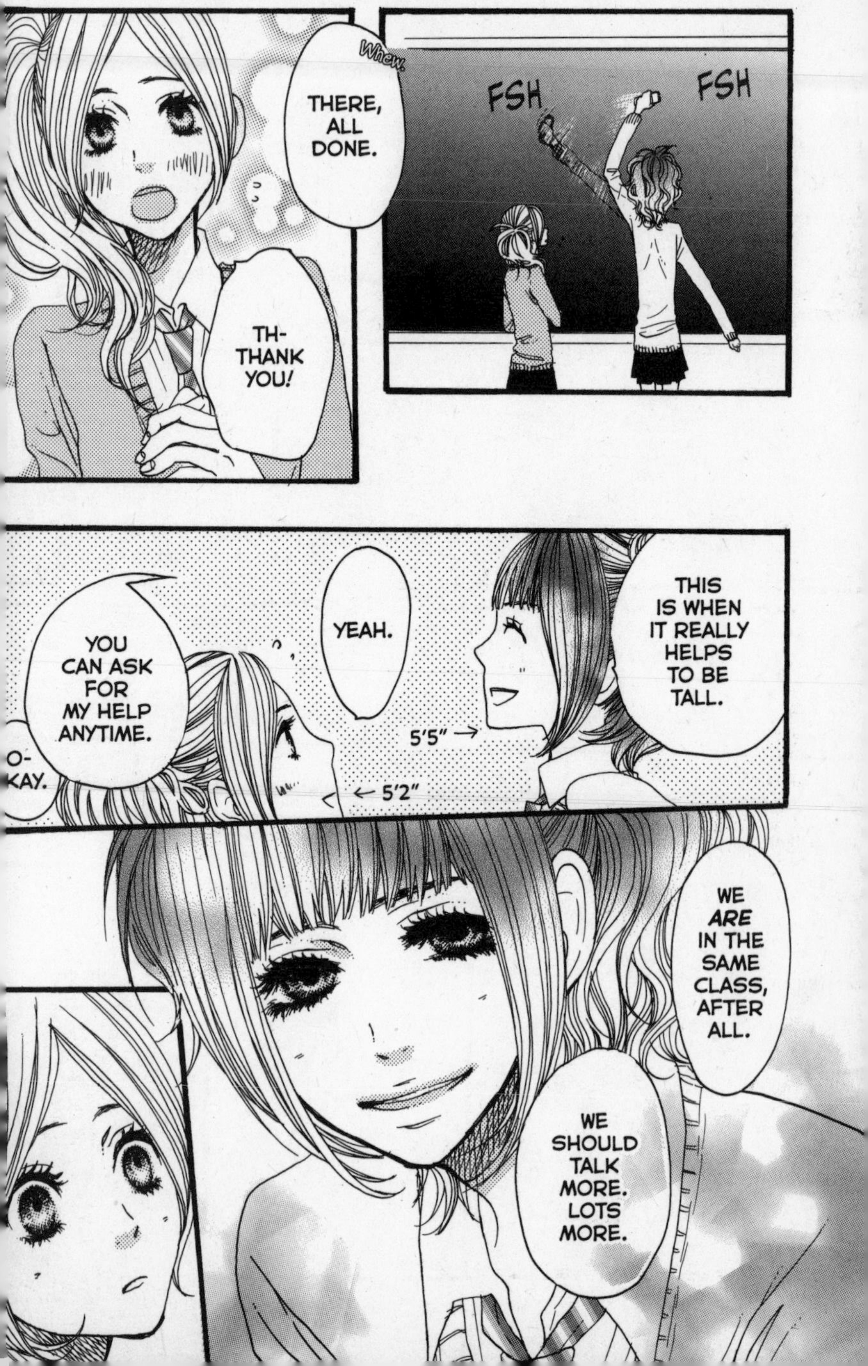
FSH FSH
Whew.
THERE, ALL DONE.
TH- THANK YOU!
THIS IS WHEN IT REALLY HELPS TO BE TALL.
5'5" →
YEAH.
← 5'2"
YOU CAN ASK FOR MY HELP ANYTIME.
O- KAY.
WE *ARE* IN THE SAME CLASS, AFTER ALL.
WE SHOULD TALK MORE. LOTS MORE.

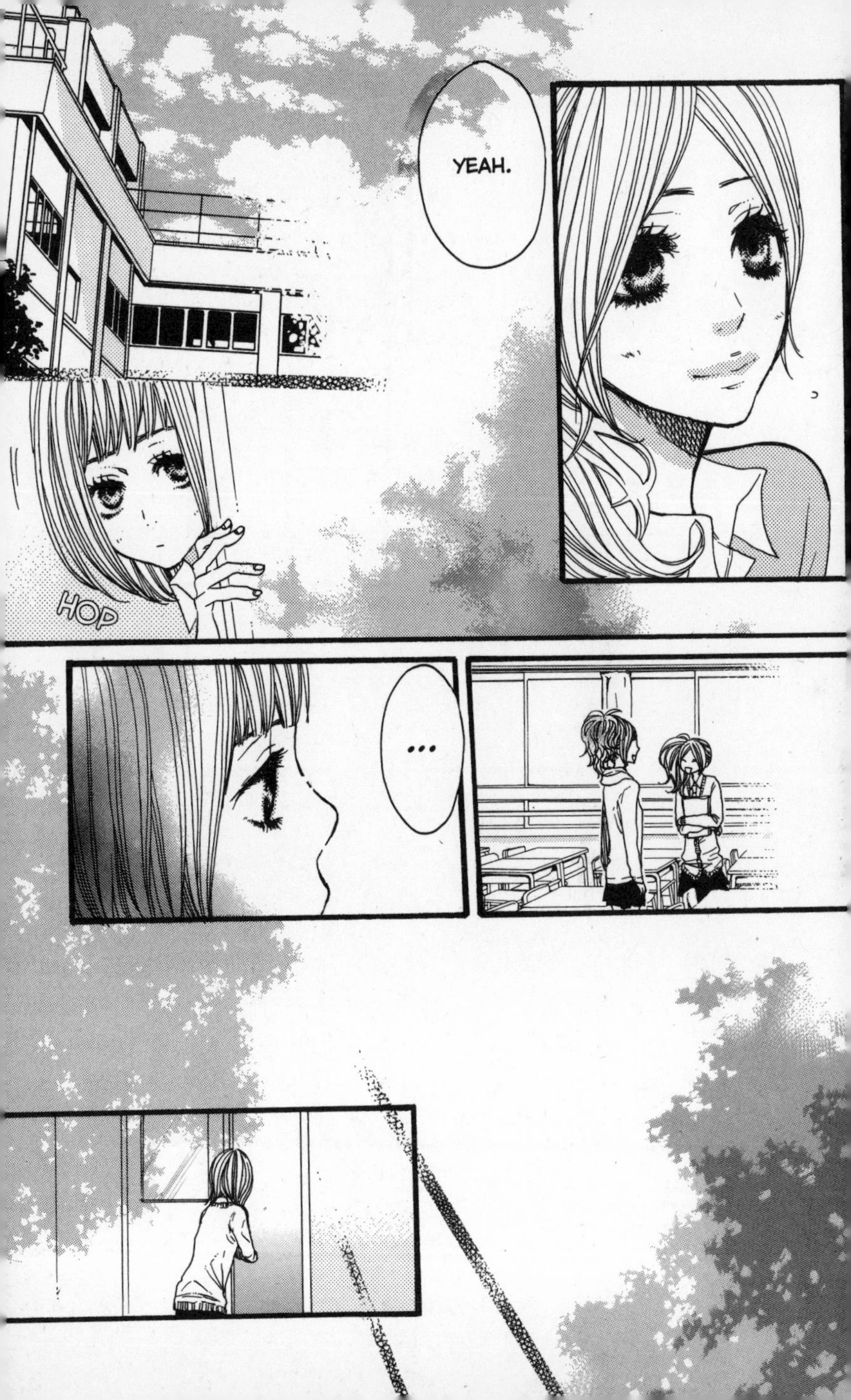
YEAH.
HOP
...

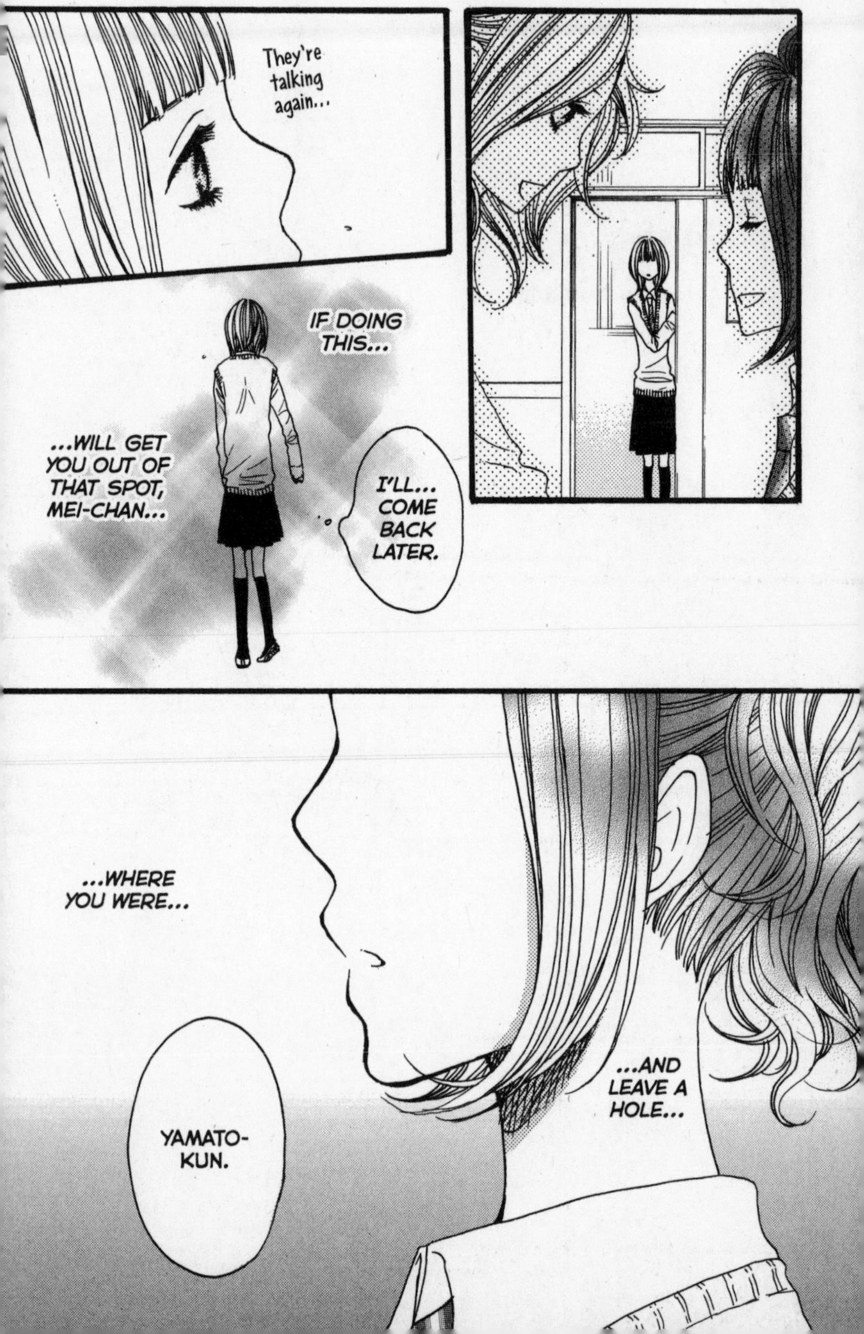
They're talking again...
IF DOING THIS...
I'LL... COME BACK LATER.
...WILL GET YOU OUT OF THAT SPOT, MEI-CHAN...
...WHERE YOU WERE...
...AND LEAVE A HOLE...
YAMATO-KUN.

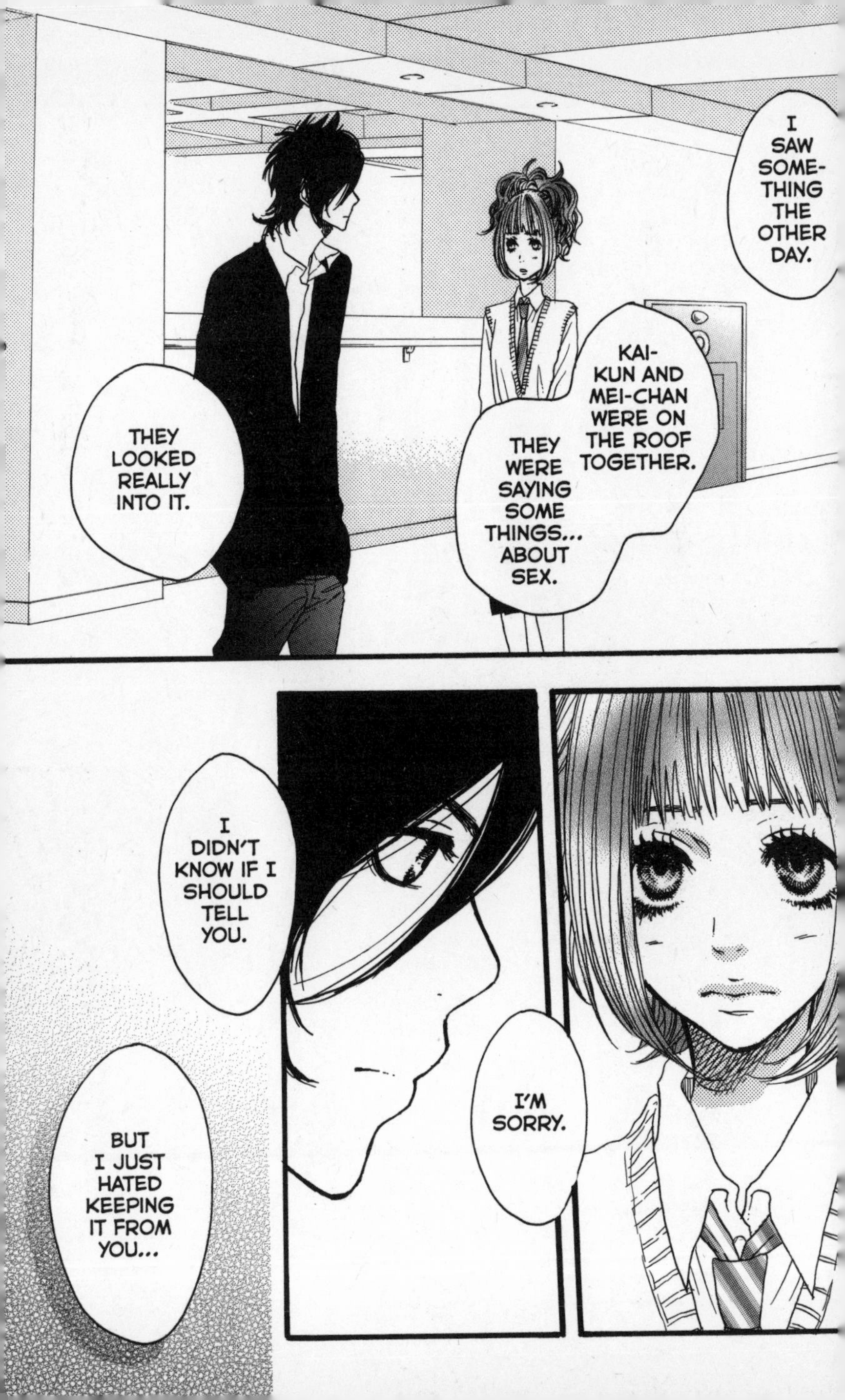
I SAW SOME-THING THE OTHER DAY.
KAI-KUN AND MEI-CHAN WERE ON THE ROOF TOGETHER.
THEY WERE SAYING SOME THINGS... ABOUT SEX.
THEY LOOKED REALLY INTO IT.
I DIDN'T KNOW IF I SHOULD TELL YOU.
BUT I JUST HATED KEEPING IT FROM YOU...
I'M SORRY.

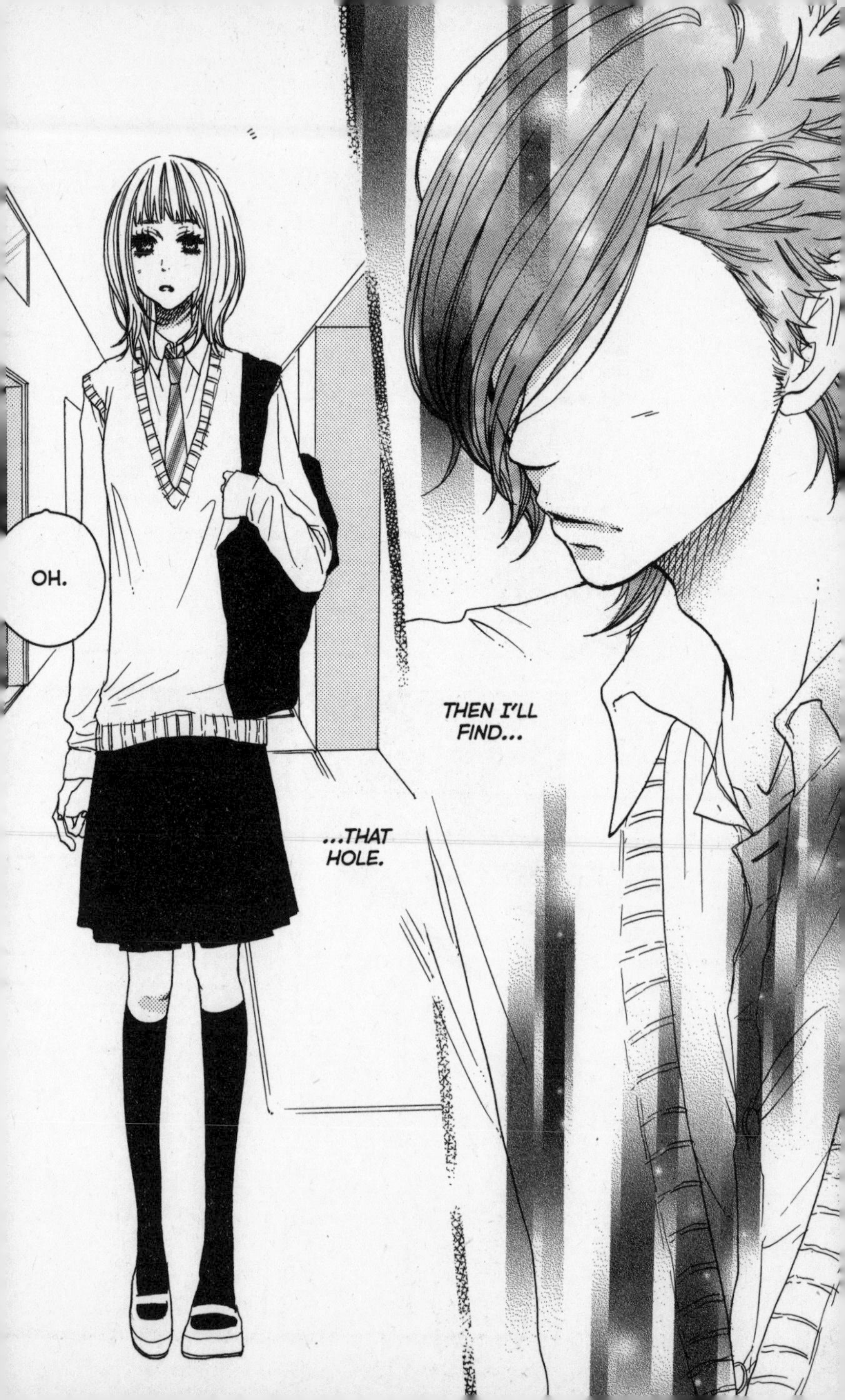
THEN I'LL FIND...
...THAT HOLE.
OH.

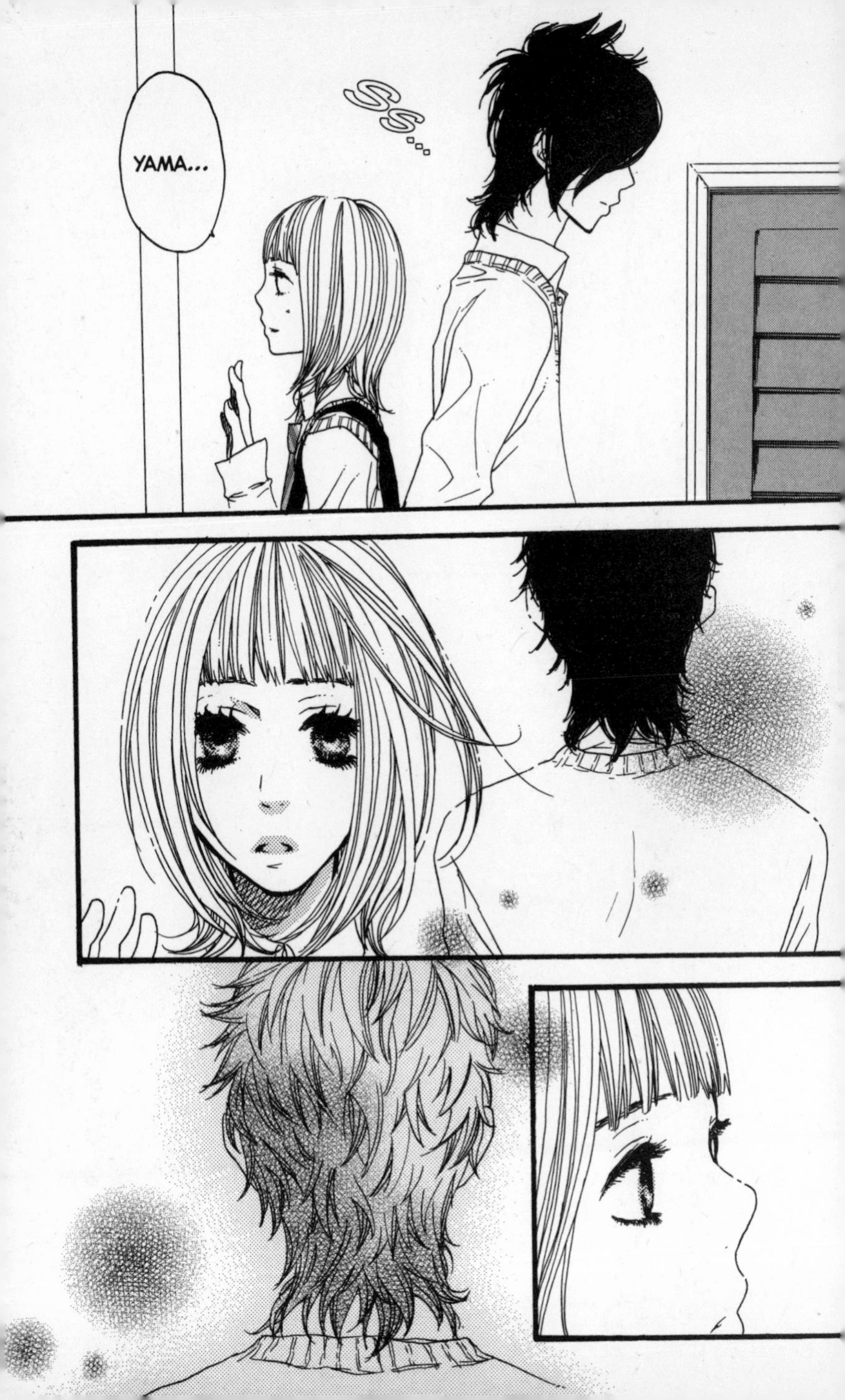
YAMA...
SS...

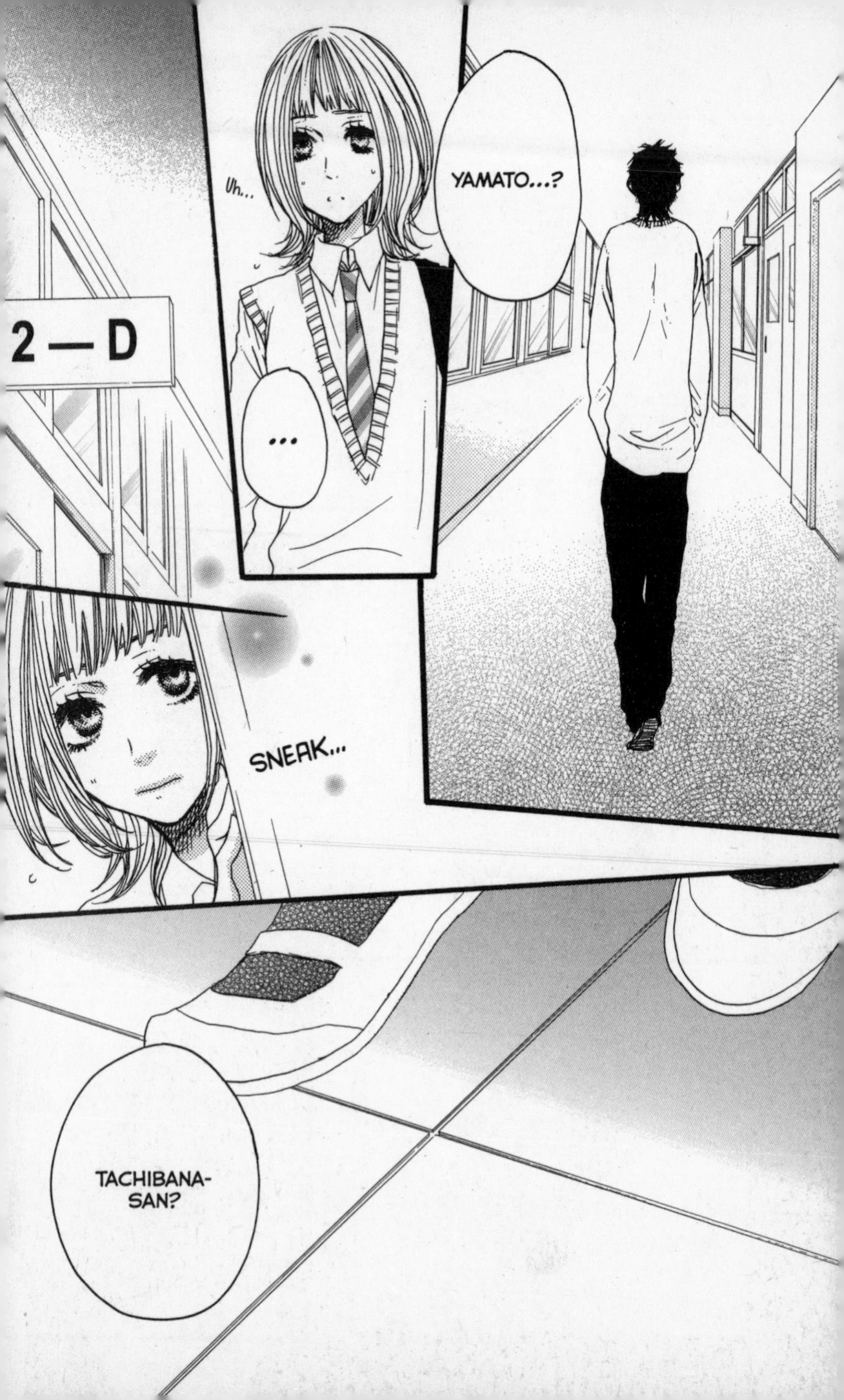
YAMATO...?
Uh...
...
2 — D
SNEAK...
TACHIBANA-SAN?

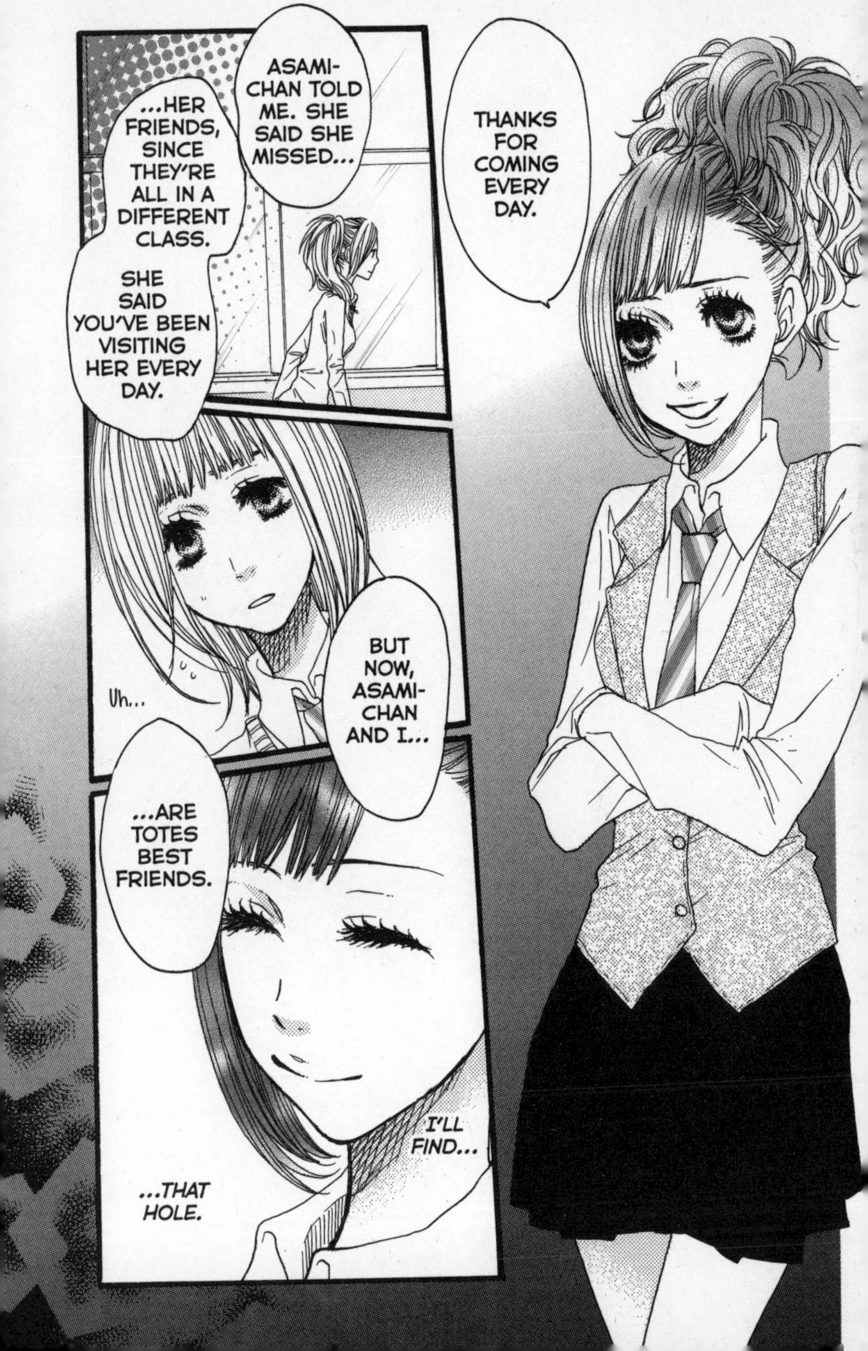
THANKS FOR COMING EVERY DAY.
ASAMI-CHAN TOLD ME. SHE SAID SHE MISSED...
...HER FRIENDS, SINCE THEY'RE ALL IN A DIFFERENT CLASS.
SHE SAID YOU'VE BEEN VISITING HER EVERY DAY.
BUT NOW, ASAMI-CHAN AND I...
Uh...
...ARE TOTES BEST FRIENDS.
I'LL FIND...
...THAT HOLE.

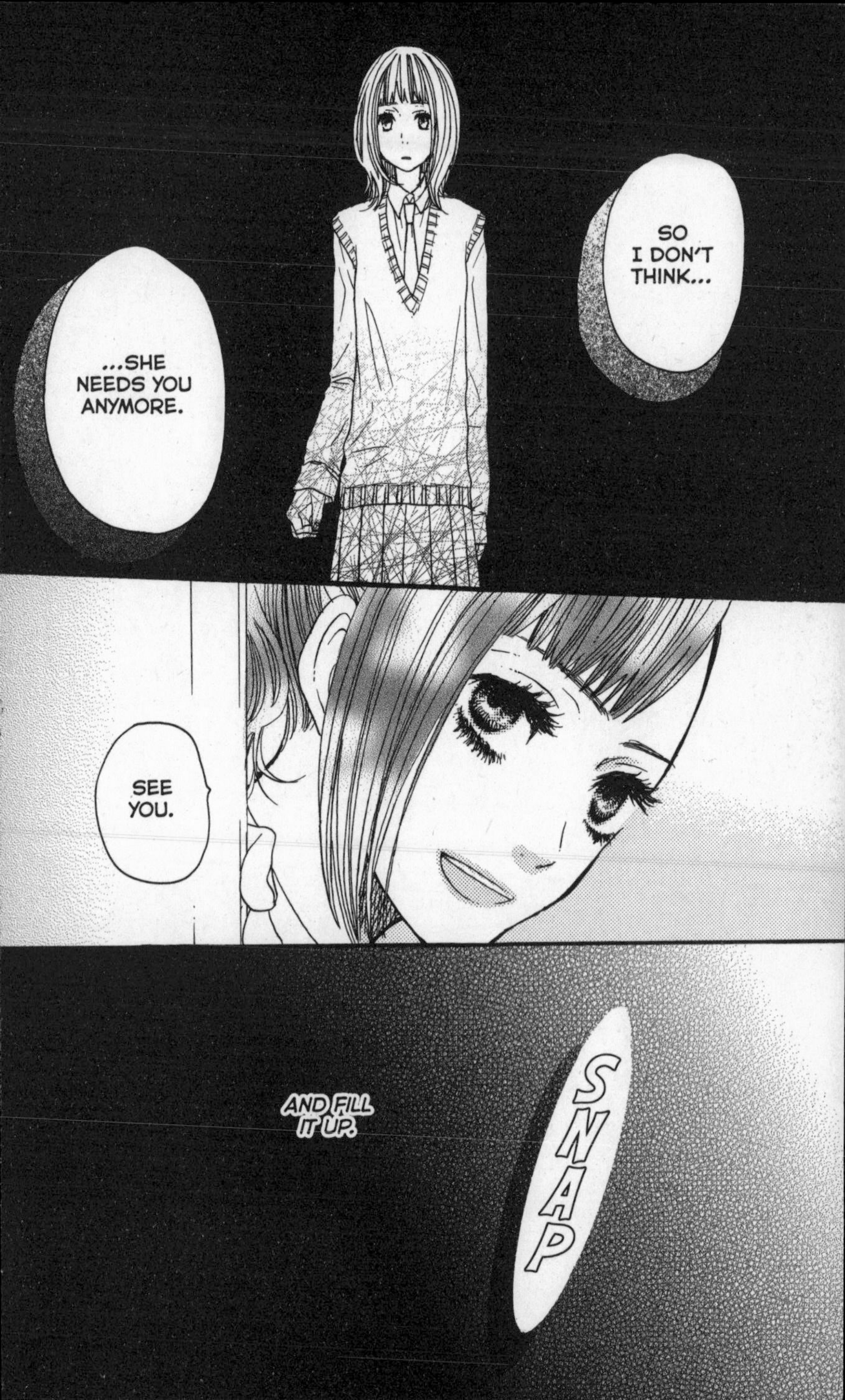
SO I DON'T THINK...
...SHE NEEDS YOU ANYMORE.
SEE YOU.
SNAP
AND FILL IT UP.

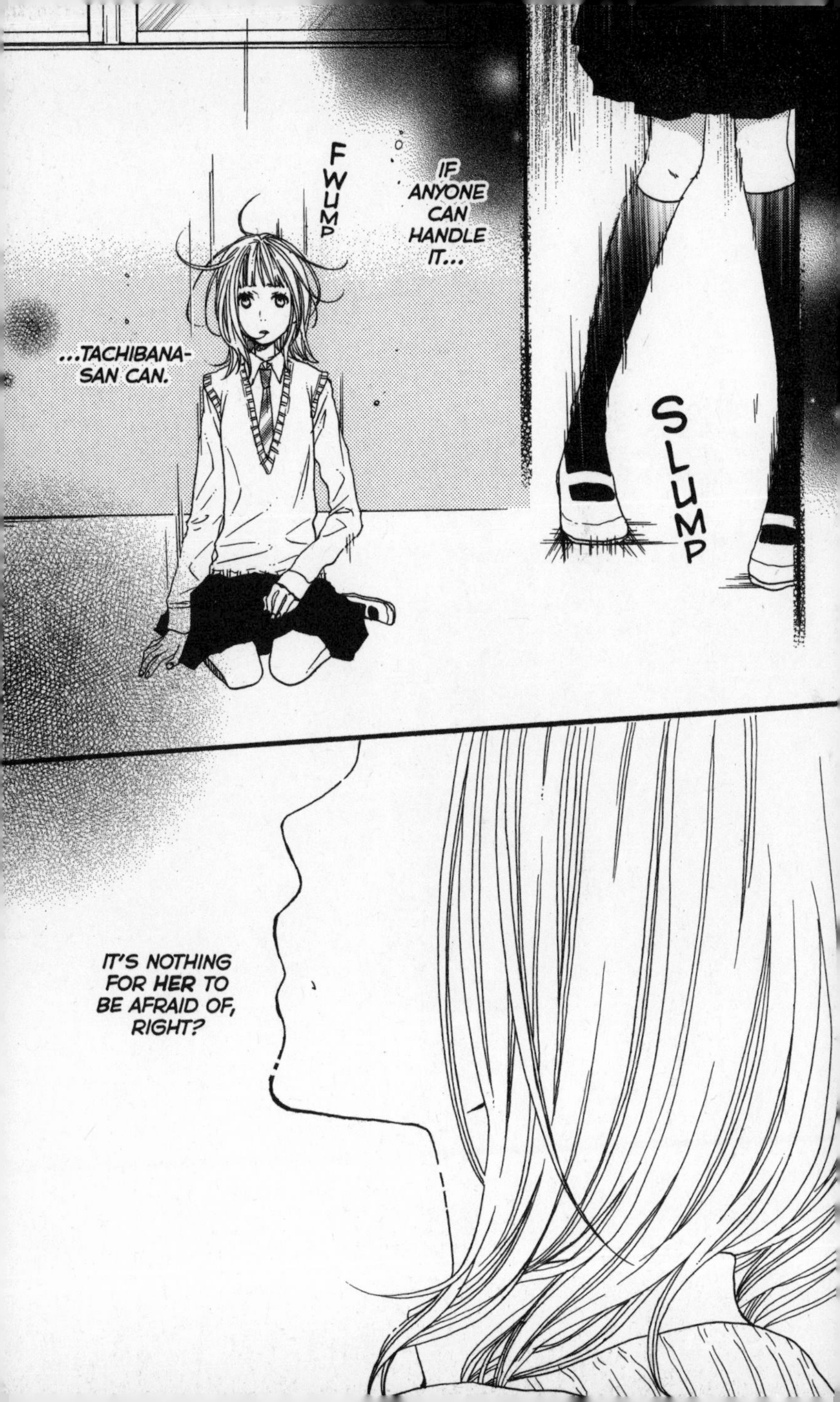
SLUMP
IF ANYONE CAN HANDLE IT...
FWUMP
...TACHIBANA-SAN CAN.
IT'S NOTHING FOR HER TO BE AFRAID OF, RIGHT?

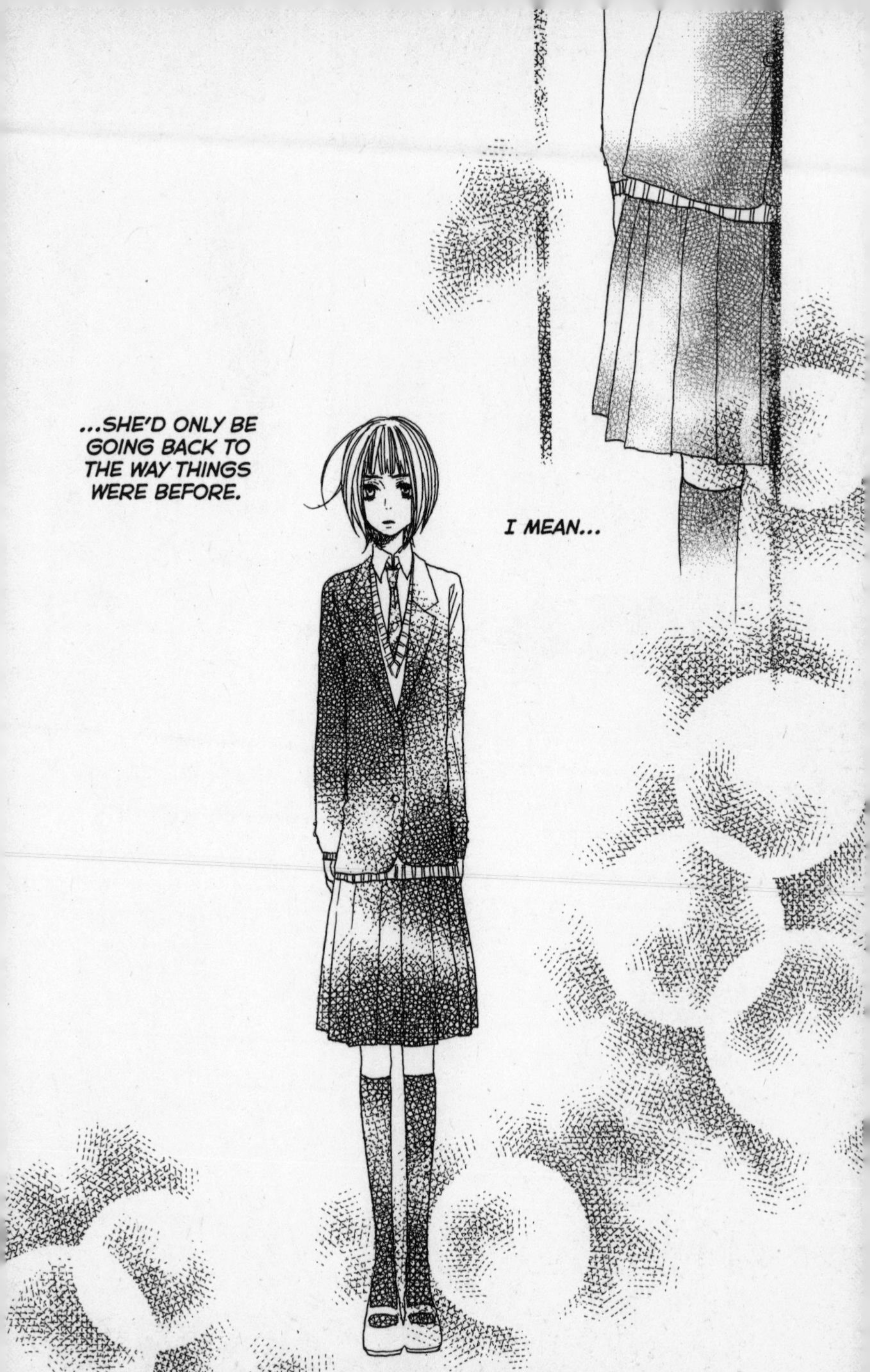
I MEAN...
...SHE'D ONLY BE GOING BACK TO THE WAY THINGS WERE BEFORE.

Chapter 18 — End

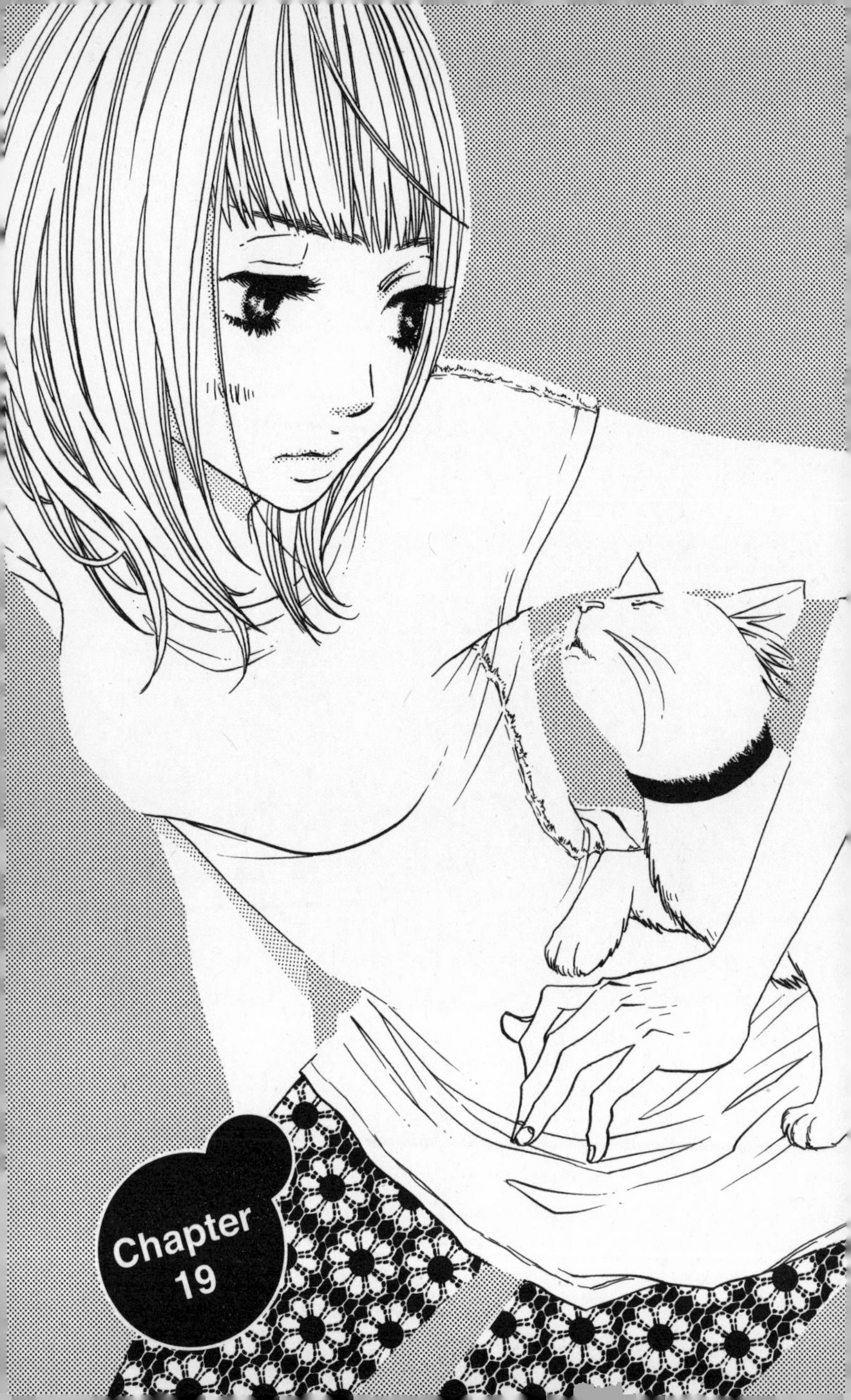
Chapter
19

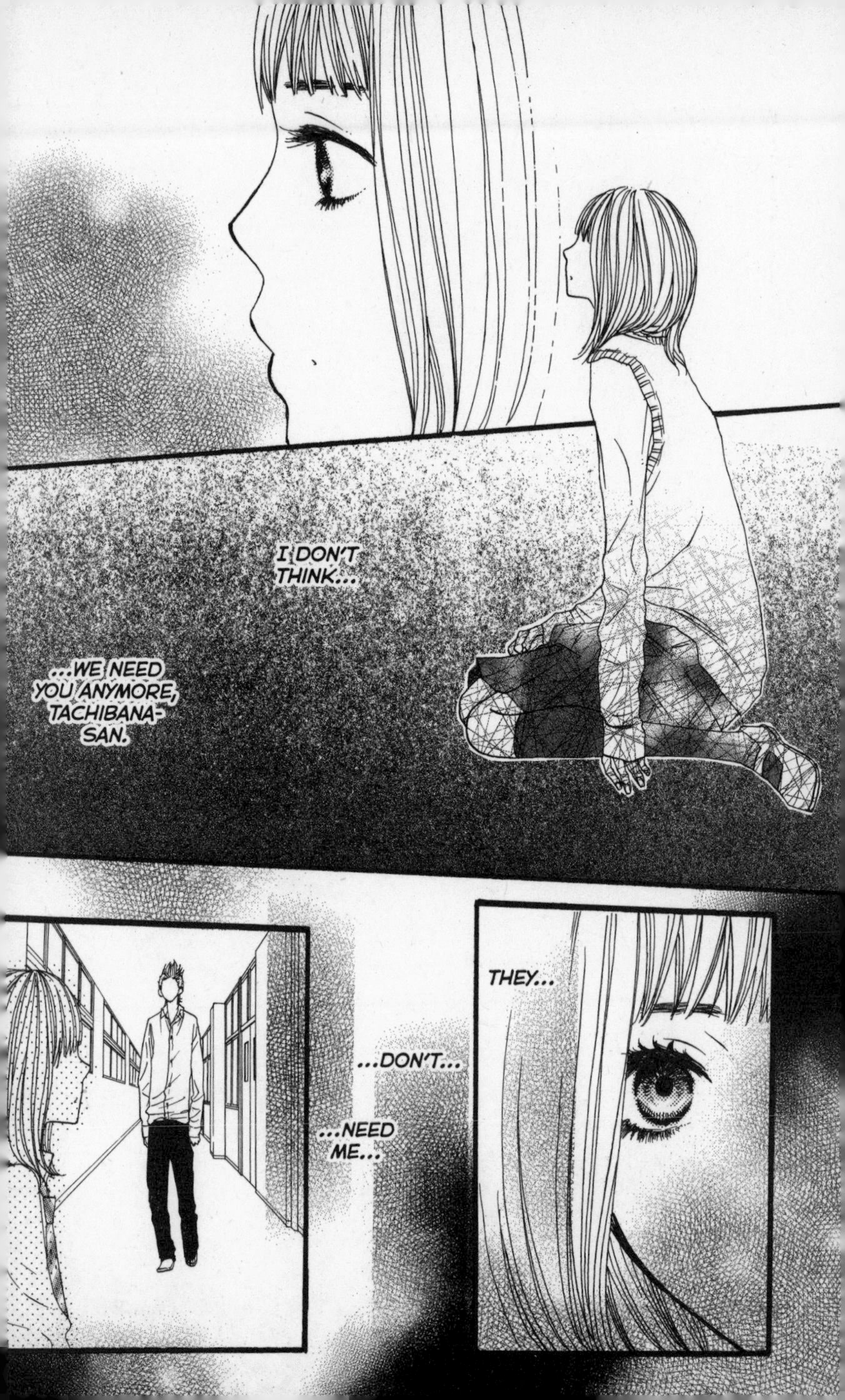
I DON'T THINK...
...WE NEED YOU ANYMORE, TACHIBANA-SAN.
THEY...
...DON'T...
...NEED ME...

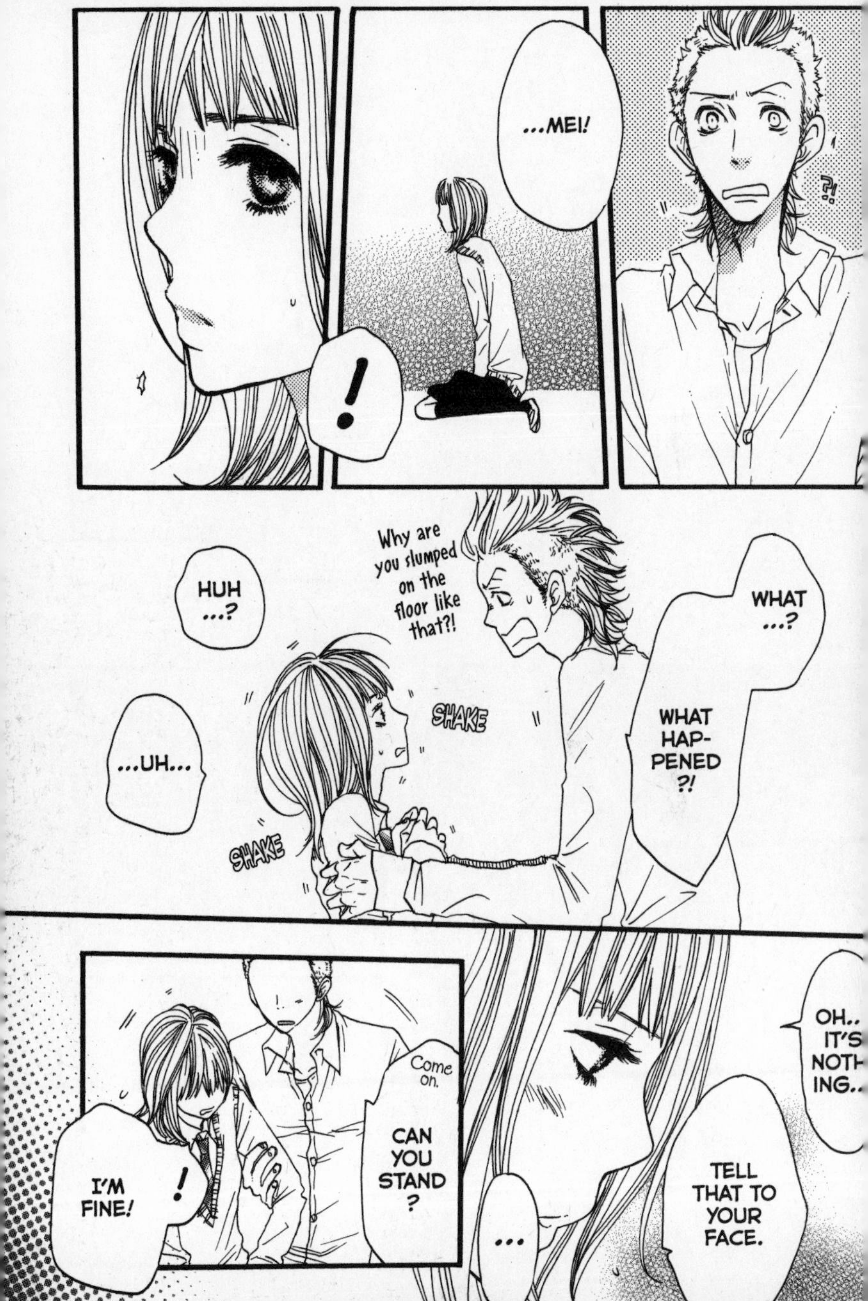
?!
...MEI!
!
WHAT ...?
WHAT HAP-PENED ?!
Why are you slumped on the floor like that?!
SHAKE
HUH ...?
...UH...
SHAKE
OH.. IT'S NOTH ING..
TELL THAT TO YOUR FACE.
...
Come on.
CAN YOU STAND ?
!
I'M FINE!

...I'M SORRY.

PAH

BUT I'M FINE.

...

GASP

I'M SCARED.

I'M SCARED.

I'M SCARED.

WHAT DO I DO?

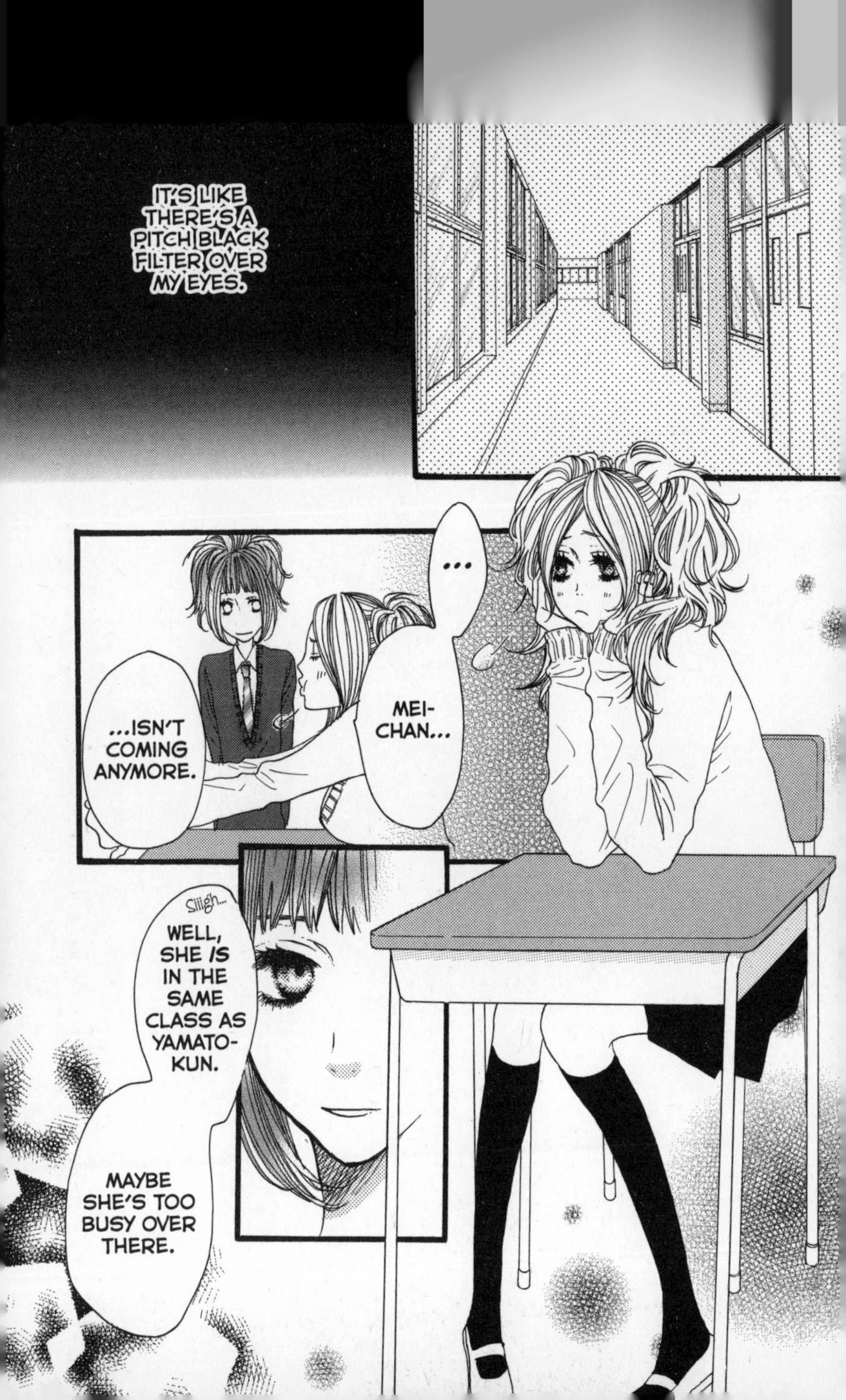
IT'S LIKE THERE'S A PITCH BLACK FILTER OVER MY EYES.
...
MEI-CHAN...
...ISN'T COMING ANYMORE.
Siiigh...
WELL, SHE *IS* IN THE SAME CLASS AS YAMATO-KUN.
MAYBE SHE'S TOO BUSY OVER THERE.

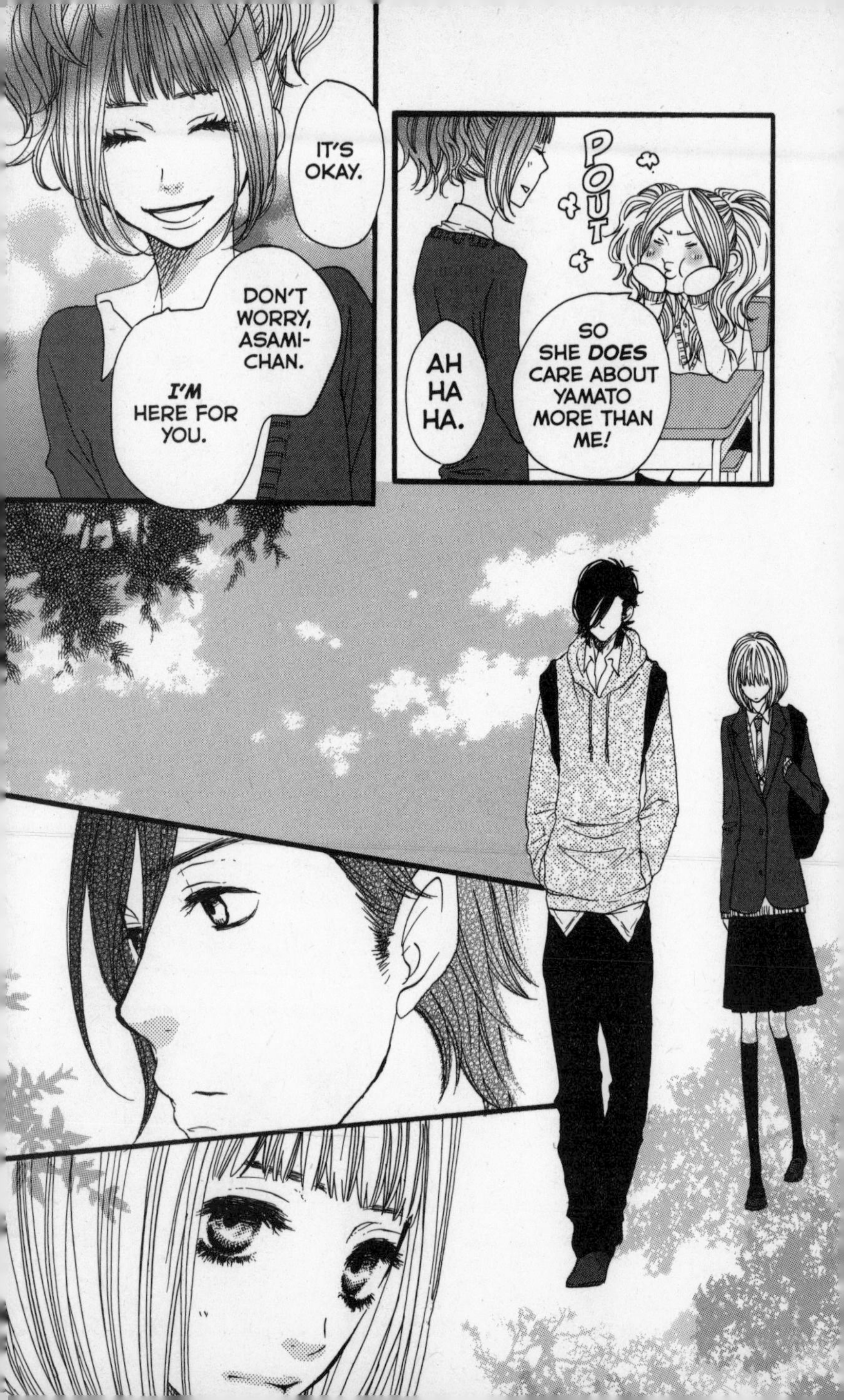
POUT
SO SHE *DOES* CARE ABOUT YAMATO MORE THAN ME!
AH HA HA.
IT'S OKAY.
DON'T WORRY, ASAMI-CHAN.
I'M HERE FOR YOU.

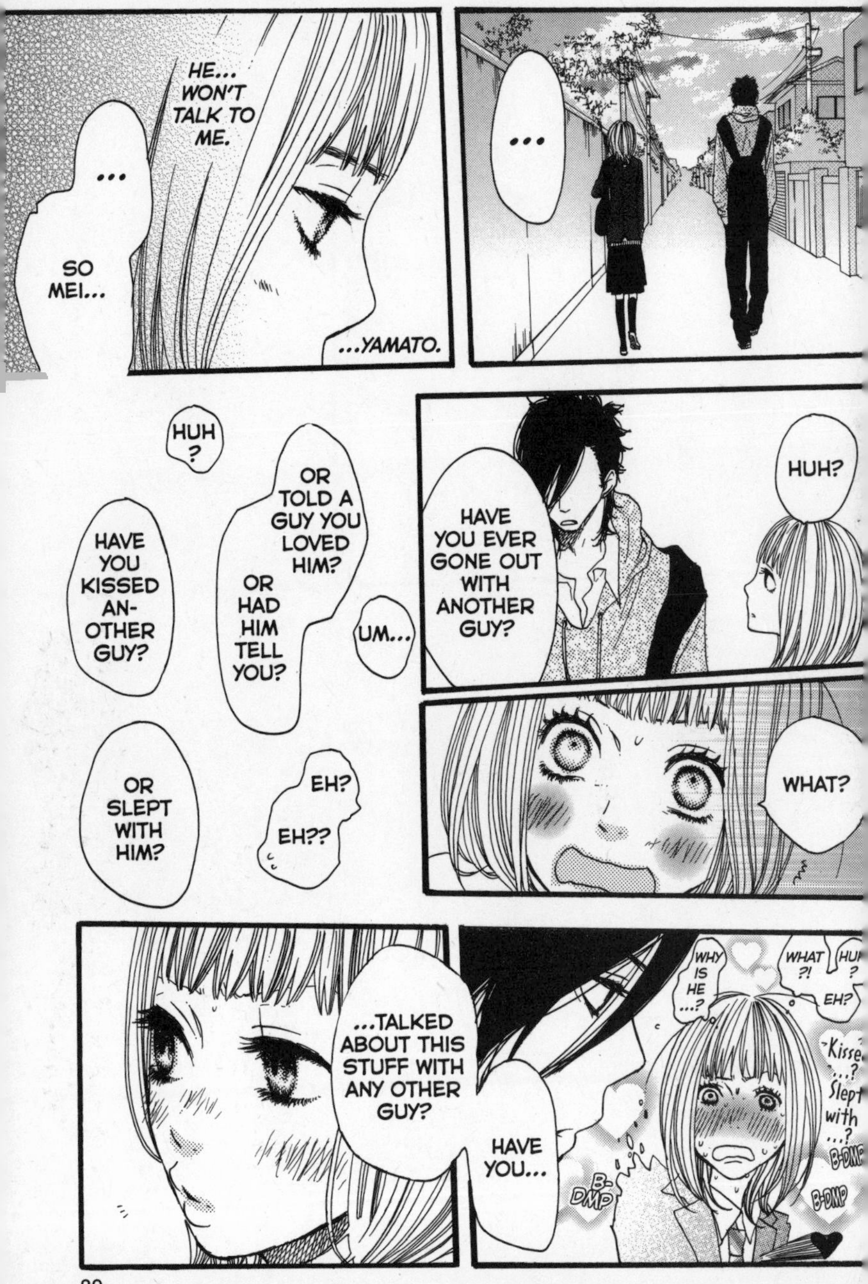
...
HE... WON'T TALK TO ME.
...YAMATO.
...
SO MEI...
HUH?
HAVE YOU EVER GONE OUT WITH ANOTHER GUY?
UM...
OR TOLD A GUY YOU LOVED HIM?
OR HAD HIM TELL YOU?
HUH?
HAVE YOU KISSED AN-OTHER GUY?
WHAT?
EH?
EH??
OR SLEPT WITH HIM?
WHAT?!
HUH?
EH?
WHY IS HE ...?
Kissed ...?
Slept with ...?
B-DMP
B-DMP
B-DMP
HAVE YOU...
...TALKED ABOUT THIS STUFF WITH ANY OTHER GUY?

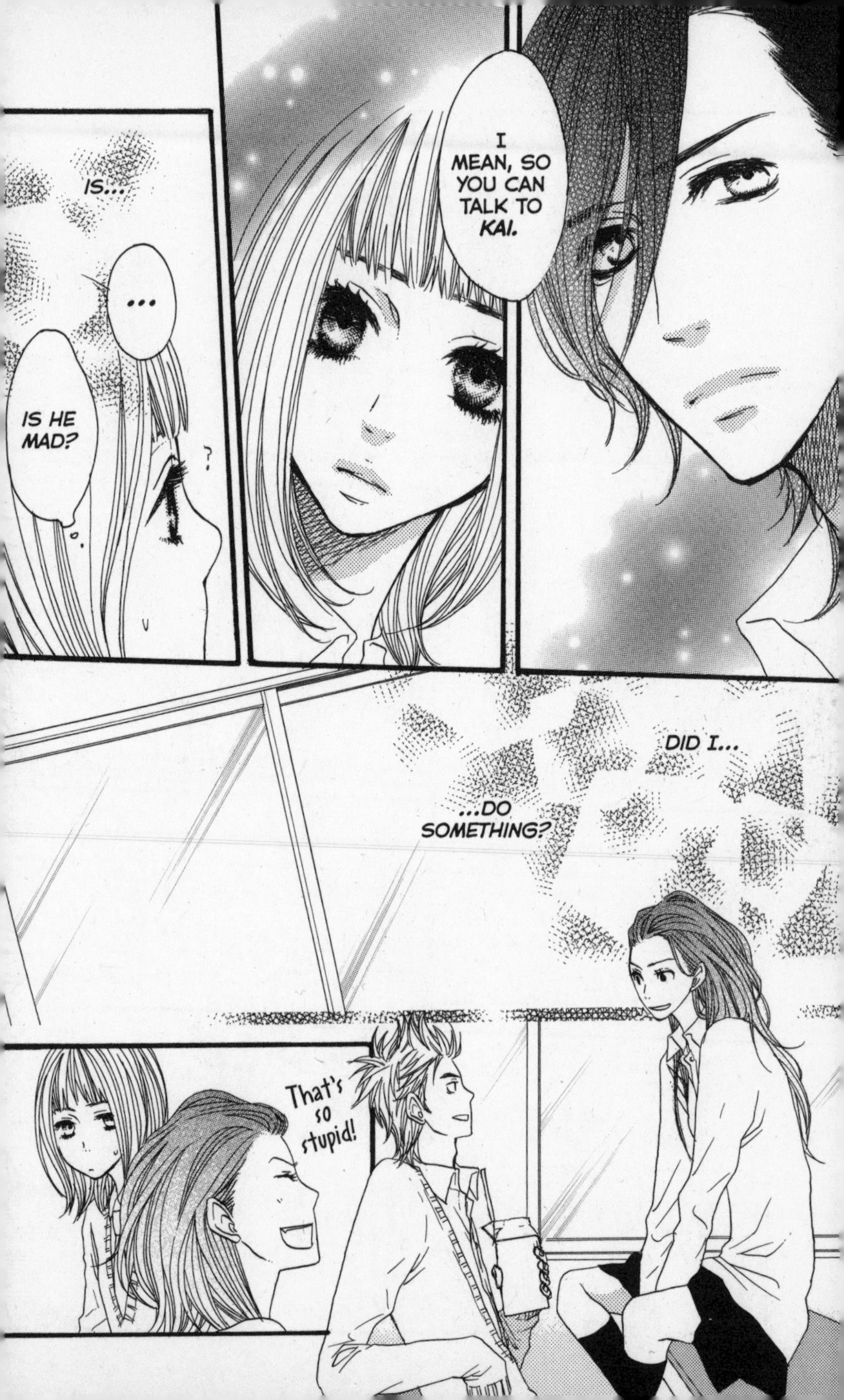
I MEAN, SO YOU CAN TALK TO KAI.
IS...
...
IS HE MAD?
DID I...
...DO SOMETHING?
That's so stupid!

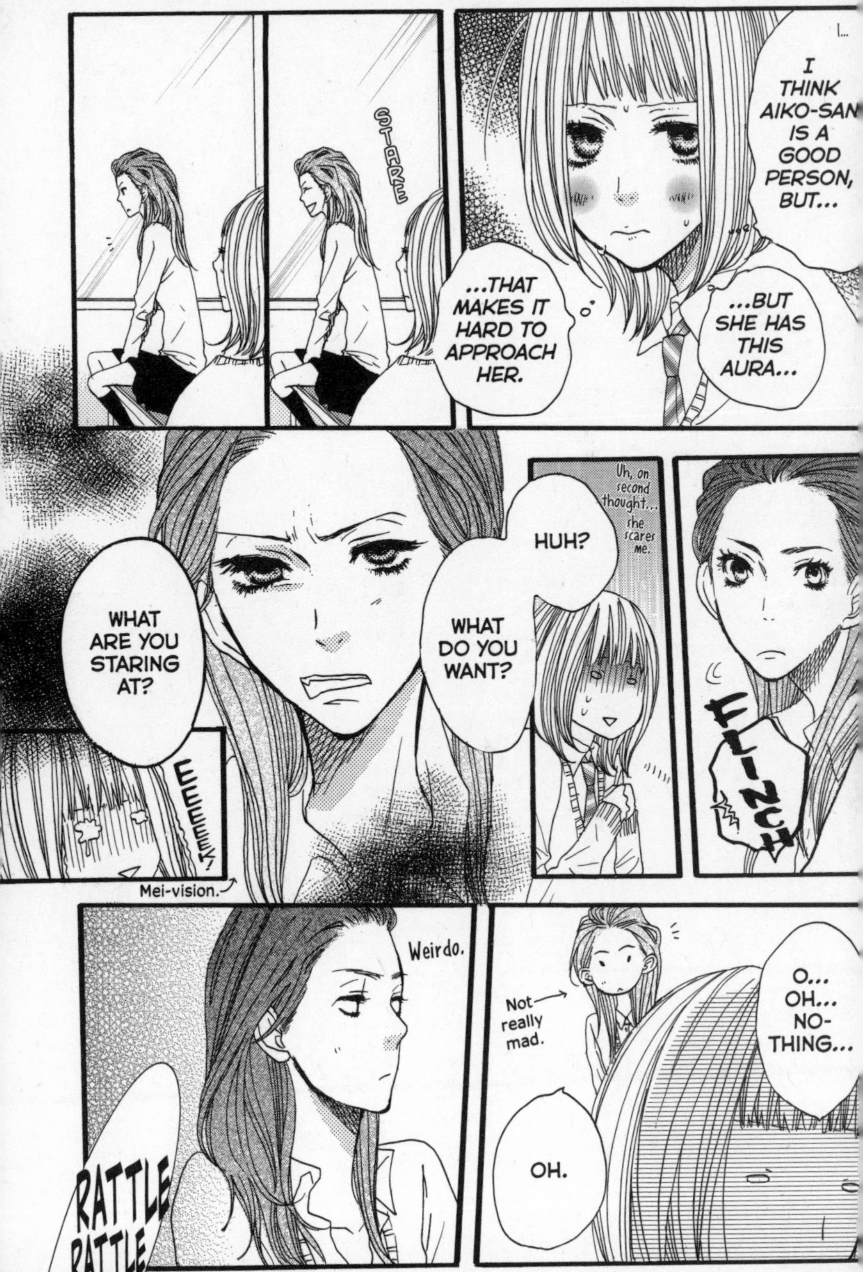
I...
I THINK AIKO-SAN IS A GOOD PERSON, BUT...
...BUT SHE HAS THIS AURA...
...THAT MAKES IT HARD TO APPROACH HER.
STARE
FLINCH
Uh, on second thought... she scares me.
HUH?
WHAT DO YOU WANT?
WHAT ARE YOU STARING AT?
EEEEEK!
Mei-vision.
O... OH... NOTHING...
Not really mad.
OH.
Weirdo.
RATTLE RATTLE

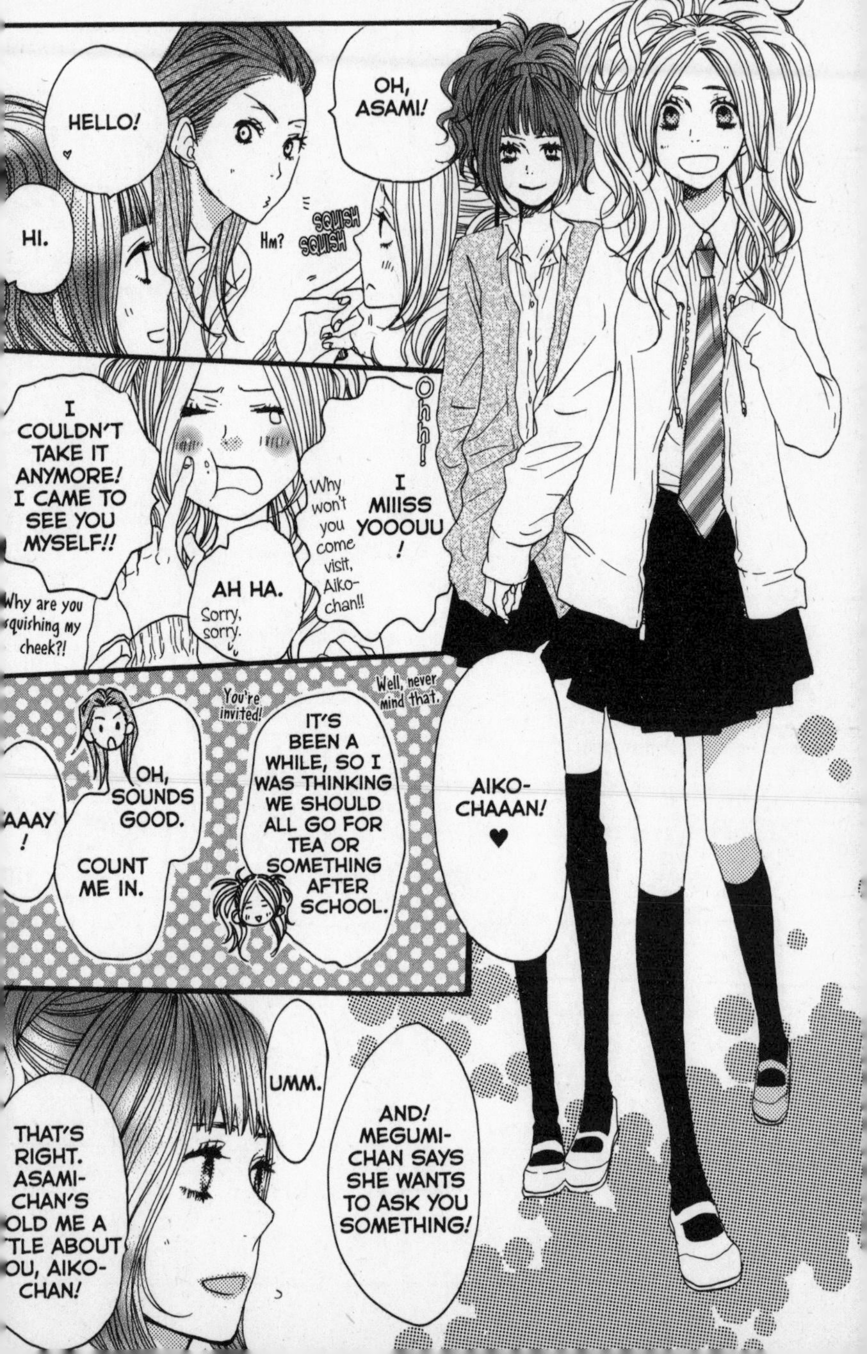
AIKO-CHAAAN! ♥
OH, ASAMI!
SQUISH SQUISH
Hm?
HELLO! ♥
HI.
Ohh!
I MIIISS YOOOUU!
Why won't you come visit, Aiko-chan!!
AH HA.
Sorry, sorry.
I COULDN'T TAKE IT ANYMORE! I CAME TO SEE YOU MYSELF!!
Why are you squishing my cheek?!
Well, never mind that.
IT'S BEEN A WHILE, SO I WAS THINKING WE SHOULD ALL GO FOR TEA OR SOMETHING AFTER SCHOOL.
You're invited!
OH, SOUNDS GOOD.
COUNT ME IN.
AAAY!
AND! MEGUMI-CHAN SAYS SHE WANTS TO ASK YOU SOMETHING!
UMM.
THAT'S RIGHT. ASAMI-CHAN'S OLD ME A TLE ABOUT OU, AIKO-CHAN!

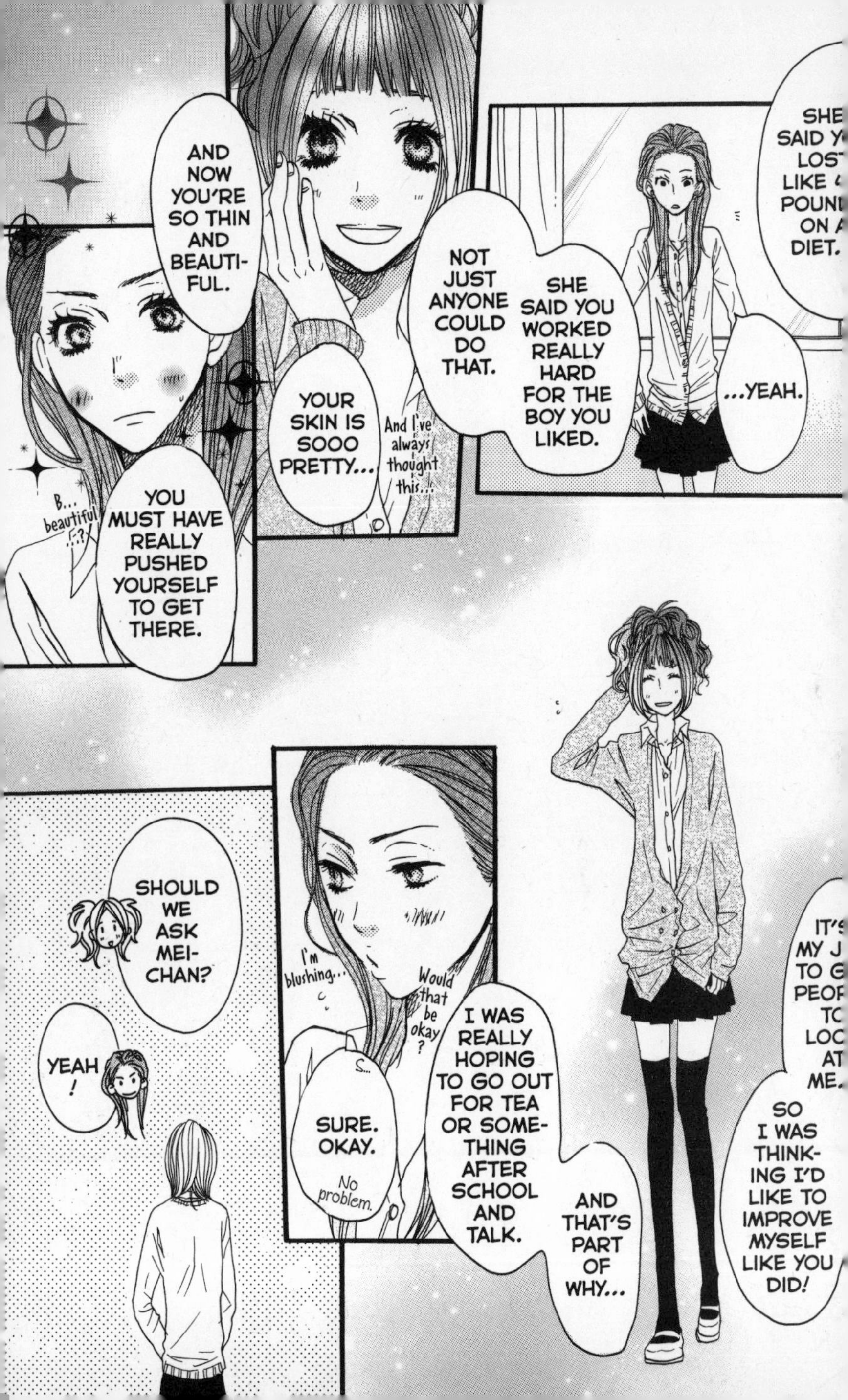
SHE SAID Y LOST LIKE 4 POUN ON A DIET.
...YEAH.
SHE SAID YOU WORKED REALLY HARD FOR THE BOY YOU LIKED.
NOT JUST ANYONE COULD DO THAT.
And I've always thought this...
YOUR SKIN IS SOOO PRETTY...
AND NOW YOU'RE SO THIN AND BEAUTIFUL.
B... beautiful...?
YOU MUST HAVE REALLY PUSHED YOURSELF TO GET THERE.
IT'S MY J TO G PEOP TO LOC AT ME.
SO I WAS THINKING I'D LIKE TO IMPROVE MYSELF LIKE YOU DID!
AND THAT'S PART OF WHY...
I WAS REALLY HOPING TO GO OUT FOR TEA OR SOMETHING AFTER SCHOOL AND TALK.
Would that be okay?
I'm blushing...
S...
SURE. OKAY.
No problem.
SHOULD WE ASK MEI-CHAN?
YEAH!

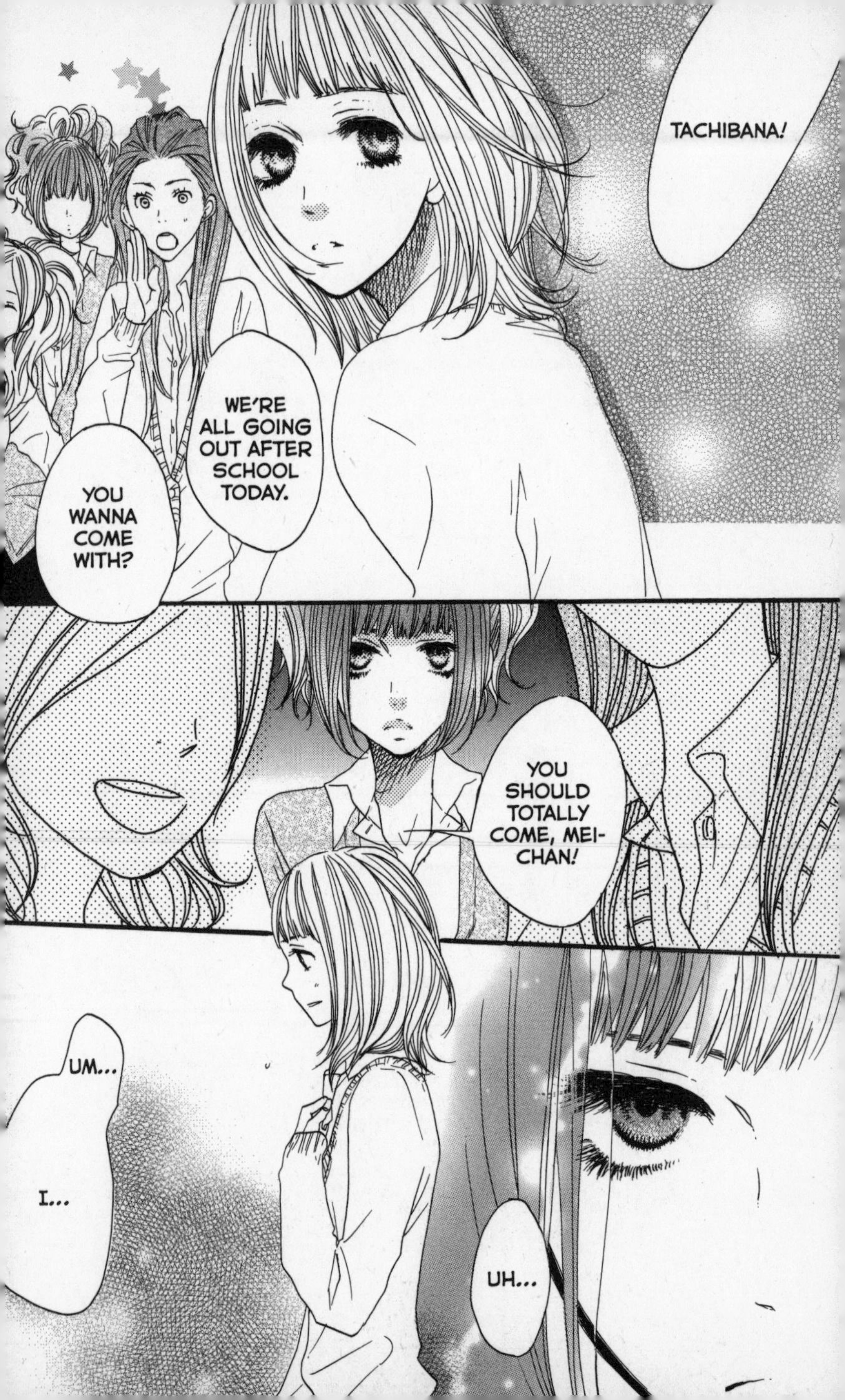
TACHIBANA!
WE'RE ALL GOING OUT AFTER SCHOOL TODAY.
YOU WANNA COME WITH?
YOU SHOULD TOTALLY COME, MEI-CHAN!
UH...
UM...
I...

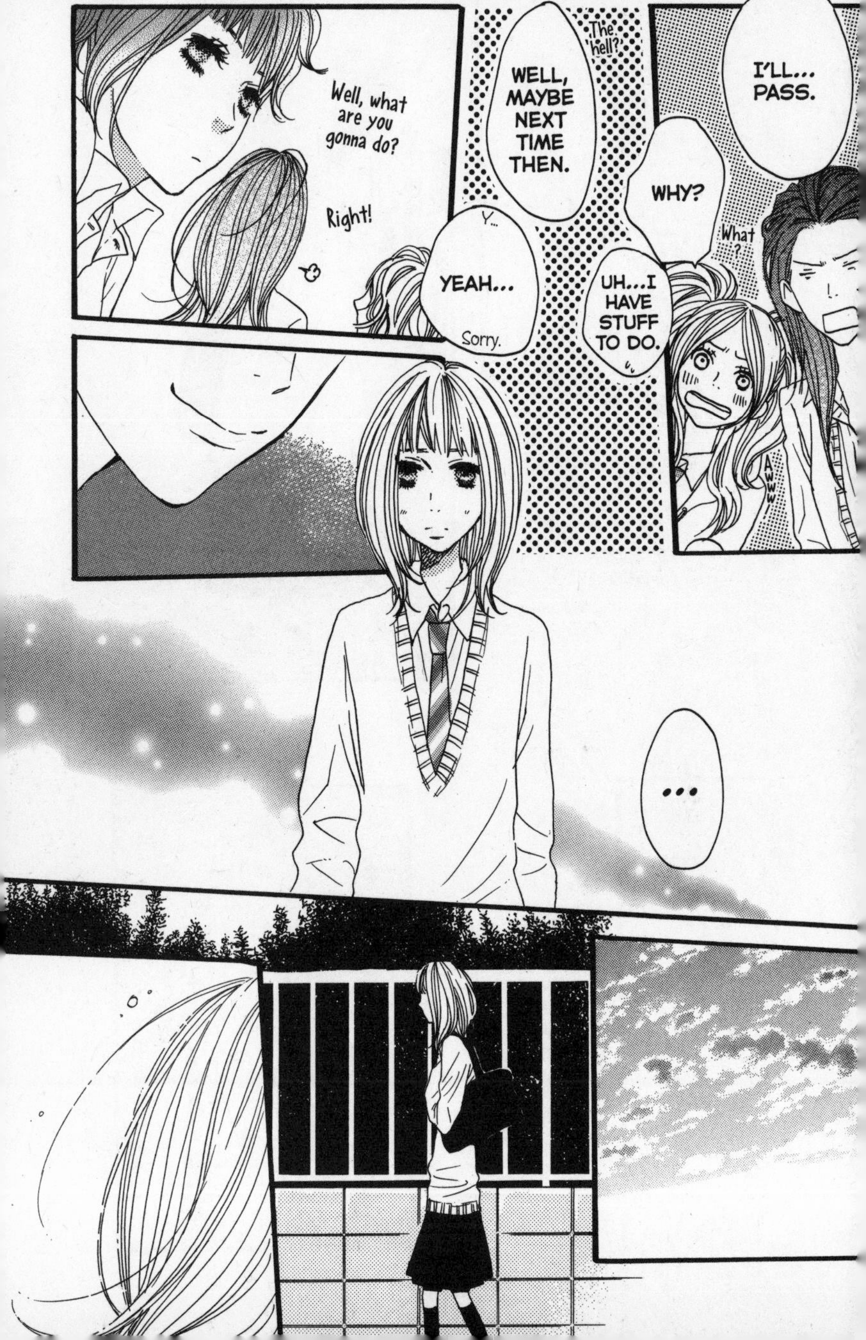
I'LL... PASS.
WHY?
What?
UH...I HAVE STUFF TO DO.
AWWW
The hell?
WELL, MAYBE NEXT TIME THEN.
Y...
YEAH...
Sorry.
Well, what are you gonna do?
Right!
...

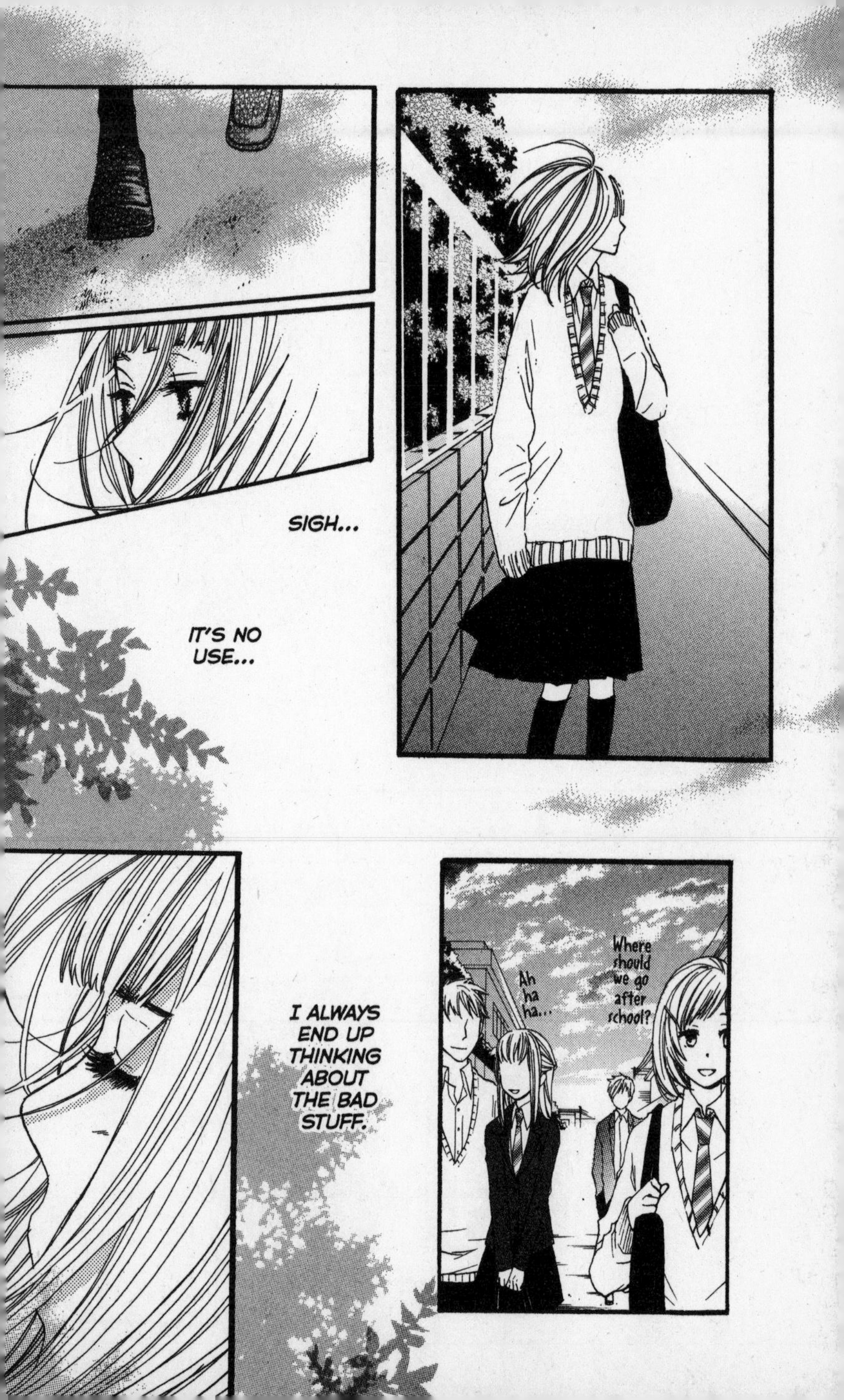
SIGH...
IT'S NO USE...
Where should we go after school?
Ah ha ha...
I ALWAYS END UP THINKING ABOUT THE BAD STUFF.

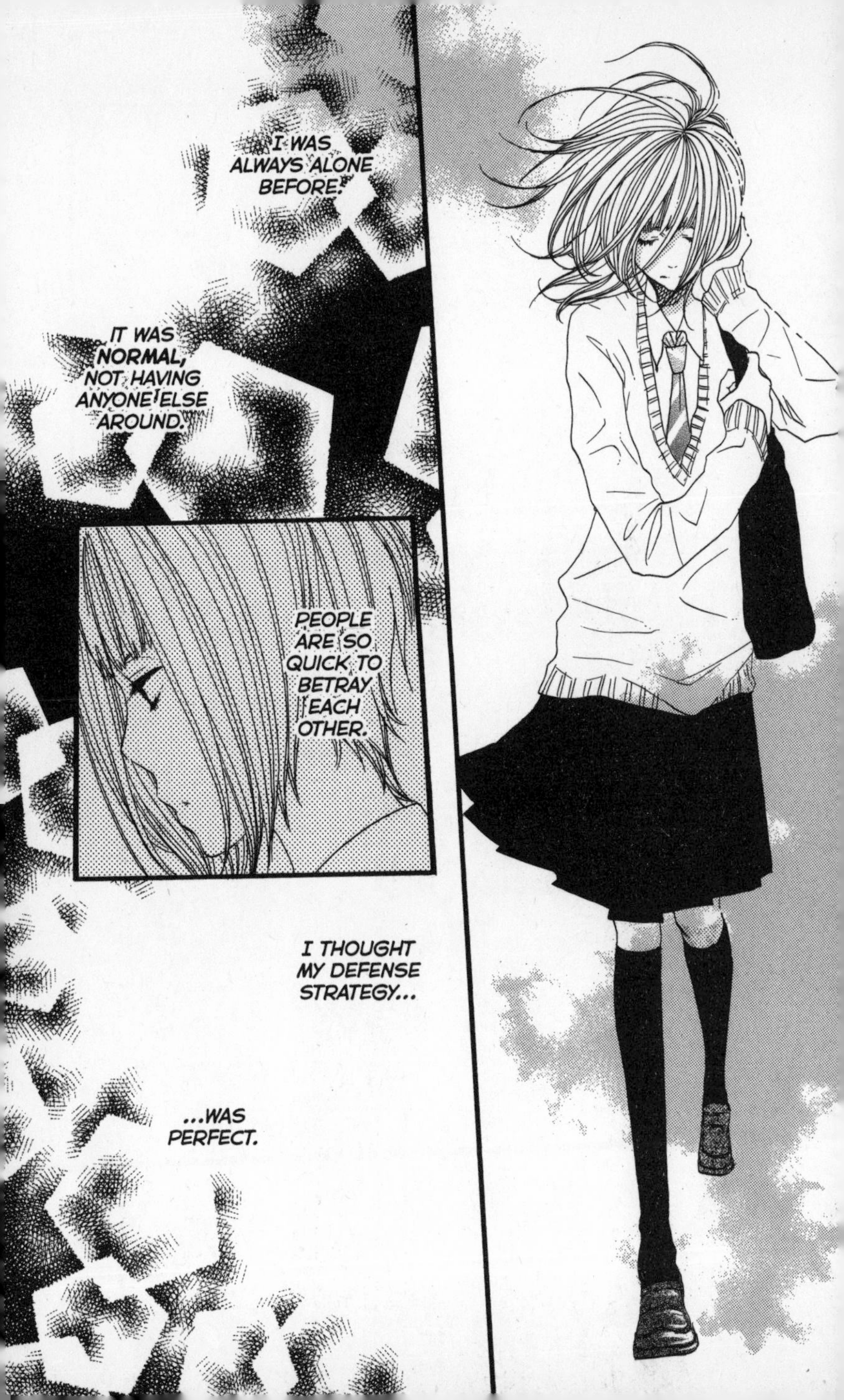
I WAS ALWAYS ALONE BEFORE.
IT WAS NORMAL, NOT HAVING ANYONE ELSE AROUND.
PEOPLE ARE SO QUICK TO BETRAY EACH OTHER.
I THOUGHT MY DEFENSE STRATEGY...
...WAS PERFECT.

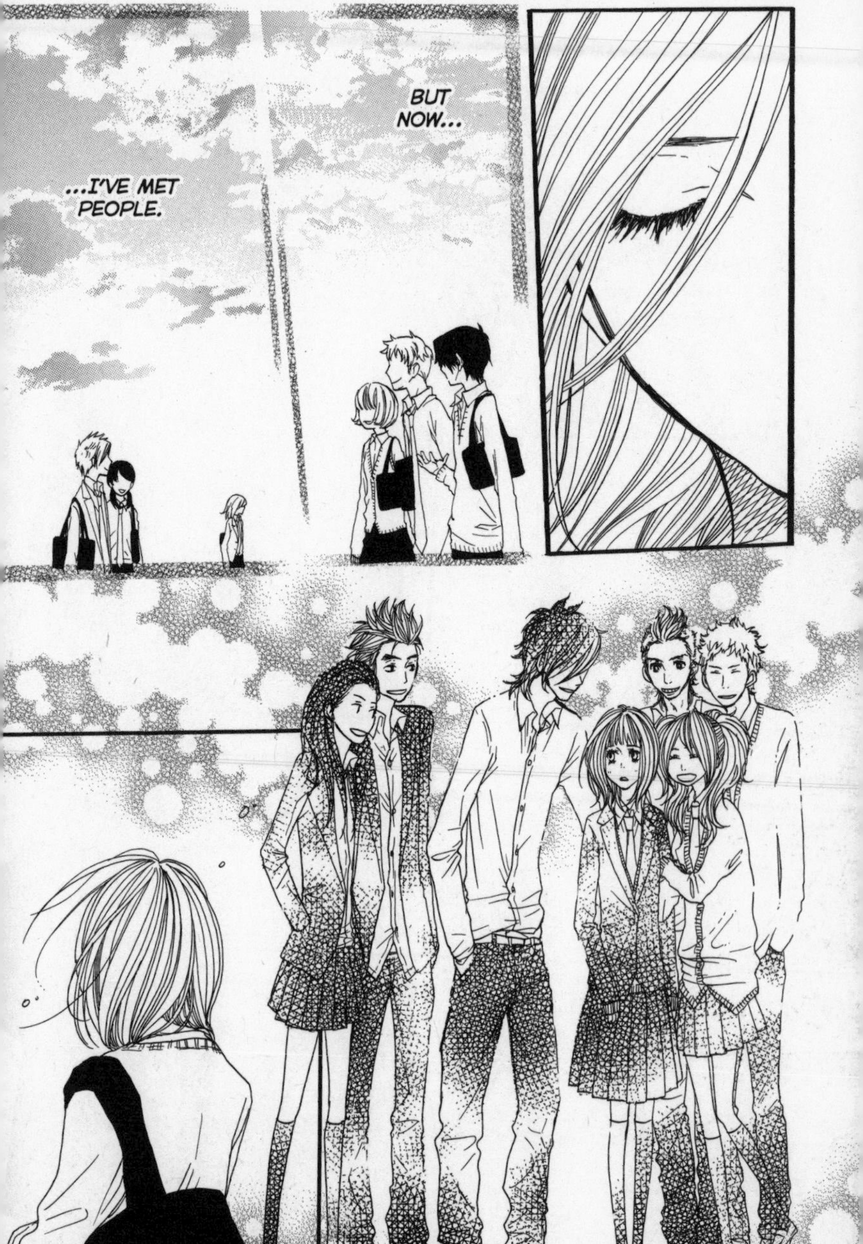
BUT NOW...
...I'VE MET PEOPLE.

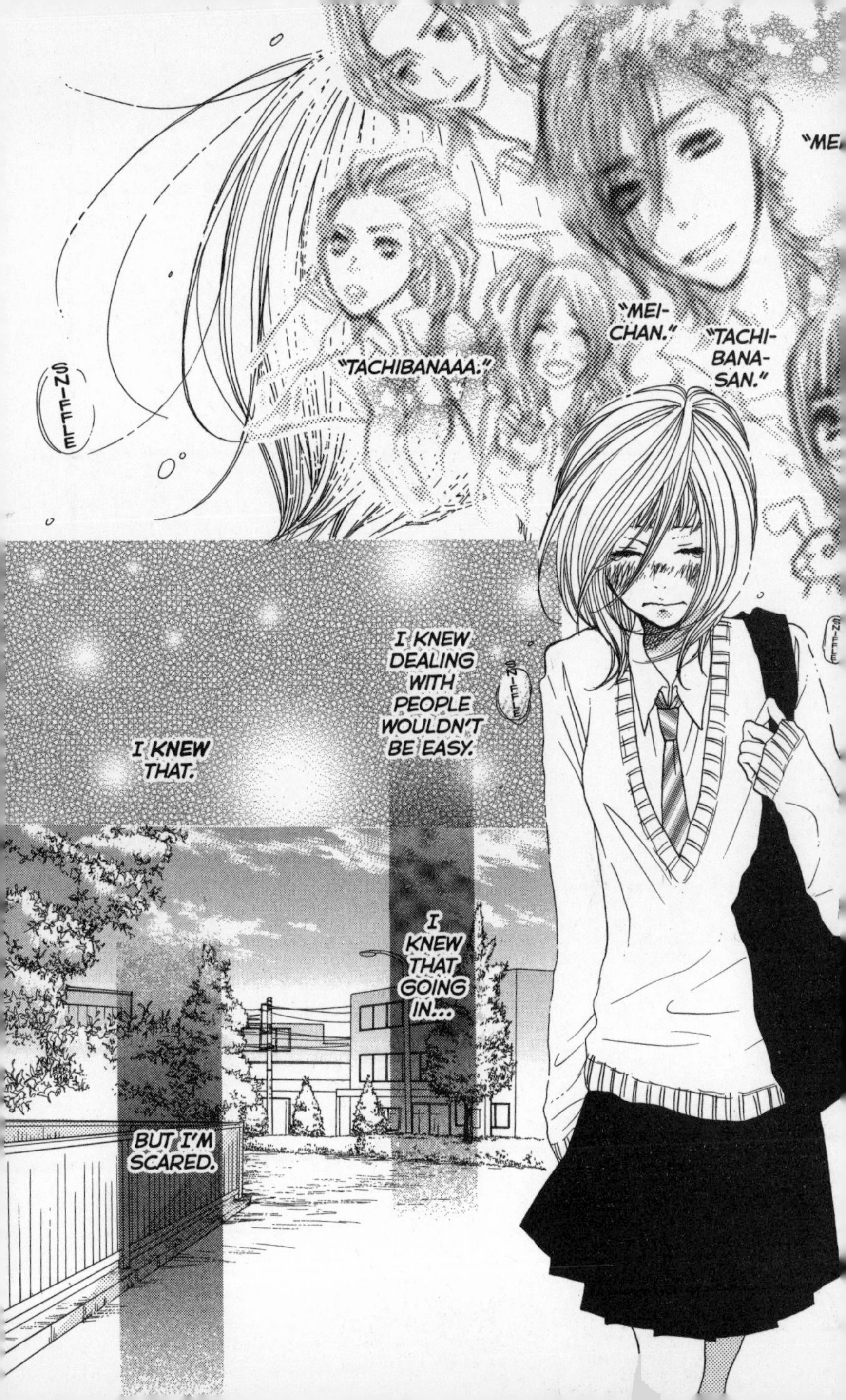
"ME
"TACHIBANA-SAN."
"MEI-CHAN."
"TACHIBANAAA."
SNIFFLE
SNIFFLE
I KNEW DEALING WITH PEOPLE WOULDN'T BE EASY.
SNIFFLE
I KNEW THAT.
I KNEW THAT GOING IN...
BUT I'M SCARED.

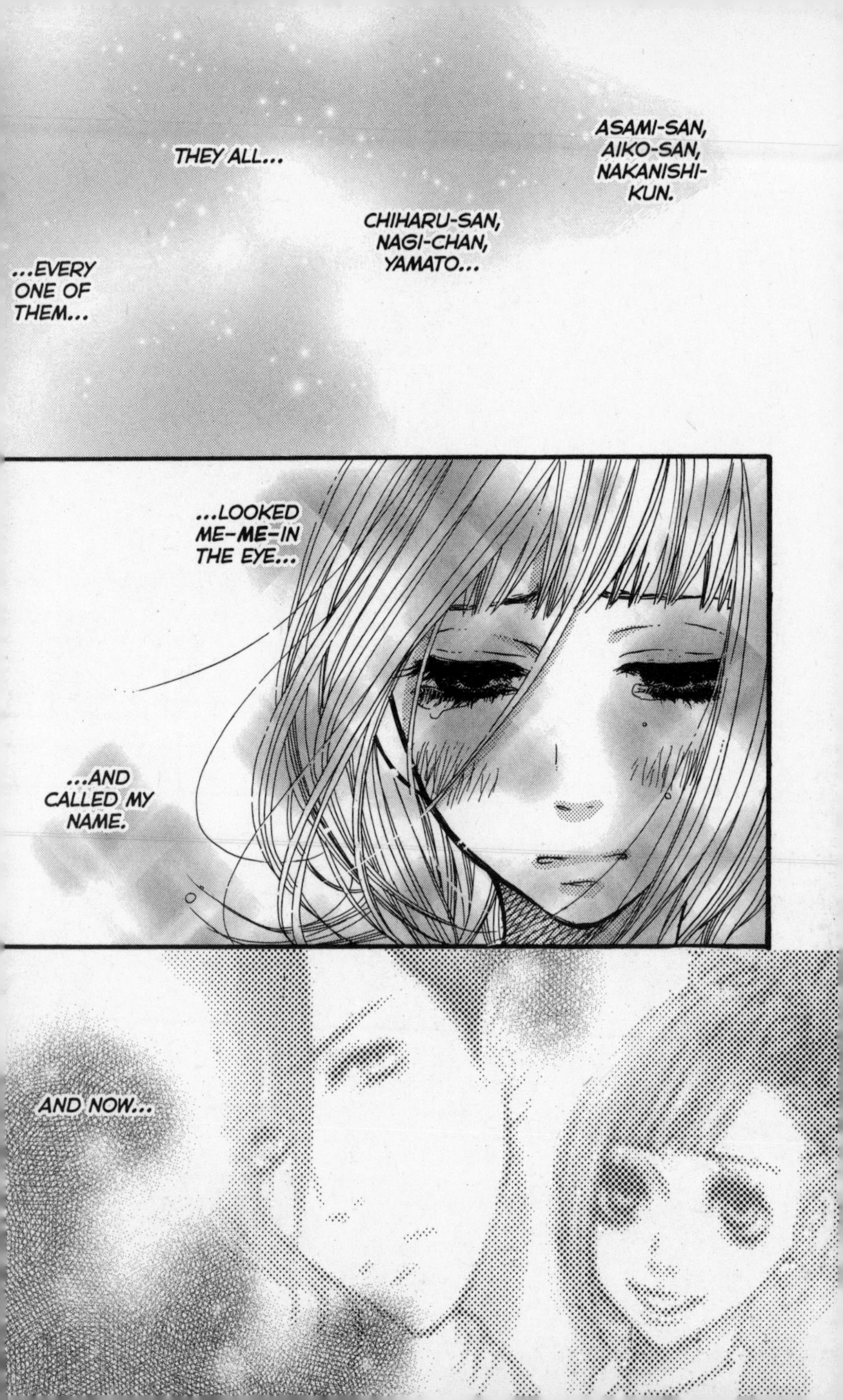
ASAMI-SAN, AIKO-SAN, NAKANISHI-KUN.
CHIHARU-SAN, NAGI-CHAN, YAMATO...
THEY ALL...
...EVERY ONE OF THEM...
...LOOKED ME-ME-IN THE EYE...
...AND CALLED MY NAME.
AND NOW...

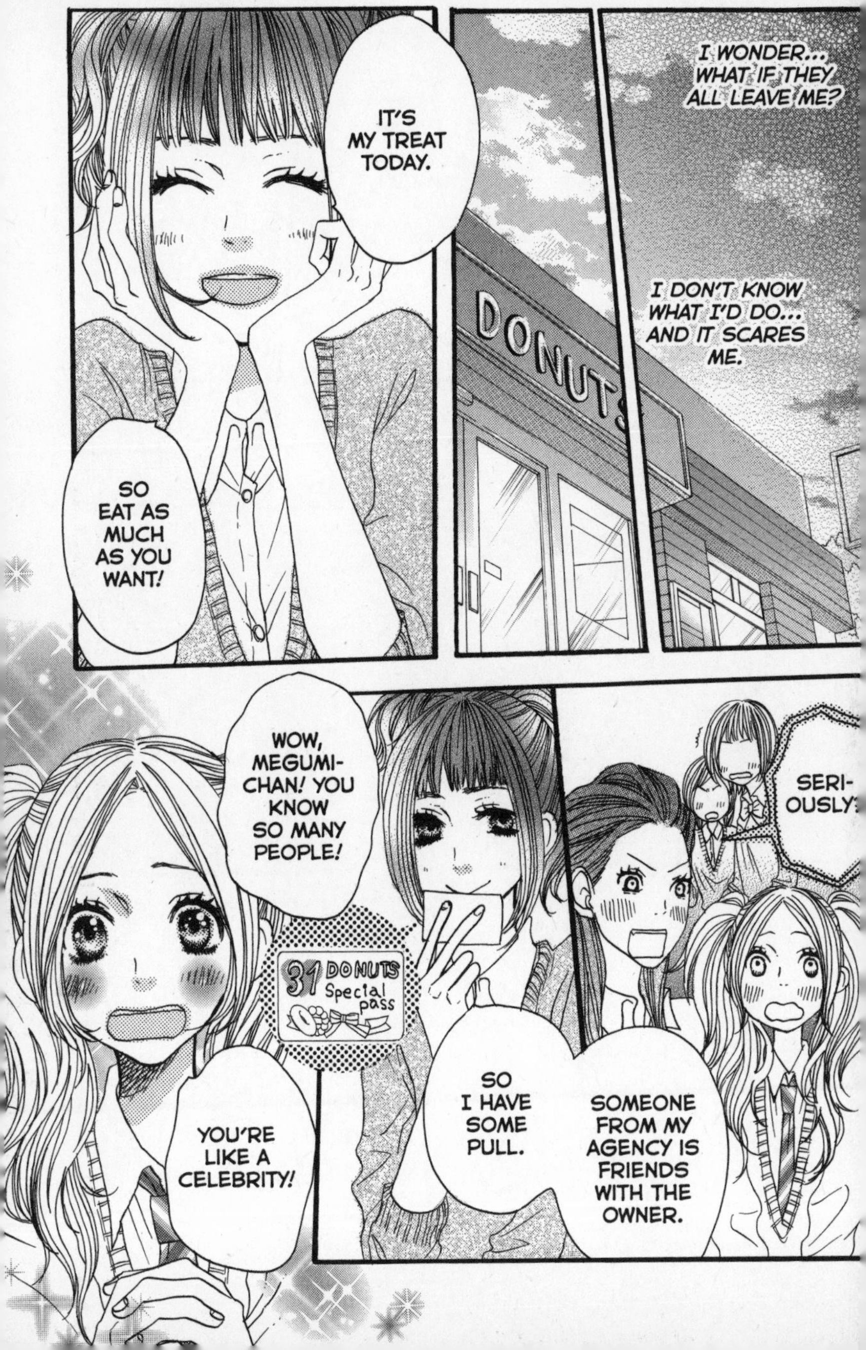
I WONDER... WHAT IF THEY ALL LEAVE ME?
I DON'T KNOW WHAT I'D DO... AND IT SCARES ME.
DONUTS
IT'S MY TREAT TODAY.
SO EAT AS MUCH AS YOU WANT!
SERI-OUSLY?
SOMEONE FROM MY AGENCY IS FRIENDS WITH THE OWNER.
SO I HAVE SOME PULL.
31 DONUTS Special pass
WOW, MEGUMI-CHAN! YOU KNOW SO MANY PEOPLE!
YOU'RE LIKE A CELEBRITY!

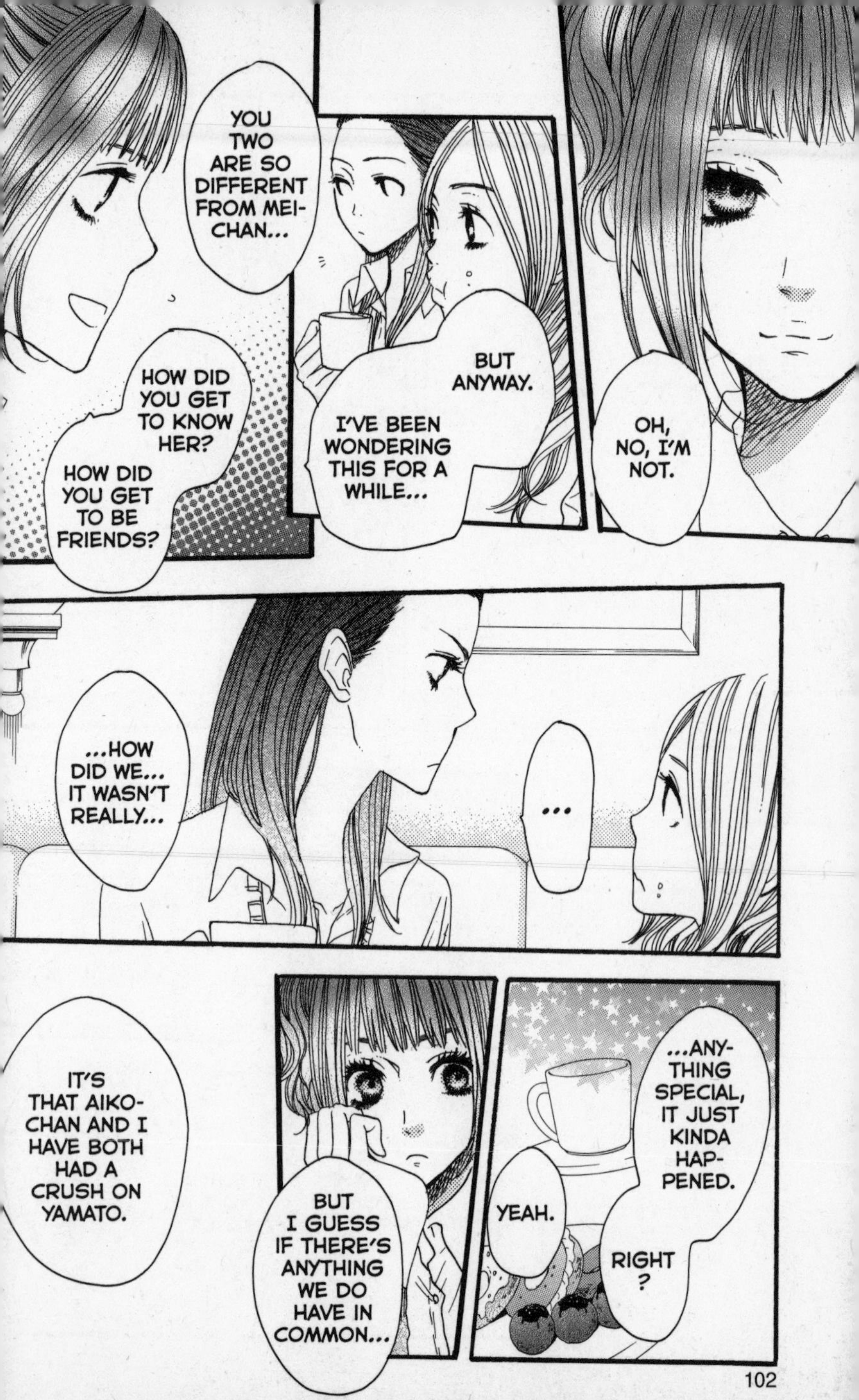
OH, NO, I'M NOT.
BUT ANYWAY.
I'VE BEEN WONDERING THIS FOR A WHILE...
YOU TWO ARE SO DIFFERENT FROM MEI-CHAN...
HOW DID YOU GET TO KNOW HER?
HOW DID YOU GET TO BE FRIENDS?
...
...HOW DID WE... IT WASN'T REALLY...
...ANY-THING SPECIAL, IT JUST KINDA HAP-PENED.
RIGHT?
YEAH.
BUT I GUESS IF THERE'S ANYTHING WE DO HAVE IN COMMON...
IT'S THAT AIKO-CHAN AND I HAVE BOTH HAD A CRUSH ON YAMATO.

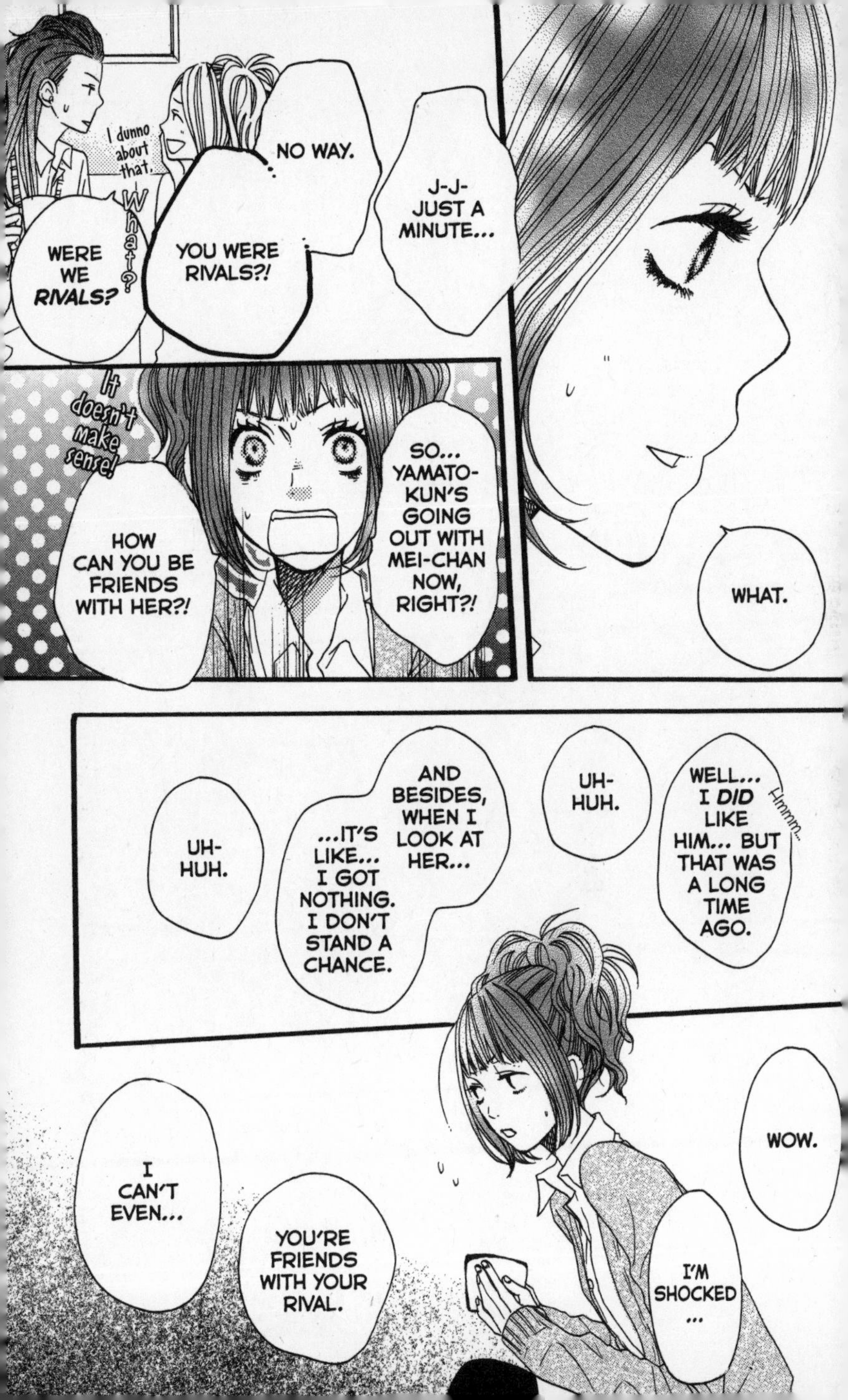
WHAT.
J-J- JUST A MINUTE...
NO WAY.
YOU WERE RIVALS?!
What?
I dunno about that.
WERE WE RIVALS?
SO... YAMATO-KUN'S GOING OUT WITH MEI-CHAN NOW, RIGHT?!
It doesn't make sense!
HOW CAN YOU BE FRIENDS WITH HER?!
WELL... I DID LIKE HIM... BUT THAT WAS A LONG TIME AGO.
Hmmm...
UH-HUH.
AND BESIDES, WHEN I LOOK AT HER...
...IT'S LIKE... I GOT NOTHING. I DON'T STAND A CHANCE.
UH-HUH.
WOW.
I'M SHOCKED...
YOU'RE FRIENDS WITH YOUR RIVAL.
I CAN'T EVEN...

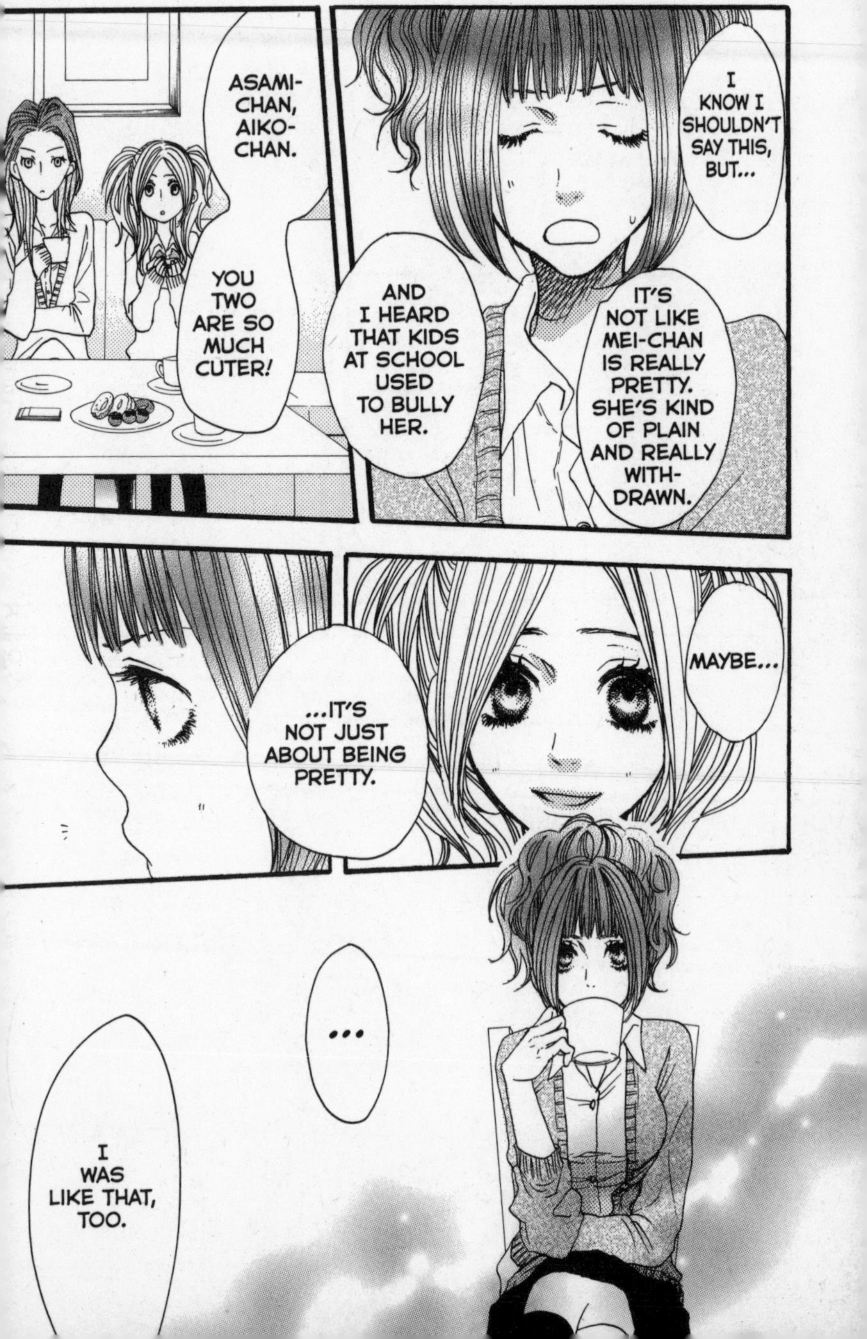
I KNOW I SHOULDN'T SAY THIS, BUT...
IT'S NOT LIKE MEI-CHAN IS REALLY PRETTY. SHE'S KIND OF PLAIN AND REALLY WITH-DRAWN.
AND I HEARD THAT KIDS AT SCHOOL USED TO BULLY HER.
ASAMI-CHAN, AIKO-CHAN.
YOU TWO ARE SO MUCH CUTER!
MAYBE...
...IT'S NOT JUST ABOUT BEING PRETTY.
...
I WAS LIKE THAT, TOO.

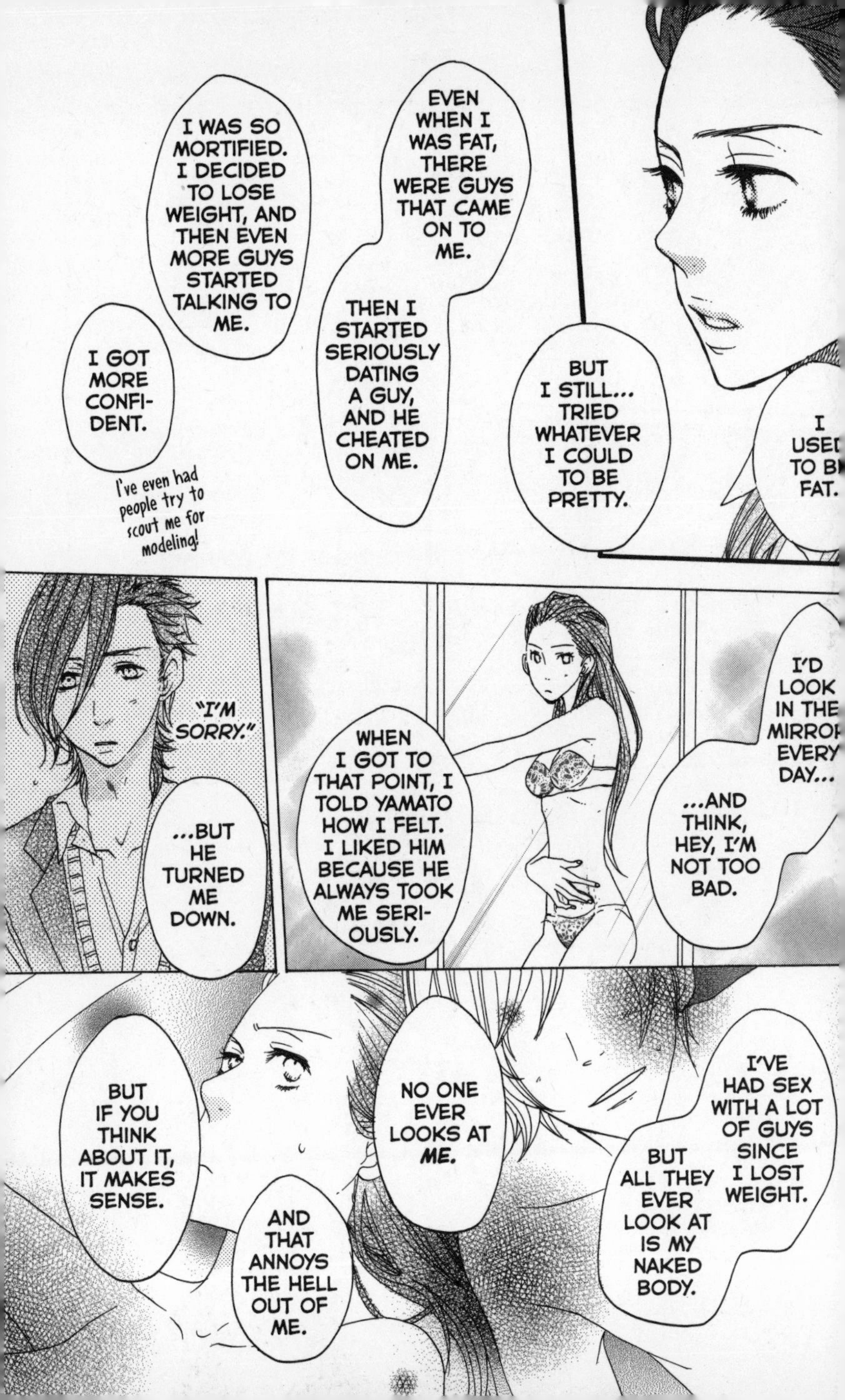

I USED TO B FAT.
BUT I STILL... TRIED WHATEVER I COULD TO BE PRETTY.
EVEN WHEN I WAS FAT, THERE WERE GUYS THAT CAME ON TO ME.
THEN I STARTED SERIOUSLY DATING A GUY, AND HE CHEATED ON ME.
I WAS SO MORTIFIED. I DECIDED TO LOSE WEIGHT, AND THEN EVEN MORE GUYS STARTED TALKING TO ME.
I GOT MORE CONFI-DENT.
I've even had people try to scout me for modeling!
I'D LOOK IN THE MIRRO EVERY DAY...
...AND THINK, HEY, I'M NOT TOO BAD.
WHEN I GOT TO THAT POINT, I TOLD YAMATO HOW I FELT. I LIKED HIM BECAUSE HE ALWAYS TOOK ME SERI-OUSLY.
"I'M SORRY."
...BUT HE TURNED ME DOWN.
I'VE HAD SEX WITH A LOT OF GUYS SINCE I LOST WEIGHT.
BUT ALL THEY EVER LOOK AT IS MY NAKED BODY.
NO ONE EVER LOOKS AT ME.
AND THAT ANNOYS THE HELL OUT OF ME.
BUT IF YOU THINK ABOUT IT, IT MAKES SENSE.

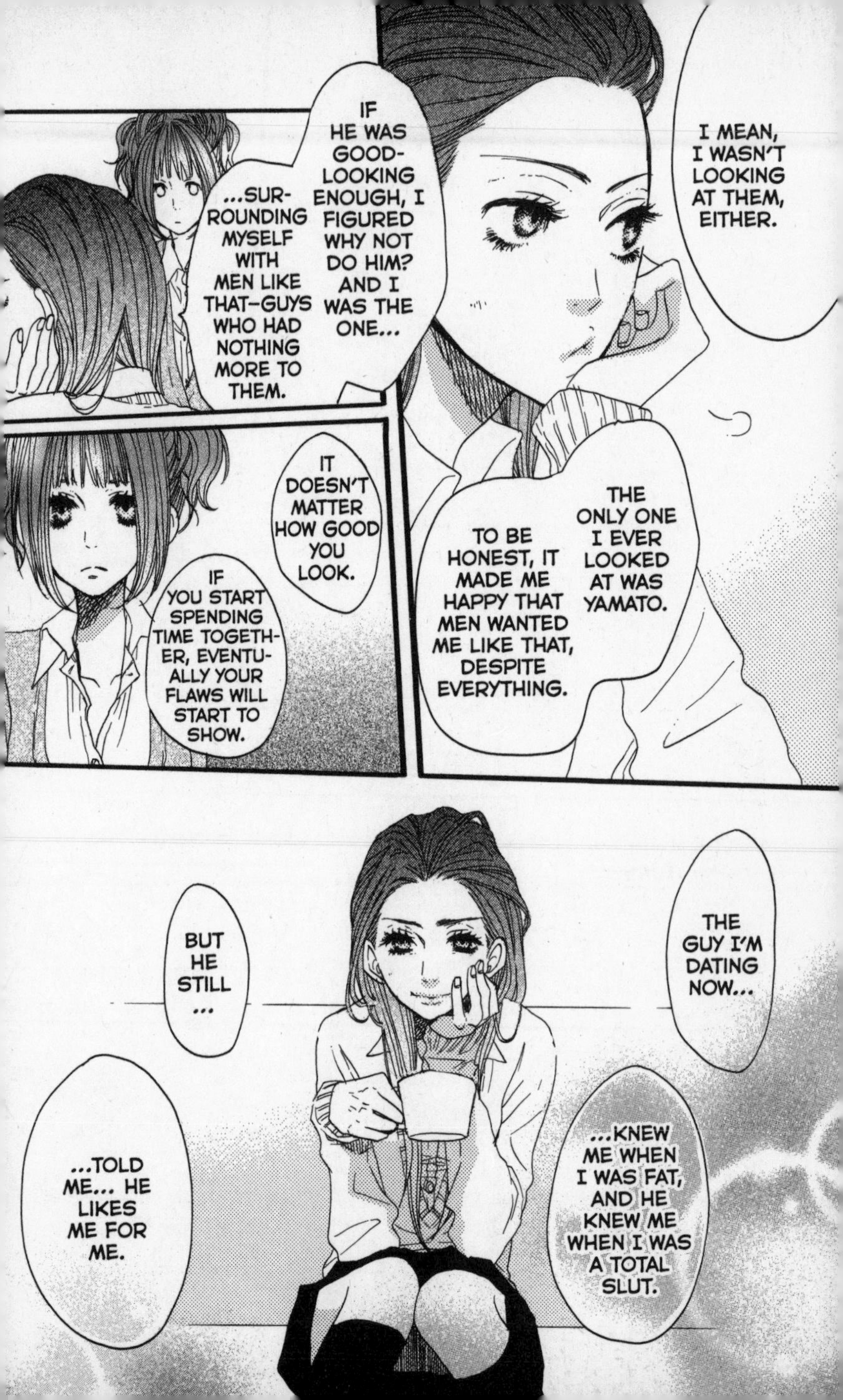
I MEAN, I WASN'T LOOKING AT THEM, EITHER.
IF HE WAS GOOD-LOOKING ENOUGH, I FIGURED WHY NOT DO HIM? AND I WAS THE ONE...
...SUR-ROUNDING MYSELF WITH MEN LIKE THAT—GUYS WHO HAD NOTHING MORE TO THEM.
THE ONLY ONE I EVER LOOKED AT WAS YAMATO.
TO BE HONEST, IT MADE ME HAPPY THAT MEN WANTED ME LIKE THAT, DESPITE EVERYTHING.
IT DOESN'T MATTER HOW GOOD YOU LOOK.
IF YOU START SPENDING TIME TOGETH-ER, EVENTU-ALLY YOUR FLAWS WILL START TO SHOW.
THE GUY I'M DATING NOW...
...KNEW ME WHEN I WAS FAT, AND HE KNEW ME WHEN I WAS A TOTAL SLUT.
BUT HE STILL ...
...TOLD ME... HE LIKES ME FOR ME.

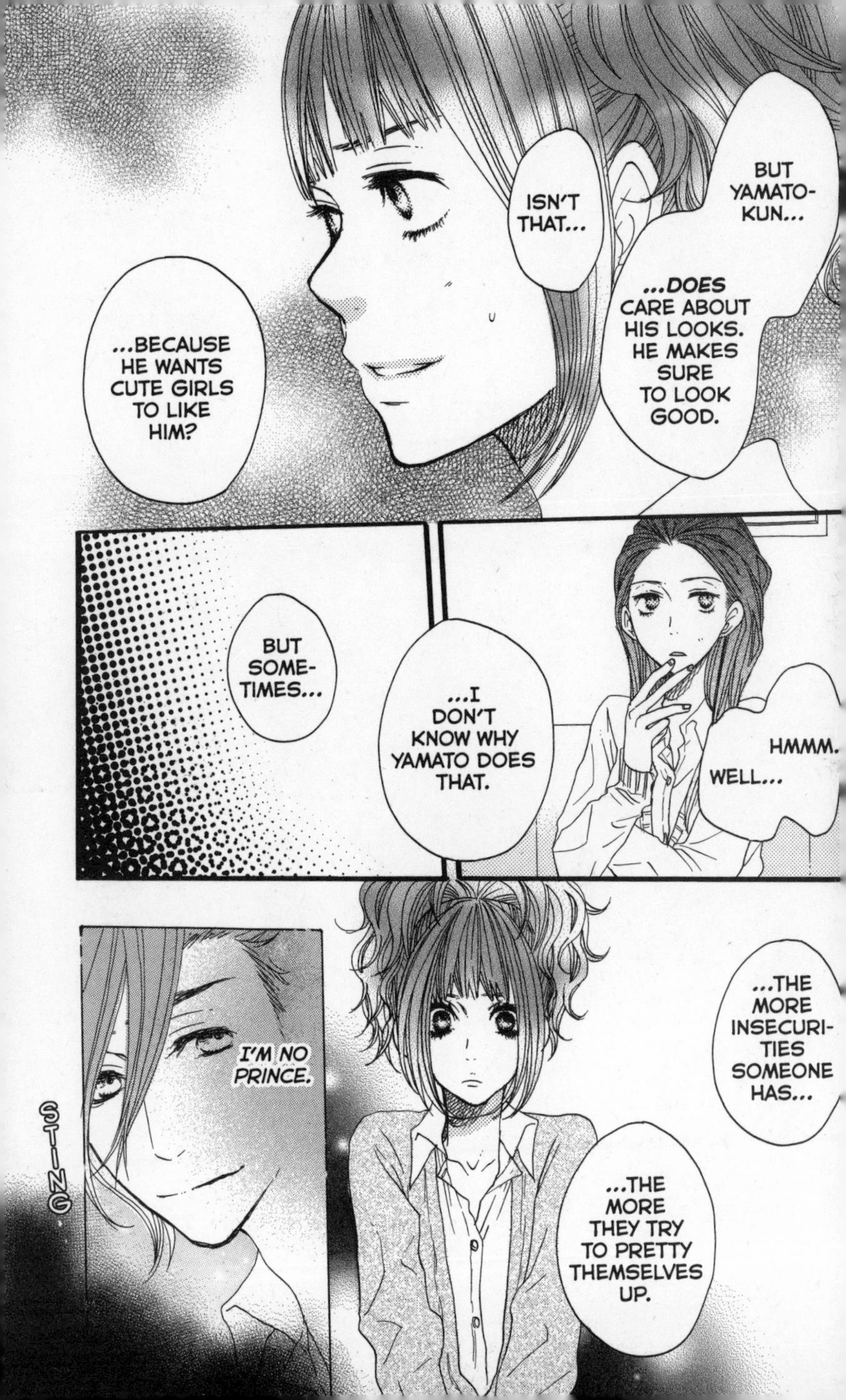
BUT YAMATO-KUN...
...DOES CARE ABOUT HIS LOOKS. HE MAKES SURE TO LOOK GOOD.
ISN'T THAT...
...BECAUSE HE WANTS CUTE GIRLS TO LIKE HIM?
HMMM.
WELL...
...I DON'T KNOW WHY YAMATO DOES THAT.
BUT SOME-TIMES...
...THE MORE INSECURITIES SOMEONE HAS...
...THE MORE THEY TRY TO PRETTY THEMSELVES UP.
I'M NO PRINCE.
STING

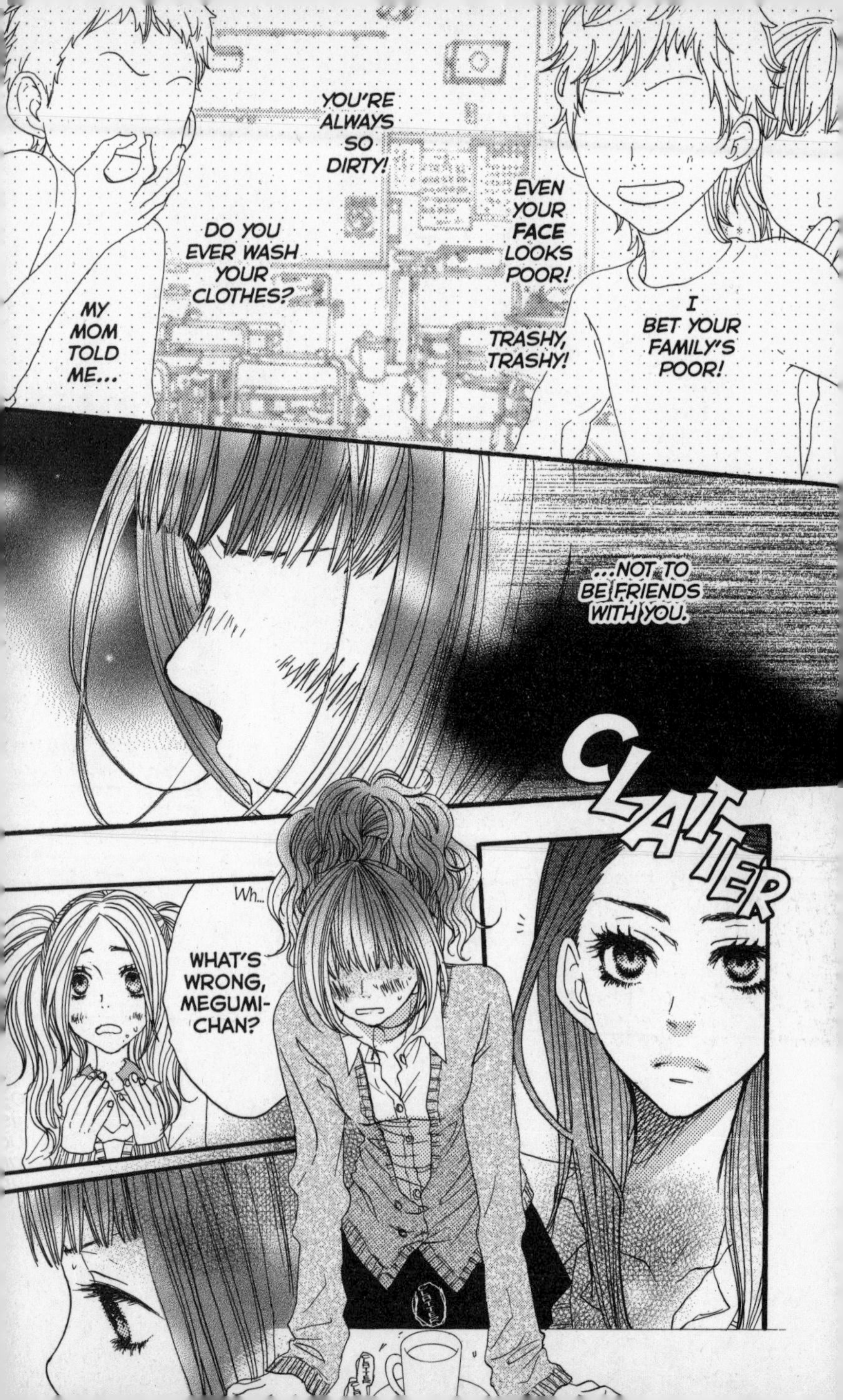
I BET YOUR FAMILY'S POOR!
TRASHY, TRASHY!
EVEN YOUR FACE LOOKS POOR!
YOU'RE ALWAYS SO DIRTY!
DO YOU EVER WASH YOUR CLOTHES?
MY MOM TOLD ME...
...NOT TO BE FRIENDS WITH YOU.
CLATTER
Wh...
WHAT'S WRONG, MEGUMI-CHAN?

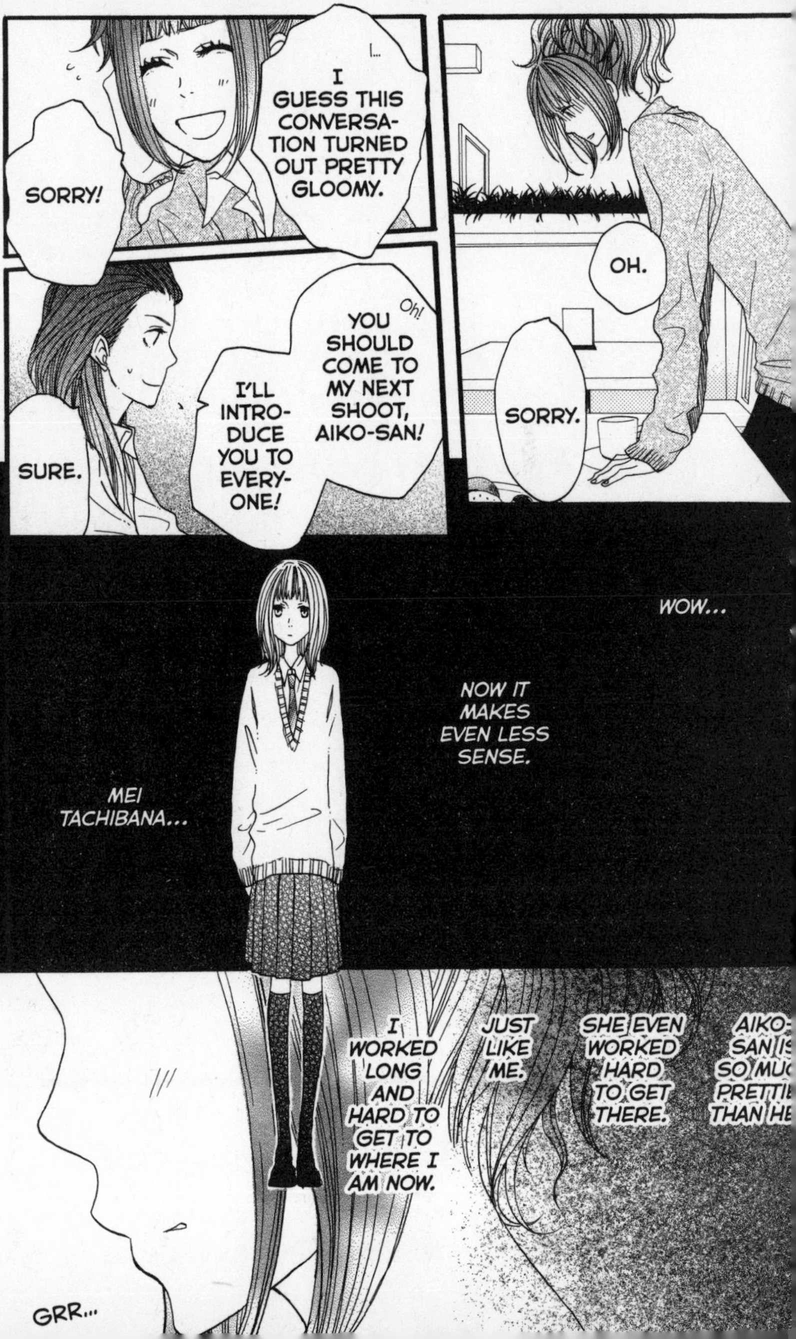
OH.
SORRY.
I...
I GUESS THIS CONVERSATION TURNED OUT PRETTY GLOOMY.
SORRY!
Oh!
YOU SHOULD COME TO MY NEXT SHOOT, AIKO-SAN!
I'LL INTRODUCE YOU TO EVERYONE!
SURE.
WOW...
NOW IT MAKES EVEN LESS SENSE.
MEI TACHIBANA...
AIKO-SAN IS SO MUC PRETTI THAN HE
SHE EVEN WORKED HARD TO GET THERE.
JUST LIKE ME.
I WORKED LONG AND HARD TO GET TO WHERE I AM NOW.
GRR...

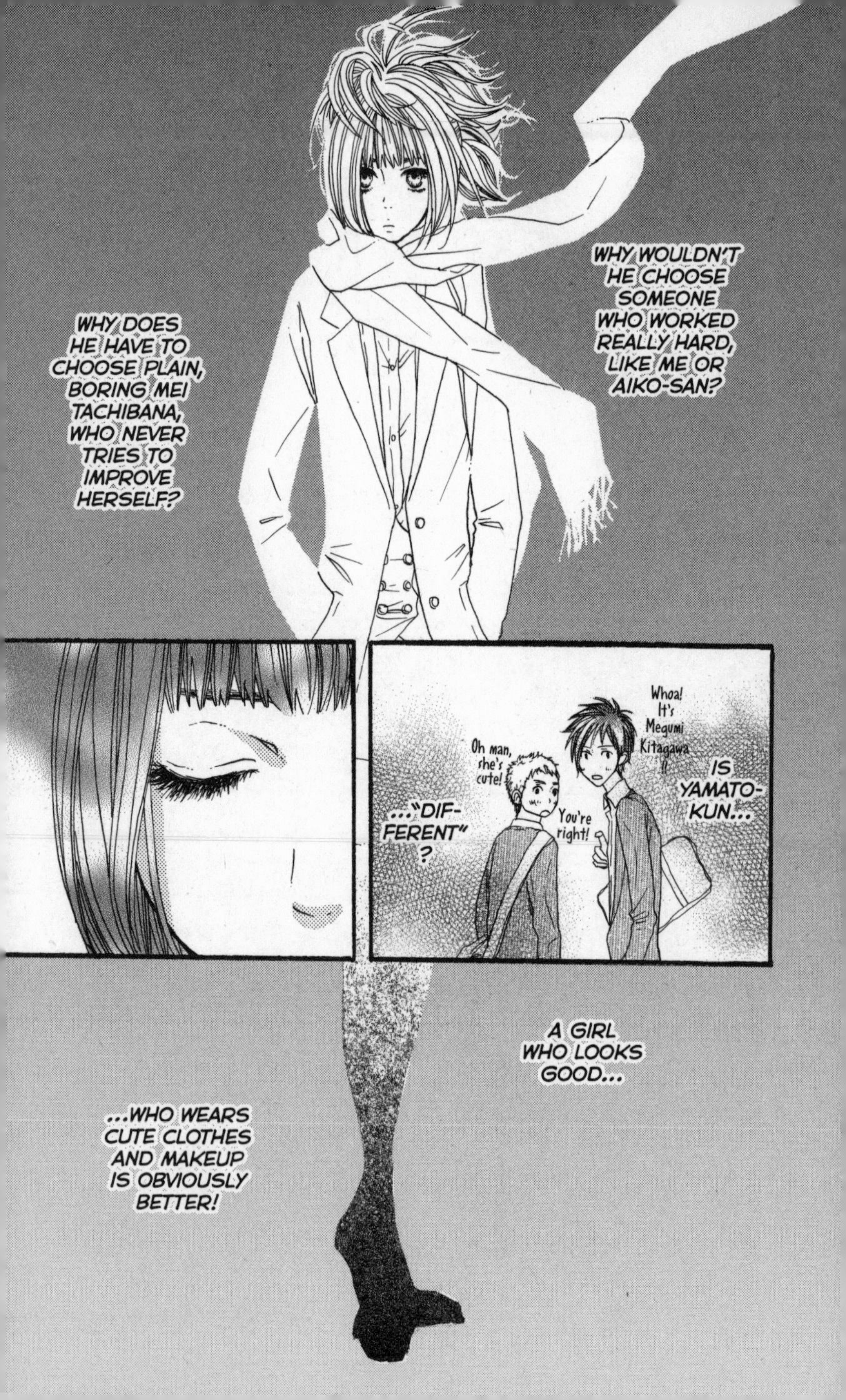
WHY WOULDN'T HE CHOOSE SOMEONE WHO WORKED REALLY HARD, LIKE ME OR AIKO-SAN?
WHY DOES HE HAVE TO CHOOSE PLAIN, BORING MEI TACHIBANA, WHO NEVER TRIES TO IMPROVE HERSELF?
Whoa! It's Megumi Kitagawa!!
IS YAMATO-KUN...
Oh man, she's cute!
You're right!
..."DIF-FERENT"?
A GIRL WHO LOOKS GOOD...
...WHO WEARS CUTE CLOTHES AND MAKEUP IS OBVIOUSLY BETTER!

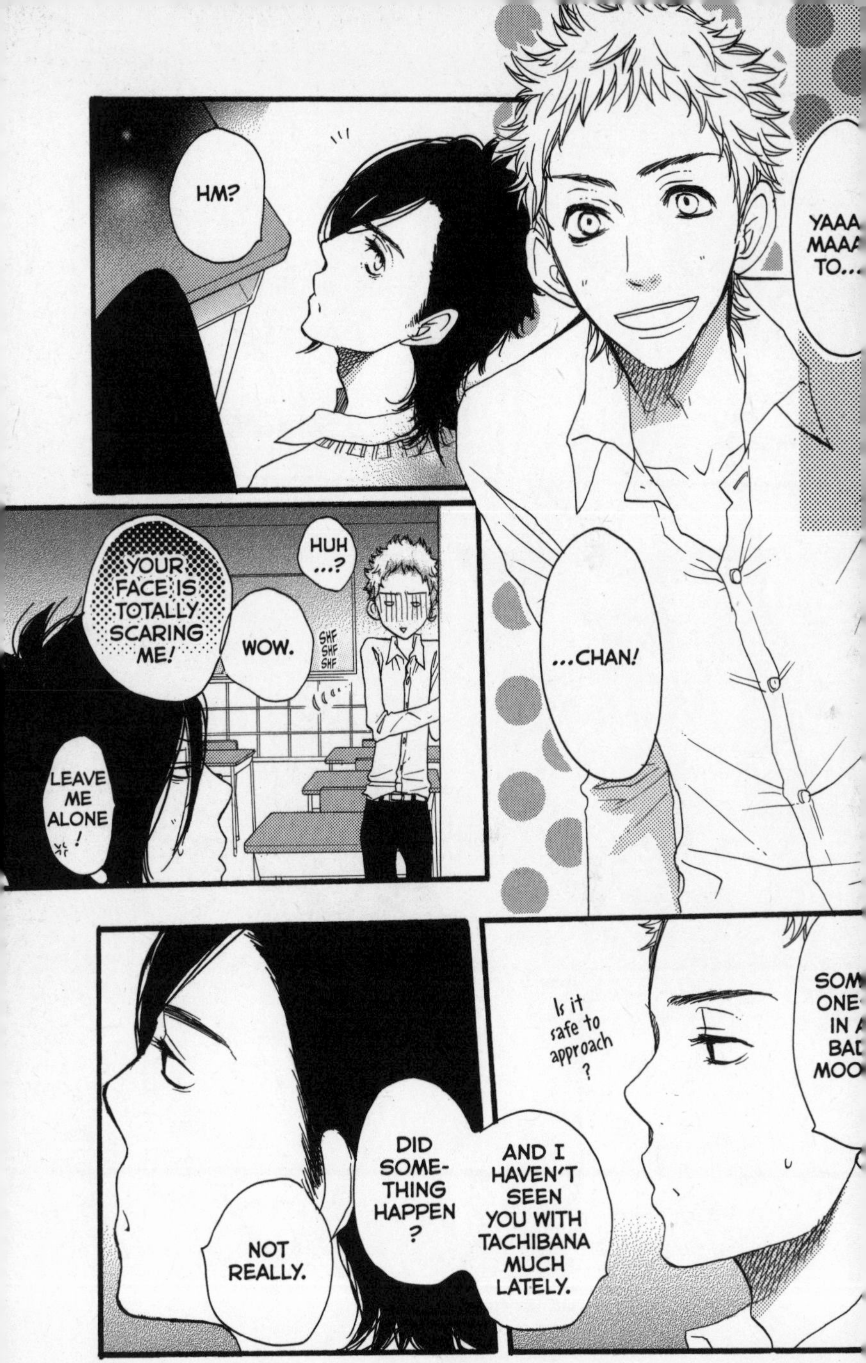
YAAA MAAA TO...
...CHAN!
HM?
HUH ...?
YOUR FACE IS TOTALLY SCARING ME!
WOW.
SHF SHF SHF
LEAVE ME ALONE!
SOM ONE- IN A BAD MOO
Is it safe to approach?
AND I HAVEN'T SEEN YOU WITH TACHIBANA MUCH LATELY.
DID SOME-THING HAPPEN?
NOT REALLY.

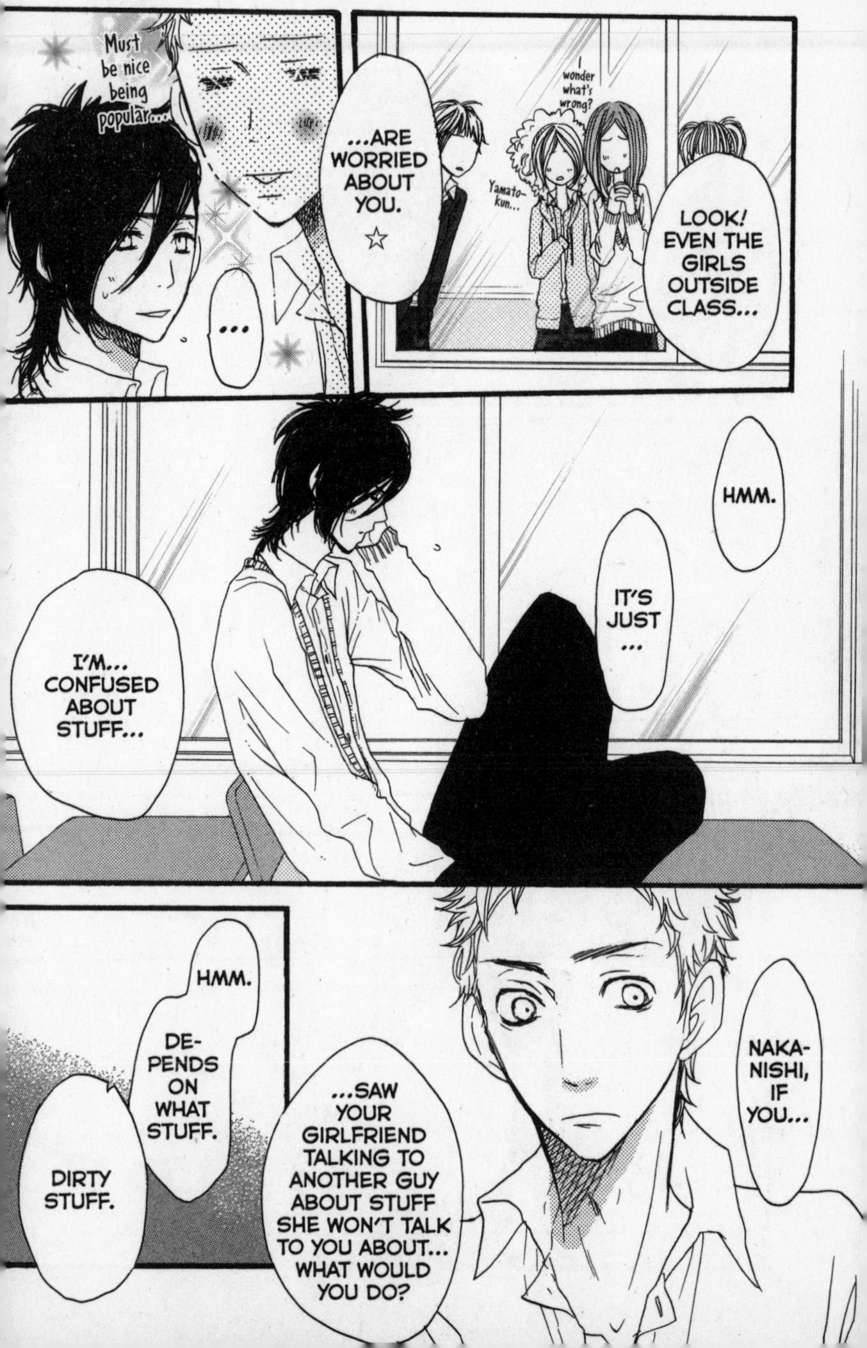
LOOK! EVEN THE GIRLS OUTSIDE CLASS...
I wonder what's wrong?
Yamato-kun...
...ARE WORRIED ABOUT YOU. ☆
Must be nice being popular...
...
HMM.
IT'S JUST ...
I'M... CONFUSED ABOUT STUFF...
NAKA-NISHI, IF YOU...
...SAW YOUR GIRLFRIEND TALKING TO ANOTHER GUY ABOUT STUFF SHE WON'T TALK TO YOU ABOUT... WHAT WOULD YOU DO?
HMM.
DE-PENDS ON WHAT STUFF.
DIRTY STUFF.

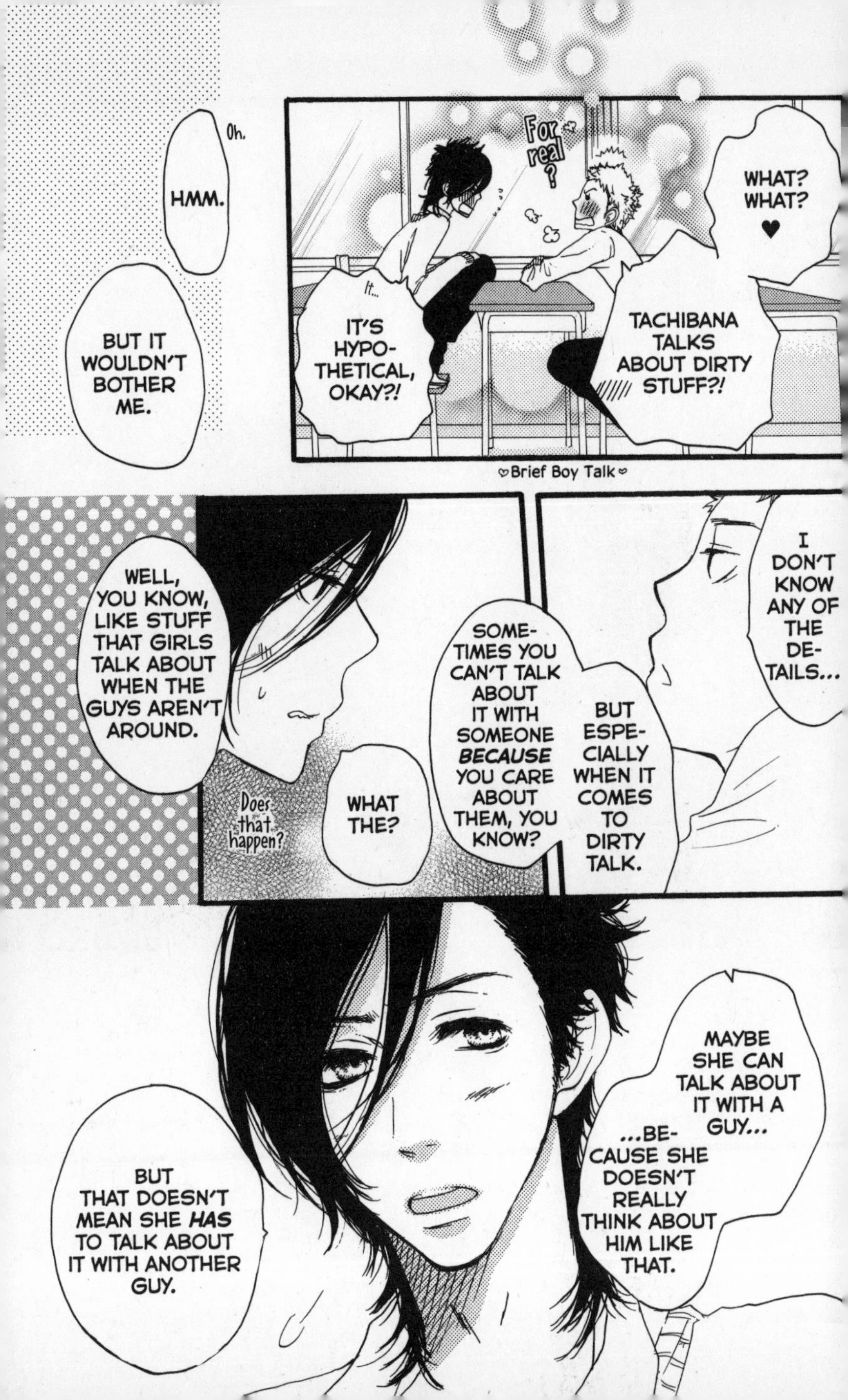
WHAT? WHAT? ♥
For real?
TACHIBANA TALKS ABOUT DIRTY STUFF?!
It...
IT'S HYPOTHETICAL, OKAY?!
Oh.
HMM.
BUT IT WOULDN'T BOTHER ME.
♡Brief Boy Talk♡
I DON'T KNOW ANY OF THE DETAILS...
SOMETIMES YOU CAN'T TALK ABOUT IT WITH SOMEONE *BECAUSE* YOU CARE ABOUT THEM, YOU KNOW?
BUT ESPECIALLY WHEN IT COMES TO DIRTY TALK.
WHAT THE?
Does that happen?
WELL, YOU KNOW, LIKE STUFF THAT GIRLS TALK ABOUT WHEN THE GUYS AREN'T AROUND.
MAYBE SHE CAN TALK ABOUT IT WITH A GUY...
...BECAUSE SHE DOESN'T REALLY THINK ABOUT HIM LIKE THAT.
BUT THAT DOESN'T MEAN SHE *HAS* TO TALK ABOUT IT WITH ANOTHER GUY.

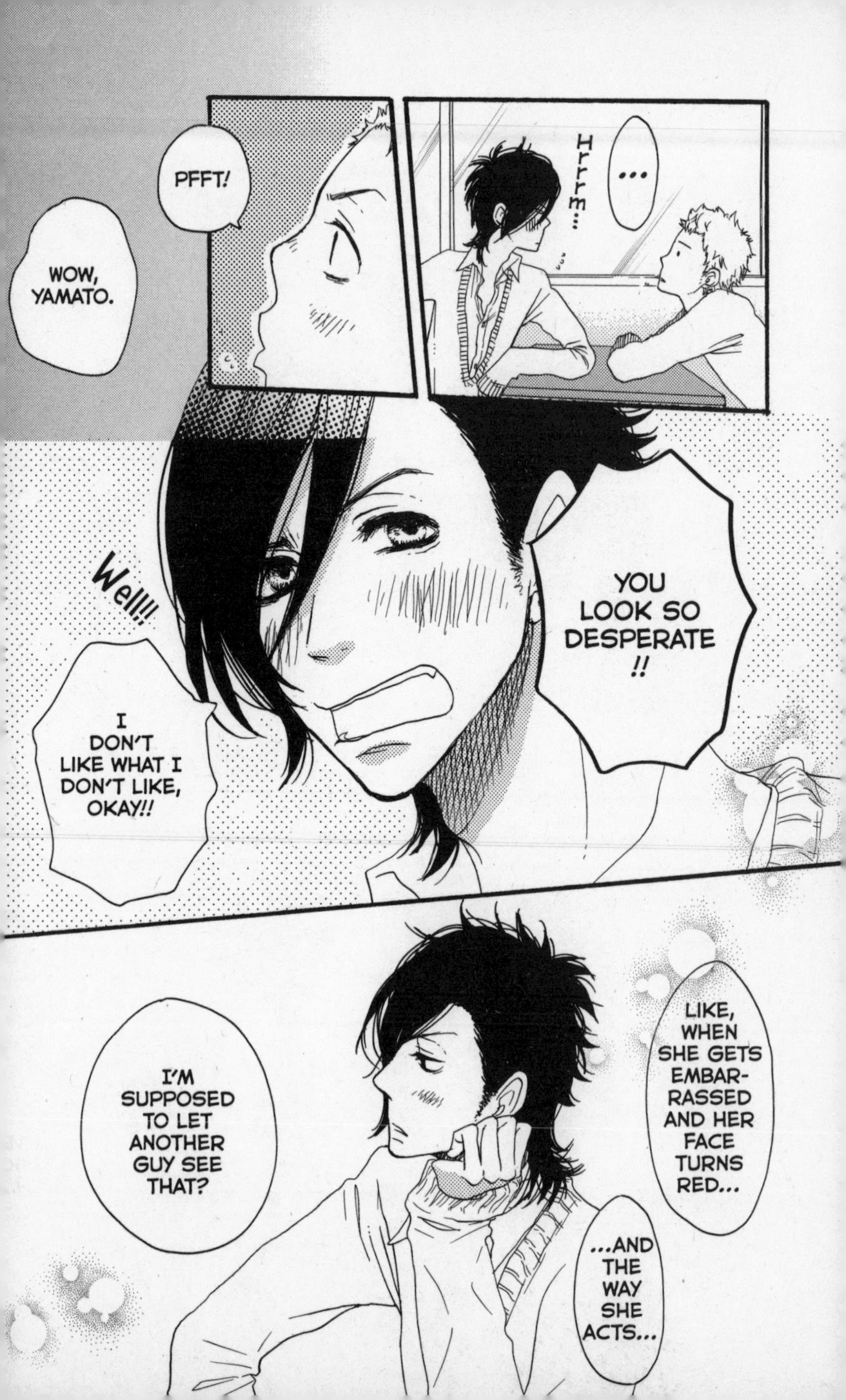
...
Hrrrm...
PFFT!
WOW, YAMATO.
YOU LOOK SO DESPERATE!!
Well!!
I DON'T LIKE WHAT I DON'T LIKE, OKAY!!
LIKE, WHEN SHE GETS EMBARRASSED AND HER FACE TURNS RED...
...AND THE WAY SHE ACTS...
I'M SUPPOSED TO LET ANOTHER GUY SEE THAT?

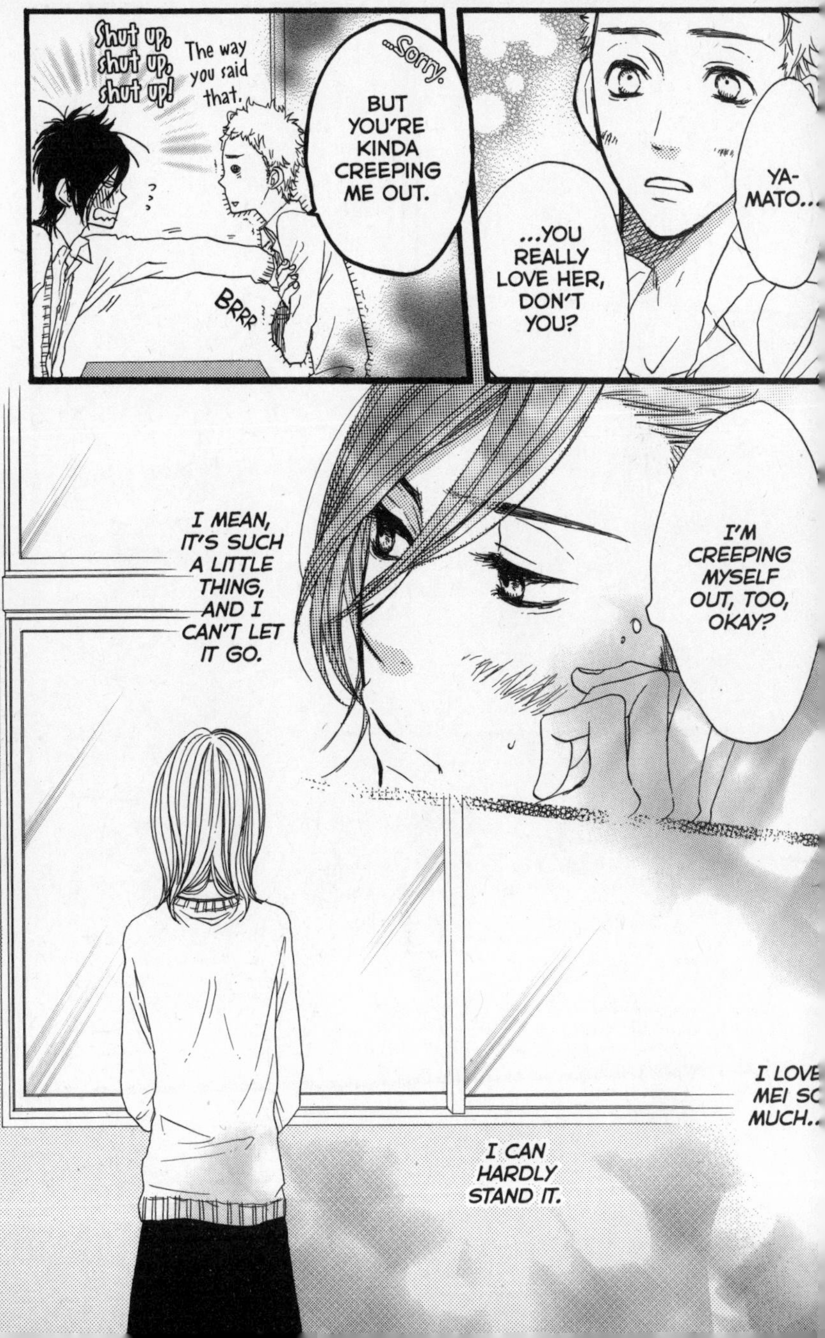
YAMATO...
...YOU REALLY LOVE HER, DON'T YOU?
...Sorry.
BUT YOU'RE KINDA CREEPING ME OUT.
The way you said that.
Shut up, shut up, shut up!
BRRR
I'M CREEPING MYSELF OUT, TOO, OKAY?
I MEAN, IT'S SUCH A LITTLE THING, AND I CAN'T LET IT GO.
I LOVE MEI SO MUCH..
I CAN HARDLY STAND IT.

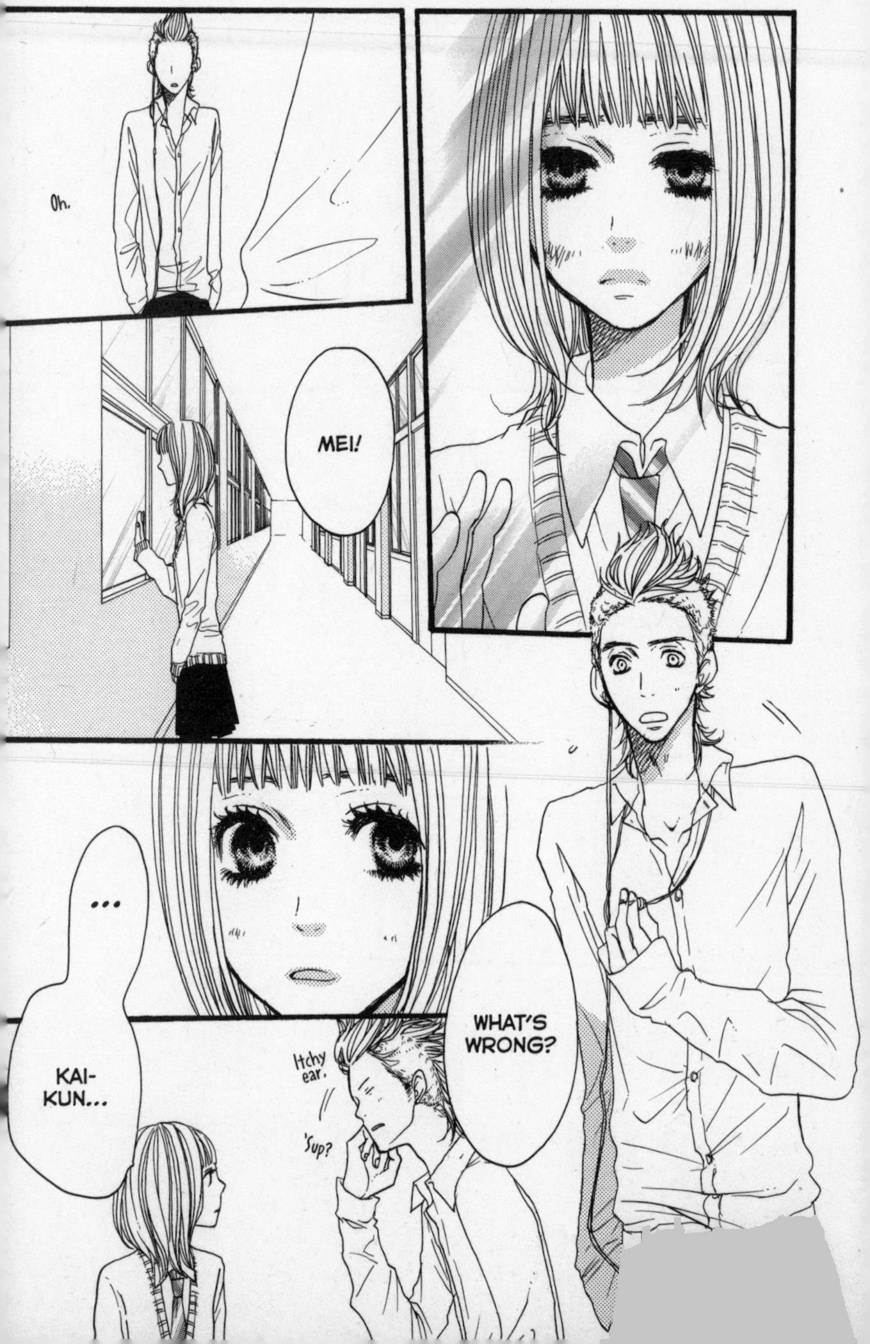
Oh.
MEI!
WHAT'S WRONG?
...
Itchy ear.
'Sup?
KAI-KUN...

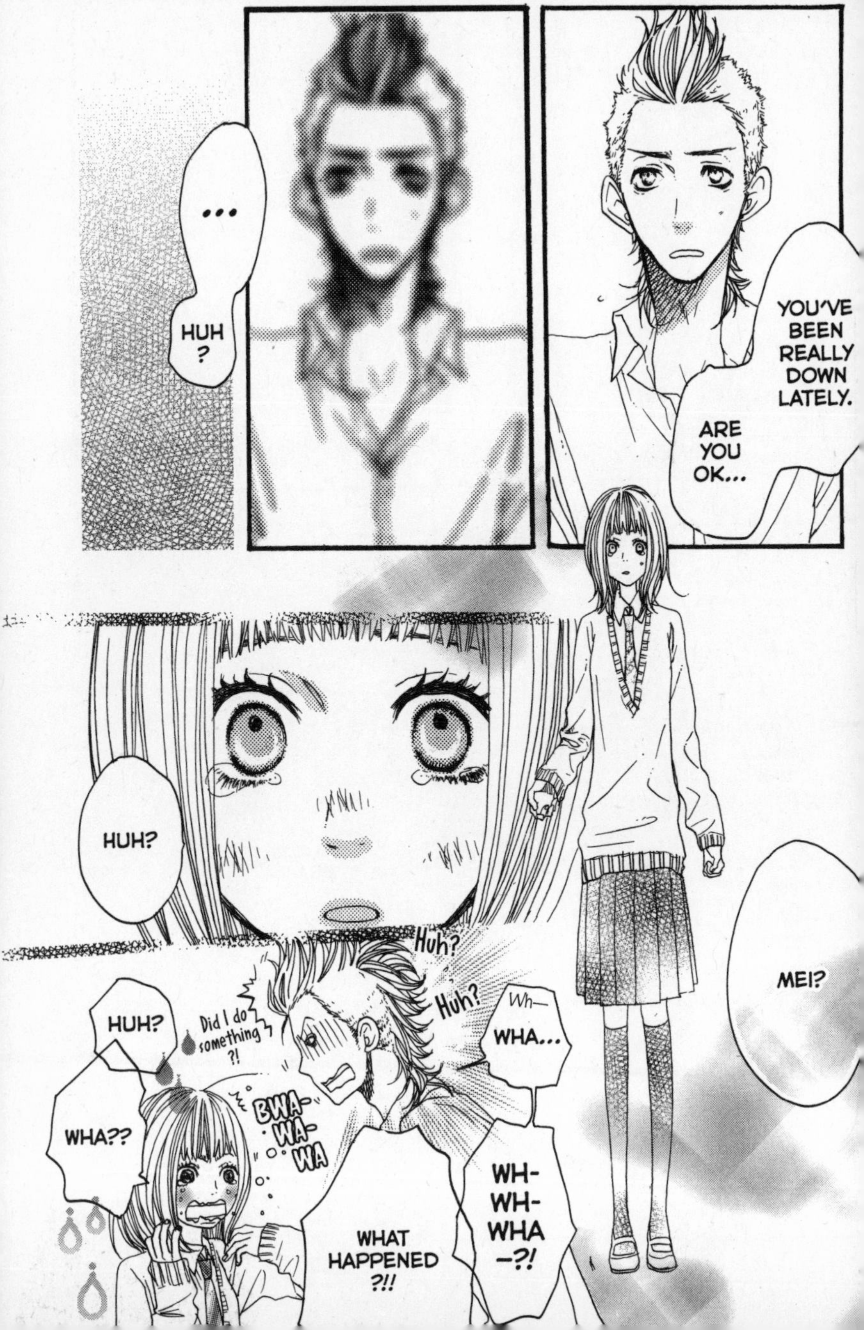

YOU'VE BEEN REALLY DOWN LATELY.
ARE YOU OK...
...
HUH?
MEI?
HUH?
Huh?
Huh?
Wh—
WHA...
WH-WH-WHA—?!
WHAT HAPPENED?!!
Did I do something?!
BWA-WA-WA
HUH?
WHA??

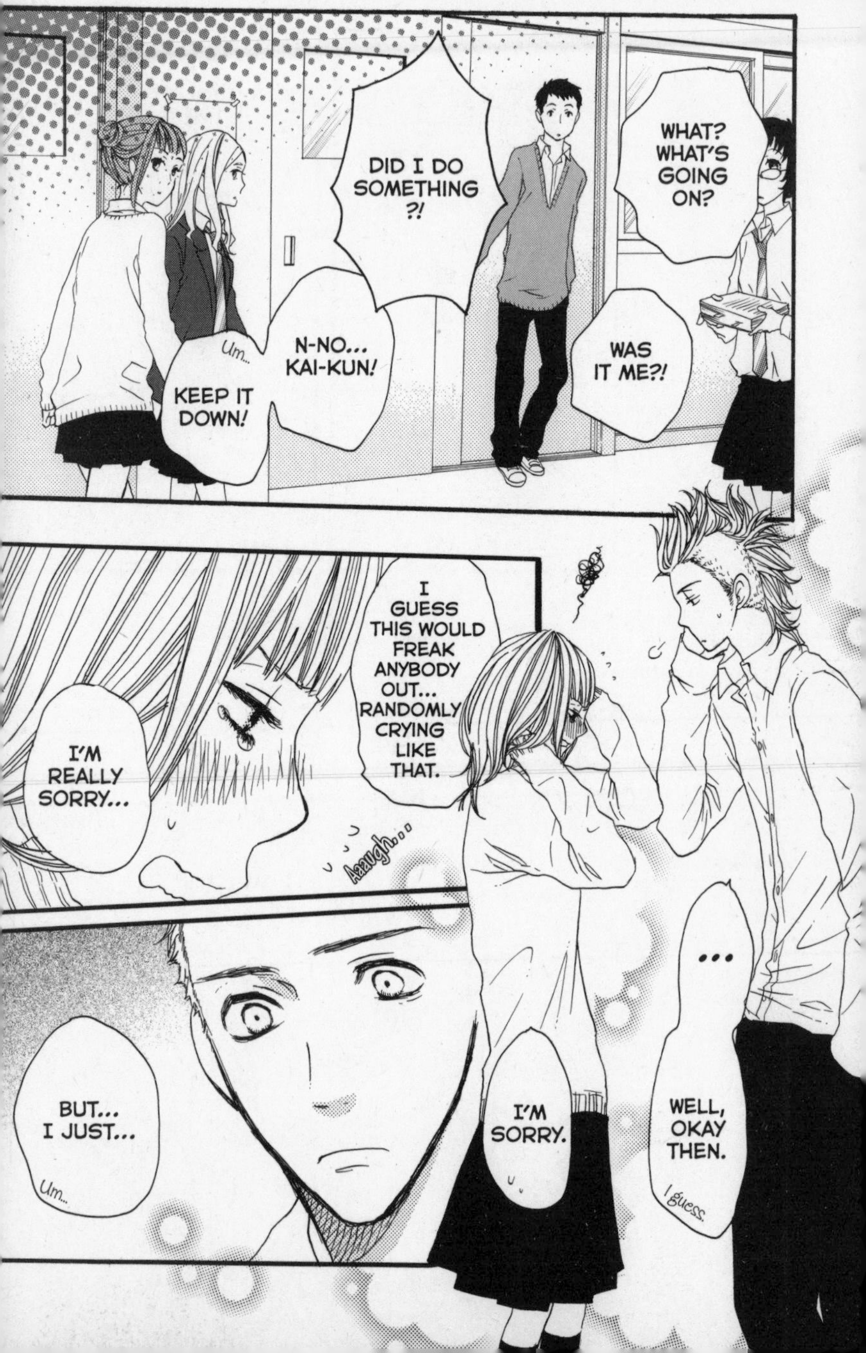
WHAT? WHAT'S GOING ON?
WAS IT ME?!
DID I DO SOMETHING ?!
N-NO... KAI-KUN!
Um...
KEEP IT DOWN!
...
WELL, OKAY THEN.
I guess.
I'M SORRY.
I GUESS THIS WOULD FREAK ANYBODY OUT... RANDOMLY CRYING LIKE THAT.
Aaaugh...
I'M REALLY SORRY...
BUT... I JUST...
Um...

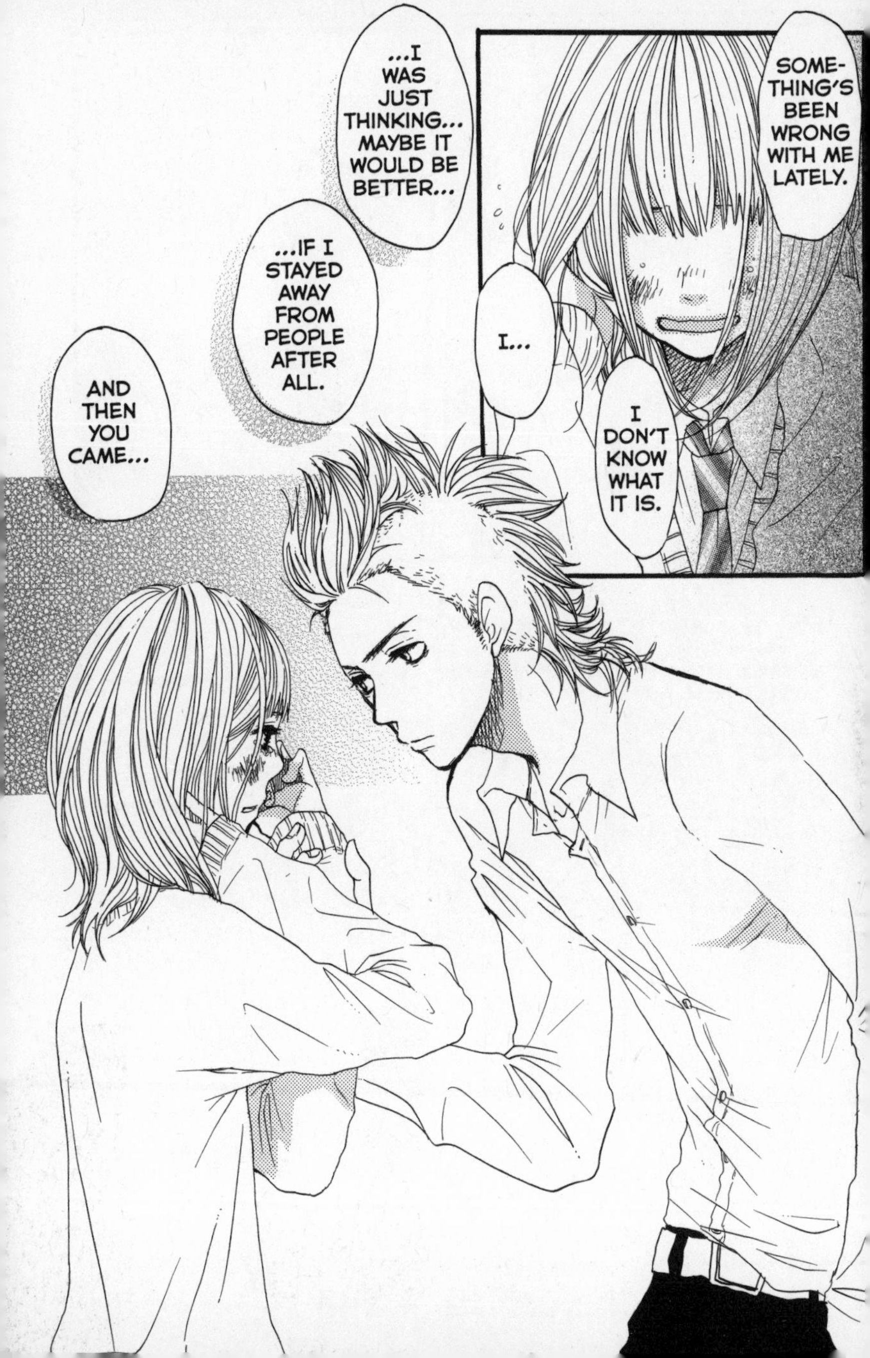
SOME-THING'S BEEN WRONG WITH ME LATELY.
I...
I DON'T KNOW WHAT IT IS.
...I WAS JUST THINKING... MAYBE IT WOULD BE BETTER...
...IF I STAYED AWAY FROM PEOPLE AFTER ALL.
AND THEN YOU CAME...

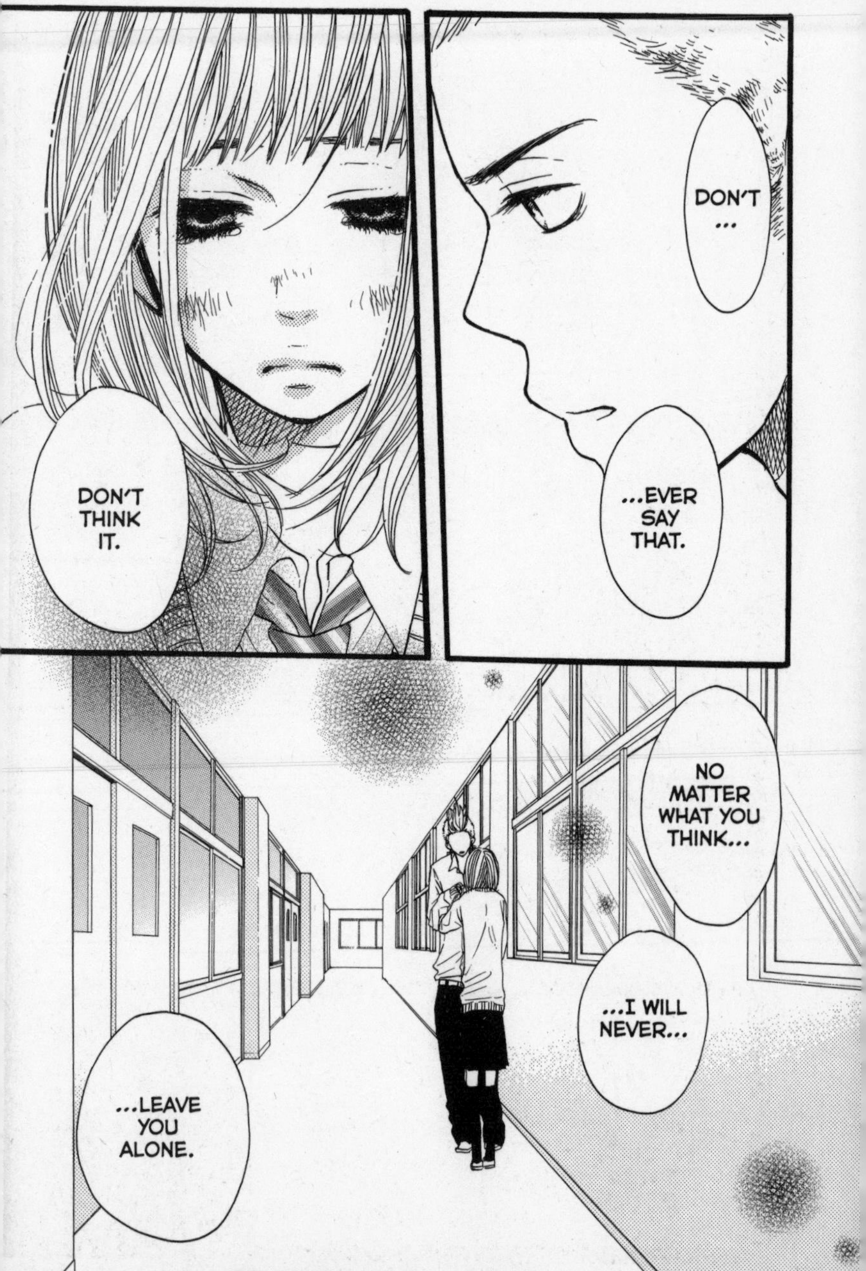
DON'T ...
...EVER SAY THAT.
DON'T THINK IT.
NO MATTER WHAT YOU THINK...
...I WILL NEVER...
...LEAVE YOU ALONE.

Chapter 19 — End

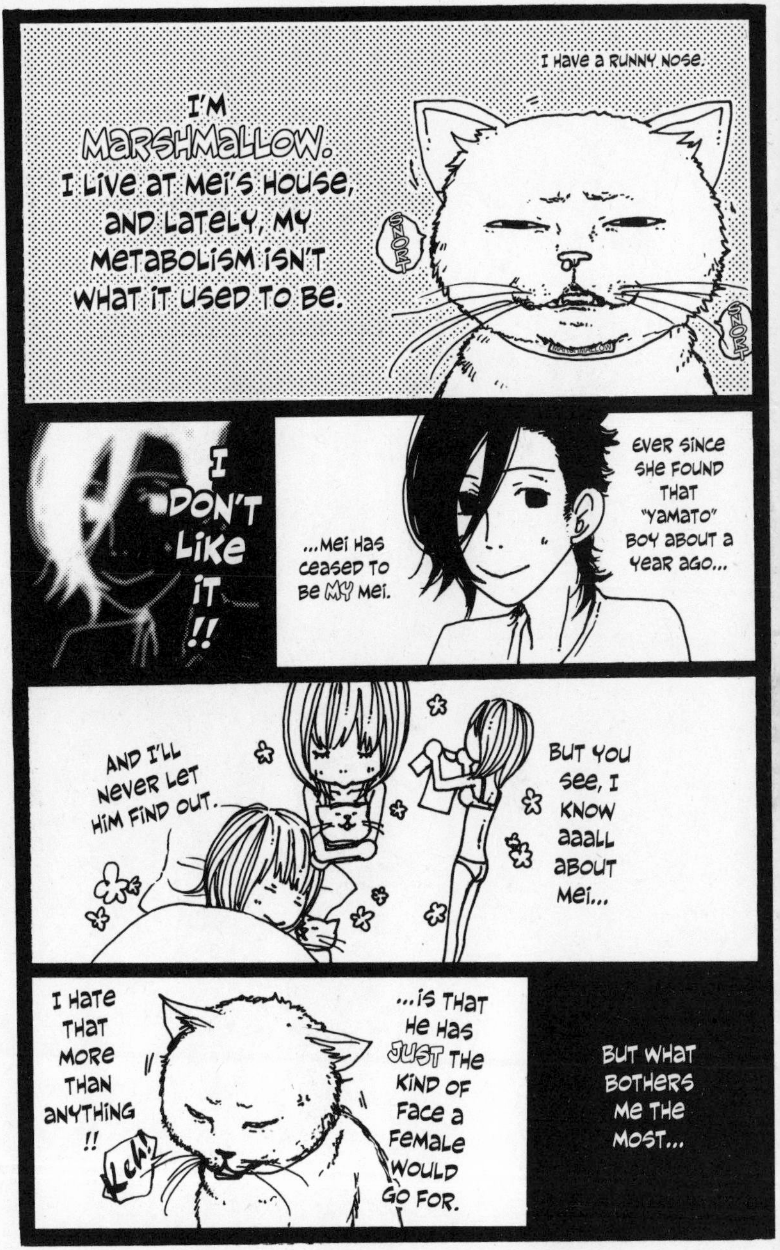
I have a runny nose.
SNORT
I'M MARSHMALLOW. I live at Mei's house, and lately, my metabolism isn't what it used to be.
MARSHMALLOW
SNORT
Ever since she found that "Yamato" boy about a year ago...
...Mei has ceased to be MY Mei.
I DON'T like it!!
But you see, I know aaall about Mei...
And I'll never let him find out.
But what bothers me the most...
...is that he has JUST the kind of face a female would go for.
I hate that more than anything!!
Kch!

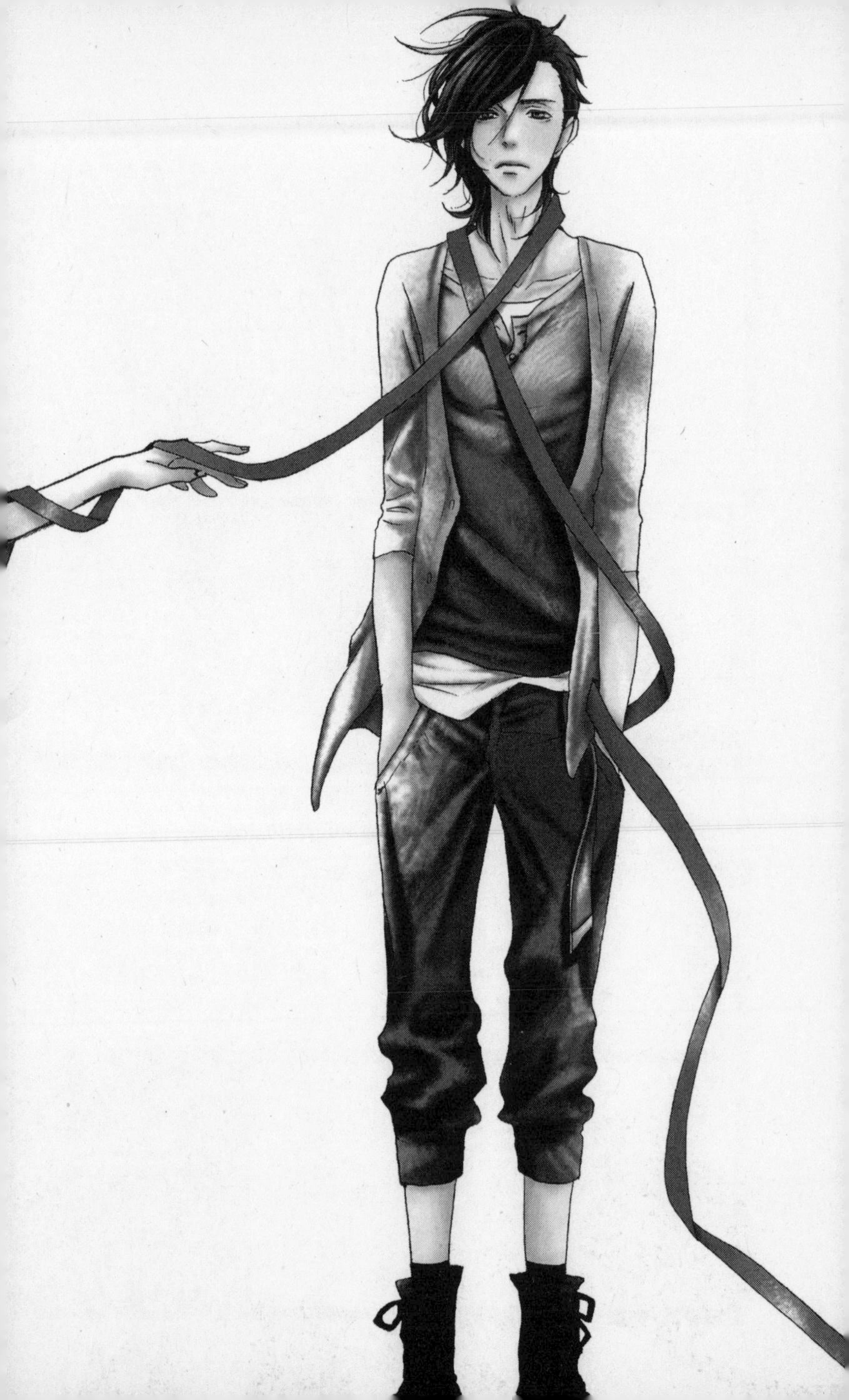

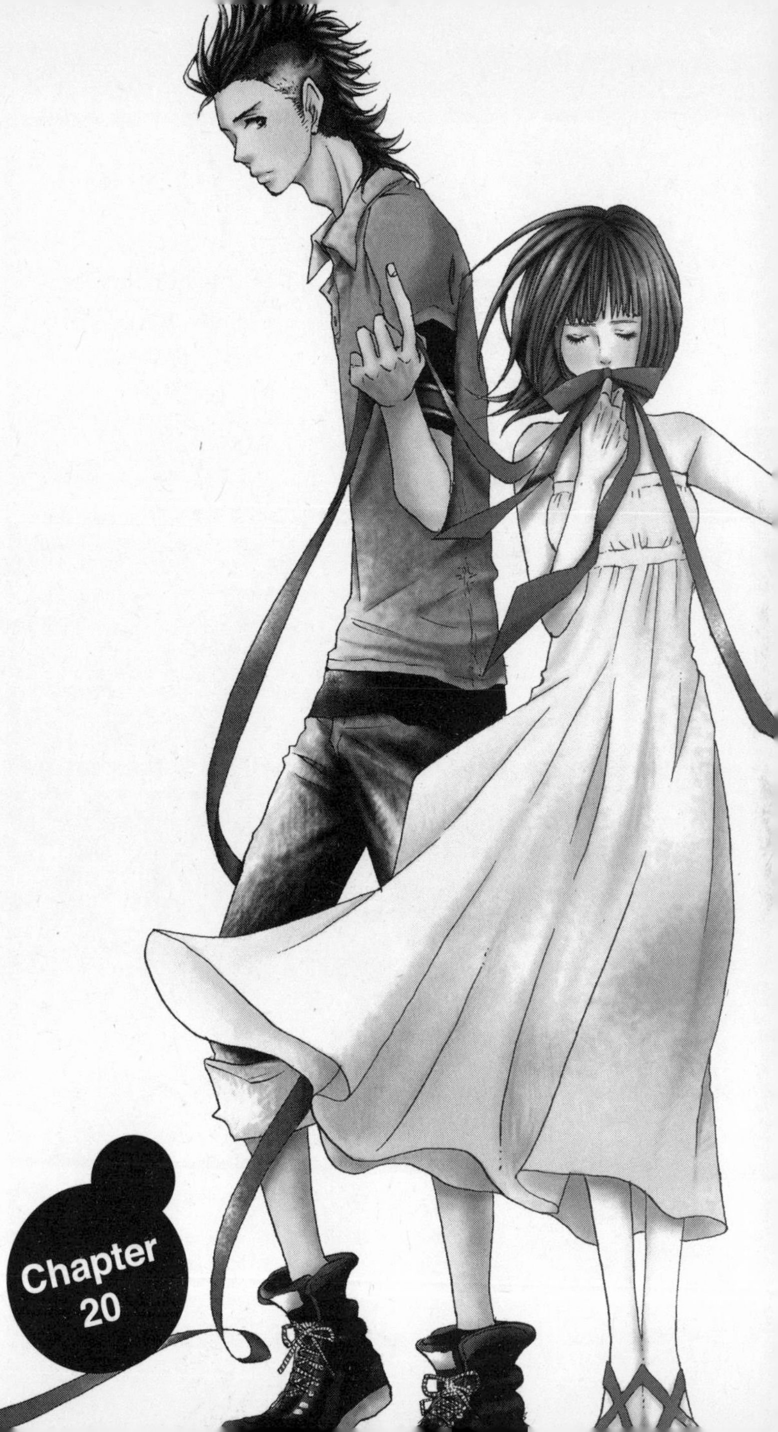
Chapter
20

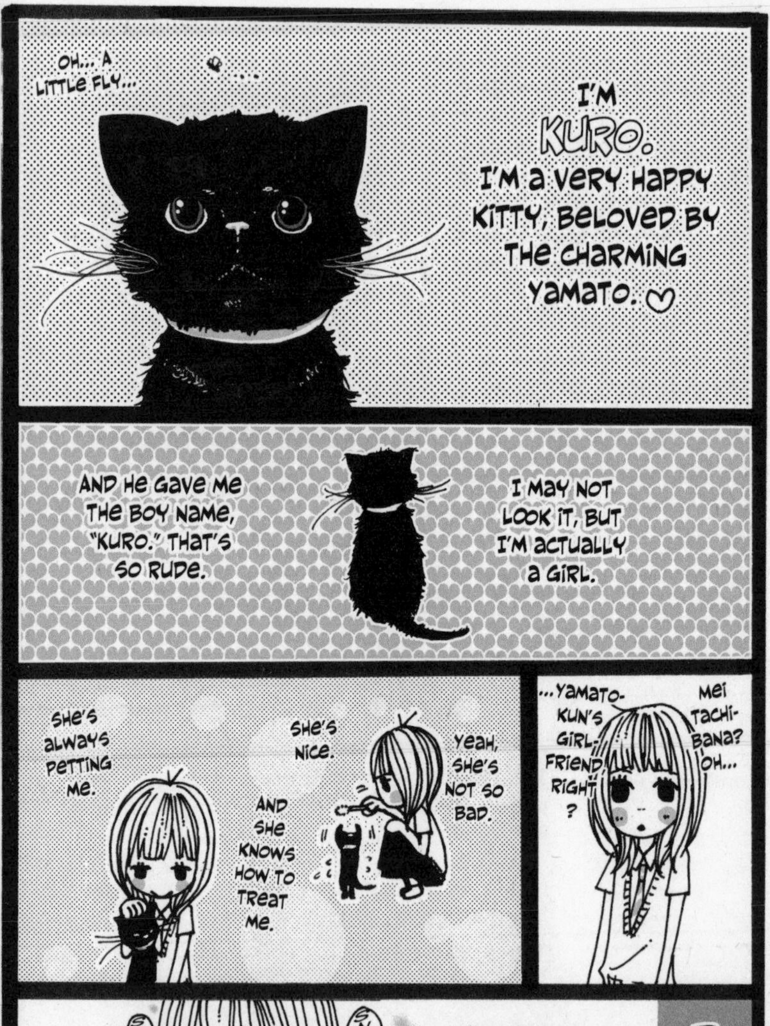
I'M KURO. I'M a VERY HAPPY KITTY, BELOVED BY THE CHARMING YAMATO. ♡
OH... A LITTLE FLY...
...
I MAY NOT LOOK IT, BUT I'M ACTUALLY A GIRL.
AND HE GAVE ME THE BOY NAME, "KURO." THAT'S SO RUDE.
MEI TACHI-BANA? OH...
...YAMATO-KUN'S GIRL-FRIEND, RIGHT?
YEAH, SHE'S NOT SO BAD.
SHE'S NICE.
AND SHE KNOWS HOW TO TREAT ME.
SHE'S ALWAYS PETTING ME.
BUT...
WHEN YAMATO-KUN ISN'T AROUND, SHE SNIFFS MY HEAD.
DO I SMELL BAD OR SOMETHING?
SNIFF
SNIFF
IT'S SO RUDE.
...

※ See Volume 2, page 48...

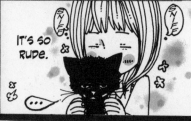

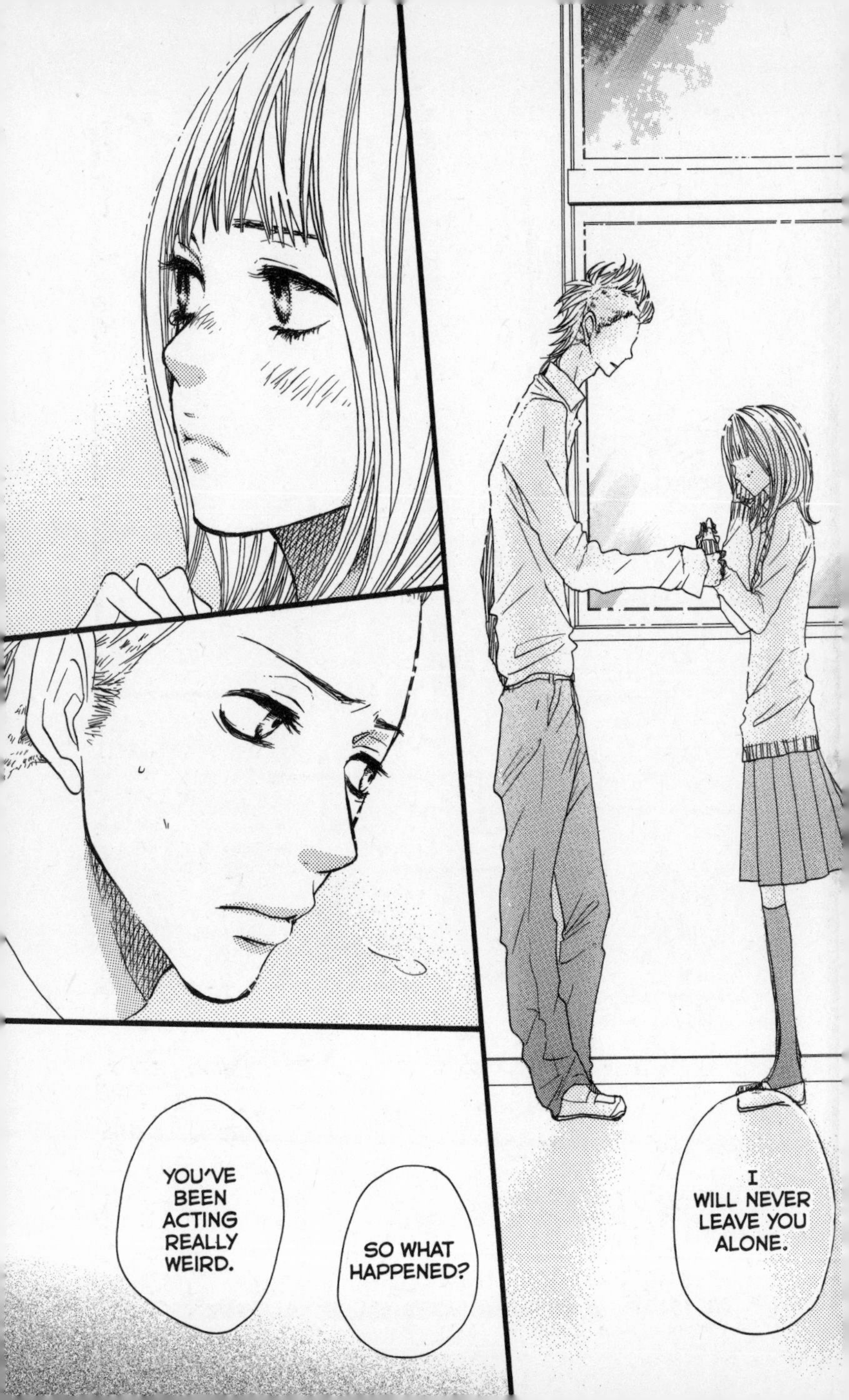
I WILL NEVER LEAVE YOU ALONE.
YOU'VE BEEN ACTING REALLY WEIRD.
SO WHAT HAPPENED?

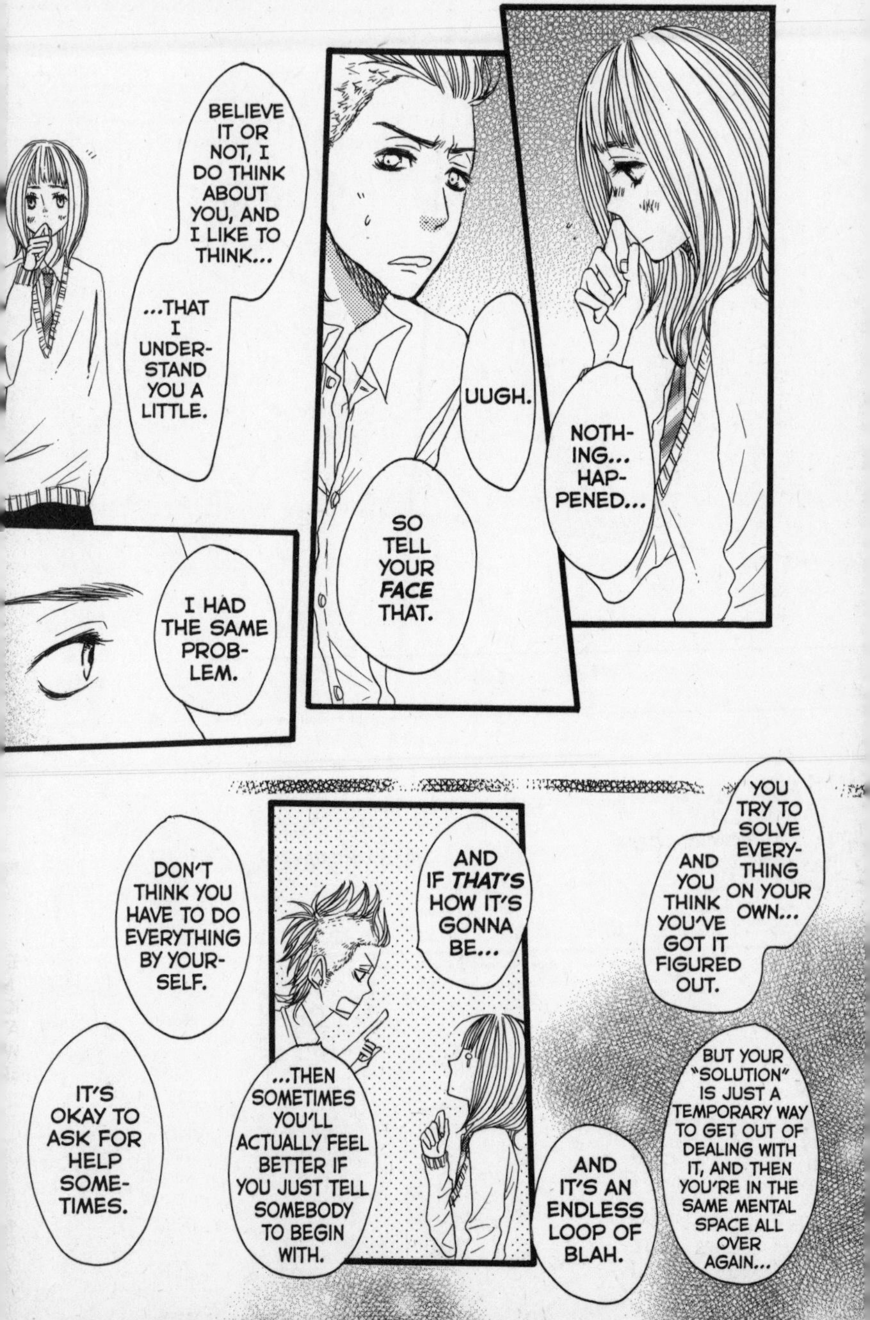
NOTHING... HAPPENED...
UUGH.
SO TELL YOUR *FACE* THAT.
BELIEVE IT OR NOT, I DO THINK ABOUT YOU, AND I LIKE TO THINK...
...THAT I UNDERSTAND YOU A LITTLE.
I HAD THE SAME PROBLEM.
YOU TRY TO SOLVE EVERYTHING ON YOUR OWN...
AND YOU THINK YOU'VE GOT IT FIGURED OUT.
BUT YOUR "SOLUTION" IS JUST A TEMPORARY WAY TO GET OUT OF DEALING WITH IT, AND THEN YOU'RE IN THE SAME MENTAL SPACE ALL OVER AGAIN...
AND IT'S AN ENDLESS LOOP OF BLAH.
AND IF *THAT'S* HOW IT'S GONNA BE...
...THEN SOMETIMES YOU'LL ACTUALLY FEEL BETTER IF YOU JUST TELL SOMEBODY TO BEGIN WITH.
DON'T THINK YOU HAVE TO DO EVERYTHING BY YOURSELF.
IT'S OKAY TO ASK FOR HELP SOMETIMES.

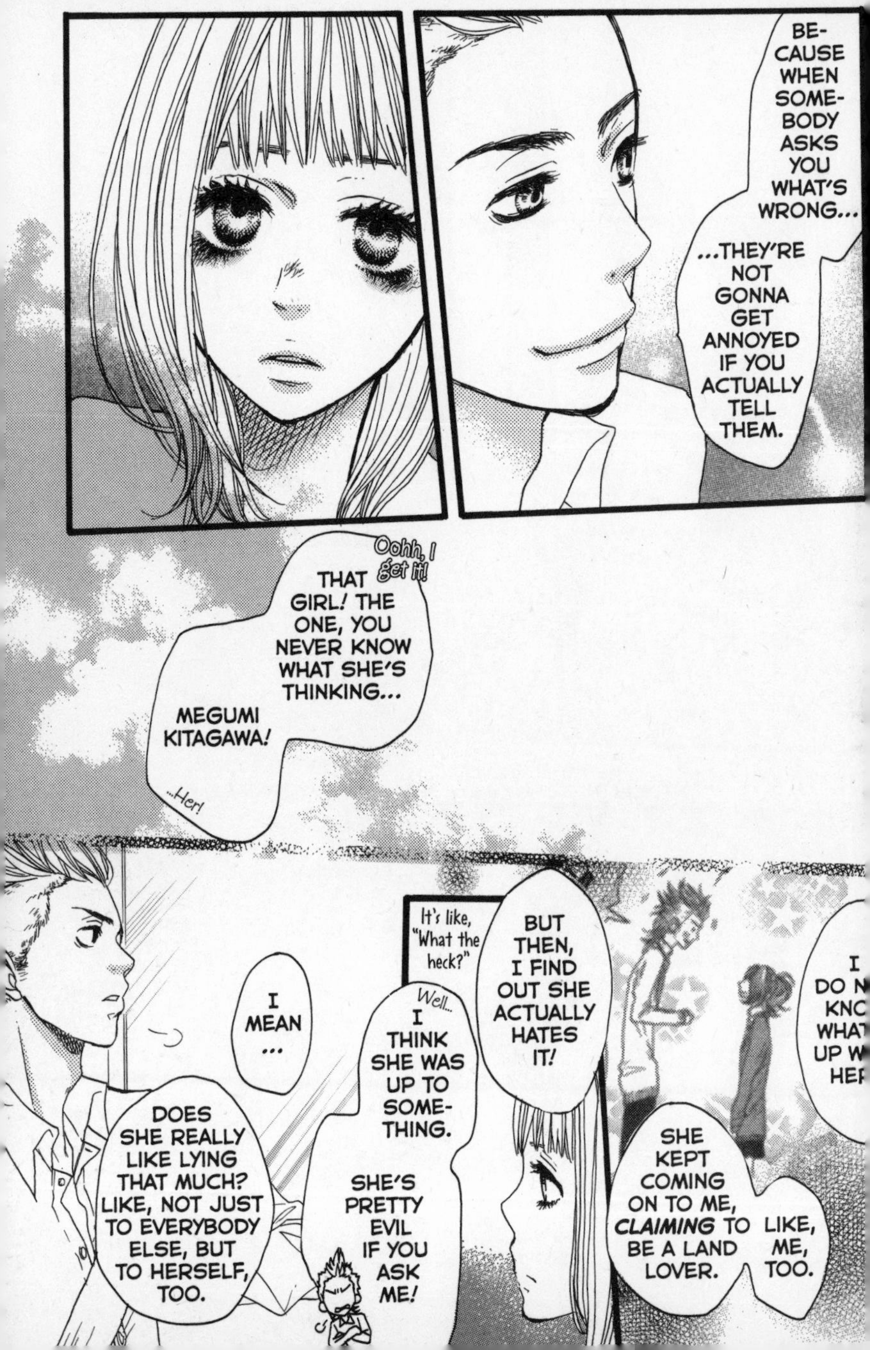
BE-CAUSE WHEN SOME-BODY ASKS YOU WHAT'S WRONG...
...THEY'RE NOT GONNA GET ANNOYED IF YOU ACTUALLY TELL THEM.
Oohh, I get it!
THAT GIRL! THE ONE, YOU NEVER KNOW WHAT SHE'S THINKING...
MEGUMI KITAGAWA!
...Her!
LIKE, ME, TOO.
SHE KEPT COMING ON TO ME, *CLAIMING* TO BE A LAND LOVER.
BUT THEN, I FIND OUT SHE ACTUALLY HATES IT!
It's like, "What the heck?"
Well... I THINK SHE WAS UP TO SOME-THING.
SHE'S PRETTY EVIL IF YOU ASK ME!
I MEAN...
DOES SHE REALLY LIKE LYING THAT MUCH? LIKE, NOT JUST TO EVERYBODY ELSE, BUT TO HERSELF, TOO.

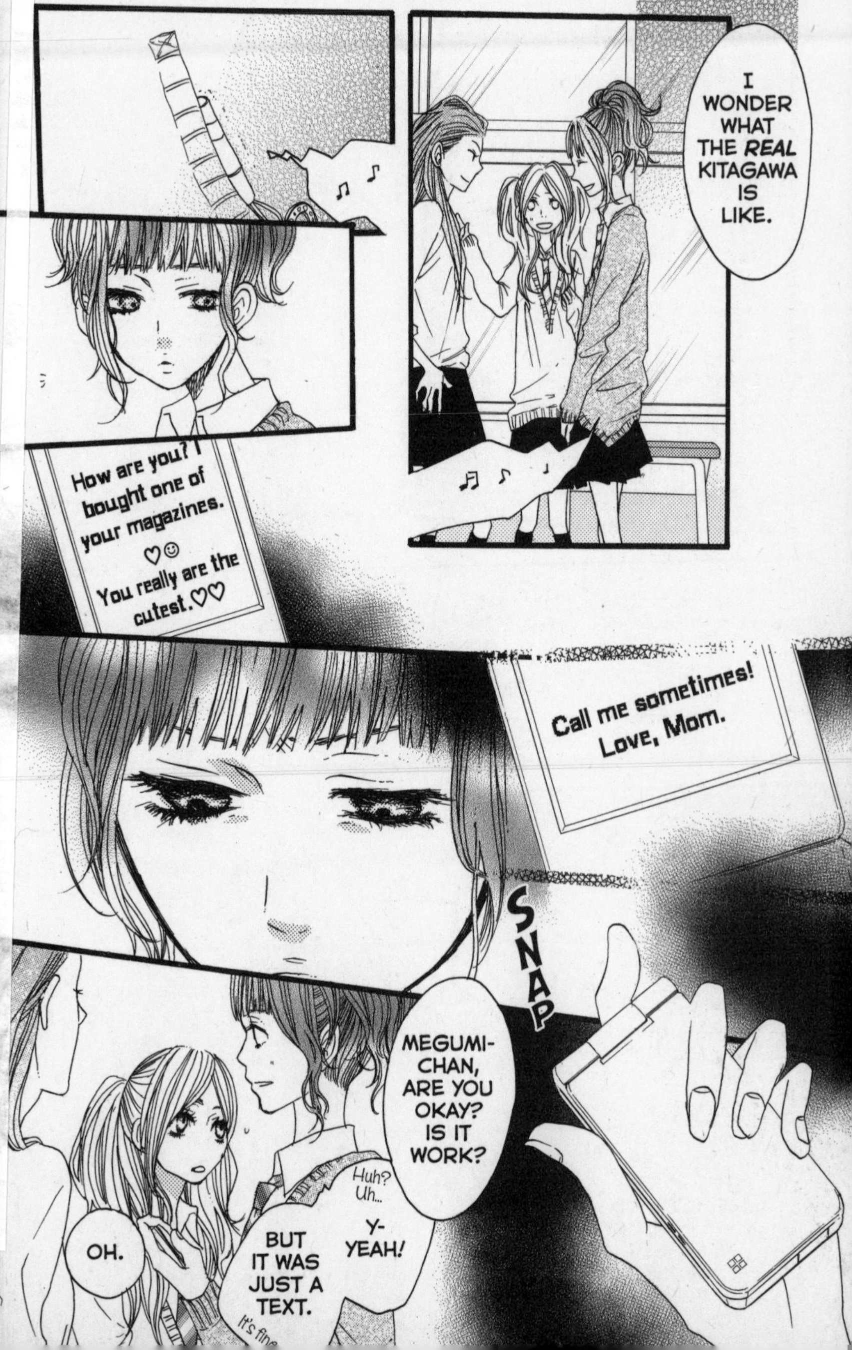
I WONDER WHAT THE REAL KITAGAWA IS LIKE.
How are you? I bought one of your magazines. ♡☺ You really are the cutest.♡♡
Call me sometimes! Love, Mom.
SNAP
MEGUMI-CHAN, ARE YOU OKAY? IS IT WORK?
Huh? Uh...
Y-YEAH!
BUT IT WAS JUST A TEXT.
OH.

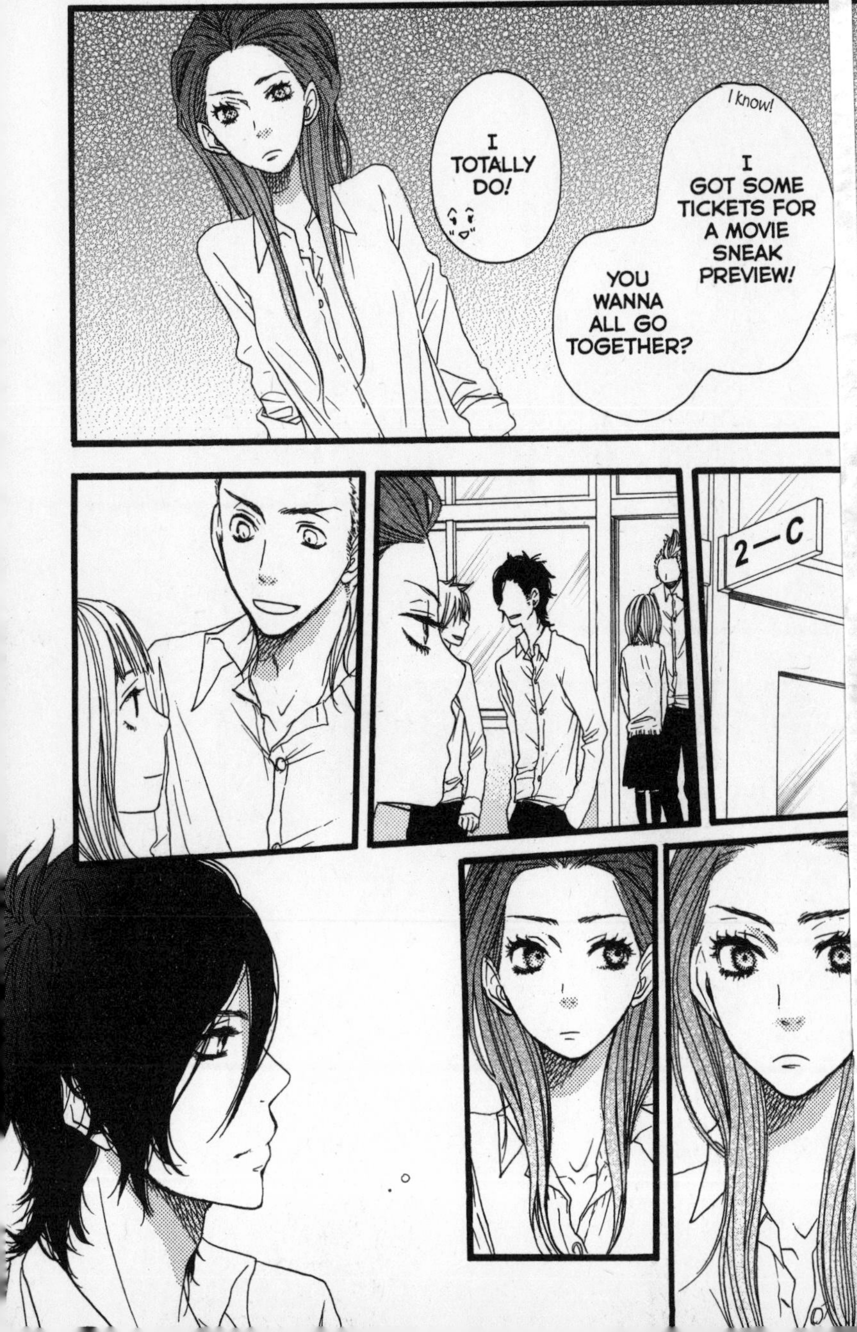
I know!
I GOT SOME TICKETS FOR A MOVIE SNEAK PREVIEW!
YOU WANNA ALL GO TOGETHER?
I TOTALLY DO!
2—C

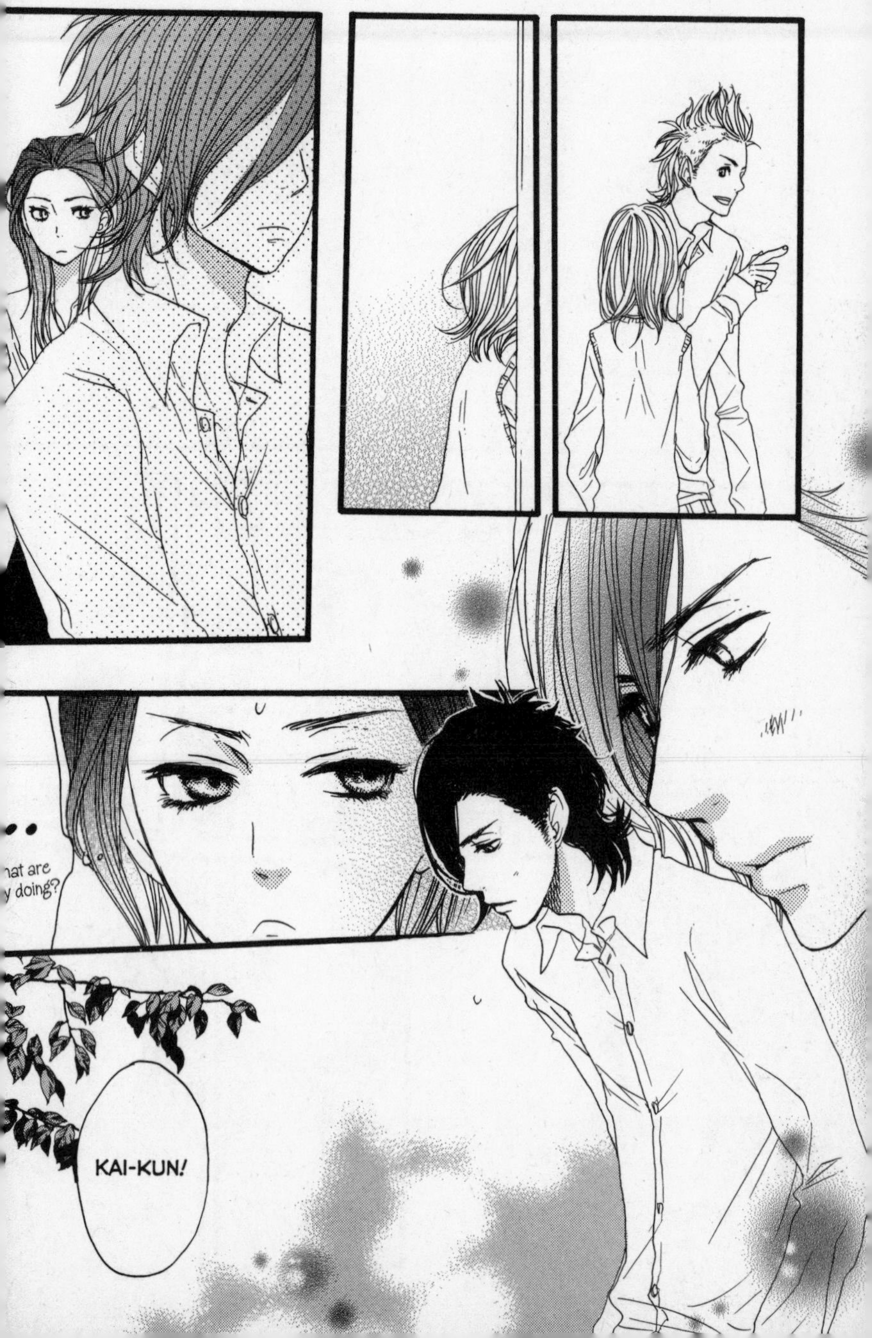

...
..hat are
..y doing?
KAI-KUN!

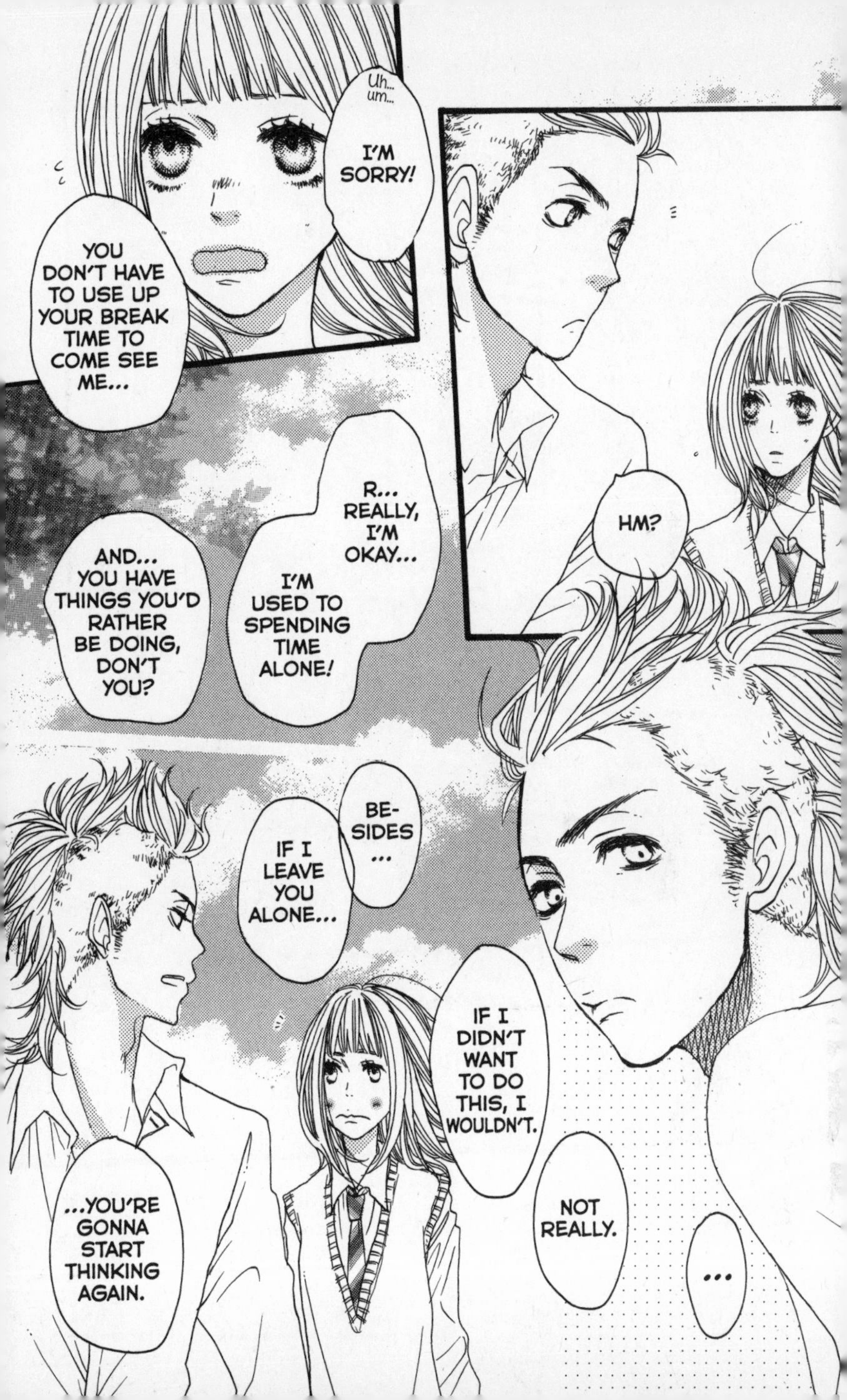
HM?
Uh... um...
I'M SORRY!
YOU DON'T HAVE TO USE UP YOUR BREAK TIME TO COME SEE ME...
R... REALLY, I'M OKAY...
I'M USED TO SPENDING TIME ALONE!
AND... YOU HAVE THINGS YOU'D RATHER BE DOING, DON'T YOU?
IF I DIDN'T WANT TO DO THIS, I WOULDN'T.
NOT REALLY.
...
BE-SIDES...
IF I LEAVE YOU ALONE...
...YOU'RE GONNA START THINKING AGAIN.

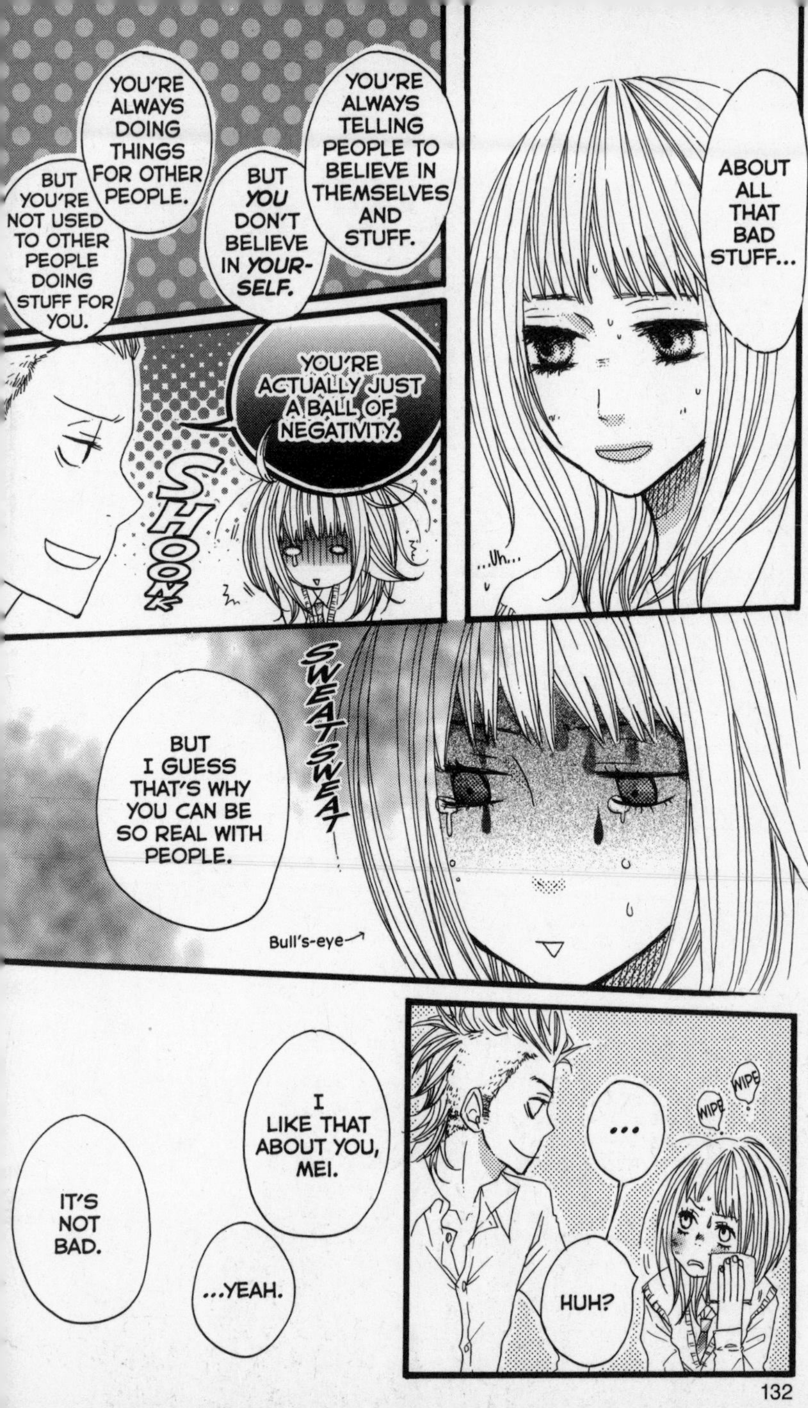
ABOUT ALL THAT BAD STUFF...
...Uh...
YOU'RE ALWAYS TELLING PEOPLE TO BELIEVE IN THEMSELVES AND STUFF.
BUT *YOU* DON'T BELIEVE IN *YOURSELF.*
YOU'RE ALWAYS DOING THINGS FOR OTHER PEOPLE.
BUT YOU'RE NOT USED TO OTHER PEOPLE DOING STUFF FOR YOU.
YOU'RE ACTUALLY JUST A BALL OF NEGATIVITY.
SHOONK
SWEAT SWEAT
BUT I GUESS THAT'S WHY YOU CAN BE SO REAL WITH PEOPLE.
Bull's-eye
...
WIPE
WIPE
HUH?
I LIKE THAT ABOUT YOU, MEI.
...YEAH.
IT'S NOT BAD.

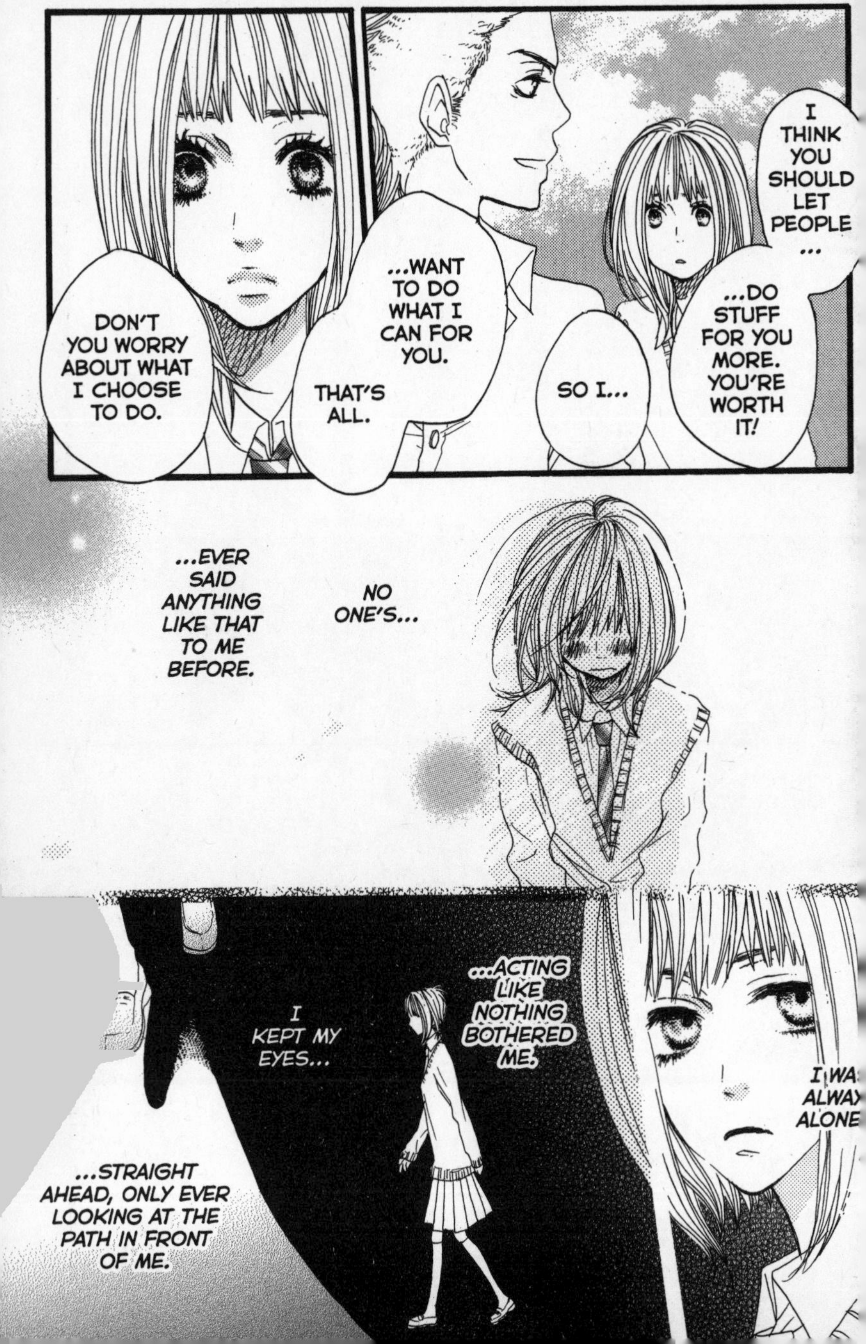
I THINK YOU SHOULD LET PEOPLE...
...DO STUFF FOR YOU MORE. YOU'RE WORTH IT!
SO I...
...WANT TO DO WHAT I CAN FOR YOU.
THAT'S ALL.
DON'T YOU WORRY ABOUT WHAT I CHOOSE TO DO.
NO ONE'S...
...EVER SAID ANYTHING LIKE THAT TO ME BEFORE.
I WA ALWAY ALONE
...ACTING LIKE NOTHING BOTHERED ME.
I KEPT MY EYES...
...STRAIGHT AHEAD, ONLY EVER LOOKING AT THE PATH IN FRONT OF ME.

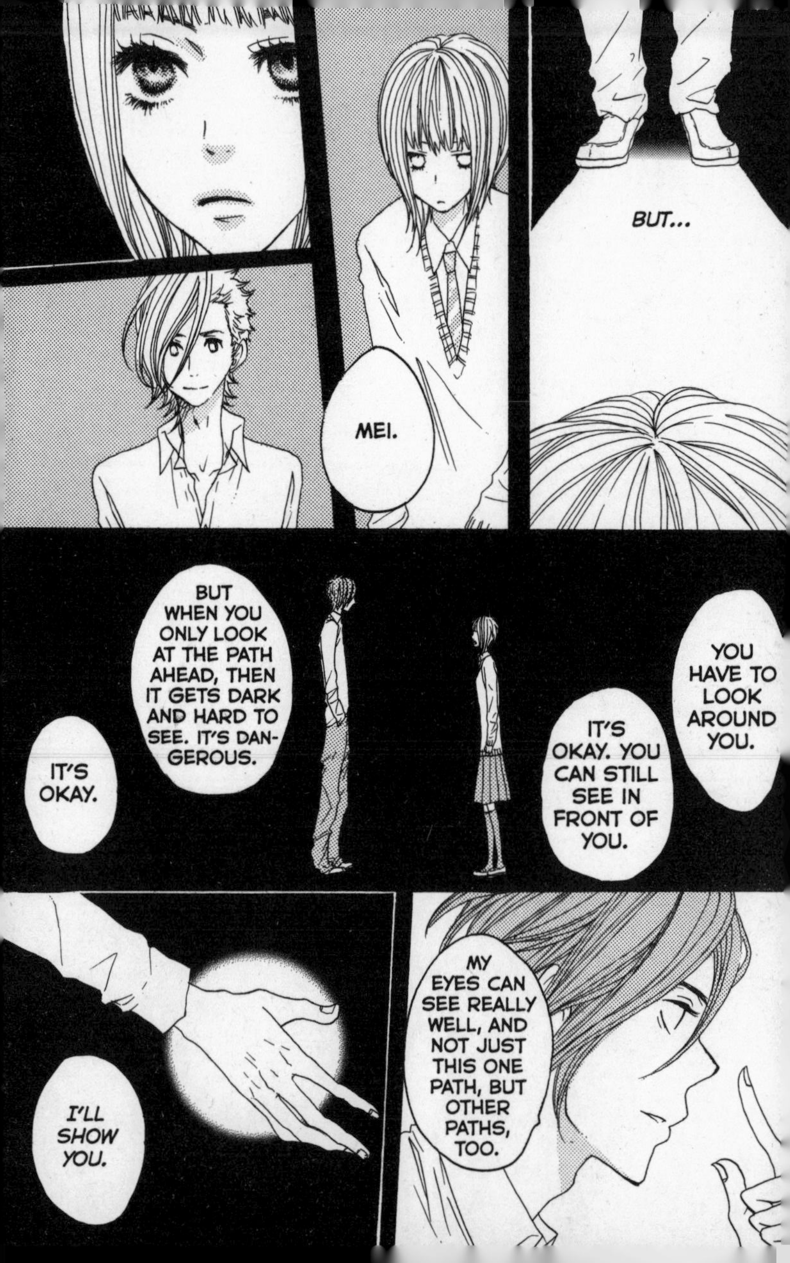
BUT...
MEI.
YOU HAVE TO LOOK AROUND YOU.
IT'S OKAY. YOU CAN STILL SEE IN FRONT OF YOU.
BUT WHEN YOU ONLY LOOK AT THE PATH AHEAD, THEN IT GETS DARK AND HARD TO SEE. IT'S DANGEROUS.
IT'S OKAY.
MY EYES CAN SEE REALLY WELL, AND NOT JUST THIS ONE PATH, BUT OTHER PATHS, TOO.
I'LL SHOW YOU.

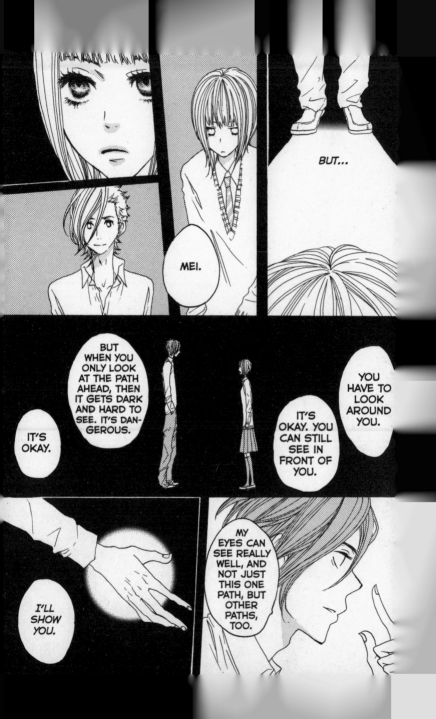

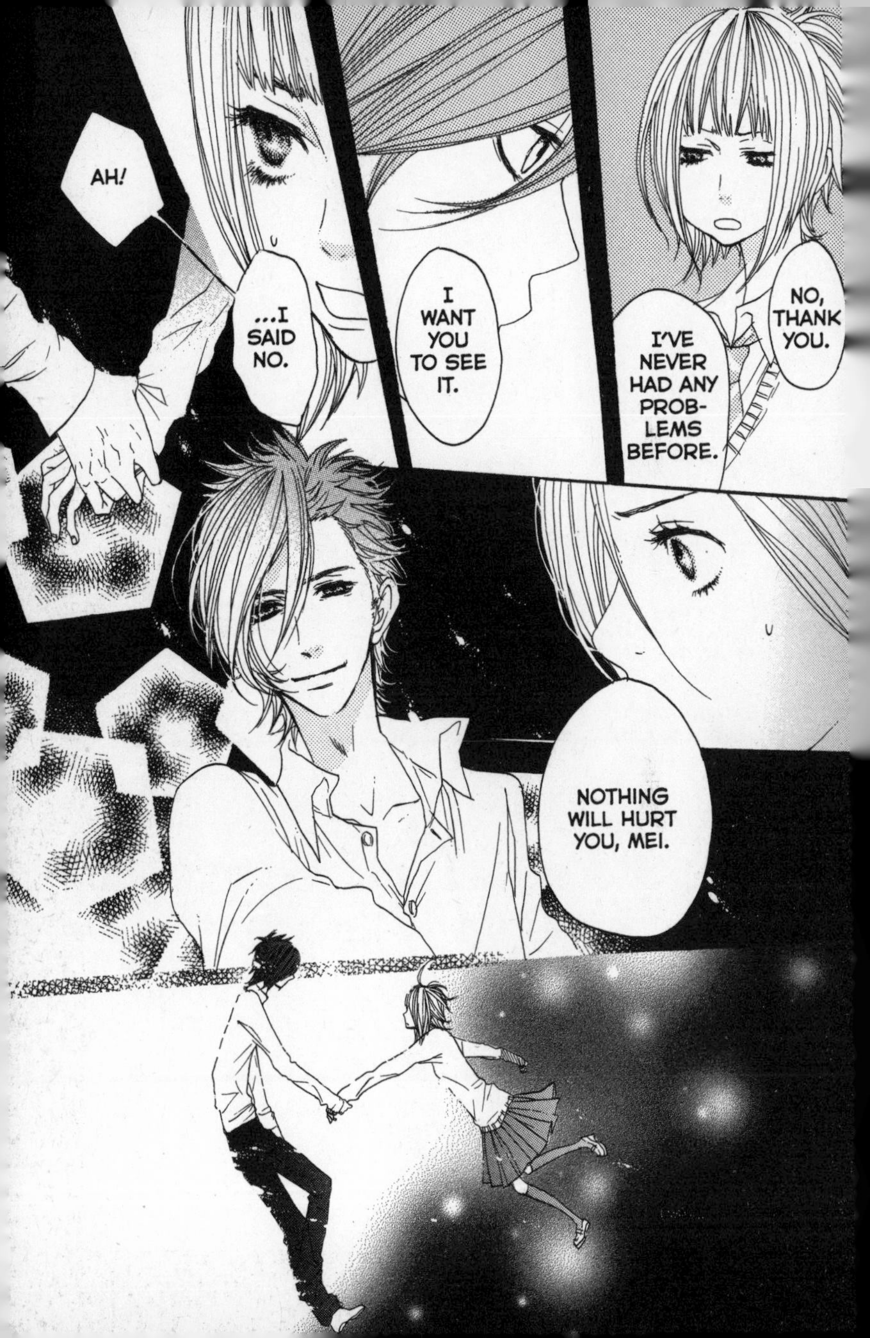
NO, THANK YOU.
I'VE NEVER HAD ANY PROB- LEMS BEFORE.
I WANT YOU TO SEE IT.
...I SAID NO.
AH!
NOTHING WILL HURT YOU, MEI.

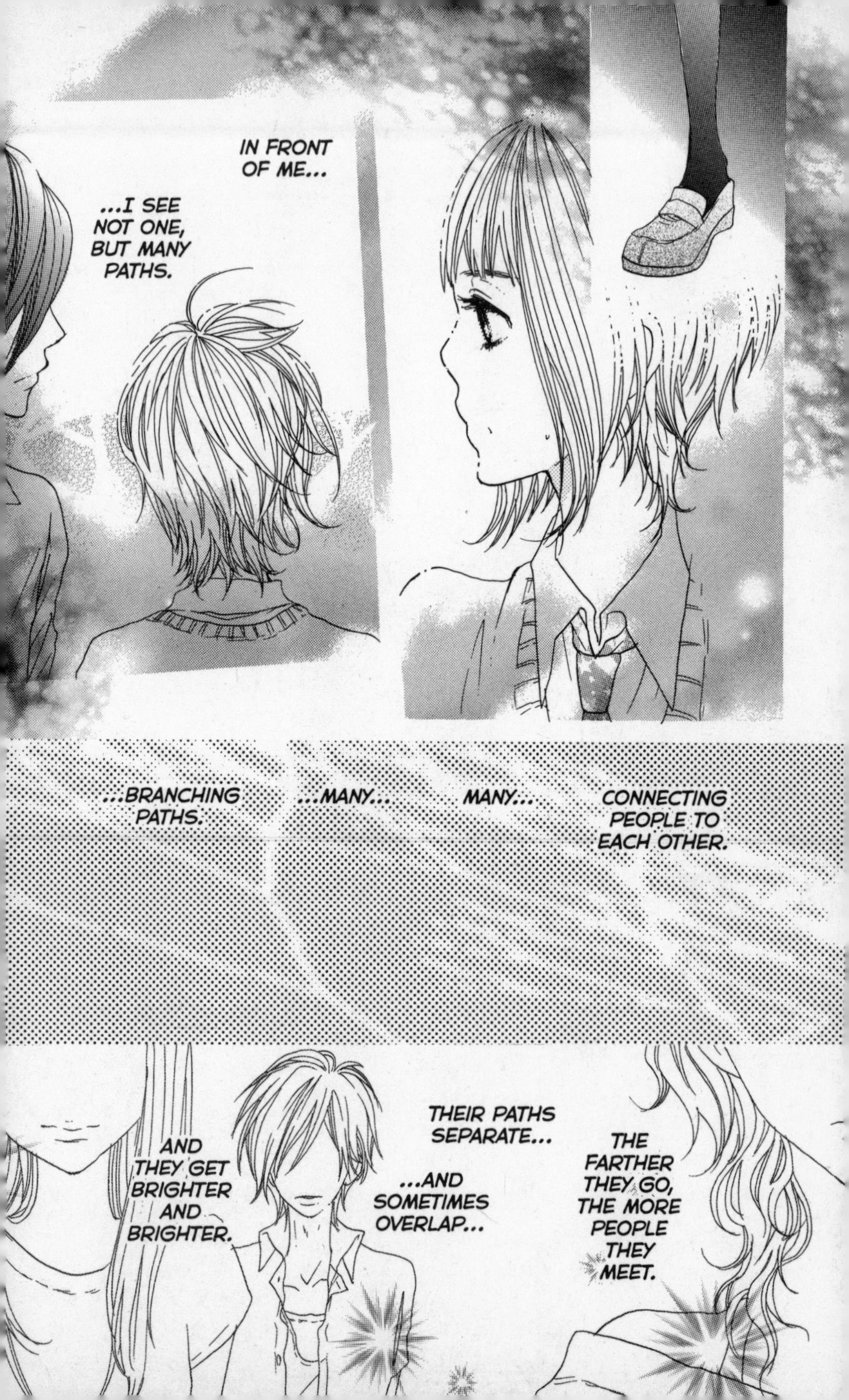
IN FRONT OF ME...
...I SEE NOT ONE, BUT MANY PATHS.
CONNECTING PEOPLE TO EACH OTHER.
MANY...
...MANY...
...BRANCHING PATHS.
THE FARTHER THEY GO, THE MORE PEOPLE THEY MEET.
THEIR PATHS SEPARATE...
...AND SOMETIMES OVERLAP...
AND THEY GET BRIGHTER AND BRIGHTER.

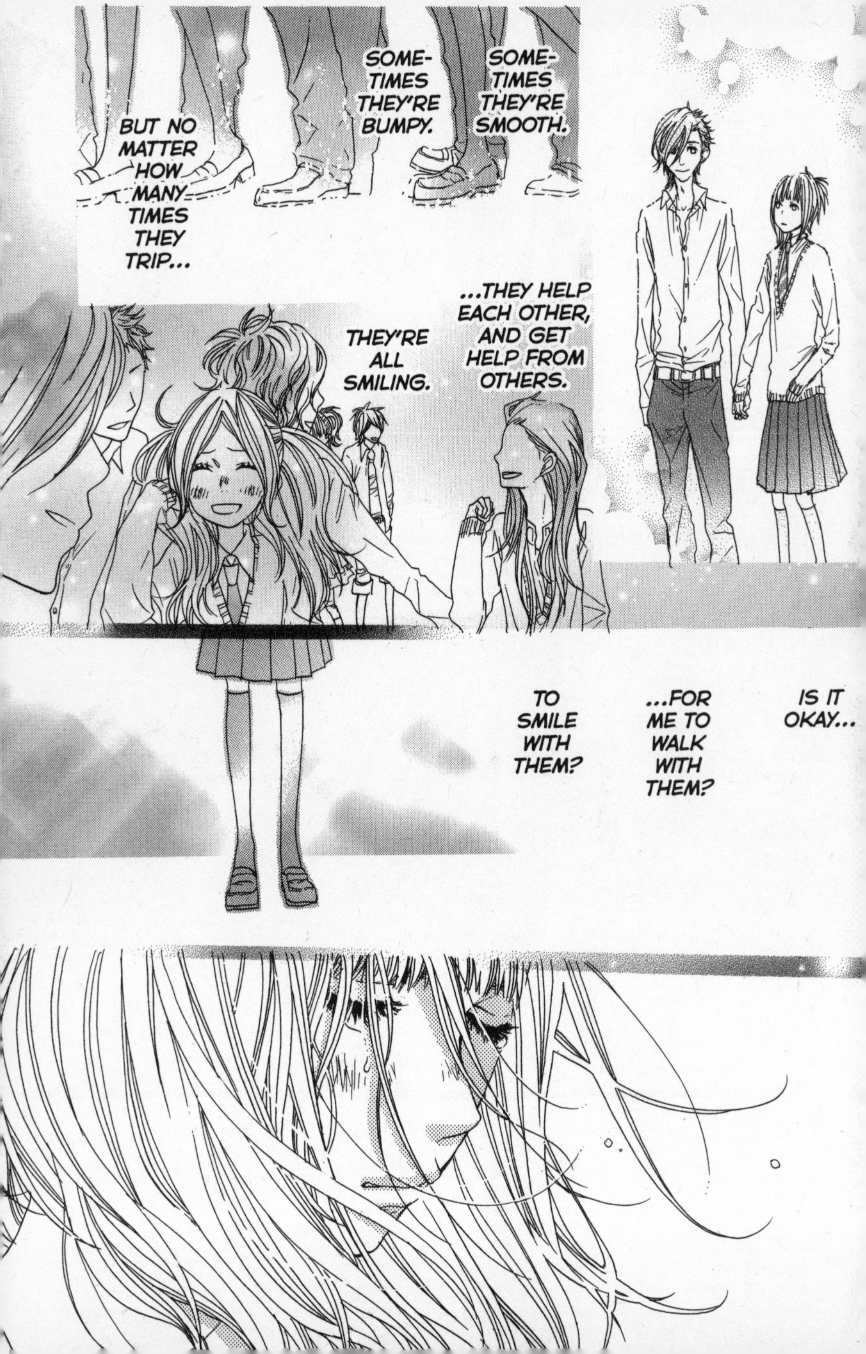
SOME-TIMES THEY'RE SMOOTH.
SOME-TIMES THEY'RE BUMPY.
BUT NO MATTER HOW MANY TIMES THEY TRIP...
...THEY HELP EACH OTHER, AND GET HELP FROM OTHERS.
THEY'RE ALL SMILING.
IS IT OKAY...
...FOR ME TO WALK WITH THEM?
TO SMILE WITH THEM?

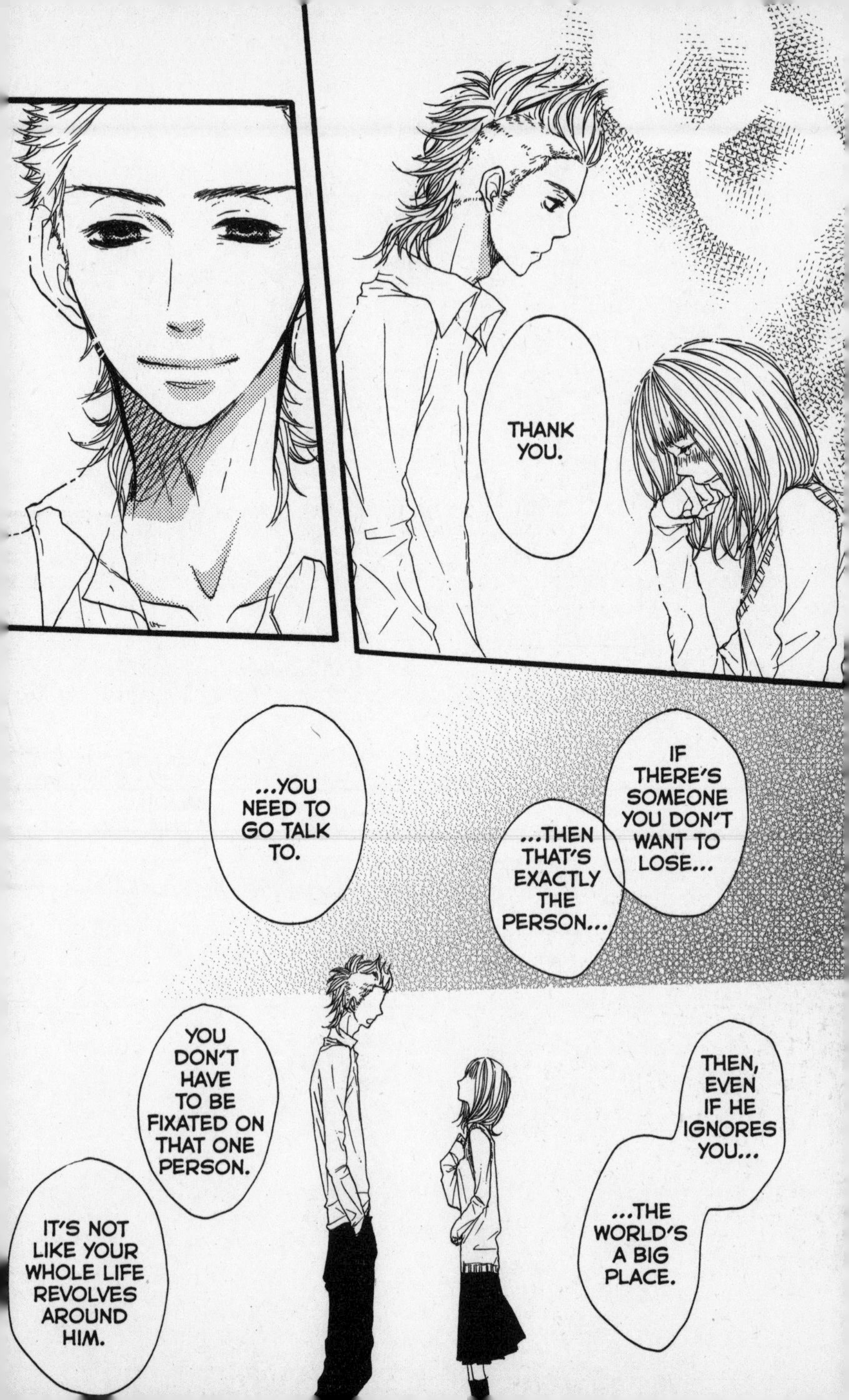
THANK YOU.
IF THERE'S SOMEONE YOU DON'T WANT TO LOSE...
...THEN THAT'S EXACTLY THE PERSON...
...YOU NEED TO GO TALK TO.
THEN, EVEN IF HE IGNORES YOU...
...THE WORLD'S A BIG PLACE.
YOU DON'T HAVE TO BE FIXATED ON THAT ONE PERSON.
IT'S NOT LIKE YOUR WHOLE LIFE REVOLVES AROUND HIM.

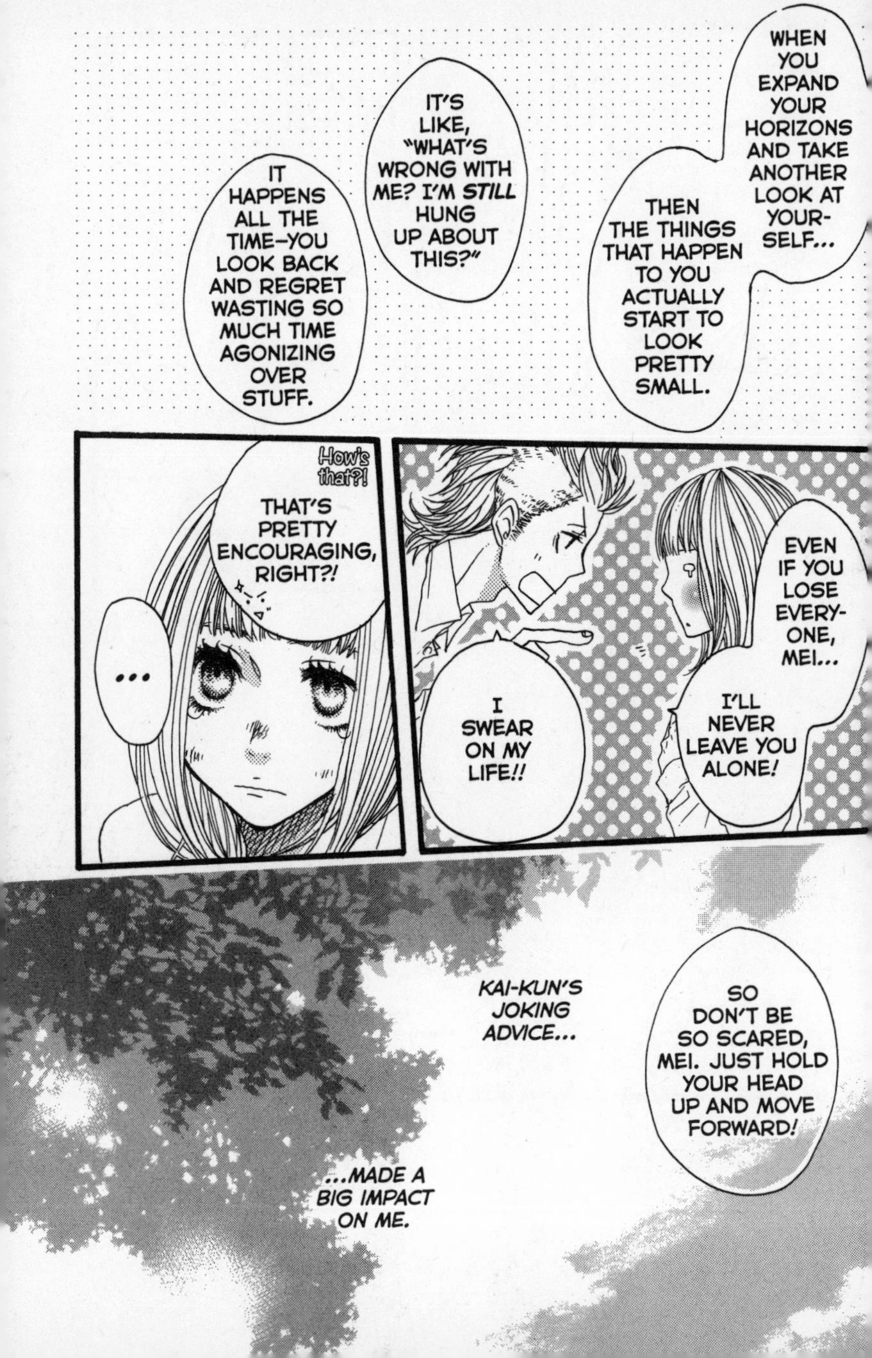
WHEN YOU EXPAND YOUR HORIZONS AND TAKE ANOTHER LOOK AT YOURSELF...
THEN THE THINGS THAT HAPPEN TO YOU ACTUALLY START TO LOOK PRETTY SMALL.
IT'S LIKE, "WHAT'S WRONG WITH ME? I'M STILL HUNG UP ABOUT THIS?"
IT HAPPENS ALL THE TIME—YOU LOOK BACK AND REGRET WASTING SO MUCH TIME AGONIZING OVER STUFF.
EVEN IF YOU LOSE EVERYONE, MEI...
I'LL NEVER LEAVE YOU ALONE!
I SWEAR ON MY LIFE!!
How's that?!
THAT'S PRETTY ENCOURAGING, RIGHT?!
...
SO DON'T BE SO SCARED, MEI. JUST HOLD YOUR HEAD UP AND MOVE FORWARD!
KAI-KUN'S JOKING ADVICE...
...MADE A BIG IMPACT ON ME.

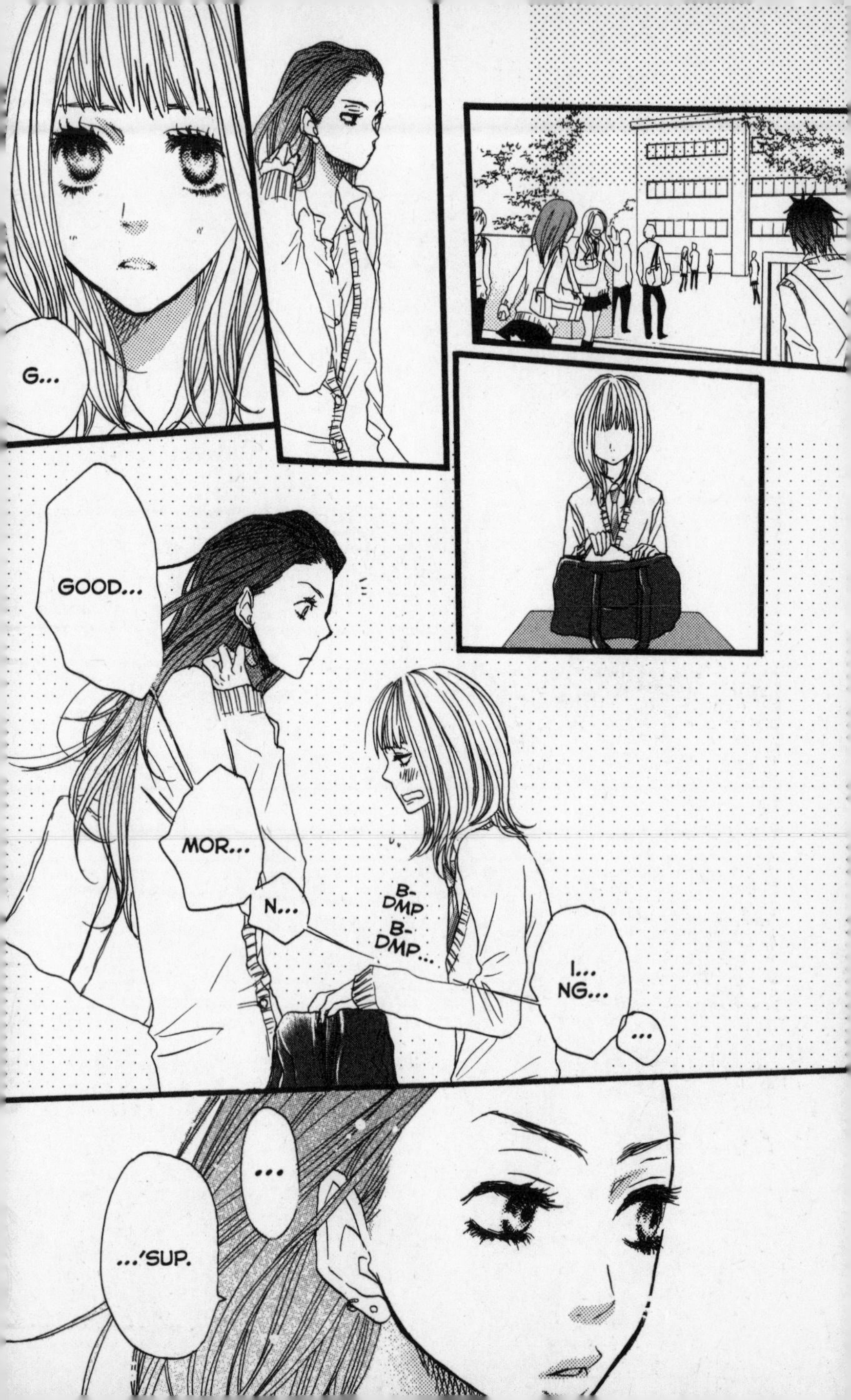
G...
GOOD...
MOR...
N...
B-DMP B-DMP...
I... NG...
...
...
...'SUP.

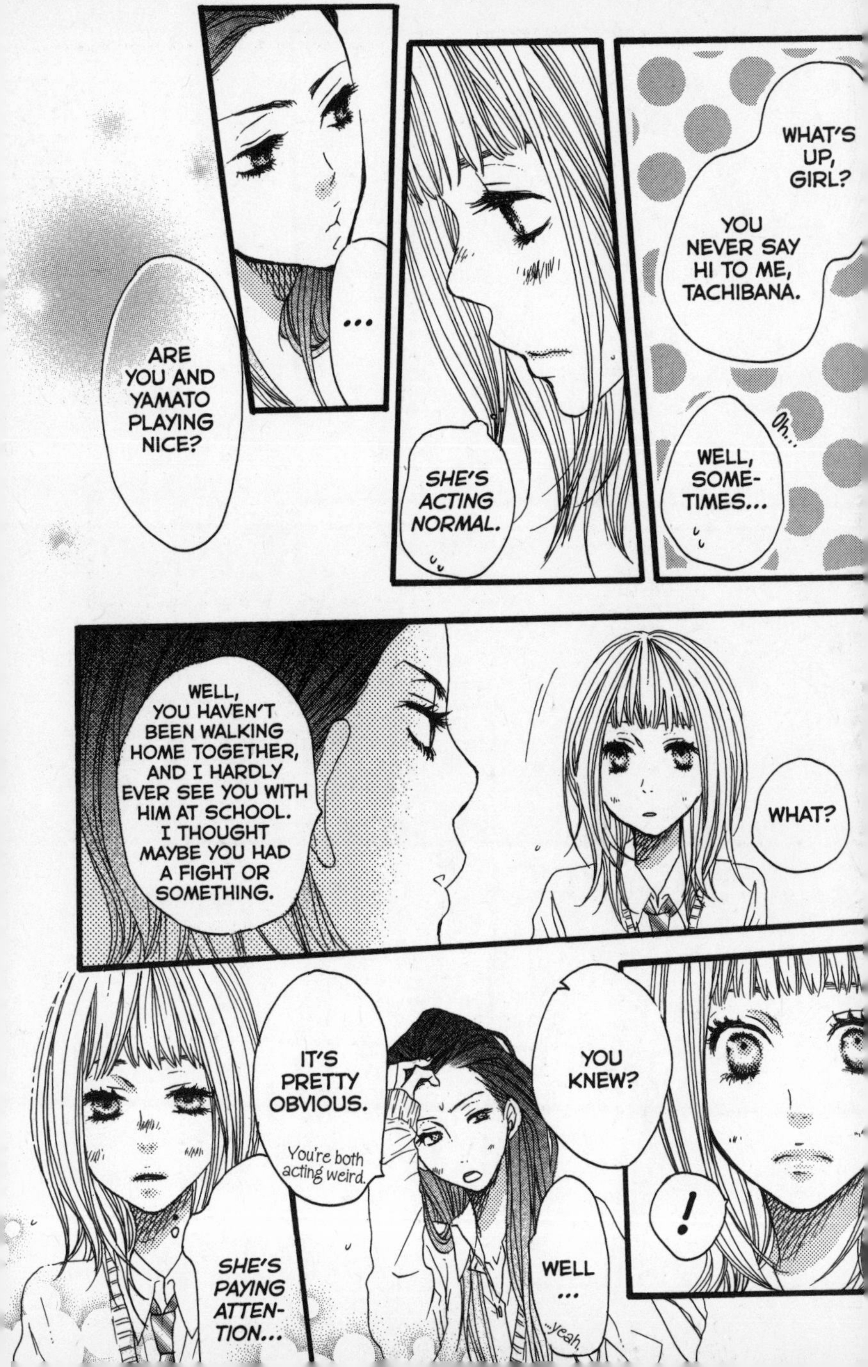
WHAT'S UP, GIRL?
YOU NEVER SAY HI TO ME, TACHIBANA.
Oh...
WELL, SOME-TIMES...
SHE'S ACTING NORMAL.
...
ARE YOU AND YAMATO PLAYING NICE?
WHAT?
WELL, YOU HAVEN'T BEEN WALKING HOME TOGETHER, AND I HARDLY EVER SEE YOU WITH HIM AT SCHOOL. I THOUGHT MAYBE YOU HAD A FIGHT OR SOMETHING.
YOU KNEW?
!
IT'S PRETTY OBVIOUS.
You're both acting weird.
WELL...
...yeah.
SHE'S PAYING ATTEN-TION...

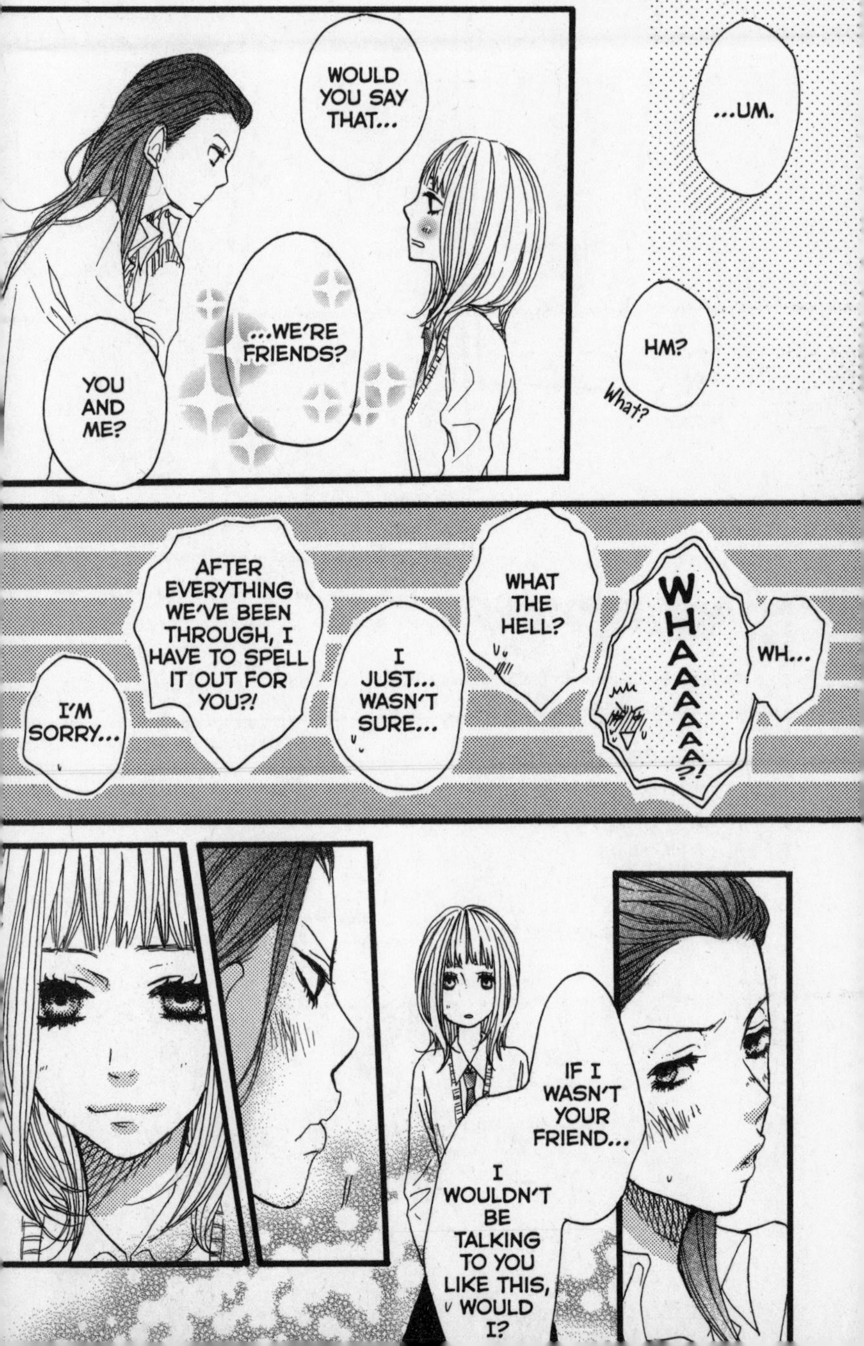
...UM.
HM?
What?
WOULD YOU SAY THAT...
...WE'RE FRIENDS?
YOU AND ME?
WH...
WHAAAAAA?!
WHAT THE HELL?
I JUST... WASN'T SURE...
AFTER EVERYTHING WE'VE BEEN THROUGH, I HAVE TO SPELL IT OUT FOR YOU?!
I'M SORRY...
IF I WASN'T YOUR FRIEND...
I WOULDN'T BE TALKING TO YOU LIKE THIS, WOULD I?

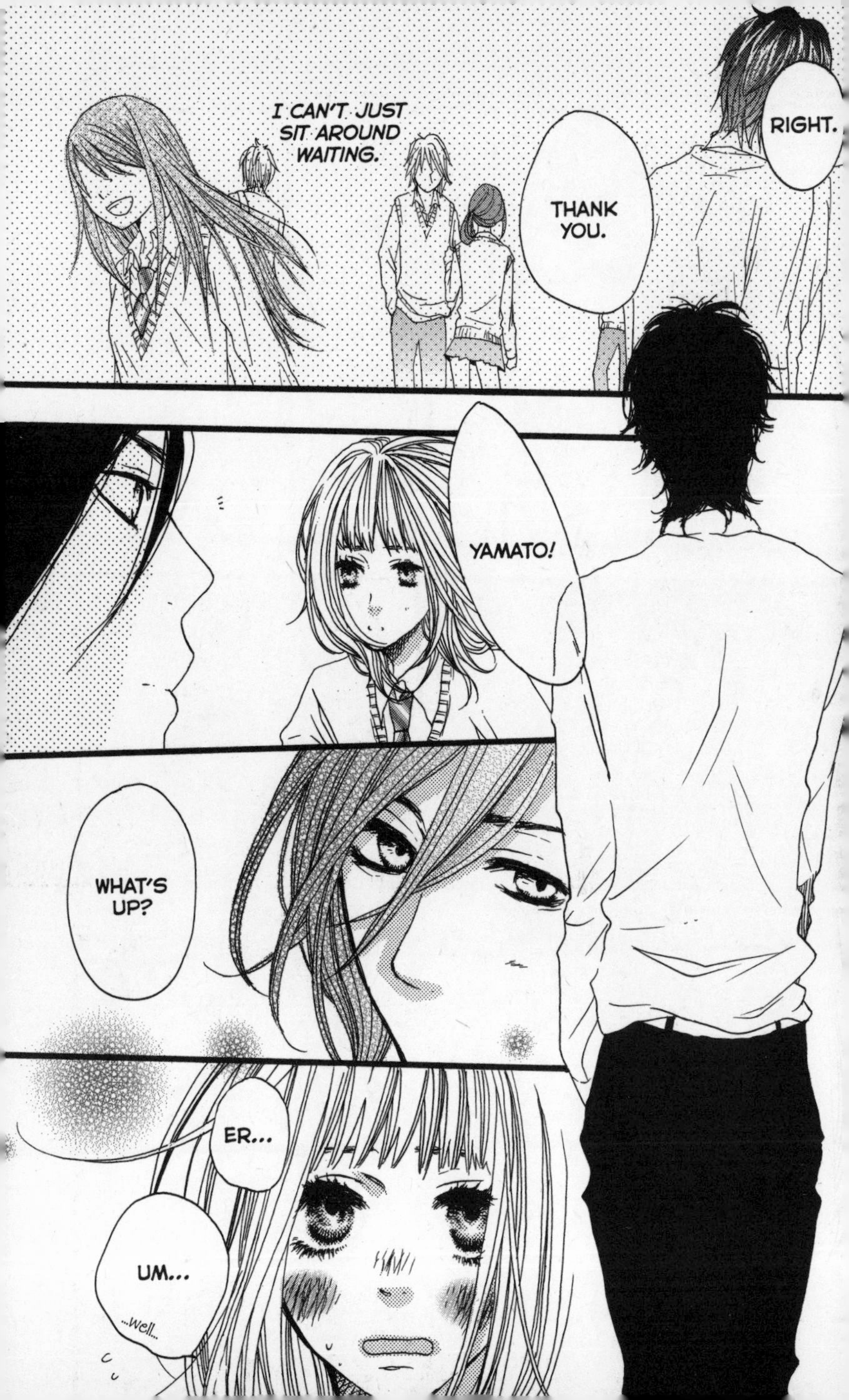
RIGHT.
THANK YOU.
I CAN'T JUST SIT AROUND WAITING.
YAMATO!
WHAT'S UP?
ER...
UM...
...well...

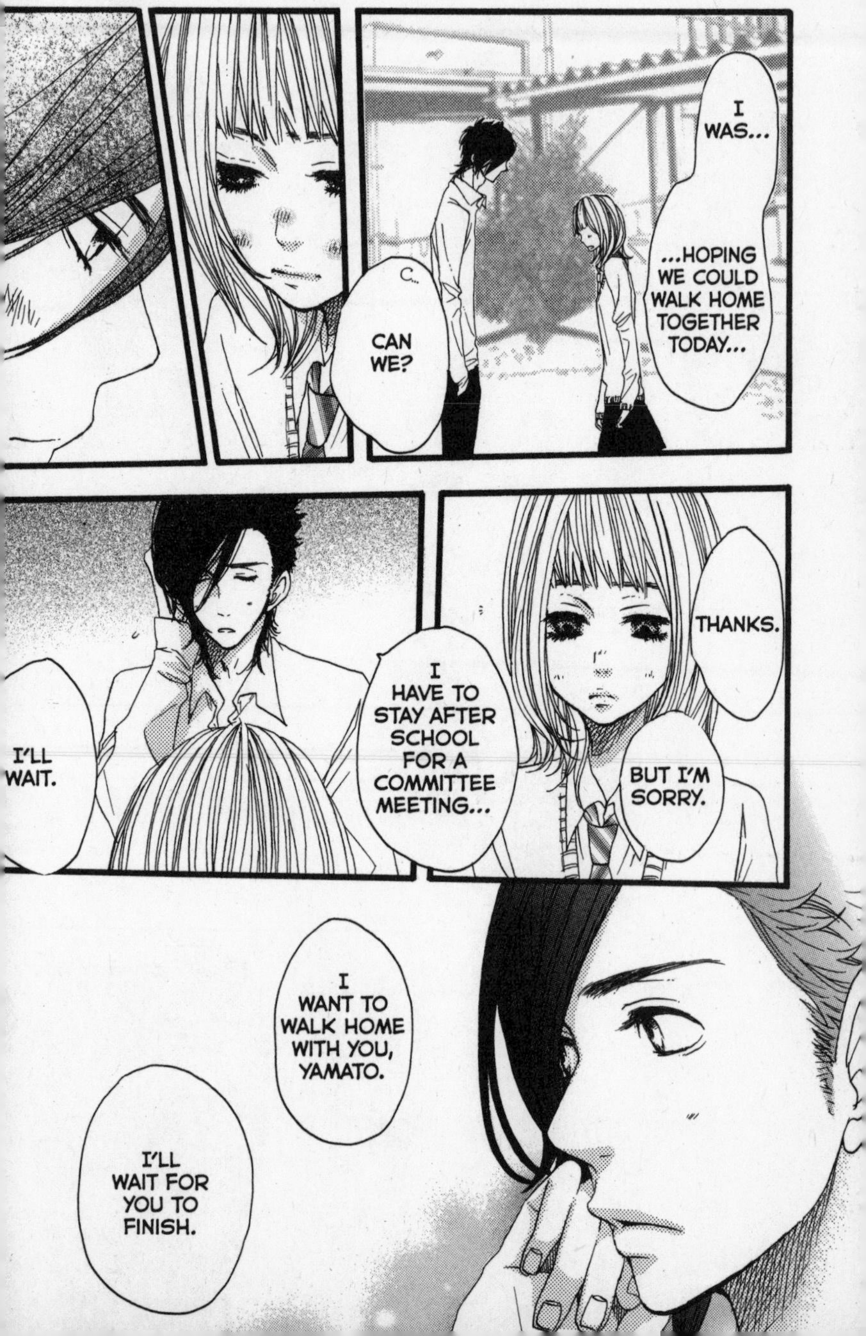
I WAS...
...HOPING WE COULD WALK HOME TOGETHER TODAY...
C..
CAN WE?
THANKS.
BUT I'M SORRY.
I HAVE TO STAY AFTER SCHOOL FOR A COMMITTEE MEETING...
I'LL WAIT.
I WANT TO WALK HOME WITH YOU, YAMATO.
I'LL WAIT FOR YOU TO FINISH.

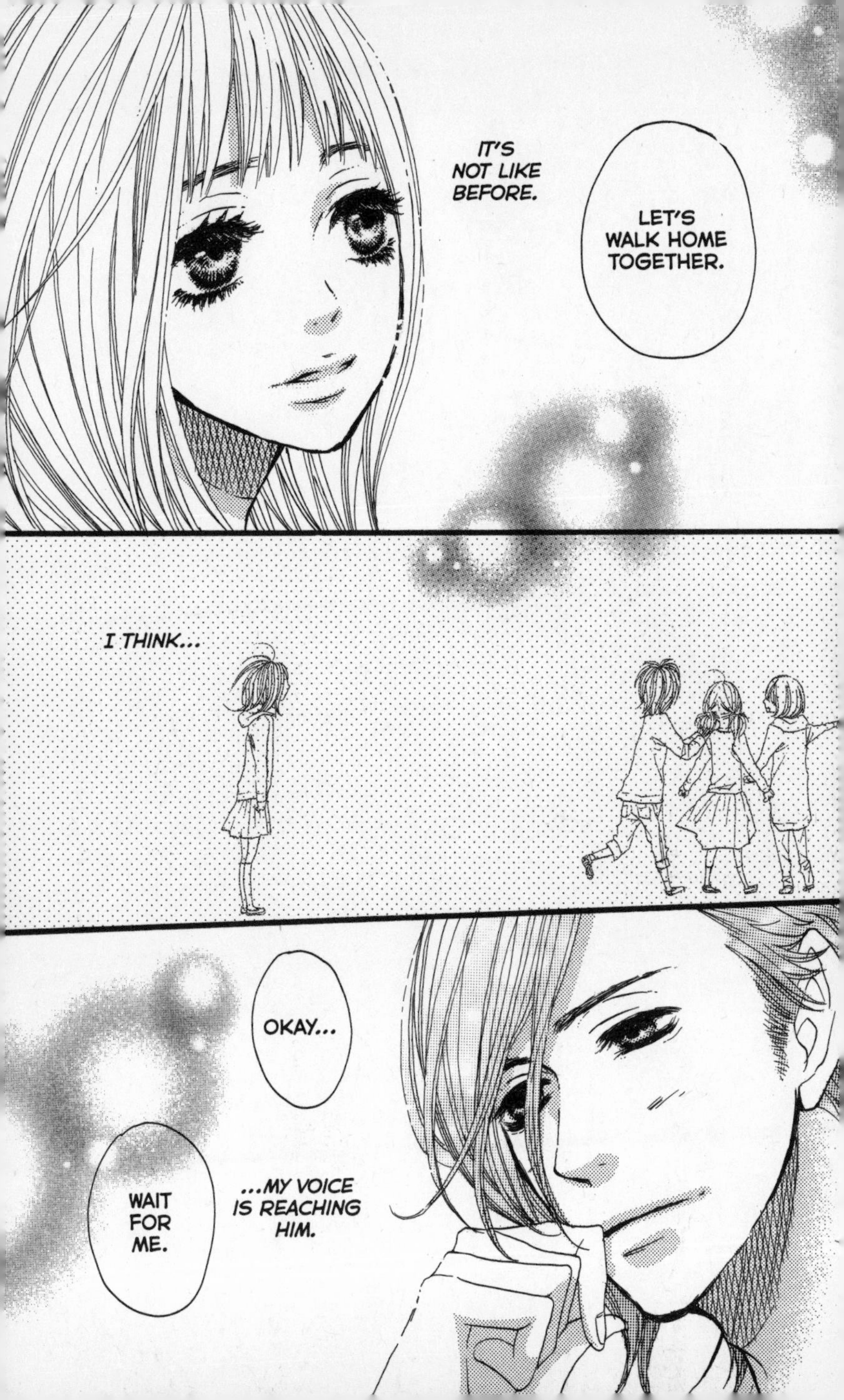
LET'S WALK HOME TOGETHER.
IT'S NOT LIKE BEFORE.
I THINK...
OKAY...
...MY VOICE IS REACHING HIM.
WAIT FOR ME.

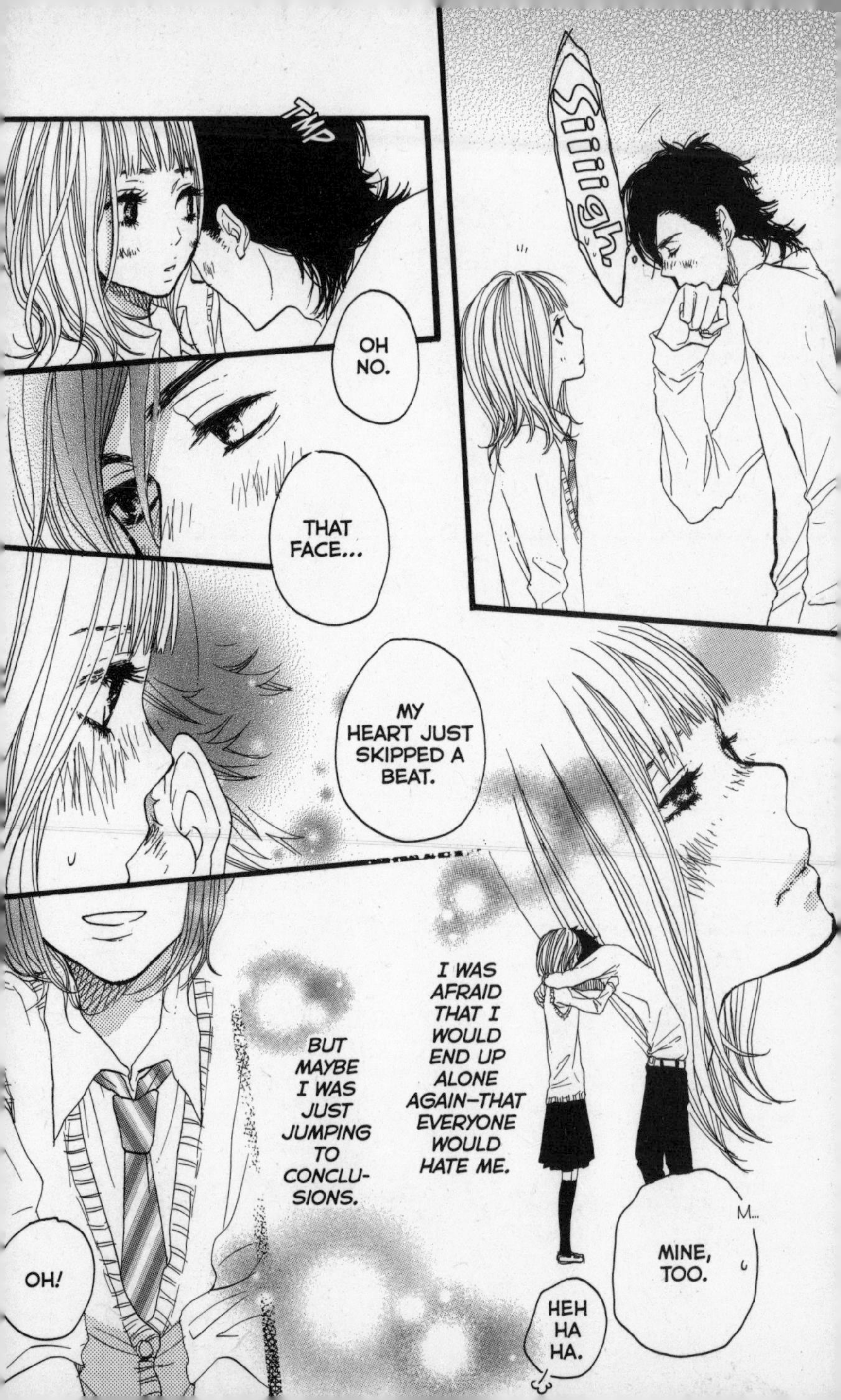
Siiiigh.
TMP
OH NO.
THAT FACE...
MY HEART JUST SKIPPED A BEAT.
M... MINE, TOO.
HEH HA HA.
I WAS AFRAID THAT I WOULD END UP ALONE AGAIN—THAT EVERYONE WOULD HATE ME.
BUT MAYBE I WAS JUST JUMPING TO CONCLU- SIONS.
OH!

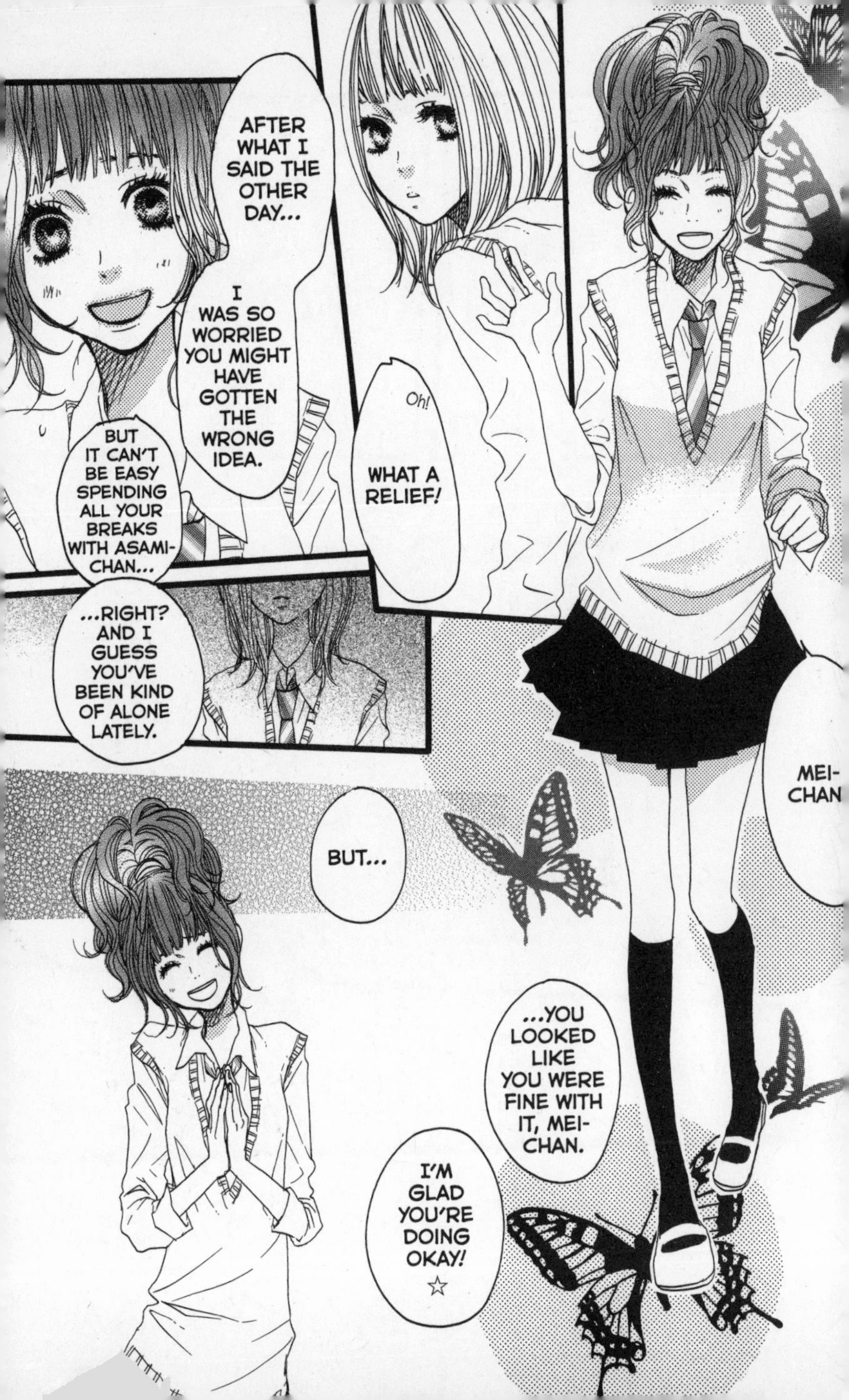
MEI-CHAN
AFTER WHAT I SAID THE OTHER DAY...
I WAS SO WORRIED YOU MIGHT HAVE GOTTEN THE WRONG IDEA.
BUT IT CAN'T BE EASY SPENDING ALL YOUR BREAKS WITH ASAMI-CHAN...
...RIGHT? AND I GUESS YOU'VE BEEN KIND OF ALONE LATELY.
BUT...
...YOU LOOKED LIKE YOU WERE FINE WITH IT, MEI-CHAN.
Oh!
WHAT A RELIEF!
I'M GLAD YOU'RE DOING OKAY! ☆

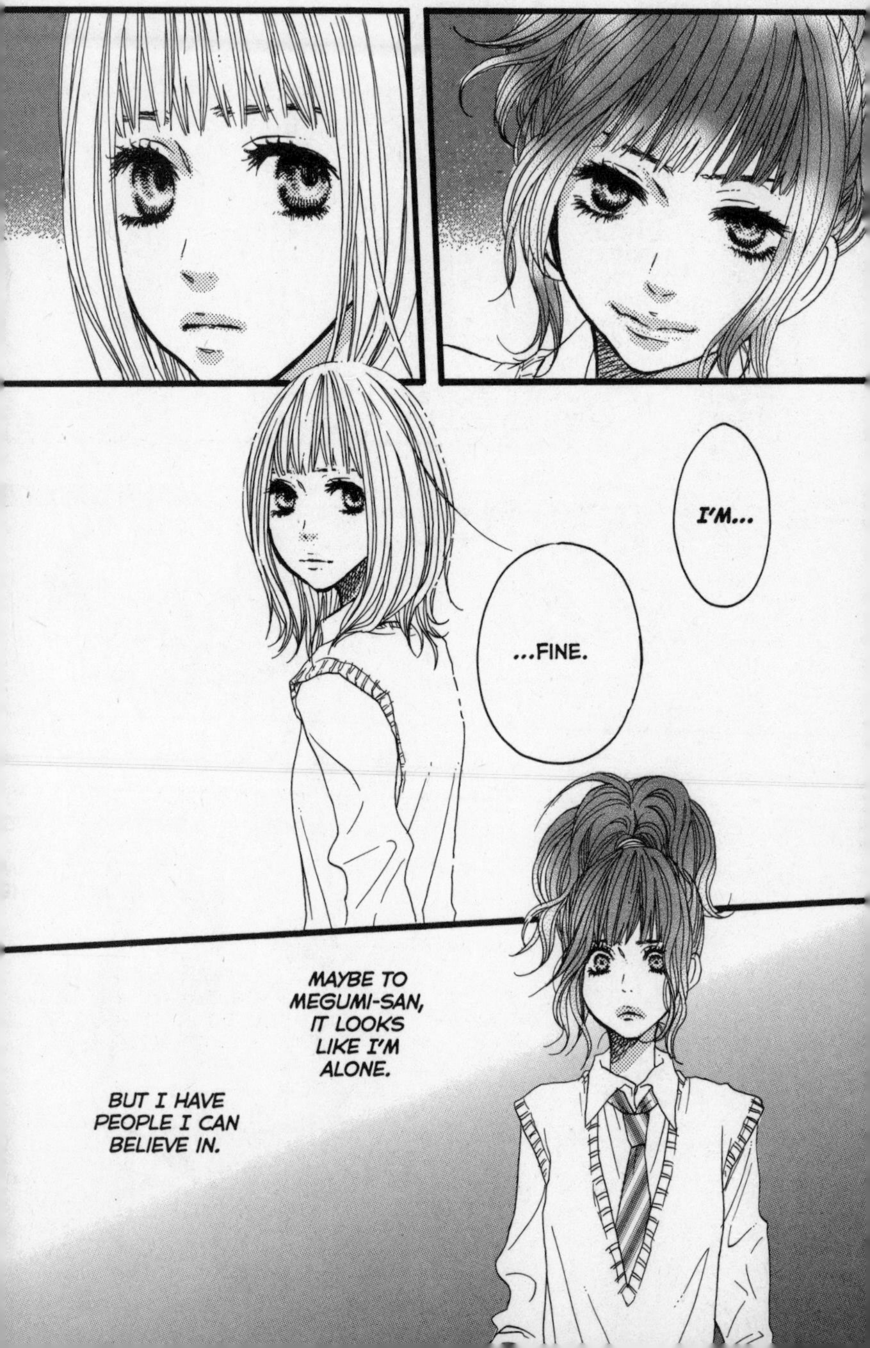
I'M...
...FINE.
MAYBE TO MEGUMI-SAN, IT LOOKS LIKE I'M ALONE.
BUT I HAVE PEOPLE I CAN BELIEVE IN.

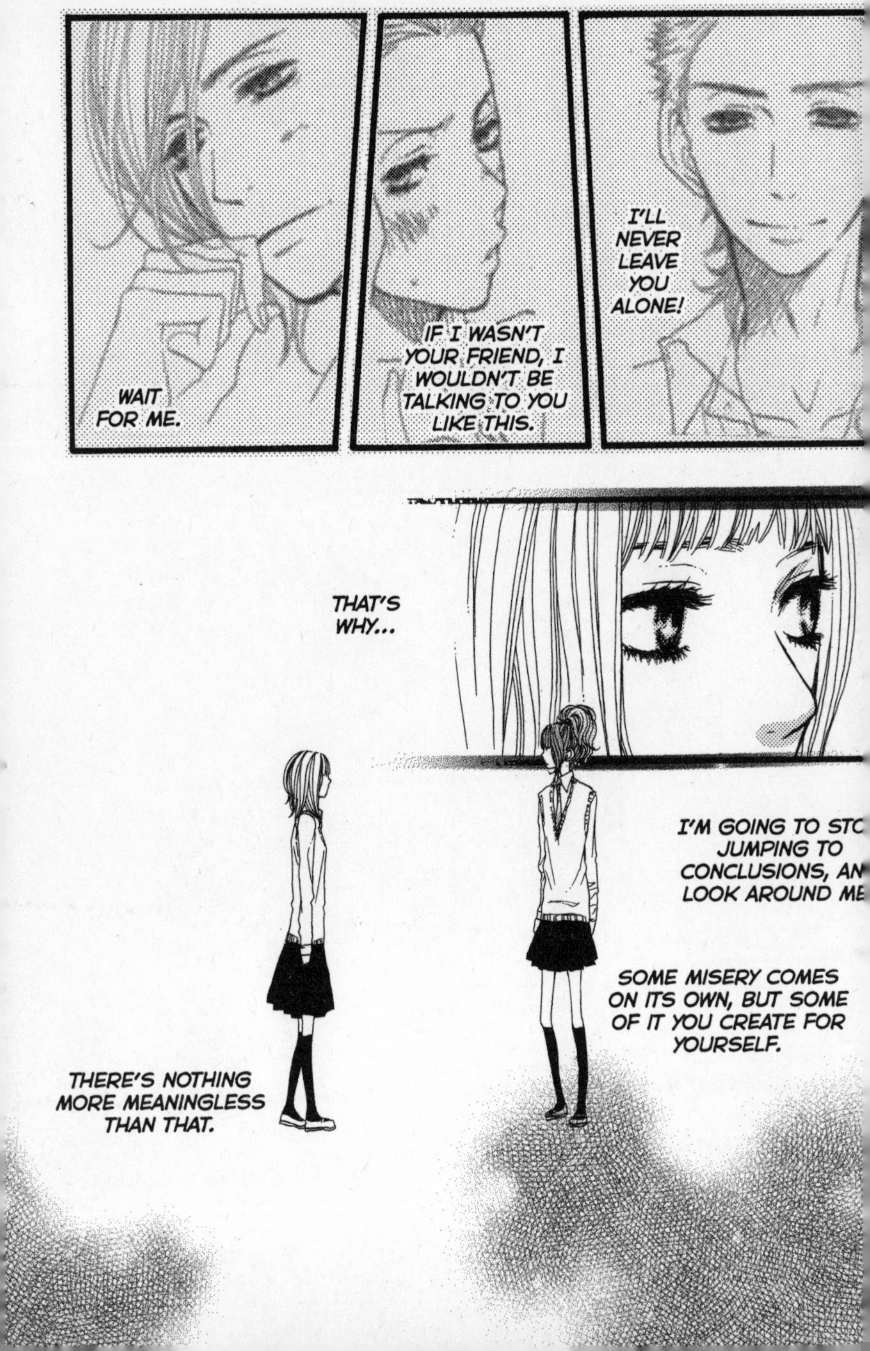
I'LL NEVER LEAVE YOU ALONE!
IF I WASN'T YOUR FRIEND, I WOULDN'T BE TALKING TO YOU LIKE THIS.
WAIT FOR ME.
THAT'S WHY...
I'M GOING TO ST
JUMPING TO
CONCLUSIONS, A
LOOK AROUND M
SOME MISERY COMES ON ITS OWN, BUT SOME OF IT YOU CREATE FOR YOURSELF.
THERE'S NOTHING MORE MEANINGLESS THAN THAT.

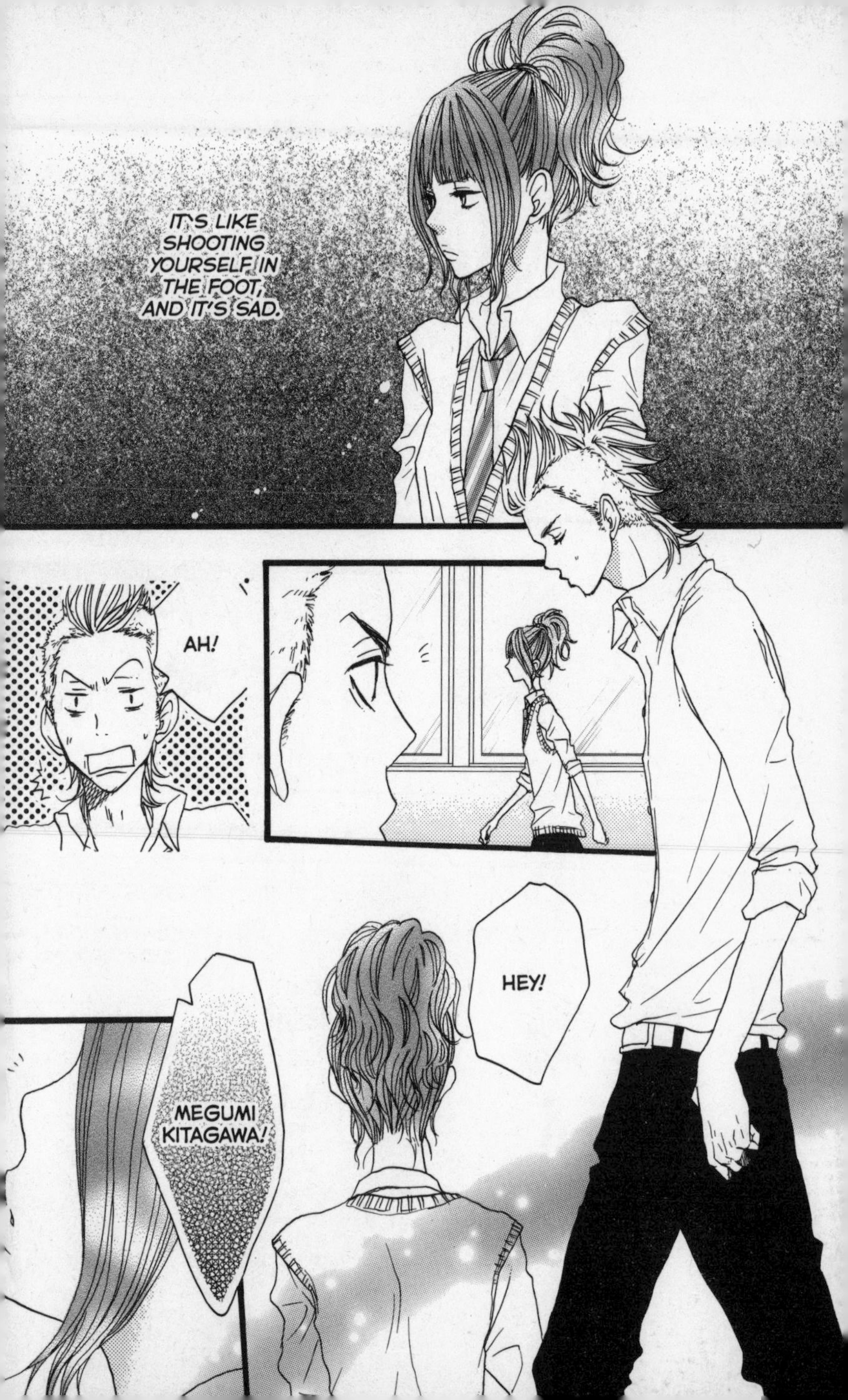
IT'S LIKE SHOOTING YOURSELF IN THE FOOT, AND IT'S SAD.
AH!
HEY!
MEGUMI KITAGAWA!

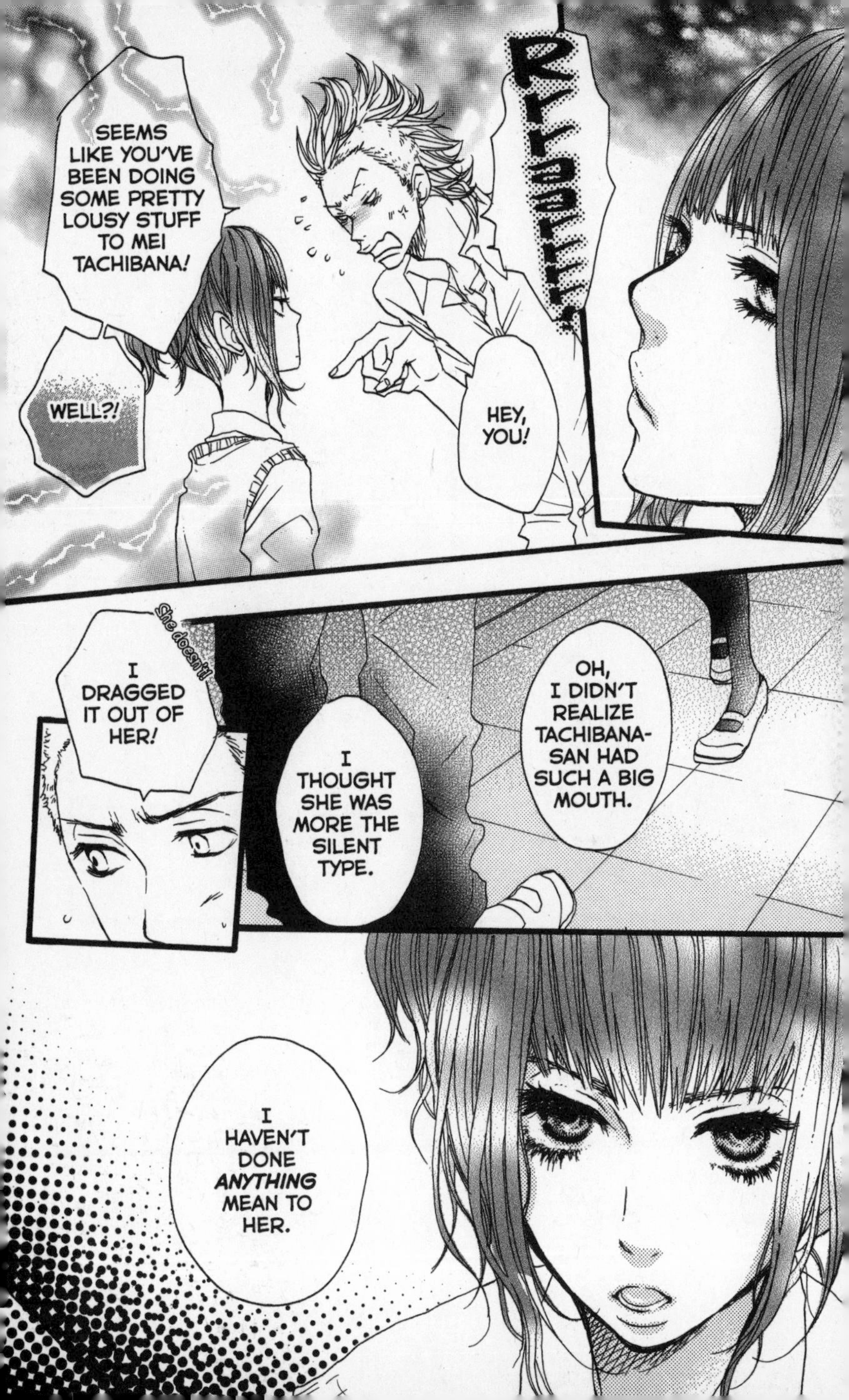
HEY, YOU!
SEEMS LIKE YOU'VE BEEN DOING SOME PRETTY LOUSY STUFF TO MEI TACHIBANA!
WELL?!
OH, I DIDN'T REALIZE TACHIBANA-SAN HAD SUCH A BIG MOUTH.
I THOUGHT SHE WAS MORE THE SILENT TYPE.
She doesn't!
I DRAGGED IT OUT OF HER!
I HAVEN'T DONE *ANYTHING* MEAN TO HER.

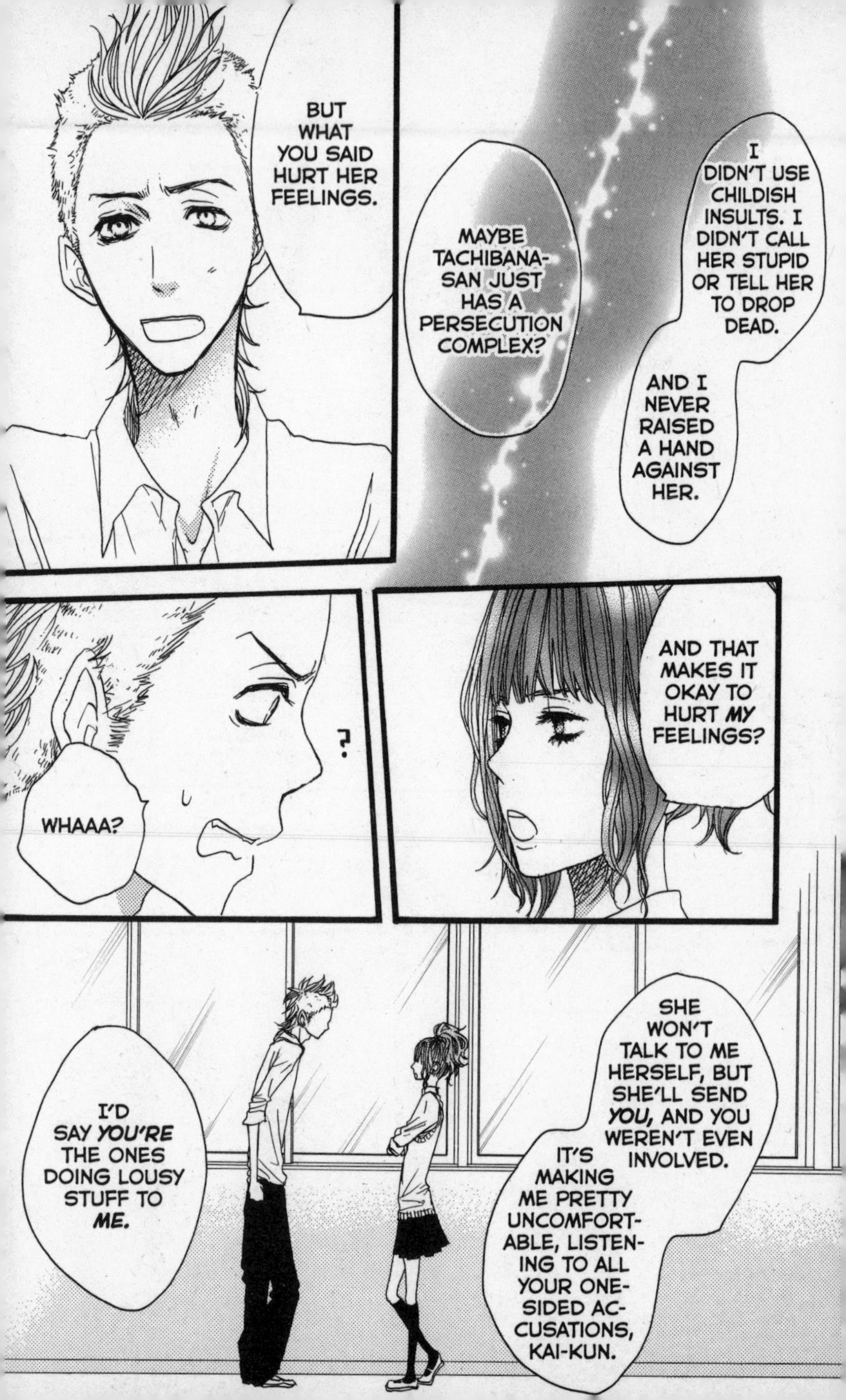
I DIDN'T USE CHILDISH INSULTS. I DIDN'T CALL HER STUPID OR TELL HER TO DROP DEAD.
AND I NEVER RAISED A HAND AGAINST HER.
MAYBE TACHIBANA-SAN JUST HAS A PERSECUTION COMPLEX?
BUT WHAT YOU SAID HURT HER FEELINGS.
AND THAT MAKES IT OKAY TO HURT *MY* FEELINGS?
?
WHAAA?
SHE WON'T TALK TO ME HERSELF, BUT SHE'LL SEND *YOU,* AND YOU WEREN'T EVEN INVOLVED.
IT'S MAKING ME PRETTY UNCOMFORTABLE, LISTENING TO ALL YOUR ONE-SIDED ACCUSATIONS, KAI-KUN.
I'D SAY *YOU'RE* THE ONES DOING LOUSY STUFF TO *ME.*

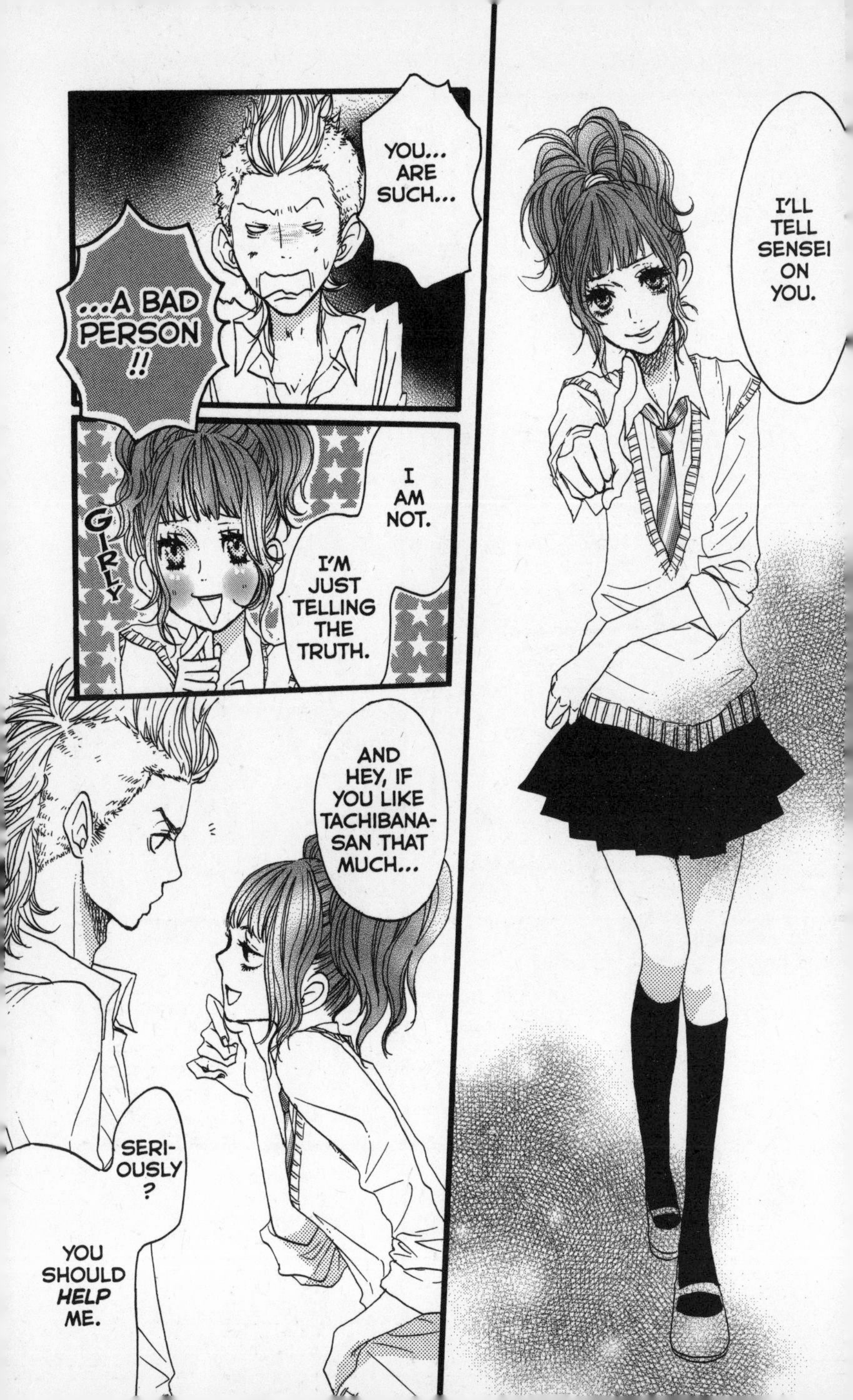
I'LL TELL SENSEI ON YOU.
YOU... ARE SUCH...
...A BAD PERSON!!
I AM NOT.
GIRLY
I'M JUST TELLING THE TRUTH.
AND HEY, IF YOU LIKE TACHIBANA-SAN THAT MUCH...
SERI-OUSLY?
YOU SHOULD *HELP* ME.

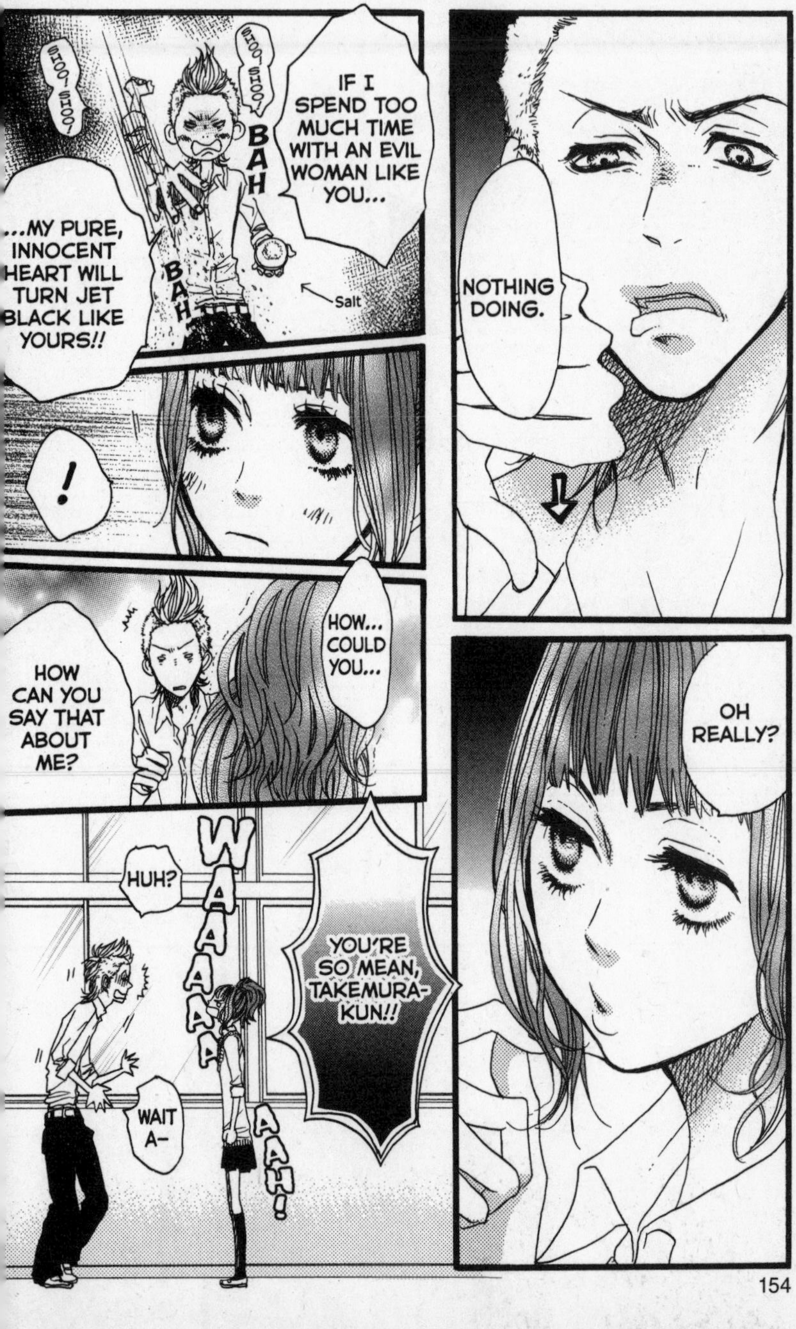
NOTHING DOING.
IF I SPEND TOO MUCH TIME WITH AN EVIL WOMAN LIKE YOU...
SHOO! SHOO!
BAH
SHOO! SHOO!
...MY PURE, INNOCENT HEART WILL TURN JET BLACK LIKE YOURS!!
BAH
Salt
!
OH REALLY?
HOW... COULD YOU...
HOW CAN YOU SAY THAT ABOUT ME?
WAAAAAAH
YOU'RE SO MEAN, TAKEMURA-KUN!!
HUH?
WAIT A-
AAAH!

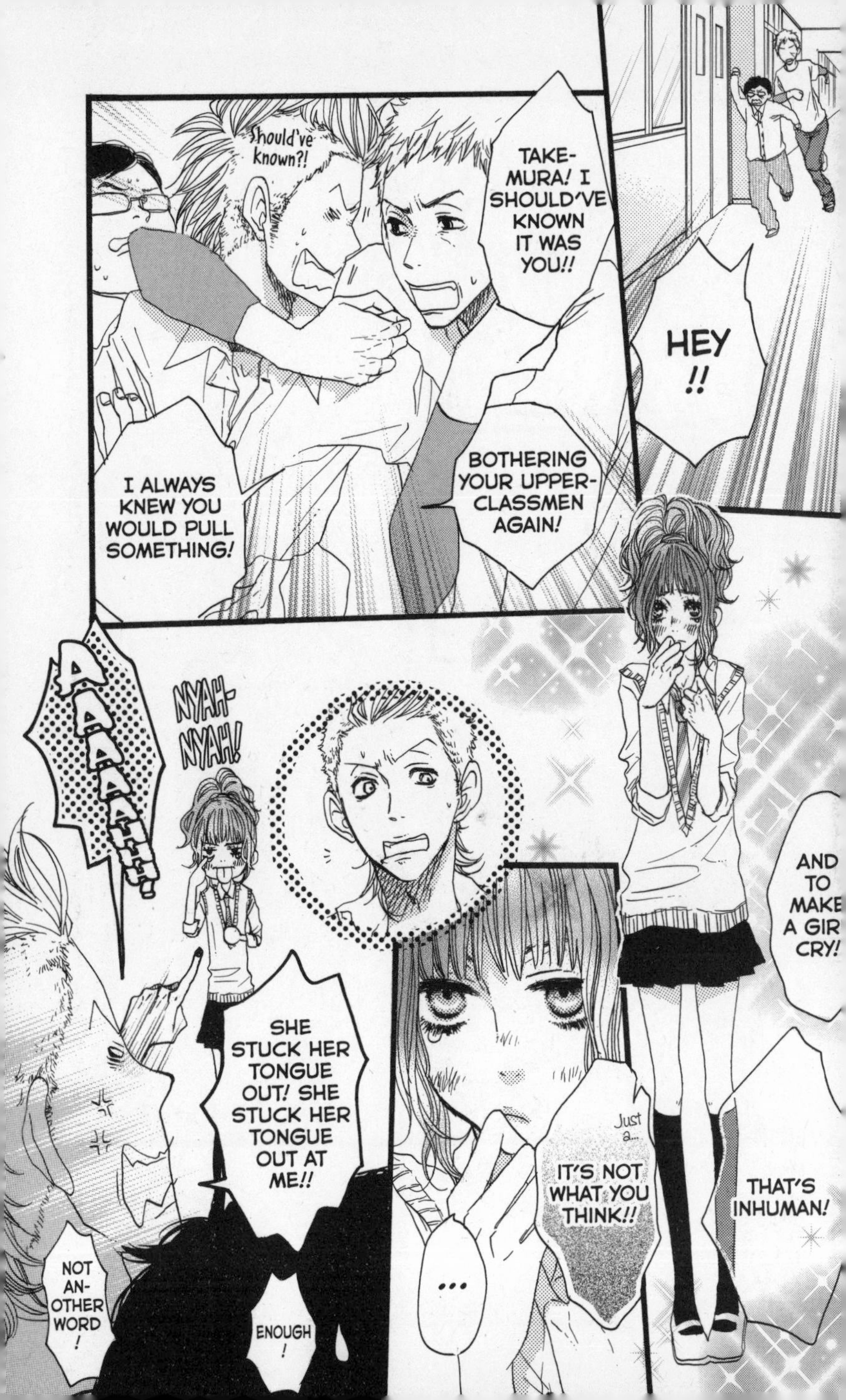
HEY!!
TAKE-MURA! I SHOULD'VE KNOWN IT WAS YOU!!
Should've known?!
BOTHERING YOUR UPPER-CLASSMEN AGAIN!
I ALWAYS KNEW YOU WOULD PULL SOMETHING!
AND TO MAKE A GIR CRY!
THAT'S INHUMAN!
Just a...
IT'S NOT WHAT YOU THINK!!
...
AAAAAHH
NYAH-NYAH!
SHE STUCK HER TONGUE OUT! SHE STUCK HER TONGUE OUT AT ME!!
ENOUGH!
NOT AN-OTHER WORD!

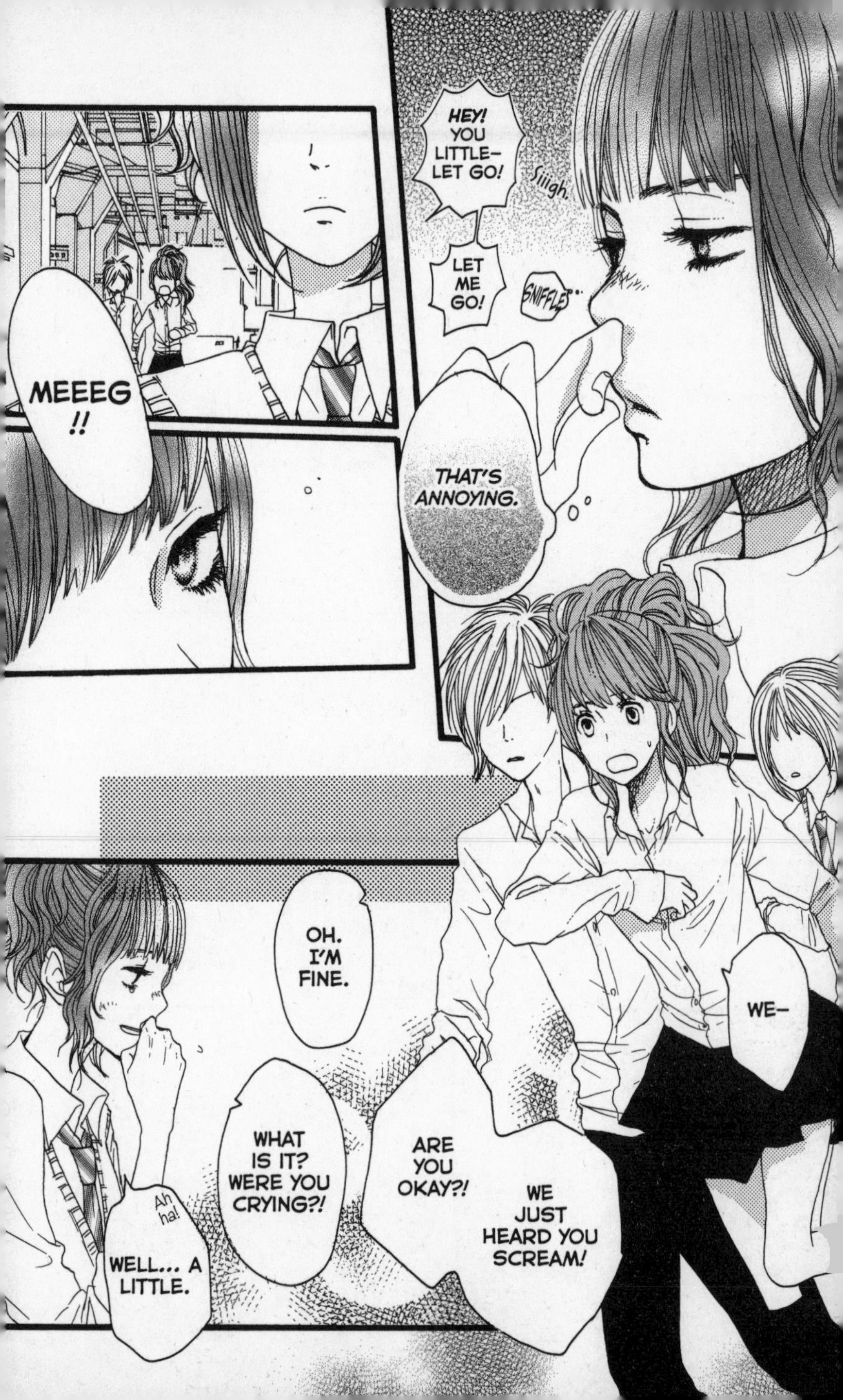

HEY! YOU LITTLE– LET GO!
Siiigh.
LET ME GO!
SNIFFLE...
THAT'S ANNOYING.
MEEEG !!
WE–
WE JUST HEARD YOU SCREAM!
ARE YOU OKAY?!
WHAT IS IT? WERE YOU CRYING?!
OH. I'M FINE.
Ah ha!
WELL... A LITTLE.

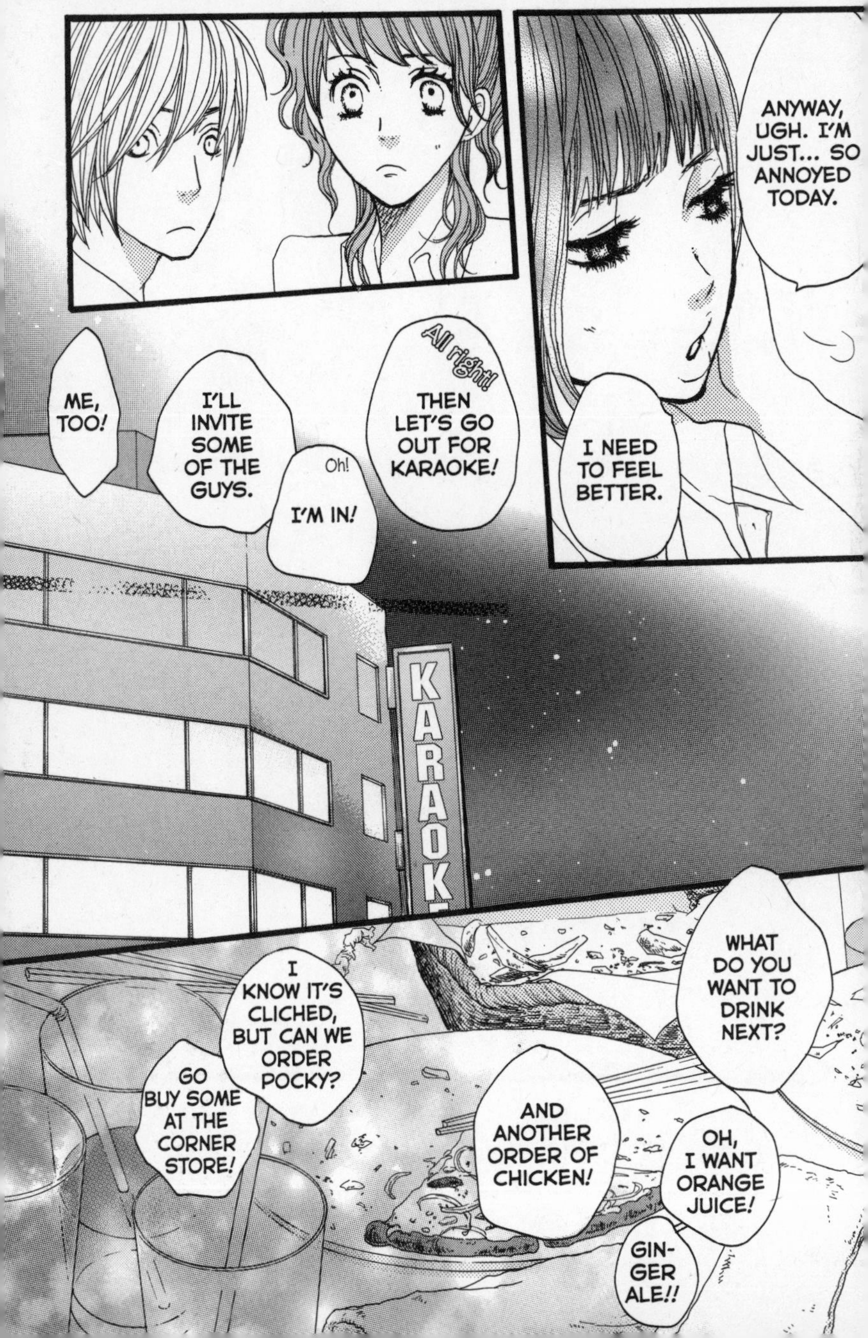
ANYWAY, UGH. I'M JUST... SO ANNOYED TODAY.
I NEED TO FEEL BETTER.
All right!
THEN LET'S GO OUT FOR KARAOKE!
Oh!
I'M IN!
I'LL INVITE SOME OF THE GUYS.
ME, TOO!
KARAOKE
WHAT DO YOU WANT TO DRINK NEXT?
OH, I WANT ORANGE JUICE!
GIN-GER ALE!!
AND ANOTHER ORDER OF CHICKEN!
I KNOW IT'S CLICHED, BUT CAN WE ORDER POCKY?
GO BUY SOME AT THE CORNER STORE!

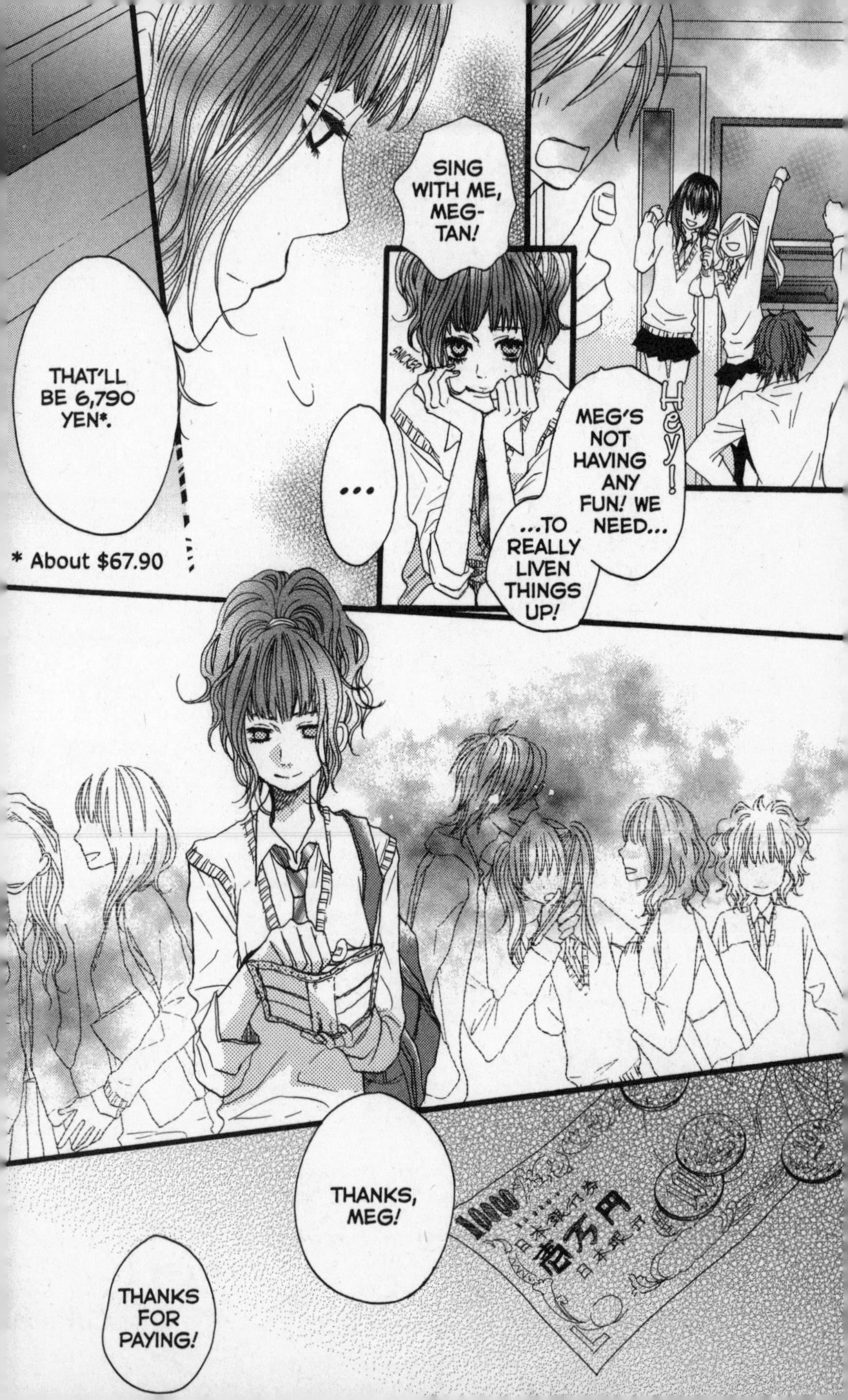
SING WITH ME, MEG-TAN!
Hey!
MEG'S NOT HAVING ANY FUN! WE NEED...
...TO REALLY LIVEN THINGS UP!
SNICKER
...
THAT'LL BE 6,790 YEN*.
THANKS, MEG!
THANKS FOR PAYING!

* About $67.90

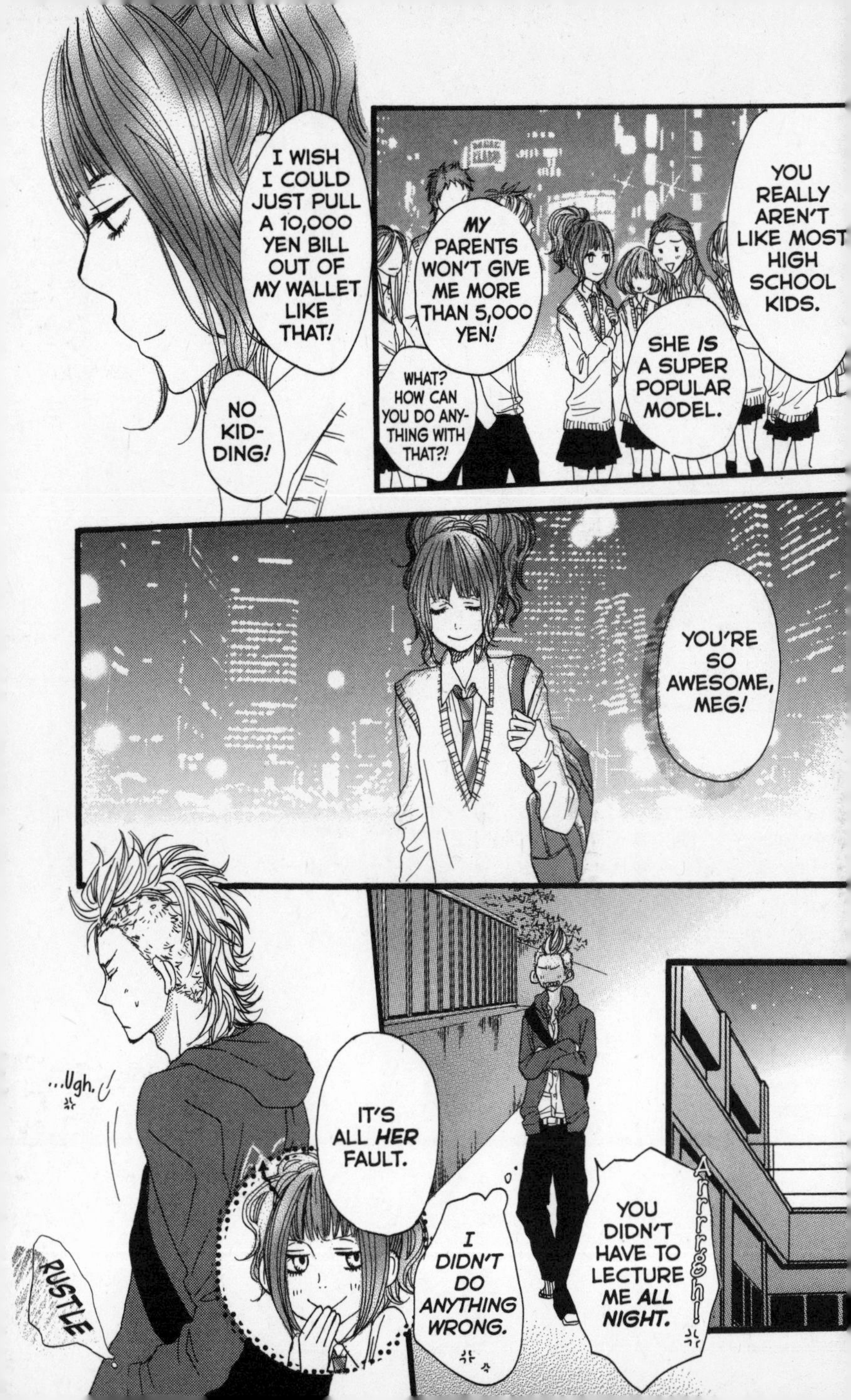
YOU REALLY AREN'T LIKE MOST HIGH SCHOOL KIDS.
SHE IS A SUPER POPULAR MODEL.
MY PARENTS WON'T GIVE ME MORE THAN 5,000 YEN!
WHAT? HOW CAN YOU DO ANYTHING WITH THAT?!
I WISH I COULD JUST PULL A 10,000 YEN BILL OUT OF MY WALLET LIKE THAT!
NO KIDDING!
YOU'RE SO AWESOME, MEG!
Arrrgh!
YOU DIDN'T HAVE TO LECTURE ME ALL NIGHT.
I DIDN'T DO ANYTHING WRONG.
IT'S ALL HER FAULT.
...Ugh.
RUSTLE

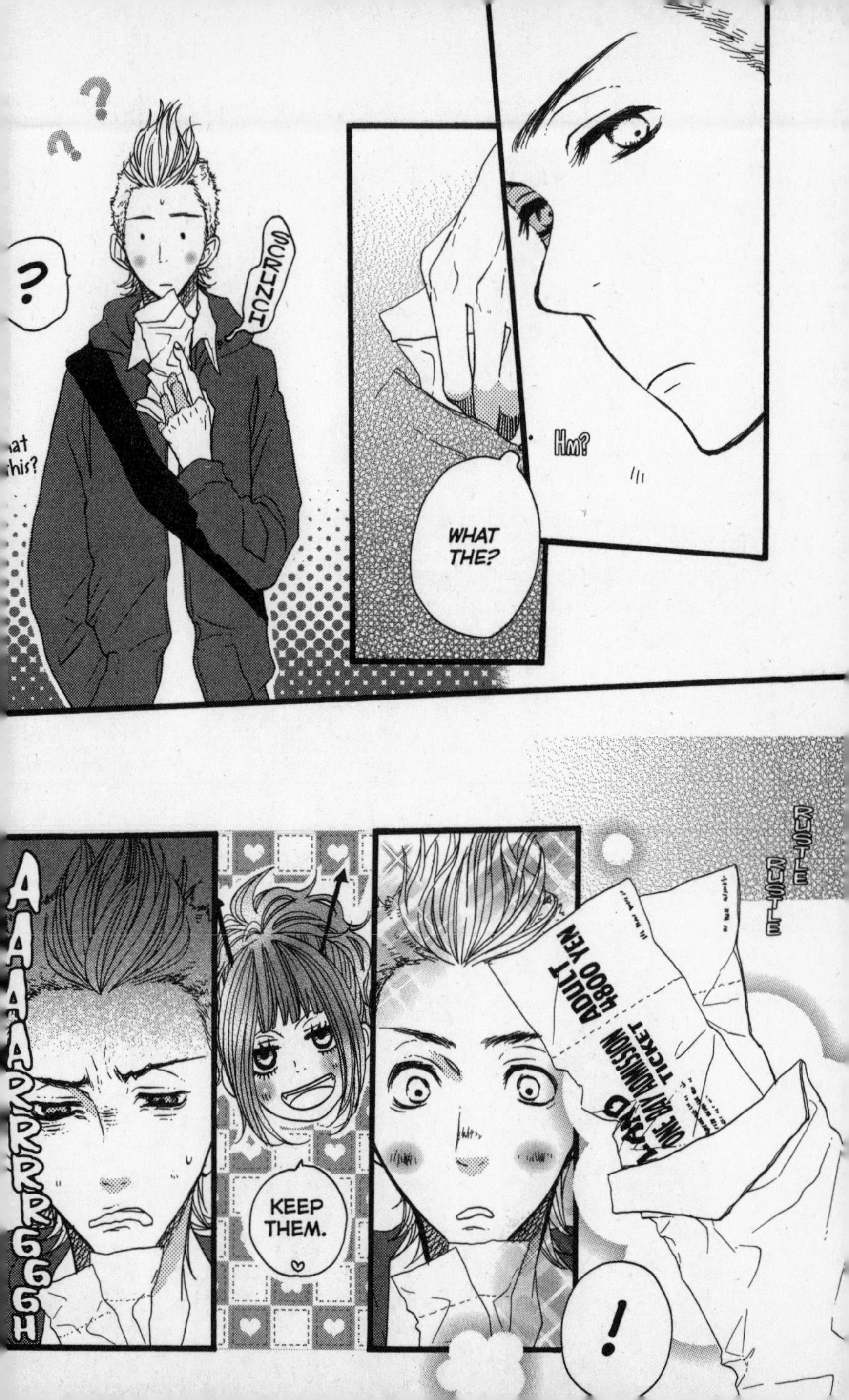
Hm?
WHAT THE?
SCRUNCH
?
RUSTLE
RUSTLE
LAND
ONE DAY ADMISSION TICKET
ADULT
4800 YEN
!
KEEP THEM.
AAAAARRRRGGGH

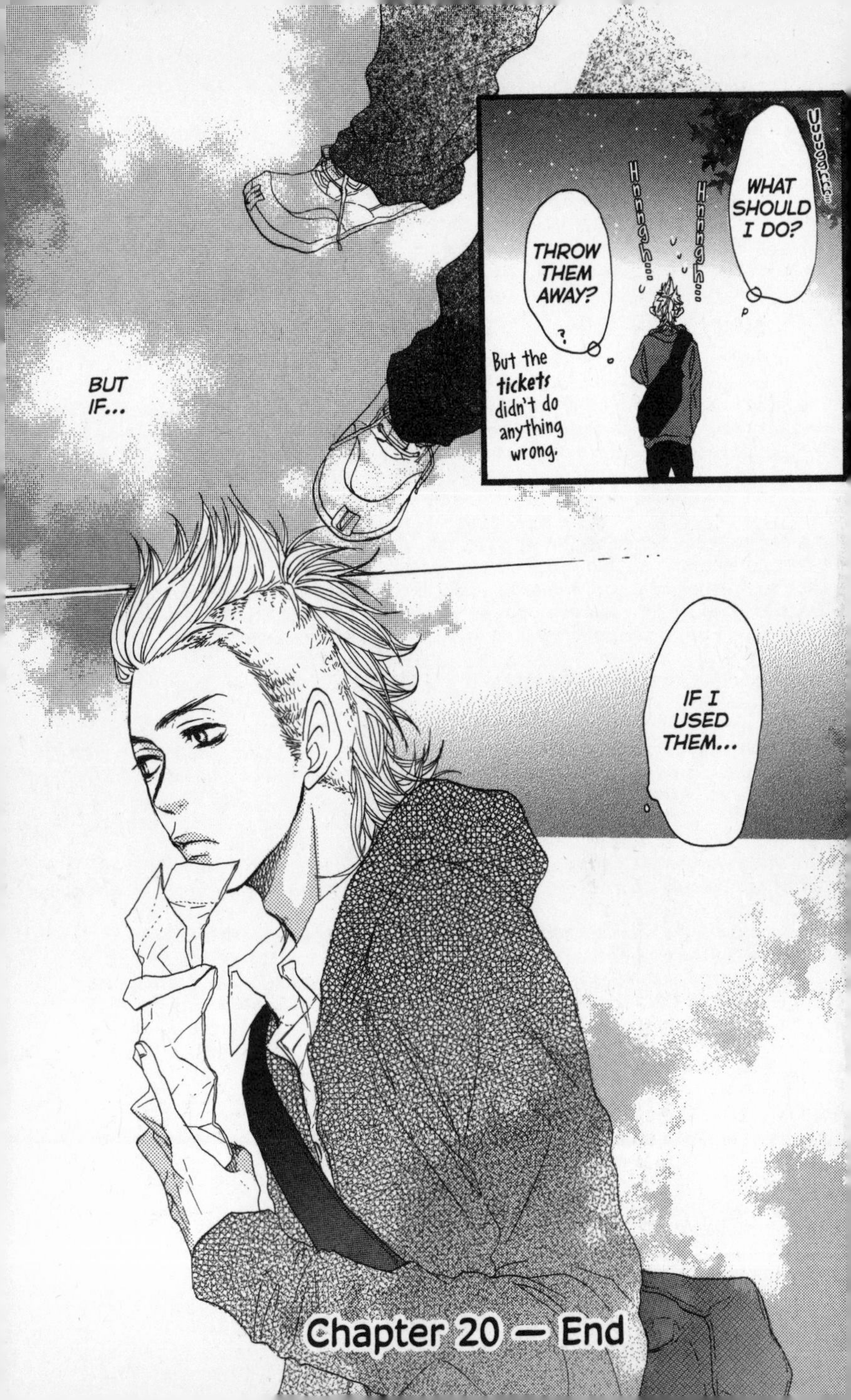
Uuuuggrrr...
WHAT SHOULD I DO?
Hnnngh...
Hnnngh...
THROW THEM AWAY?
But the tickets didn't do anything wrong.
BUT IF...
IF I USED THEM...
Chapter 20 — End

Hello, I'm Kanae Hazuki, and this is volume five. Time sure flies.

That reminds me, when volume four came out, I got to go to Tokyo and Yokohama for my first autograph sessions. I've been a manga artist for a while, but I never even dreamed that I would be asked to sign autographs; I didn't know if anyone would come, and it's not like I have a super cool autograph, so in my head, I was panicking a little. When my editor told me about it, I wondered if they really wanted me. But when I got to the venue, there was a line of readers who already had autograph tickets!!! I was so happy, but I was also really nervous, and my hand was shaking so badly I couldn't write a decent autograph, so I took forever.

Even so, you all still gave me kind words and waited patiently for me, and that made me really happy. And I loved all the treats and flowers you gave me. But in the end, what I love the most is all your heartfelt, handwritten letters! A lot of you wrote that my manga really got you thinking, or that you've been through the same things...and all kinds of stories about yourselves. That made me so, so very happy.

I think a lot of people out there have a hard time telling people about themselves. And there are even fewer people who can talk openly to people they've never met. But despite all that, you told me about yourselves, and I really appreciate that. Getting to meet all of you in person, and getting courage and energy from reading your letters really is the source of power for my manga. Thank you, thank you so much. I hope I get more opportunities to meet you all in person like this.

As for things that have been happening to me lately...

This has been a long-held dream of mine, but actually I bought a condo. I've lived in apartments up until now, and I thought it was about time I had a workroom. And of course, there's my mother. I may have written this before, but I was raised by a single mother. Then I reached a rebellious phase that went on forever, and I was always depending on her financially, so I really caused her a lot of grief. That went on, almost up until she died. I never got married, I never got a stable job, I never did anything worthwhile before I had to say goodbye to my mother. When I wondered where I would go from there, I remembered my mother when she was well.

The furniture she had was all abnormally large. The size of our home was not proportional to the size of the furniture. Not only that, but it was all designed to look big and imposing. Because of that, it felt very oppressive at home, and I was always mad about that. But thinking about it now, I don't have any memory, as far as I know, of living in a single-family home or a beautiful condo. Maybe my mother dreamed of one day owning a home. When I realized that, buying a home became my next clear goal. And this March, that dream became a reality.

I thought, "When I move, the first thing I want is for Mom to see the house." That being the case, even though it's been years since she passed away, I haven't had her entombed; I've kept her ashes with me. Next, I have to make a proper grave for my mother! The best one I can get!! Until then, I will keep drawing manga, so I can show her what I've done, and so that she can be proud in the next life to say that I'm her daughter.

I hope you'll keep reading!

—Kanae Hazuki, June 2010

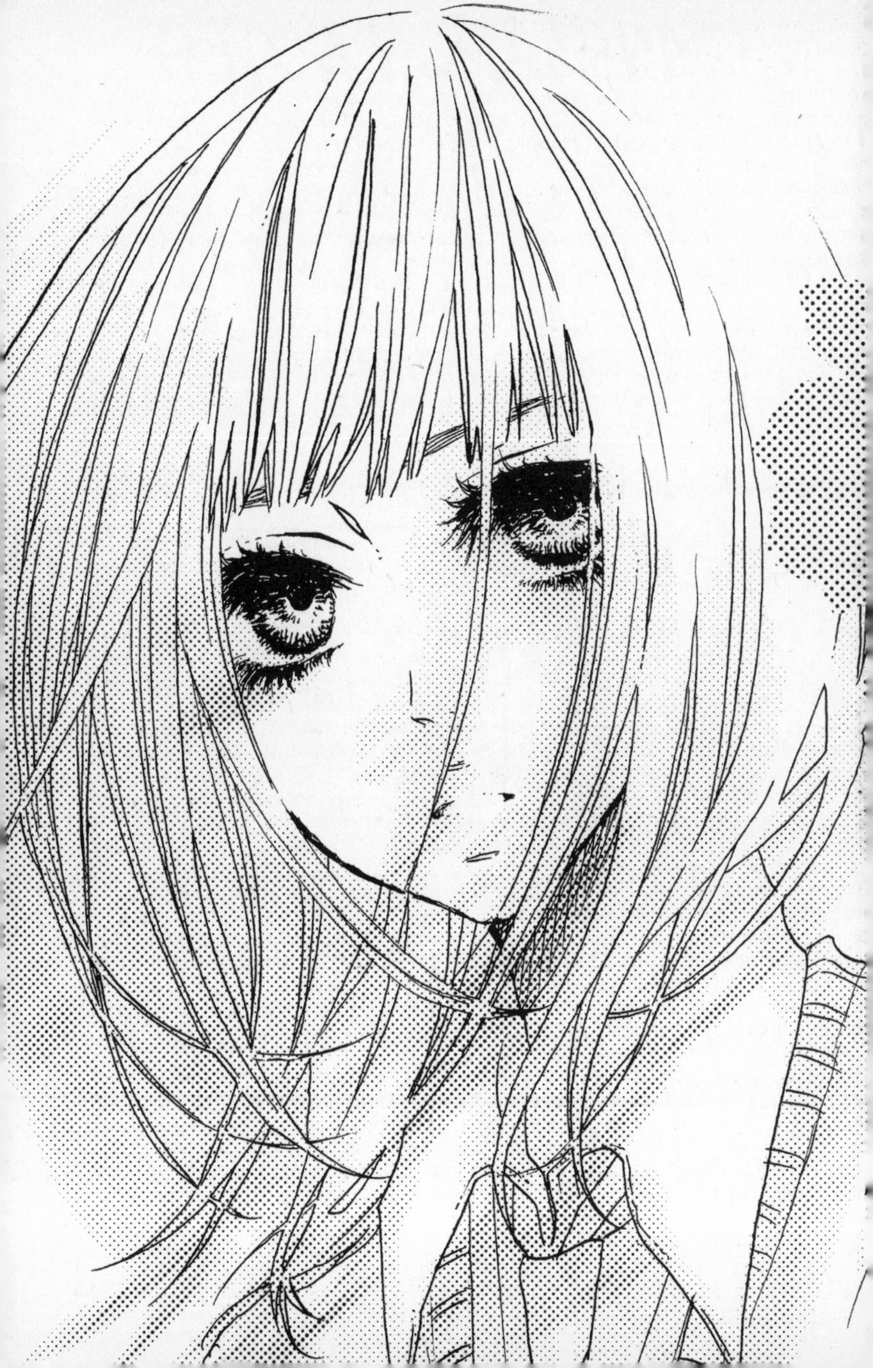

TRANSLATION NOTES

Page 8: Tirol chocolates

Although the name was partially redacted in the Japanese version, it would be obvious to most native Japanese readers that Tirol chocolates are the treat in question. Tirol chocolates are small chocolates that cost 20 or 30 yen, and come in a variety of flavors and packaging, thus making them quite collectible. The main flavor is chocolate with a coffee-nougat center.

Page 24: PDAs

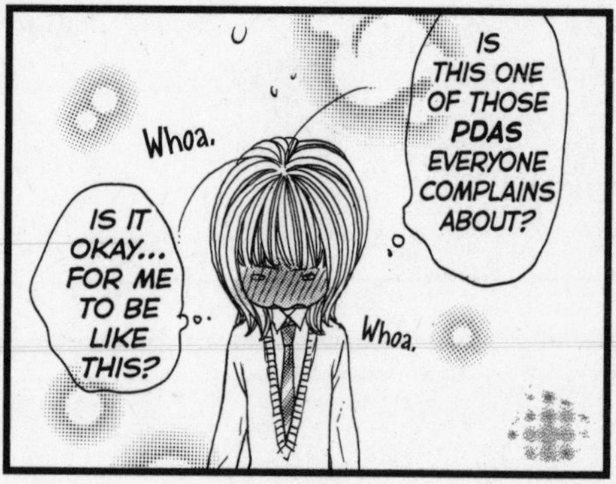
IS THIS ONE OF THOSE PDAS EVERYONE COMPLAINS ABOUT?
Whoa.
Whoa.
IS IT OKAY... FOR ME TO BE LIKE THIS?

Most of our readers probably know that PDA stands for "public display of affection." The Japanese term Mei used is *bakappuru*, which doesn't refer to the display so much as the people performing it. It's a combination of the Japanese word *baka* (stupid) and the English "couple," Japan-ified to *kappuru*. The word refers to a couple that is overly affectionate in public, ergo a *bakappuru* is a couple that would annoy others into calling them stupid with their frequent PDA.

Page 46: Love a duck

This is an expression of surprise, which the translators chose because it has the word "duck" in it, and because surely Yamato is surprised at Kai's sudden confession. The original Japanese merely said "duck," or rather, a Japanese word for duck, kamo. Kamo is also short for "kamo shirenai," which is part of what Kai said to Yamato, and means "maybe," "I think," "I cannot know if," etc.

Say I Love You. 6

preview

The following pages contain a preview of *Say I Love You* Vol. 6, coming to print and digital formats from Kodansha Comics in February 2015. Check out our website for more details!

KANAE HAZUKI

6

Say I Love You.

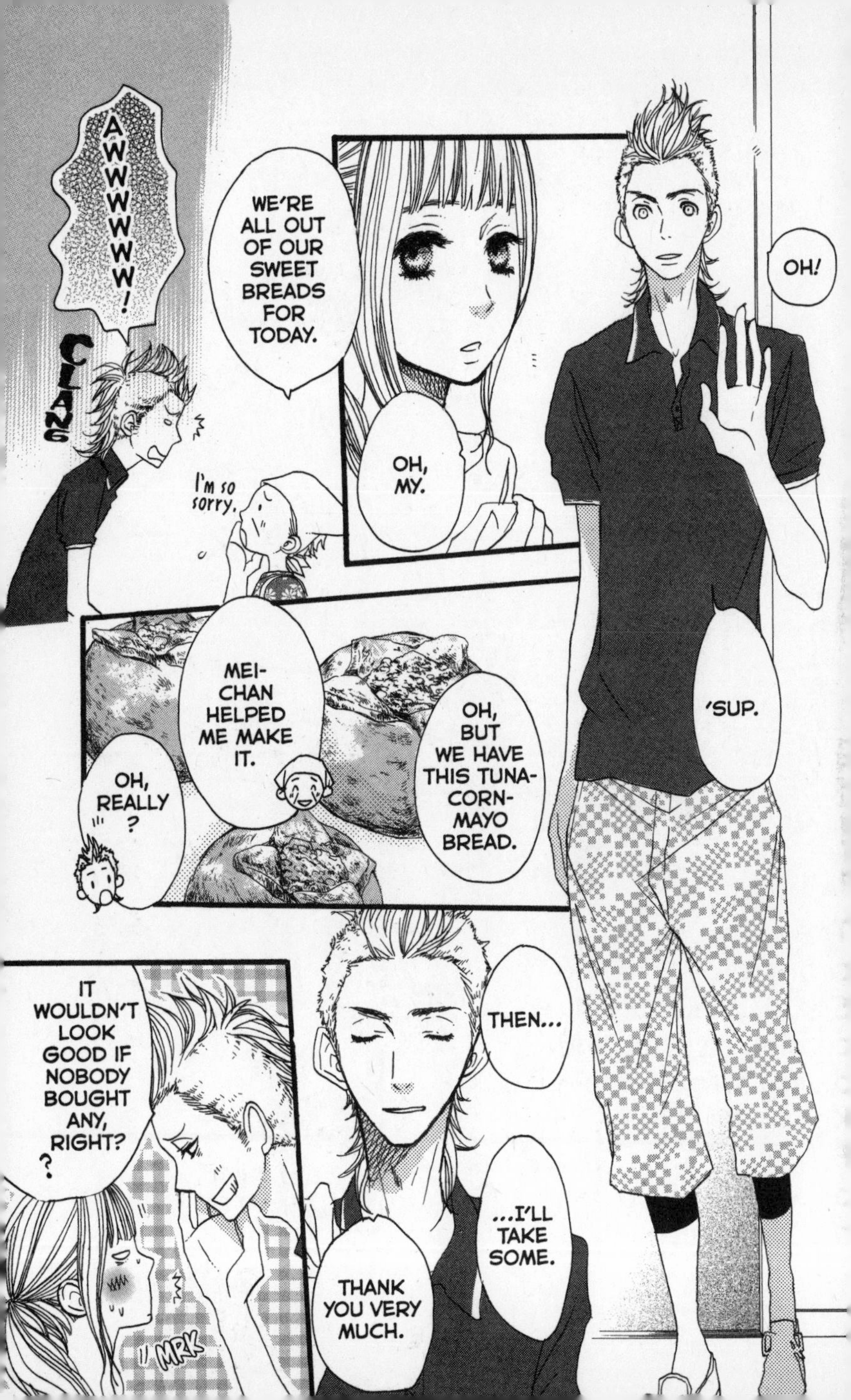
OH!
'SUP.
WE'RE ALL OUT OF OUR SWEET BREADS FOR TODAY.
OH, MY.
AWWWWWW!
CLANG
I'm so sorry.
OH, BUT WE HAVE THIS TUNA-CORN-MAYO BREAD.
MEI-CHAN HELPED ME MAKE IT.
OH, REALLY?
THEN...
...I'LL TAKE SOME.
THANK YOU VERY MUCH.
IT WOULDN'T LOOK GOOD IF NOBODY BOUGHT ANY, RIGHT?
MRK

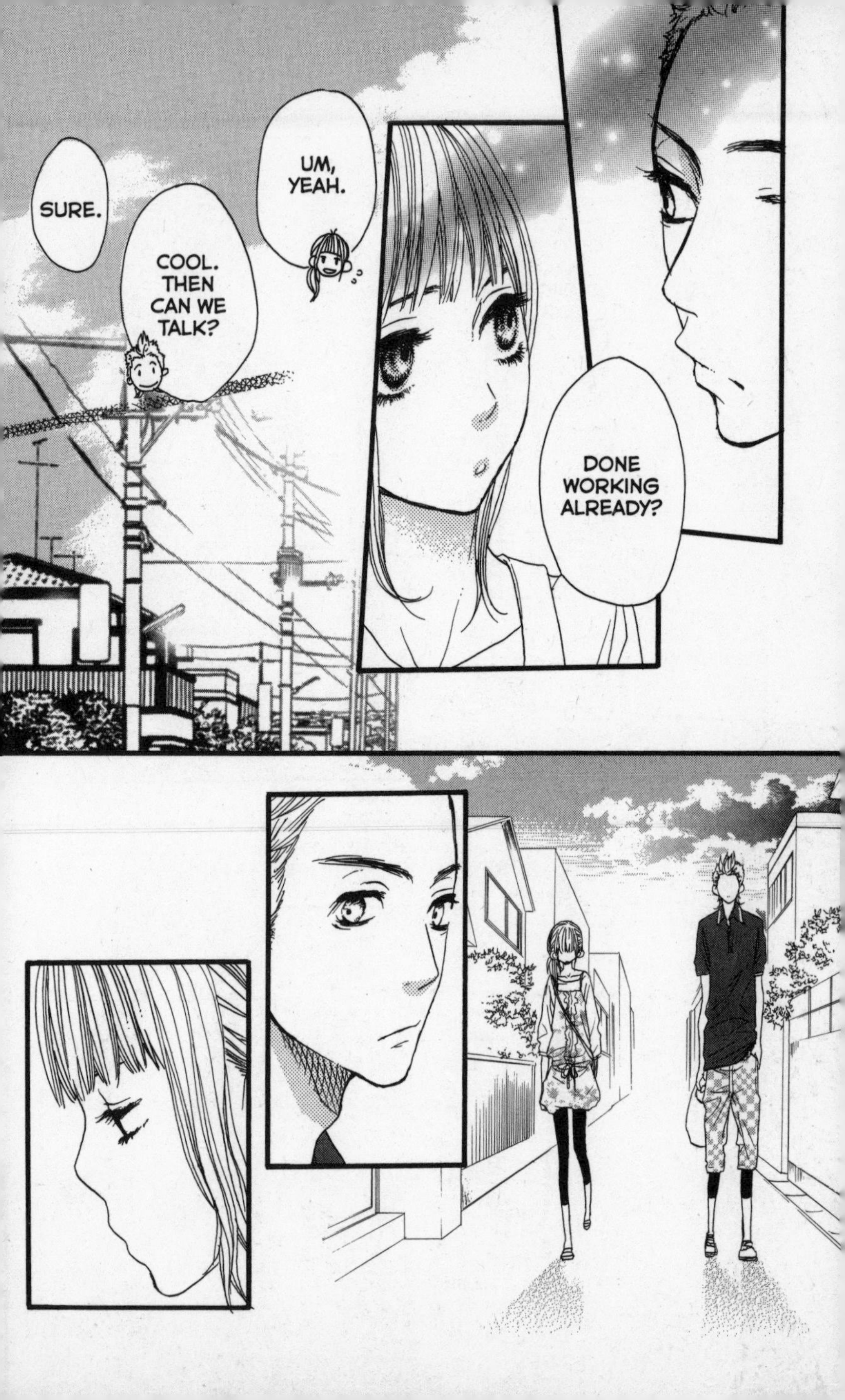
DONE WORKING ALREADY?
UM, YEAH.
COOL. THEN CAN WE TALK?
SURE.

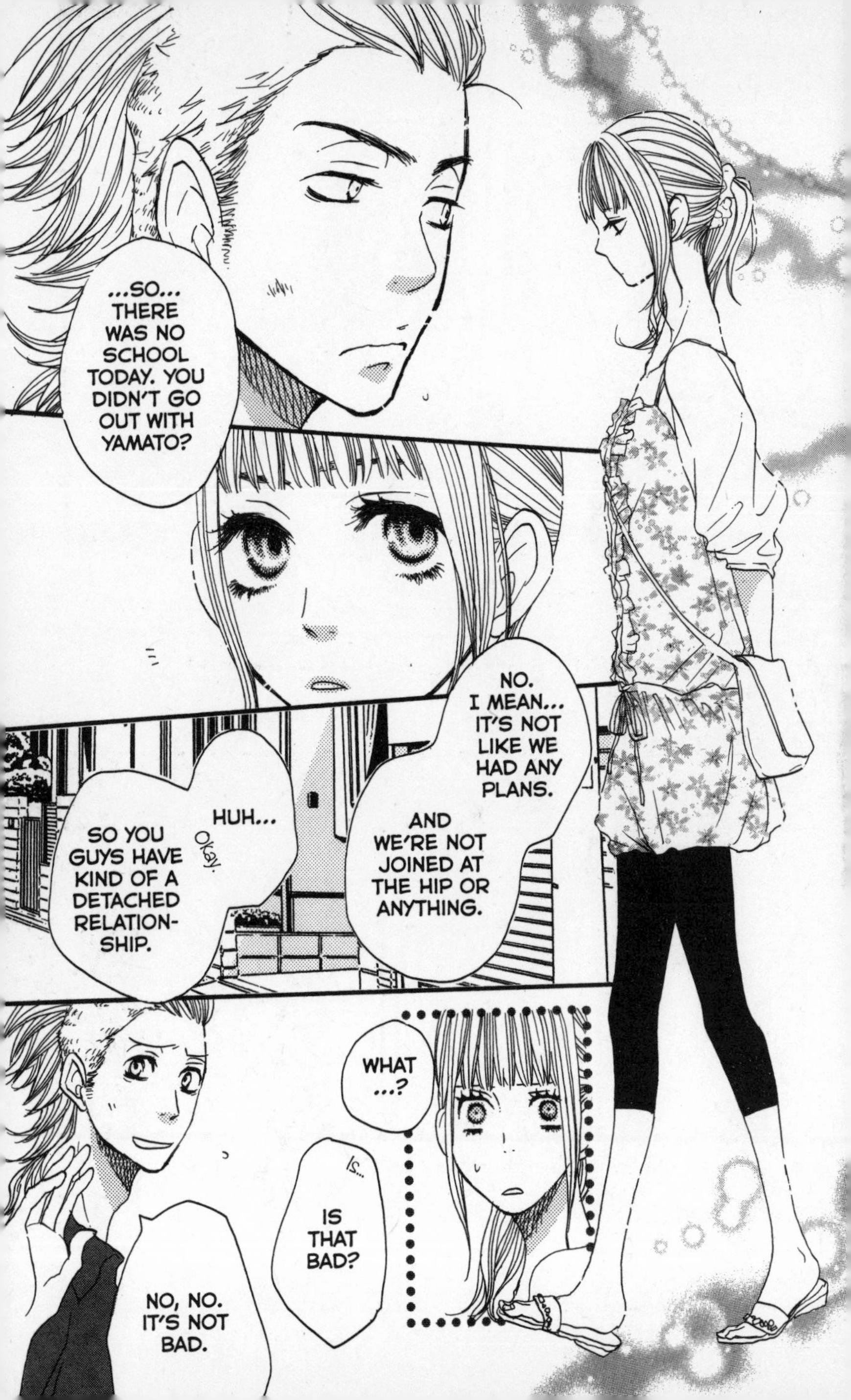
...SO... THERE WAS NO SCHOOL TODAY. YOU DIDN'T GO OUT WITH YAMATO?
NO. I MEAN... IT'S NOT LIKE WE HAD ANY PLANS.
AND WE'RE NOT JOINED AT THE HIP OR ANYTHING.
HUH...
OKAY.
SO YOU GUYS HAVE KIND OF A DETACHED RELATIONSHIP.
WHAT ...?
IS...
IS THAT BAD?
NO, NO. IT'S NOT BAD.

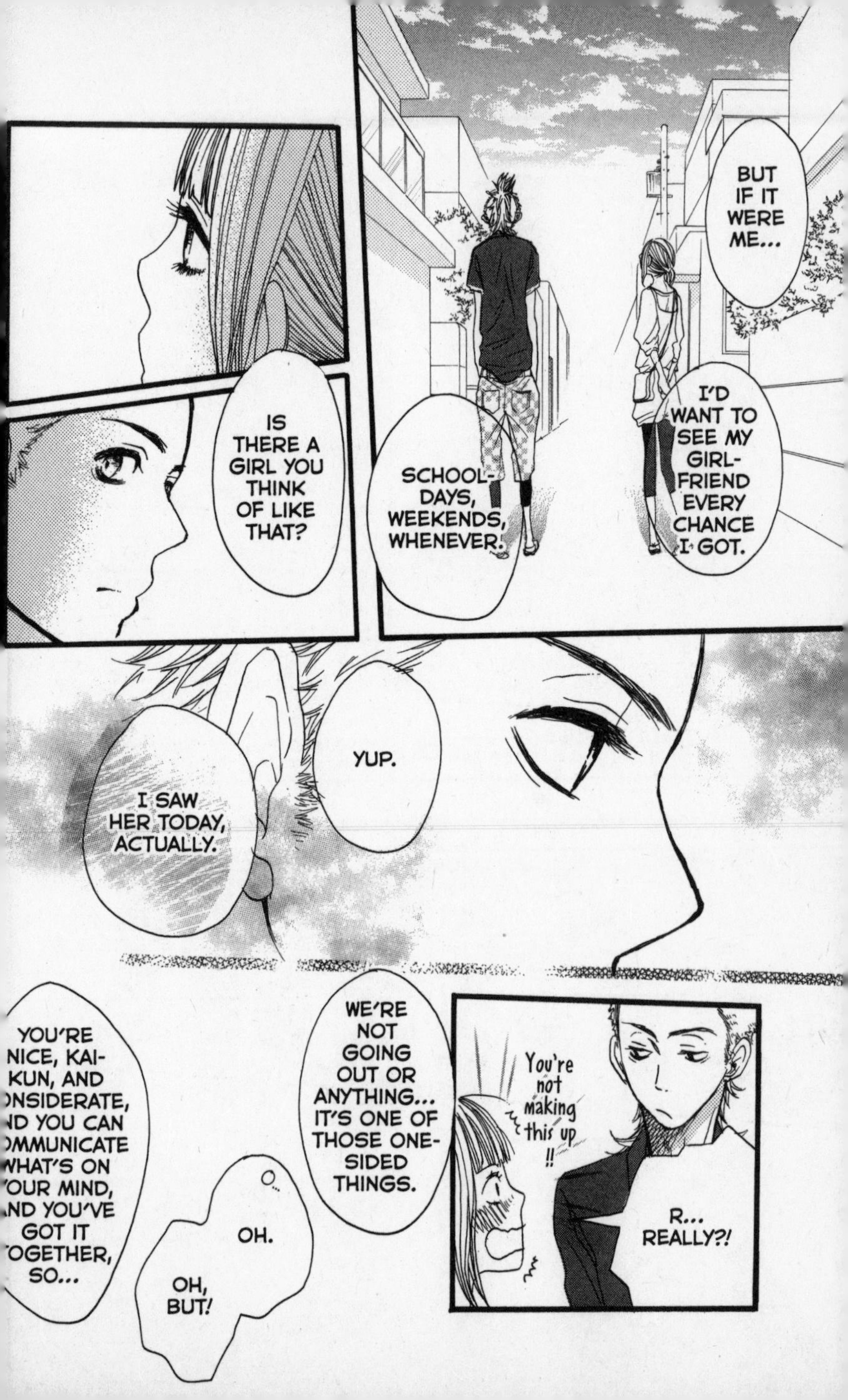
BUT IF IT WERE ME...
I'D WANT TO SEE MY GIRL-FRIEND EVERY CHANCE I GOT.
SCHOOL-DAYS, WEEKENDS, WHENEVER.
IS THERE A GIRL YOU THINK OF LIKE THAT?
YUP.
I SAW HER TODAY, ACTUALLY.
R... REALLY?!
You're not making this up !!
WE'RE NOT GOING OUT OR ANYTHING... IT'S ONE OF THOSE ONE-SIDED THINGS.
O...
OH.
OH, BUT!
YOU'RE NICE, KAI-KUN, AND NSIDERATE, ND YOU CAN MMUNICATE WHAT'S ON OUR MIND, ND YOU'VE GOT IT OGETHER, SO...

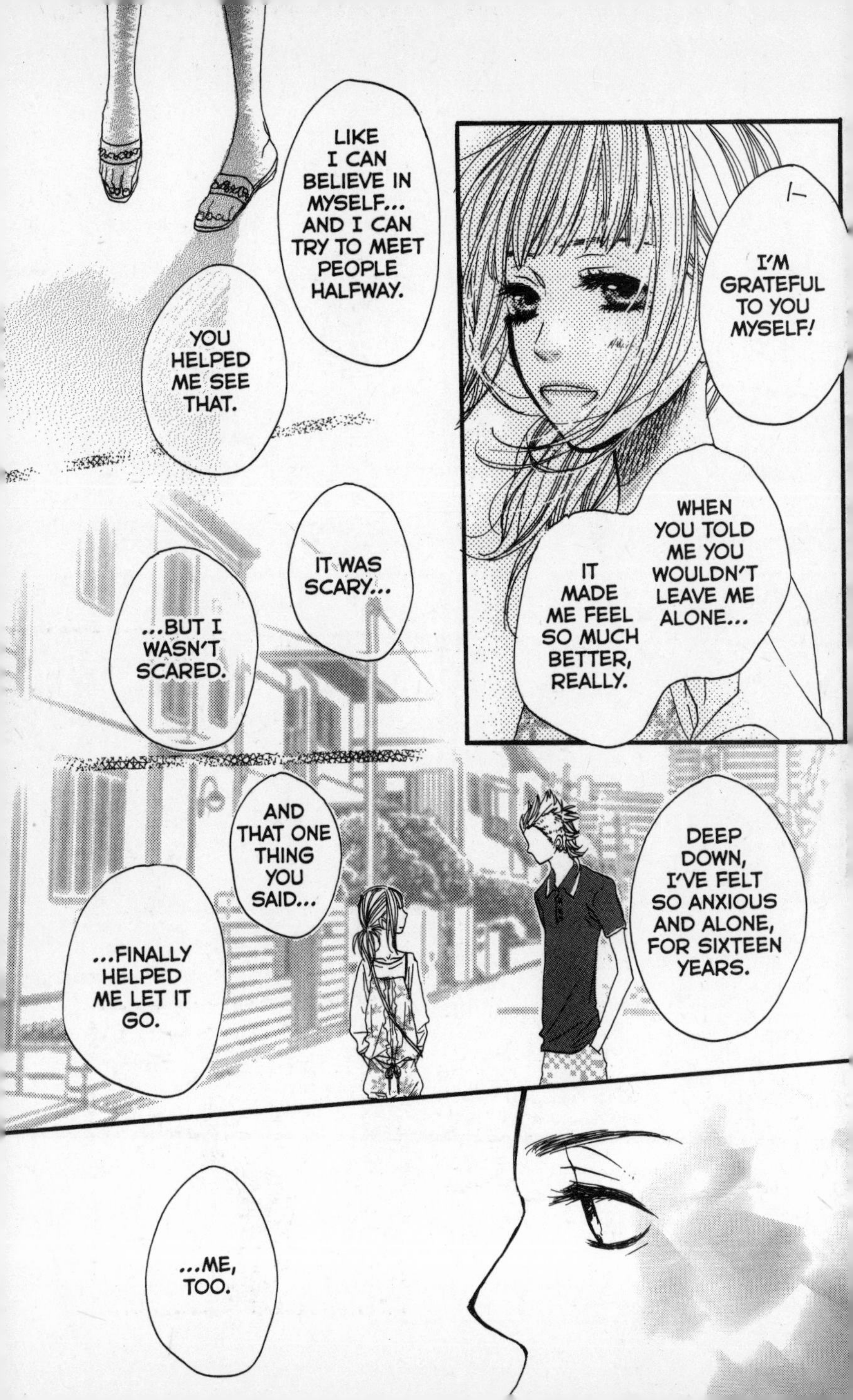
I—
I'M GRATEFUL TO YOU MYSELF!
WHEN YOU TOLD ME YOU WOULDN'T LEAVE ME ALONE...
IT MADE ME FEEL SO MUCH BETTER, REALLY.
LIKE I CAN BELIEVE IN MYSELF... AND I CAN TRY TO MEET PEOPLE HALFWAY.
YOU HELPED ME SEE THAT.
IT WAS SCARY...
...BUT I WASN'T SCARED.
DEEP DOWN, I'VE FELT SO ANXIOUS AND ALONE, FOR SIXTEEN YEARS.
AND THAT ONE THING YOU SAID...
...FINALLY HELPED ME LET IT GO.
...ME, TOO.

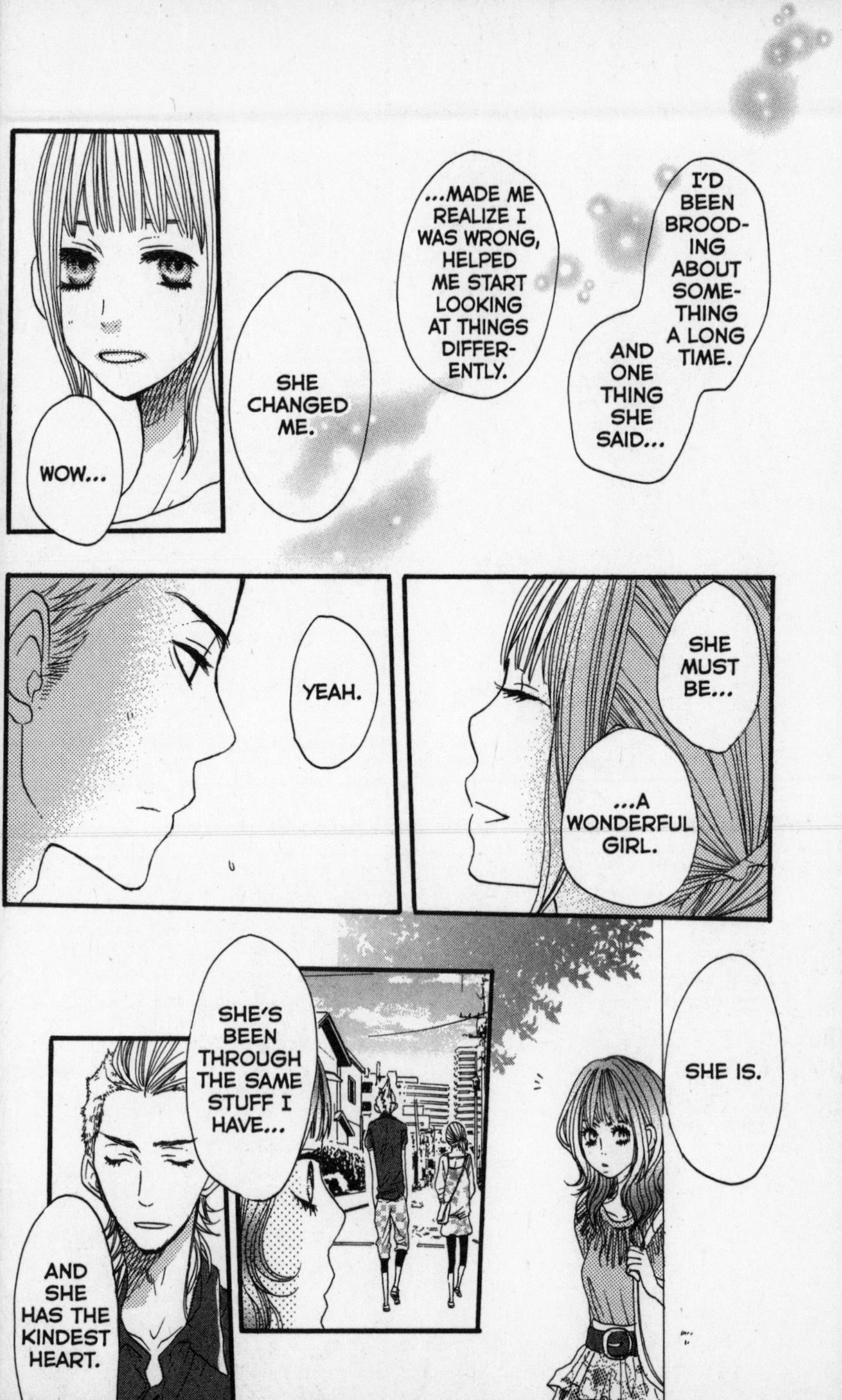
I'D BEEN BROOD-ING ABOUT SOME-THING A LONG TIME.
AND ONE THING SHE SAID...
...MADE ME REALIZE I WAS WRONG, HELPED ME START LOOKING AT THINGS DIFFER-ENTLY.
SHE CHANGED ME.
WOW...
SHE MUST BE...
...A WONDERFUL GIRL.
YEAH.
SHE IS.
SHE'S BEEN THROUGH THE SAME STUFF I HAVE...
AND SHE HAS THE KINDEST HEART.

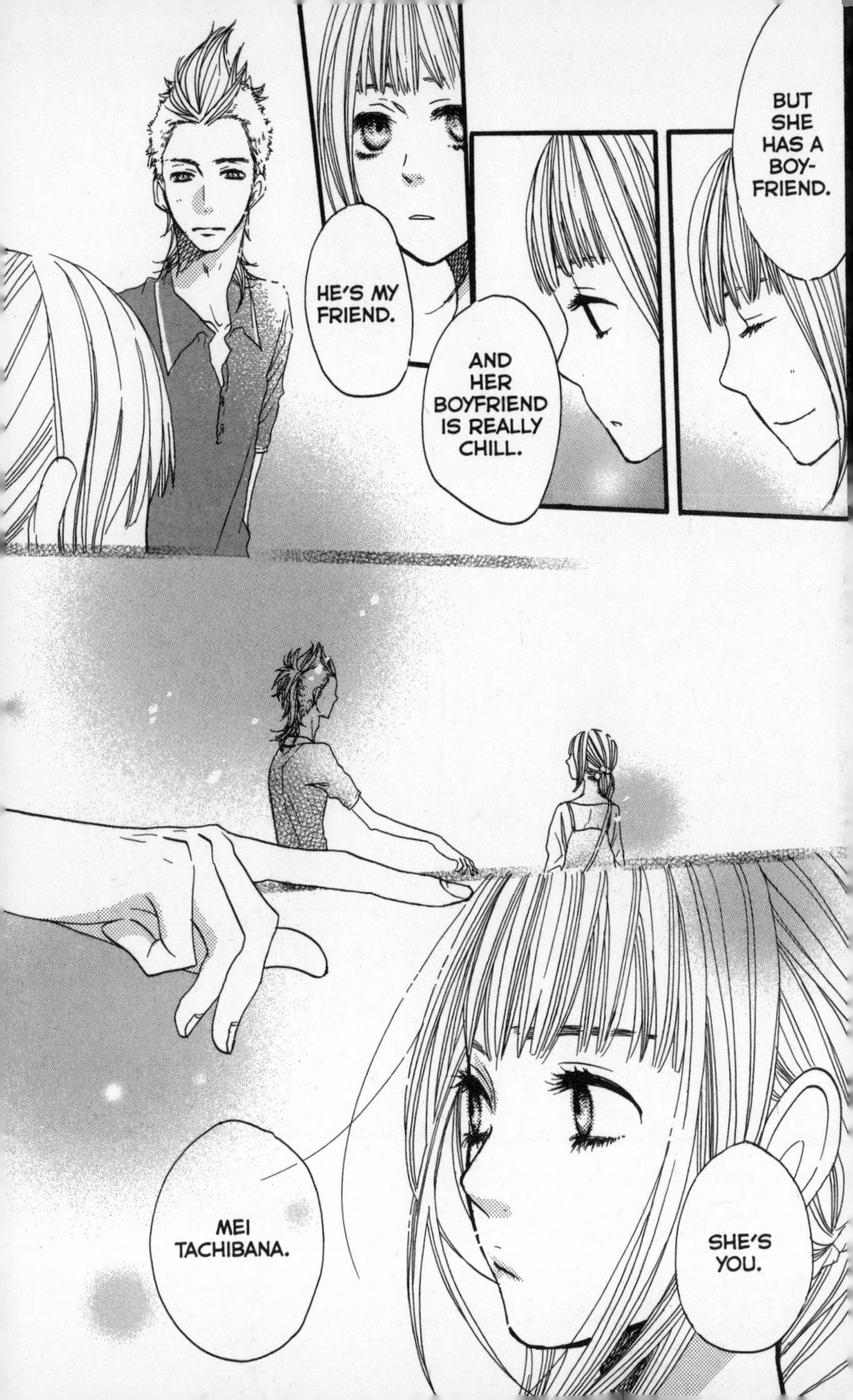
BUT SHE HAS A BOY-FRIEND.
AND HER BOYFRIEND IS REALLY CHILL.
HE'S MY FRIEND.
SHE'S YOU.
MEI TACHIBANA.

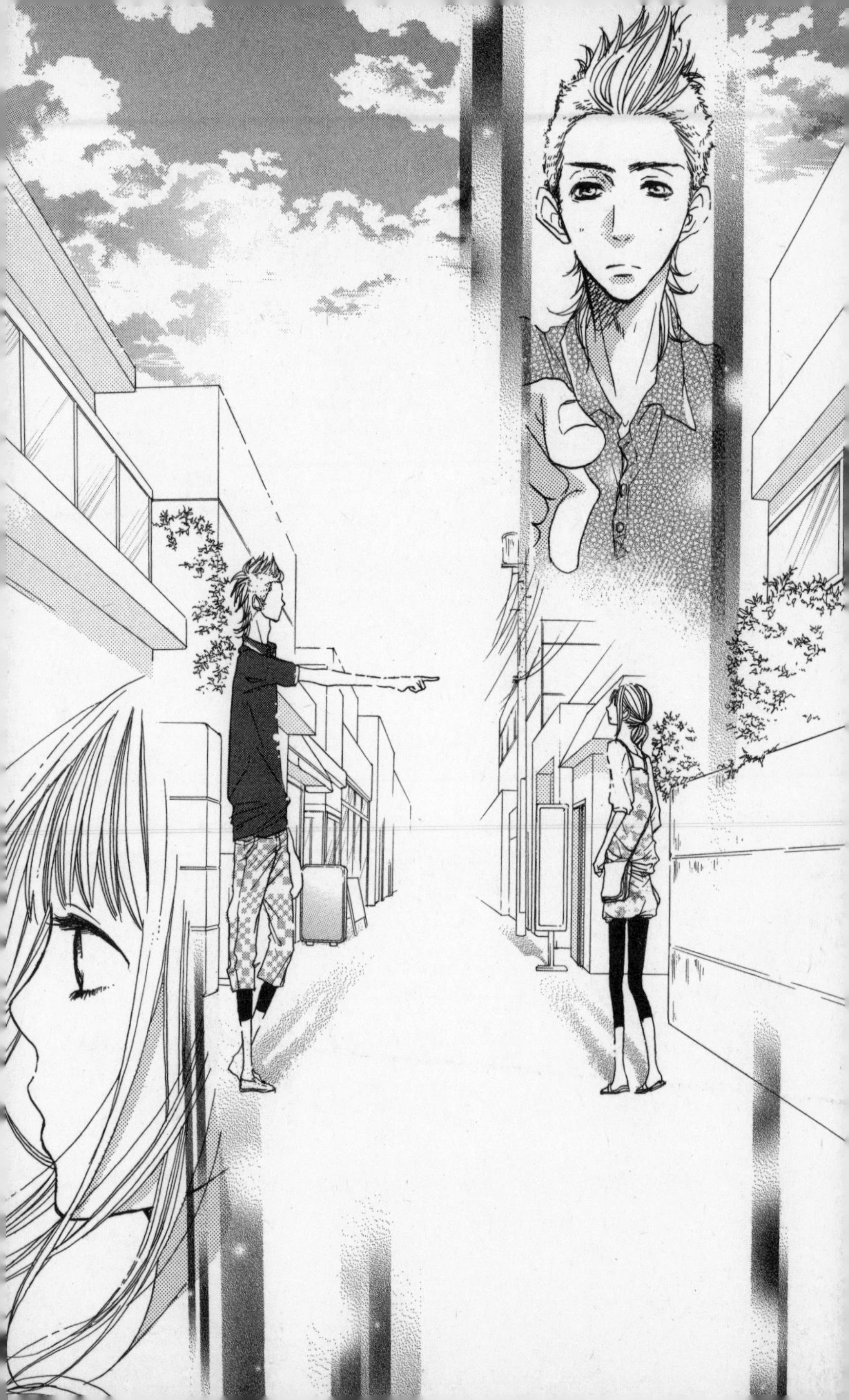

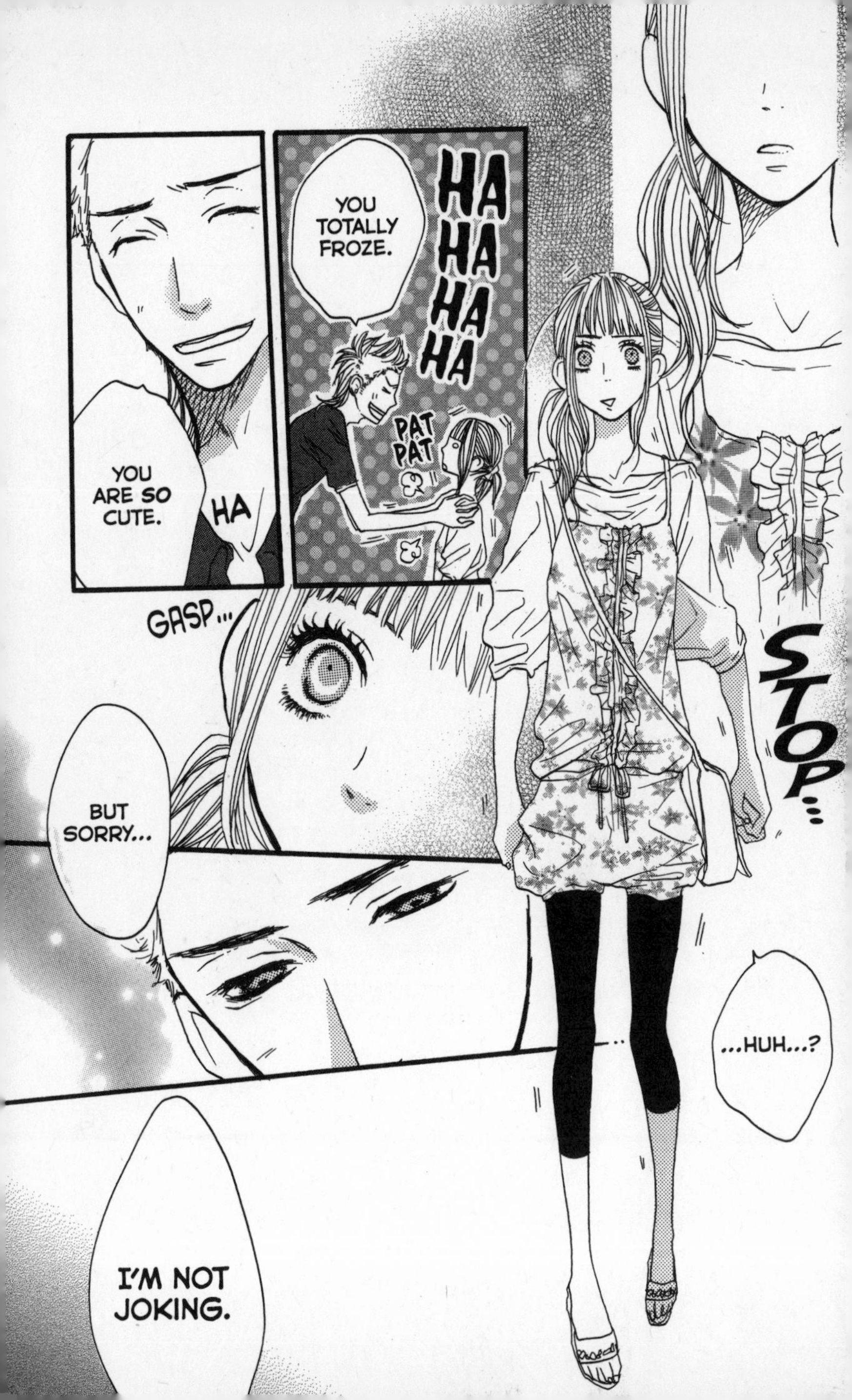
STOP...
...HUH...?
YOU TOTALLY FROZE.
HA HA HA HA
PAT PAT
YOU ARE SO CUTE.
HA
GASP...
BUT SORRY...
I'M NOT JOKING.

Say I Love You. volume 5 is a work of fiction. Names, characters, places, and incidents are the products of the author's imagination or are used fictitiously. Any resemblance to actual events, locales, or persons, living or dead, is entirely coincidental.

A Kodansha Comics Trade Paperback Original

Published in the United States by Kodansha Comics, an imprint of Kodansha USA Publishing, LLC, New York.

Publication rights for this English edition arranged through Kodansha Ltd, Tokyo.

First published in Japan in 2010 by Kodansha Ltd., Tokyo as *Sukitte iinayo.* volume 5.

ISBN 978-1-61262-606-2

Printed in the United States of America.

www.kodanshacomics.com

9 8 7 6 5 4 3 2 1
Translation: Alethea and Athena Nibley
Lettering: John Clark
Editing: Ben Applegate